An Introduction to Web Matrix

An Introduction to Web Matrix:

ASP.NET Development for Beginners

Colin Hardy
Simon Stobart

ELSEVIER
BUTTERWORTH
HEINEMANN

AMSTERDAM BOSTON HEIDELBERG LONDON NEW YORK OXFORD
PARIS SAN DIEGO SAN FRANCISCO SINGAPORE SYDNEY TOKYO

Butterworth-Heinemann
An imprint of Elsevier
Linacre House, Jordan Hill, Oxford OX2 8DP
200 Wheeler Road, Burlington, MA 01803

First published 2003

British Library Cataloguing in Publication Data
A catalogue record for this book is available from the British Library

ISBN   0 7506 60767

For information on all Butterworth-Heinemann publications
visit our website at www.bh.com

Printed and bound in Great Britain

Contents

Chapter 6

Chapter 7

Chapter 8

Chapter 9

Chapter 10

Chapter 11

Index

1

Introduction

1.1 Introduction

ASP.NET is the Microsoft solution to the creation of dynamic, high performance web applications. ASP.NET has been designed to allow you to create real world web applications quickly and easily and is a significant improvement over its predecessor ASP. ASP.NET is supported by a free community-supported development tool called ASP.NET Web Matrix. The tool is a WYSIWYG (What You See Is What You Get) application which being only 1.2 Mb in size can be downloaded quickly and easily from the Web. This book explains how to obtain, install and configure the ASP.NET Web Matrix tool, describes how to make use of the rich features that the tool provides and illustrates how to begin to develop ASP.NET dynamic web applications.

1.2 Why ASP.NET?

There are a number of different programming languages available for the creation of dynamic web applications, so why choose ASP.NET? Well according to Microsoft ASP.NET "combines unprecedented developer productivity with performance, reliability, and deployment". But what does this all mean? Well in practice ASP.NET enables the creation of web applications quickly and easily. In addition ASP.NET pages work in all web browsers including Netscape, Opera, AOL and Internet Explorer. How does it do this? Well the web server translates your ASP.NET pages into standard Hyper-Text Markup Language (HTML) which can then be displayed by the web browsers. In addition ASP.NET provides support for a number of programming languages. It comes with in built support for Visual Basic.NET, C#.NET and Jscript.NET. This gives you a huge amount of flexibility in your choice of programming language. Within this book we shall be using the VB.NET language in our examples. Another benefit of ASP.NET is that you can make use of any text editor (even Notepad) to create your web pages. However, there is a dedicated tool to enable you to create your ASP.NET pages quickly and easily and this is known as Web Matrix.

1.3   Why Web Matrix?

Why use Web Matrix? Well. It is free and that in itself is often a good enough reason for many people, given that software on the whole is quite expensive. However, just because something is free doesn't mean that it is any good. Fortunately, Web Matrix is both easy to use and powerful, making it useful for the beginner and experienced developer alike. To give you some idea of what the Web Matrix tool provides, consider the following taken from the Microsoft ASP.NET web site (www.asp.net):

ASP.NET Page Designer	Rapidly create ASP.NET pages using the rich WYSIWYG designer. Drag and drop ASP.NET Server controls from the Toolbox onto your page. Select individual server controls to get in-place designer editing support as well as full property grid customization.
SQL and MSDE Database Management	Integrated support to create and edit SQL and MSDE databases. Create new databases, add/edit/delete tables and stored procedures, and edit data content all directly within the Web Matrix tool.
Easy Data Binding	Easy to create data bound pages without writing code. Drop SQL tables on your page to create data-bound grids, or start with Data Page templates for reports or Master/Detail pages. Code builders help you generate code to select, insert, update and delete SQL data.
Project-less File	Supports both FTP-based and file-based workspaces that allow developers to easily organize and edit their ASP.NET applications. Simply double-click a file within the workspace tree to open it for editing. No FrontPage server extensions or project system required.

Development Web Server   Develop and test your ASP.NET applications, without requiring IIS. Includes a lightweight personal web server that serves most web content, including ASP.NET pages and XML Web Services, for local requests.

Community Integration   Provides a built-in gateway to the ASP.NET community right within the tool allowing you to browse community web sites and search the ASP.NET Forums and Newsgroups for help.

1.4   Is this book for you?

While there are a large number of books on ASP.NET, there are very few on the ASP.NET Web Matrix tool. Microsoft have thoughtfully provided an on-line tutorial located at: http://www.asp.net/webmatrix/tour/getstarted/intro.aspx. While, this is very good and is aimed at the beginner in most cases it assumes quite a lot of the beginner and as such our book provides both an easier introduction to the topic as well as going further than the on-line tutorial.

We have assumed that the reader of this book can use the Microsoft Windows operating system and is familiar with the installation of software through simple wizards. We also assume that the reader has some experience of creating simple web pages using HTML and understands general web terminology. No experience of ASP.NET programming or use of the Web Matrix tool is assumed and we take a simple step by step approach to introducing the reader to these technologies.

Where appropriate we have included some exercises at the end of certain chapters for you to practice what you have learnt. Model solutions to these are included towards the end of the book.

1.5   How this book is organised

This book has been written for you to read from start to finish. Later chapters build upon the knowledge and ideas introduced in previous ones. It may be the case that you are using the development environment at say a college or University where ASP.NET and Web Matrix have been installed for you. In which case you can skip the chapter on obtaining and installing the development software.

The remainder of this book is divided into the following chapters. Chapter 2 describes where to obtain and how to install the ASP.NET and Web Matrix software. Chapter 3 provides a brief introduction to the Web Matrix tool. Assisting you in the creation of your first and very simple ASP.NET web page. Chapter 4 provides a more in depth look into the different components making up the Web Matrix tool. Chapter 5 introduces the basic HTML elements which can be used to construct web pages. Chapter 6 introduces the elements which are used to construct ASP.NET forms. Chapter 7 examines the different controls which ASP.NET provides to enable the validation of user input. Chapter 8 introduces the VB.NET programming language. Chapter 9 provides two further more complex VB.NET examples of dynamic web pages. Chapter 10 describes how to install and create an SQL database. Chapter 11 introduces some simple SQL, a language used to communicate with databases. Chapter 12 describes how to interact with databases using ASP.NET. Chapter 13 describes the Web Matrix and ASP.NET on-line communities and explains where you can go for further help and information. Finally Chapter 14 provides the model solutions to the previous chapter exercises.

So what are you waiting for? Let's get started by obtaining the software we need and installing it.

2

Installing the environment

2.1   Introduction

Before we can begin to get started and develop some ASP.NET applications we need to gather together the different software components which we need in order to begin successful ASP.NET programming. In this chapter we describe what these different software components are, where they can be found and how they can be installed.

2.2   What do we need to get started?

To begin ASP.NET development we need an operating system which is capable of supporting ASP.NET development. To support this development the operating system must have the .NET framework installed. The .NET framework is only supported by Windows 2000 or Windows XP (Home or Professional). If you have an earlier operating system you should upgrade to either of those listed above. The .NET framework is an extension to the operating system which enables ASP.NET programs to be created.

The next step is to obtain a copy of the Web Matrix development environment. You don't actually need a copy of Web Matrix to begin ASP.NET development. In fact if you own a copy of Windows 2000 or Windows XP Professional then all you need to begin development has been included along with the operating system. However, Web Matrix is a sophisticated, easy to use and convenient development environment which is useful for beginners and professional developers alike. We have based this book around using the Web Matrix environment and thus because Web Matrix does not come bundled with the Windows operating system we need to download and install this software.

The final item of software which we need to obtain is an SQL Server or MSDE (Microsoft Server Database Engine). You will need a copy of MSDE installed on your computer in order to create databases and link these to your ASP.NET programs. We shall be examining how to do that in later chapters of this book as you will not need this software initially, however you should obtain this now and install it so that you will be ready to start database development when we get there.

2.3   Obtaining and installing the required software

The great thing about obtaining and installing the .NET framework and Web Matrix tool is that Microsoft have made things easy for you as everything can be found at the same   web site. Using a web browser type in the web address www.asp.net and press enter. Figure 2.1 illustrates the web page which should be displayed in your browser window.

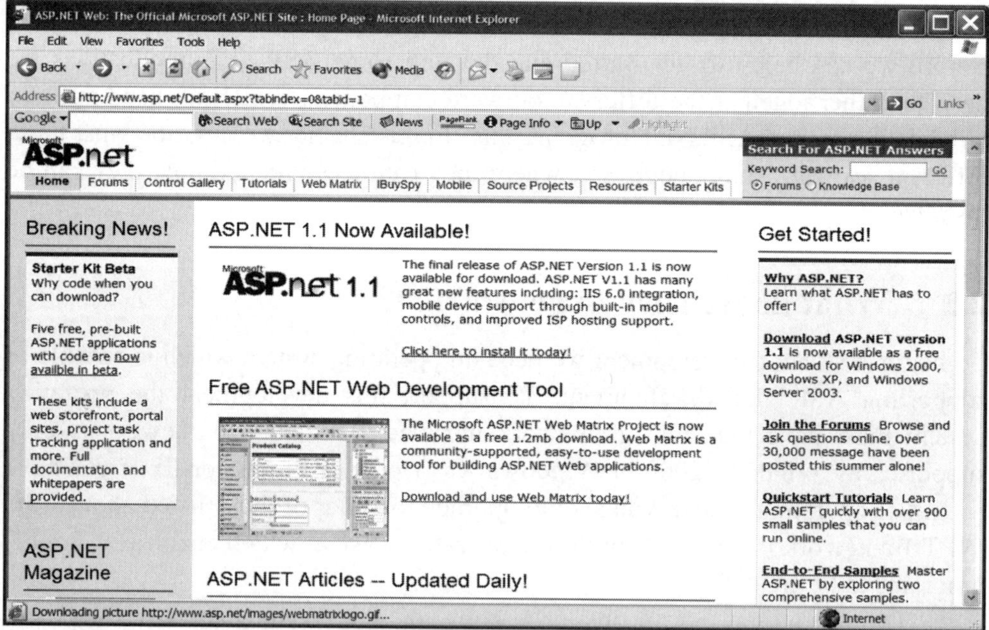

Figure 2.1: ASP.NET official web site

Of course the web site may look a little different to that shown in Figure 2.1 as good web sites are always being updated. However, for us the most important thing on the web page is the text "Free ASP.NET Web Development Tool" and below that a link which invites us to "Download and use Web Matrix today!". Clicking this link will result in the web page shown in Figure 2.2 being displayed.

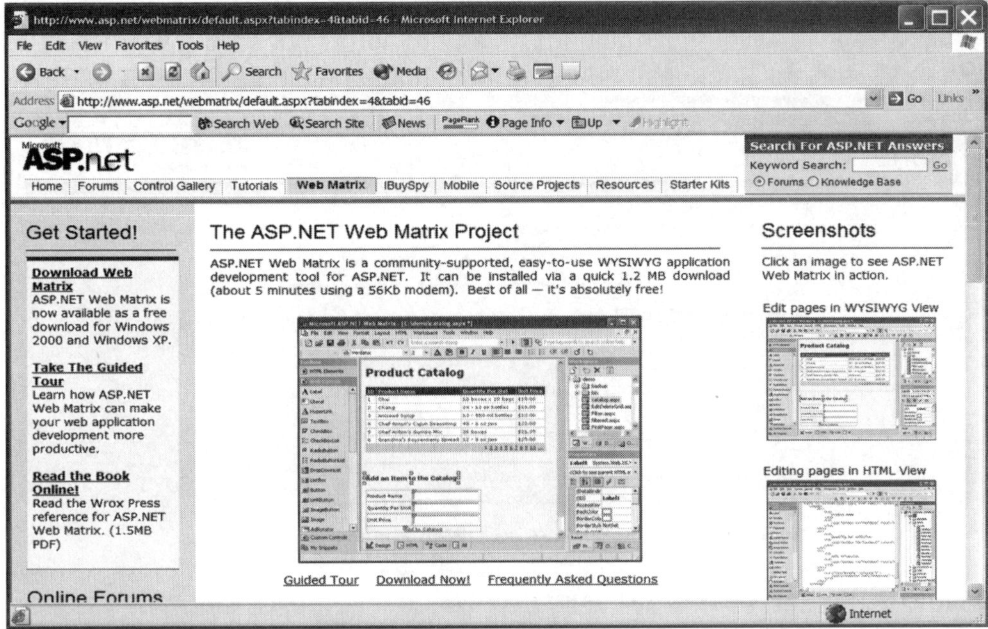

Figure 2.2: ASP.NET Web Matrix home page

The web page shown in Figure 2.2 is the home page for the ASP.NET Web Matrix tool. In addition to providing information on the Web Matrix tool, some example screen shots, a guided tour to some of the tools, basic features and answering the most frequently asked questions, it also provides a link to enable us to download the Web Matrix software. This link can be found below the main central graphic and is entitled "Download Now!".

Click this hyperlink and a web page similar to that shown in Figure 2.3 should be displayed. This web page explains that the process of installing the Web Matrix tool is a three part process. The first of which is to check if the .NET framework has been correctly installed. The second part is the downloading and installation of the Web Matrix tool. Finally, the third step is the installation of any free optional components. Amongst these is the MSDE SQL server which we will need to install.

Okay, let's start the installation process. The first thing to do is to check if the .NET framework is installed on your computer. Without this the Web Matrix tool will refuse to install. To do this click the link "Click here to see if you have the .NET Framework installed". Although the .NET framework comes with Windows 2000 and Windows XP it is not usually activated. To install it follow the instructions shown on the web page. As we have already installed the .NET framework we get a web page with the message .NET framework found displayed.

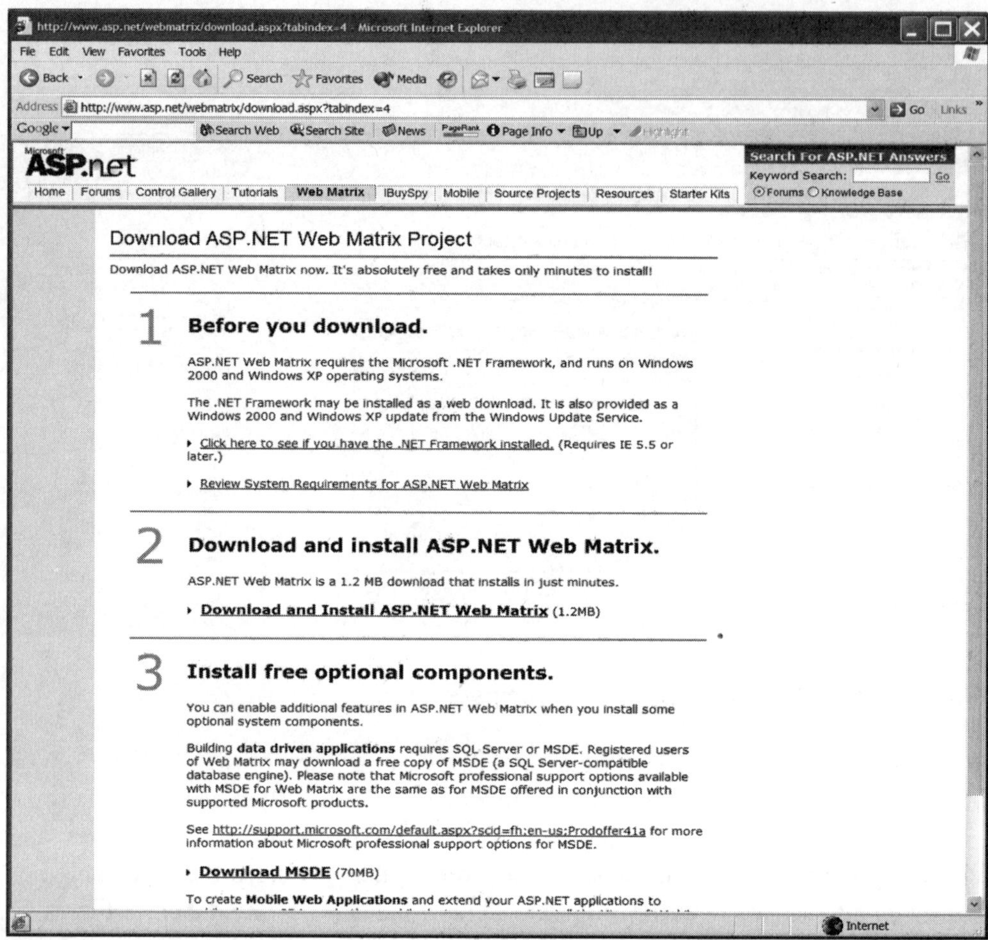

Figure 2.3: Steps involved with installation of the Web Matrix project

Having installed the .NET framework we are now ready to install the Web Matrix tool. Return to the web page shown in Figure 2.3 and select the "Download and Install ASP.NET Web Matrix" link. The web page displayed is shown in Figure 2.4. To download the Web Matrix tool you must first register with Microsoft. This is a three step process. The first of which requires you to enter your email address and country where you live on a simple web form. When you have done this click the Next >> link.

The second step in this process should then be displayed. This is illustrated in Figure 2.5. This step asks you to enter a Forums User Name in the form field provided. The forum is a means of communicating with other ASP.NET developers. Enter a user name and click the Next >> link.

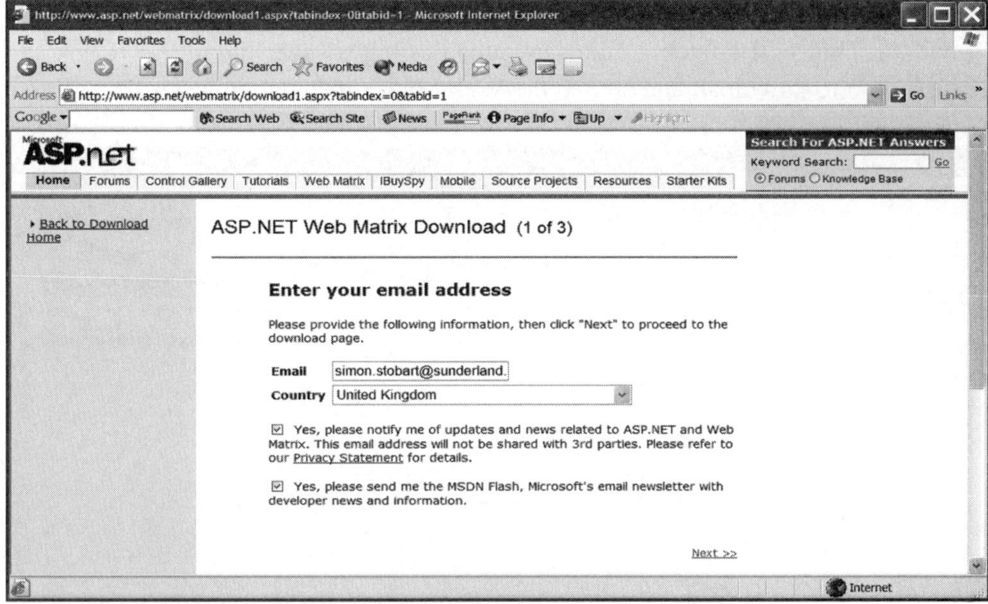

Figure 2.4: Installing ASP.NET Web Matrix step 1

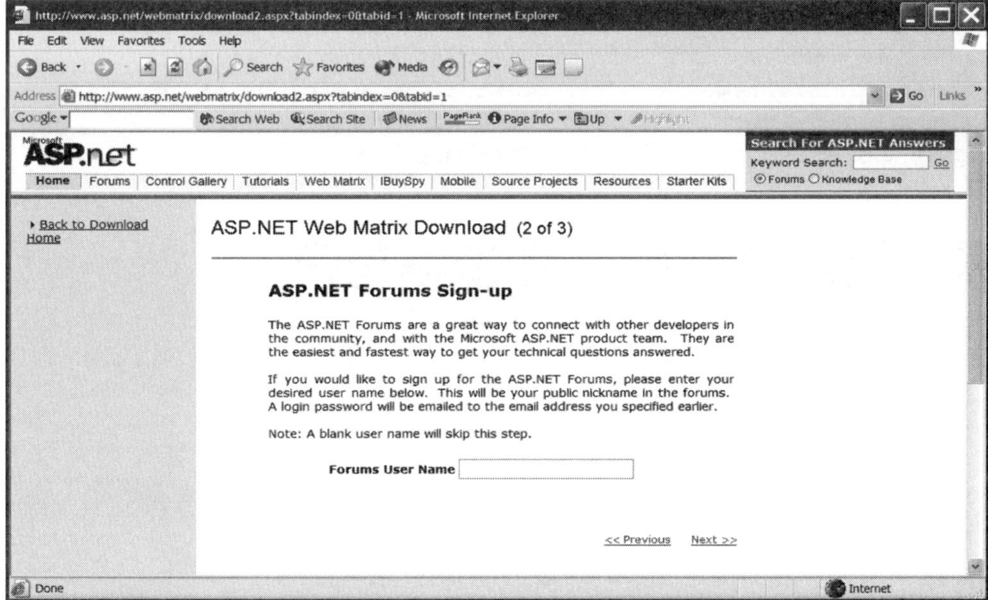

Figure 2.5: Installing ASP.NET Web Matrix step 2

Figure 2.6 illustrates the final step in the Web Matrix registration/installation process. Click the link "Download ASP.NET Web Matrix Project Technology Preview". This will launch a File Download window, see Figure 2.7. Click the Open button to download and launch the Web Matrix installation wizard.

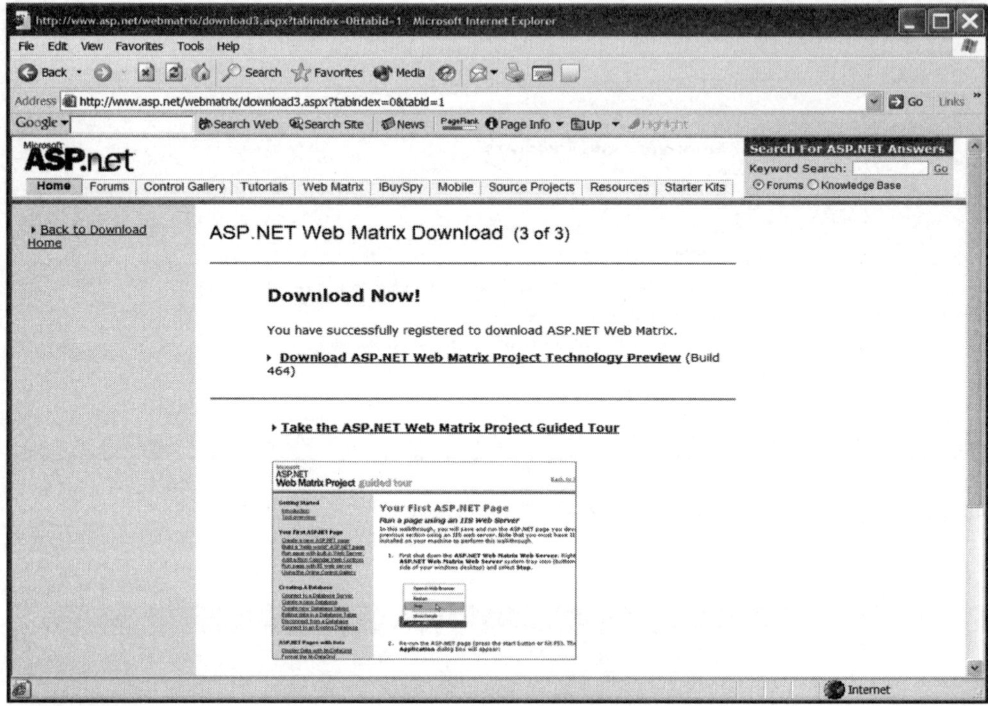

Figure 2.6: Installing ASP.NET Web Matrix step 2

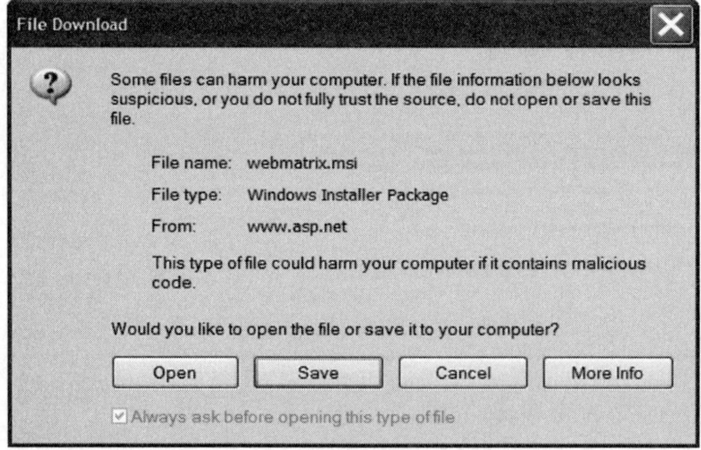

Figure 2.7: File Download window

Having installed the Web Matrix tool, the final component which we require is the MSDE SQL server. Return to the web page shown in Figure 2.3 and click the link "Download MSDE" under step 3. This will display the web page shown in Figure 2.8.

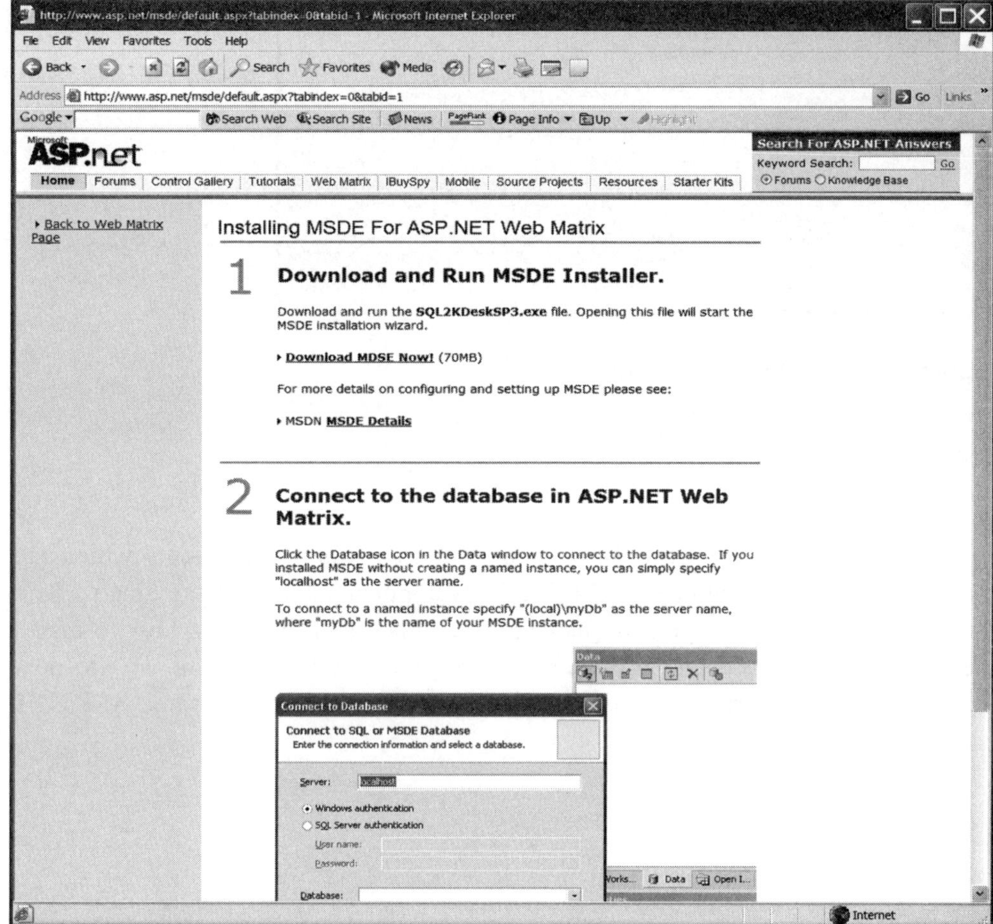

Figure 2.8: Downloading the MSDE

Clicking the link "Download MSDE Now!" will launch the File Download window. This is shown in Figure 2.9. Click the Open button. This will download the MSDE application and launch the setup wizard. Note however that while the Web Matrix tool is quite small and will download quite quickly the MSDE SQL server is 70 MB in length and will take much longer to download.

When you have installed this application you are now ready to continue with your ASP.NET development.

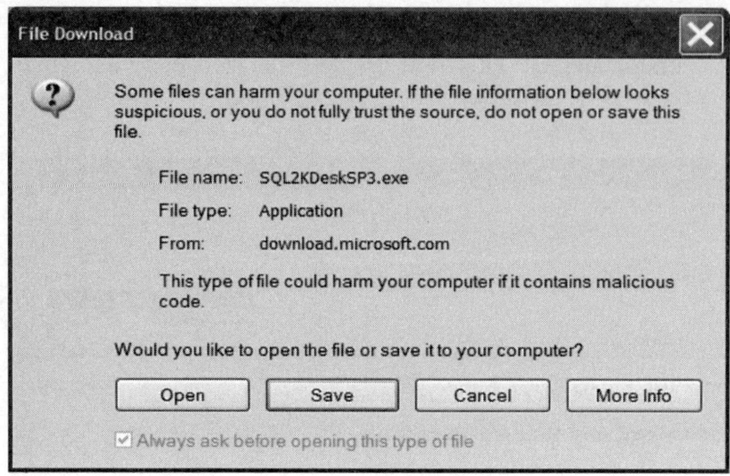

Figure 2.9: File Download window

2.4   Summary

In this chapter we have described the different software components which are required in order to commence ASP.NET development. We have explained where these different software applications can be obtained and illustrated how to install them. Having obtained and installed our development environment we are now ready to begin learning how to use the Web Matrix tool and create some ASP.NET programs.

3

Introduction to the Web Matrix tool

3.1   Introduction

The Web Matrix tool is a powerful dynamic web development environment with a sophisticated graphical user interface. The Web Matrix tool contains many features to help the novice and professional developer alike. In this chapter we shall begin by showing you how to start using the Web Matrix tool. We shall then provide a brief tour of the different components that make up the tool. Finally, we shall explain the development process and illustrate how to create a simple ASP.NET web page.

3.2   Starting the tool

To start the Web Matrix tool, locate the ASP.NET Web Matrix program on your Programs menu, by firstly clicking the Start button. On our computer the Web Matrix tool can be found on a third level menu, under the title "Microsoft ASP.NET Web Matrix", but this may be located elsewhere on your computer. Figure 3.1 illustrates the Web Matrix program menu item.

Clicking the ASP.NET Web Matrix program menu item launches the Web Matrix environment. After a few seconds you should be presented with the Web Matrix tool, shown in Figure 3.2. When you first launch the Web Matrix tool an Add New File window is launched, as shown in more detail in Figure 3.2. This window allows you to select what kind of dynamic page you wish to build and what programming language you are going to use to build it.

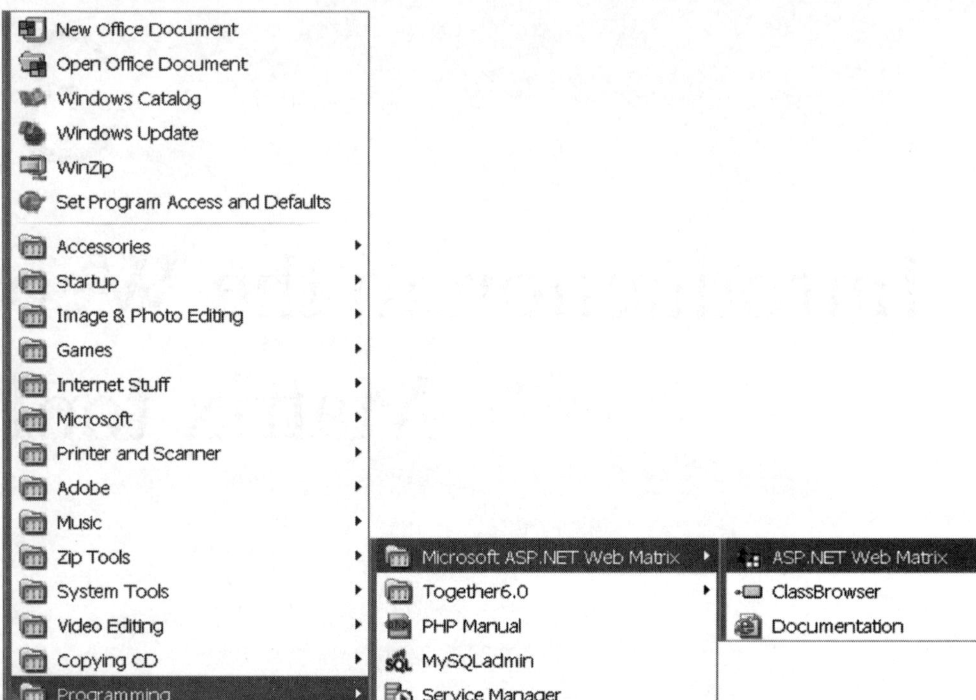

Figure 3.1: Locating Web Matrix on the start menu

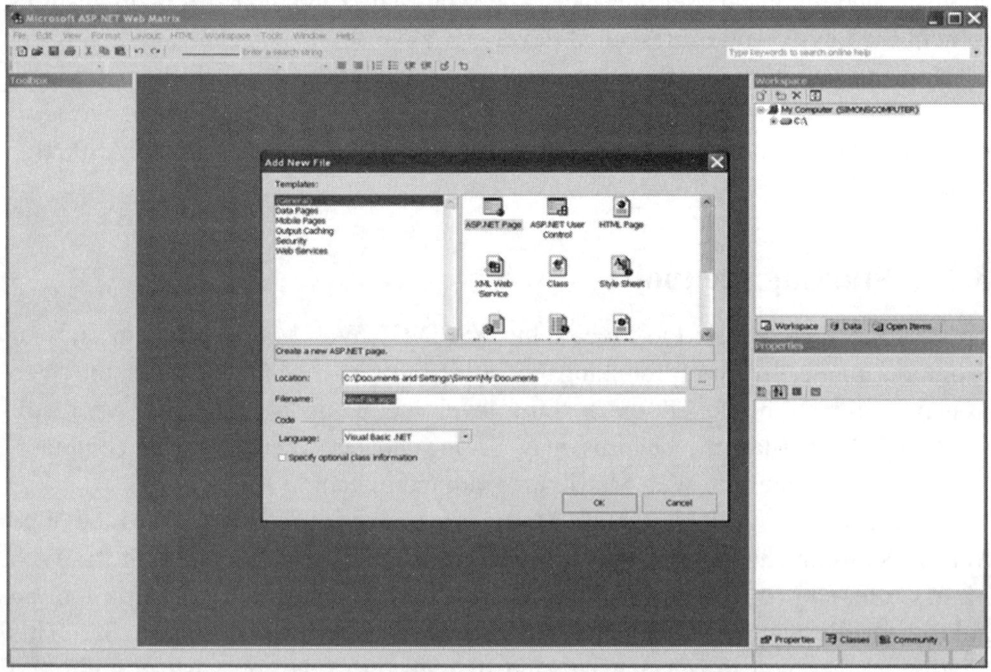

Figure 3.2: Launching Web Matrix

As this is our first time using the tool, we shall keep things simple. We shall leave the Template set to ASP.NET Page. We have changed the Location to save the documents to:

You may wish to choose a different location to save your documents. We will also change the Filename from NewFile.aspx to first.aspx. We shall also leave the programming Language set to Visual Basic .NET. It is worth mentioning that Visual Basic is often referred to simply as VB and Visual Basic .NET is often referred to as VB.NET. Figure 3.3 illustrates what the pop-up window should look like just before we click the OK button.

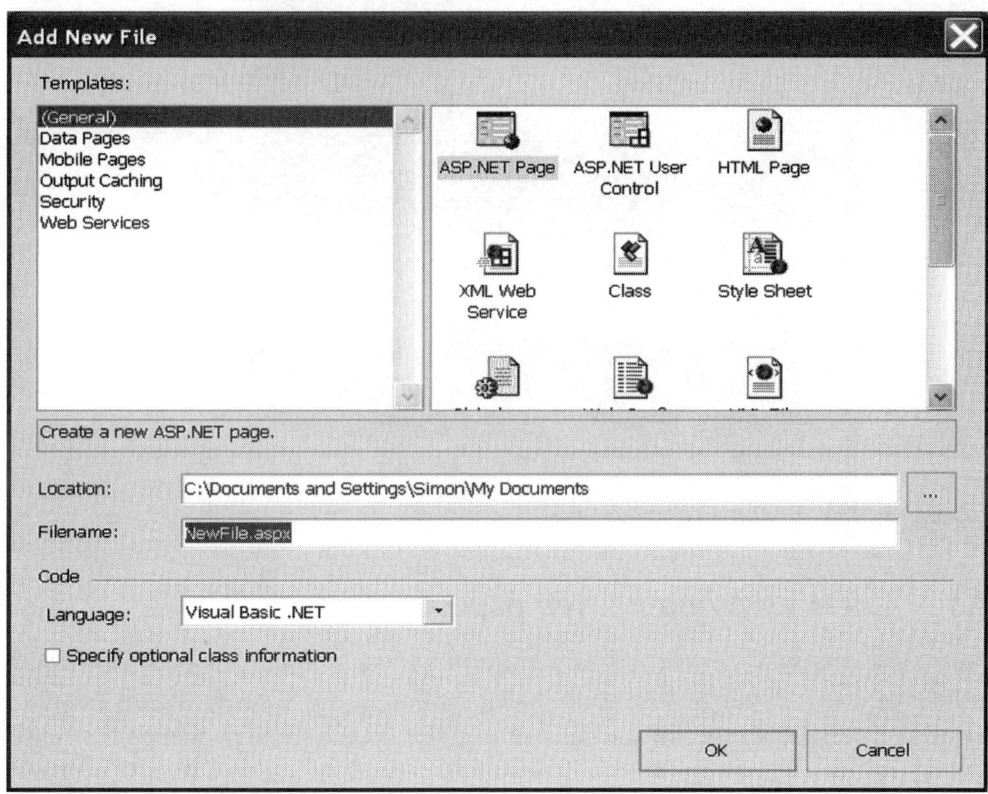

Figure 3.3: Add New File window

After the OK button has been clicked the Web Matrix tool completes its start-up operations the tool is now ready for you the developer to begin using it. Figure 3.4 illustrates what the tool should now look like. You should be able to recognise some familiar components that make up the tool. These components include the drop-down menus and buttons along the top of the application.

However, you will also note that the tool contains a number of other components that can be a little confusing to the novice user.

Don't worry if you don't yet understand what each of the different components do, as we shall introduce each of these in turn and explain their function.

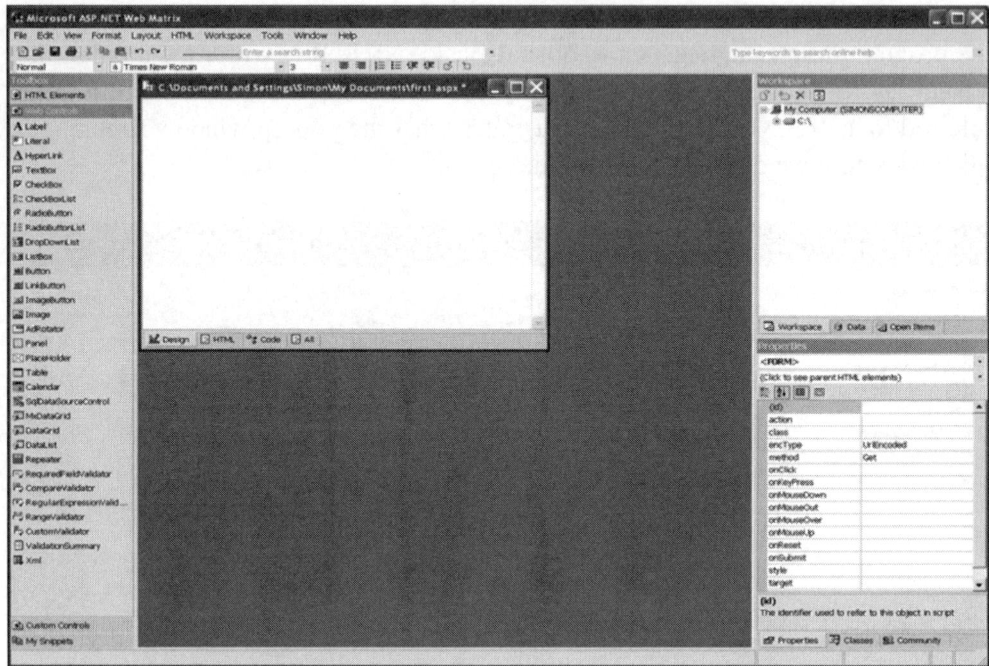

Figure 3.4: Web Matrix ready to use

3.3   Creating dynamic web pages

Essentially, the Web Matrix tool is a piece of software which has been developed to help us create dynamic web pages using ASP.NET more easily than is possible by using a generic text editor such as Notepad. Of course some people prefer to use text editors instead of specific development environments such as Web Matrix and that is their choice. Because the Web Matrix environment has been developed to assist in ASP.NET dynamic web development it consists of a variety of tools (components) which assist the developer in creating Hyper-Text Markup Language (HTML) and ASP.NET code (which we shall learn about later) as well as managing files and databases. All this is presented within a drag and drop graphical user interface which once you get used to it is easy to use, but to the beginner the number of different functions and components can be a little confusing.

3.4   The Web Matrix components

As mentioned the Web Matrix tool consists of a number of separate components, which together form the complete development environment. In this section we shall examine briefly these different components. If you examine Figure 3.5 you will see that this is same image as shown in Figure 3.4 but each of the different components making up the tool has been labelled with an identifying letter.

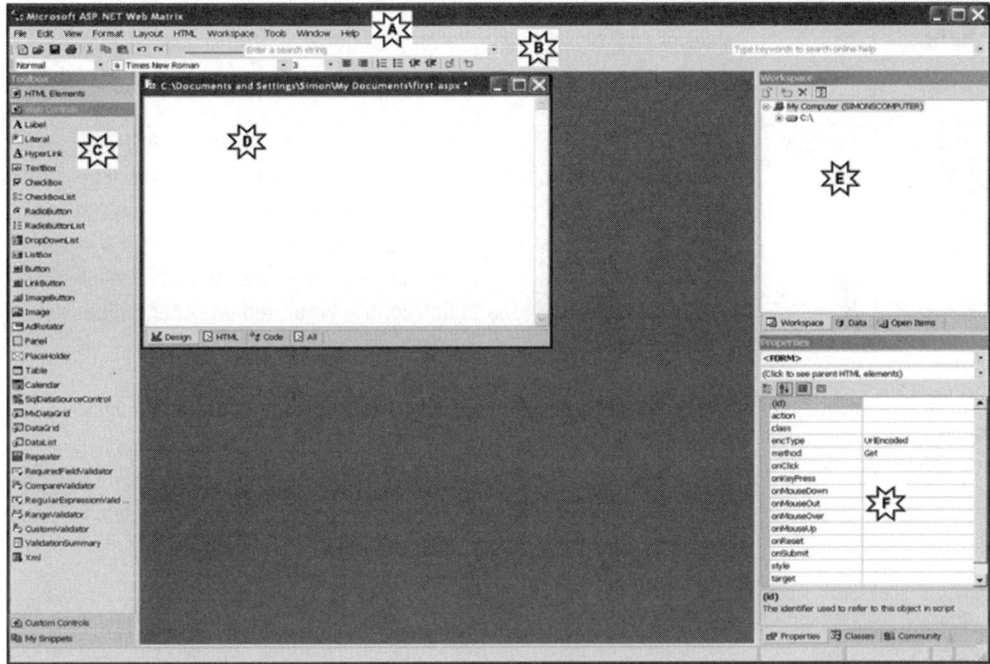

Figure 3.5: Web Matrix tool with highlighted components.

Table 3.1 lists each of these components and includes a brief description of what the component does. This table has been adapted from the Microsoft Web Matrix Project getting started guide available at the following web page: http://www.asp.net/webmatrix/tour/getstarted/tooloverview.aspx.

3.5   Creating and viewing your first simple page

The Web Matrix tool is an environment to help us develop dynamic web pages using the ASP.NET programming language. ASP.NET is a framework that encompasses a number of programming languages to allow us to create dynamic, interactive, web pages and complete on-line applications. One of the languages that forms part of ASP.NET is Visual Basic (VB) and this is the language that we have chosen to create our web pages with.

Key	Name	Description
A	Menu Bar	The area displayed across the top of the main ASP.NET Web Matrix window directly below the title bar. The Menu Bar includes a set of menu titles. Each menu title provides access to a drop-down menu composed of a collection of menu items, or choices. Menus display a list of commands available to the user.
B	Toolbar	The area displayed across the top of the main ASP.NET Web Matrix window directly below the Menu Bar. A toolbar is a panel that contains a set of controls, designed to provide quick access to specific commands or options.
C	Toolbox	The area displayed across the left side of the main ASP.NET Web Matrix window directly next to the Document window. The items available from the Toolbox change depending upon which page designer you are using. A Toolbox is a panel that contains a set of controls and tools you use while designing your web application. Each set of controls and tools is functionally organised on separate tabs within the Toolbox.
D	Document	The area displayed in the middle of the main ASP.NET Web Matrix window directly between the Toolbox and the Workspace and Properties windows. The Document window is dynamically created when you open or create files. The list of open Document windows appears in the window menu, with the top-most window listed last.
E	Workspace	The area displayed on the top right of the main ASP.NET Web Matrix window directly above the Properties window. The Workspace window provides you with an organised view of your file system and open files as well as ready access to any databases you have created.
F	Properties	The area displayed on the bottom right of the main ASP.NET Web Matrix window directly below the Workspace window. Properties define the state, behaviour, and appearance of an ASP.NET page, document or control. Most graphical controls contain properties that can be changed to define their visual appearance.

Table 3.1: Web Matrix components (from the www.asp.net site)

We are ready to create our first ASP.NET web page. As this is our first web page we shall keep things as simple as possible while still trying to illustrate the dynamic potential that the ASP.NET framework provides. Therefore, we shall create a web page that consists of a simple button and when someone clicks the mouse on the button the text *"Hello There!"* will be displayed on the web page next to the button.

The first step in creating our web page is to place a *Label* onto our Document window. A *Label* is a form control, which is used to display some text on the web page. A form is the means by which interaction with the web page user occurs. Labels display text to the user and are one of many form controls. *Buttons*, which we shall be using shortly are another form control and allow the user to *"Submit"* the form. We will be looking at forms and their controls in much greater detail later. But for now let's add the *Label* control. To do this we select the Web Controls tab of the Toolbox (which is on the left side of the Web Matrix tool) to list the web controls, by left clicking on the Web Controls tab. Note that the tabs making up the Toolbox may appear at the top or bottom of the Toolbox component. We then click and hold the left mouse button down on the Web Control tab *"Label"* and drag and drop this onto the Document window by moving the mouse and releasing the left button. This results in a *Label* being added to the Document window, as shown in Figure 3.6.

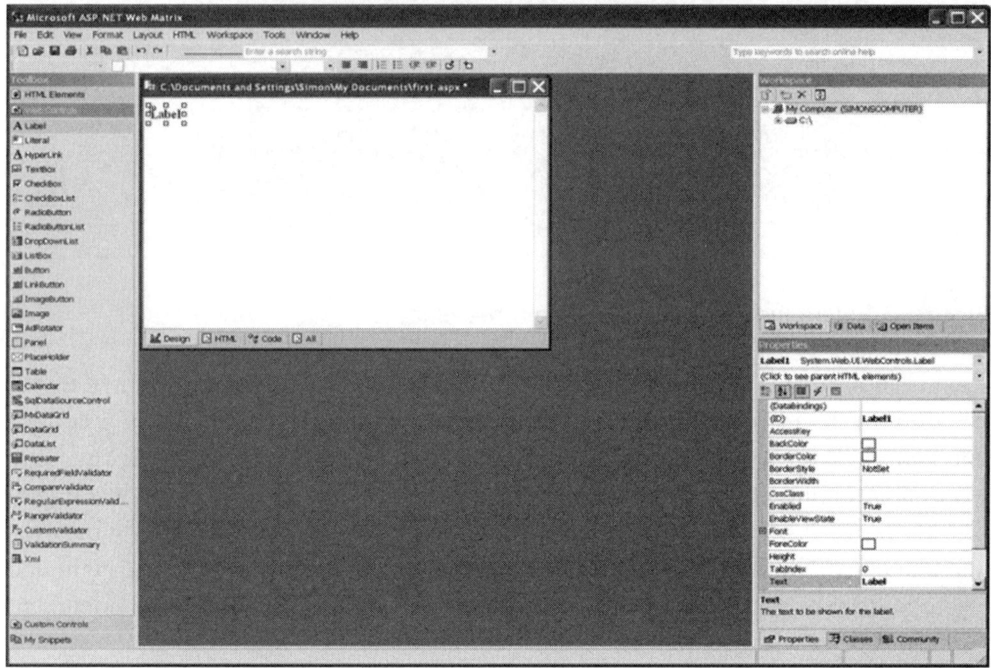

Figure 3.6: Creating a Label

Having added a *Label* control to our page we are now ready to add a *Button* control. First we need to place a new-line character after the *Label* so that the *Button* control appears below and not alongside the *Label*. To do this click the mouse to the right of the placed *Label* control and press the enter key. To add the

Button we select then drag a *Button* control onto the document from the Toolbox. As mentioned *Buttons* are a form control their sole purpose is to allow web page users to click them. When the user clicks the button this causes an "event" to occur and the ASP.NET environment is then able to respond to what the user has done or simply to do something itself. This is illustrated in Figure 3.7.

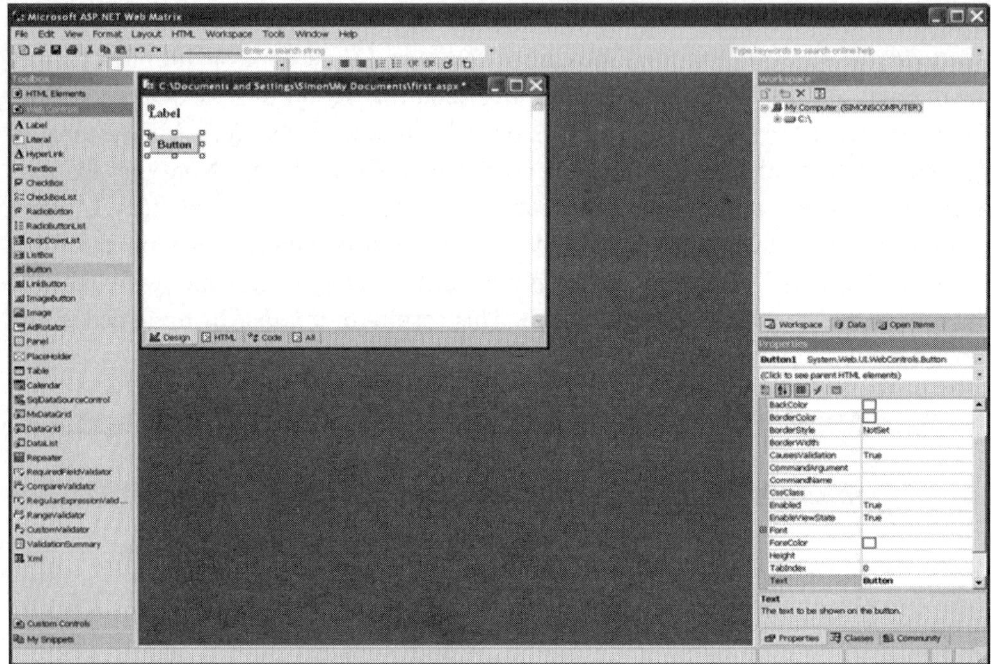

Figure 3.7: Creating a Document with three objects

It doesn't matter if you haven't placed the controls on separate lines it will not stop the script from working. If you want to correct the placement of a control you can click on it with the mouse and delete it by pressing the delete key. It is worth mentioning at this point that you cannot drag and drop objects anywhere you like on the Web Matrix document component window. In fact the window behaves just like a text editor or word processor, objects and text are placed left to right and top to bottom of the window. When you drag and drop objects onto the document window the Web Matrix tool creates the corresponding HTML code, which will be interpreted by our web browser. You can view the HTML code that has been generated by clicking on the HTML tab at the bottom of the Document window. The HTML code generated for these objects is shown in Figure 3.8.

```
C:\Documents and Settings\Simon\My Documents\first.aspx *

<html>
<head>
</head>
<body>
    <form runat="server">
        <p>
            <asp:Label id="Label1" runat="server">Label</asp:Label>
        </p>
        <p>
            <asp:Button id="Button1" runat="server" Text="Button"></asp:Button>
        </p>
        <!-- Insert content here -->
    </form>
</body>
</html>

Design   HTML   Code   All
```

Figure 3.8: Generated HTML

So far we have added two form controls to our web page. However, we mentioned at the start of this section that what we wanted to create a web page which presented a button to the user and when clicked displayed the text *"Hello There"* next to it. In order to accomplish this we need to add some VB.NET code, which tells the browser to display something on the Label when the Button is clicked. To do this click the Document window Design tab and then double click the Button object with the left mouse button. The code associated with this control is displayed in the Document window, as shown in Figure 3.9.

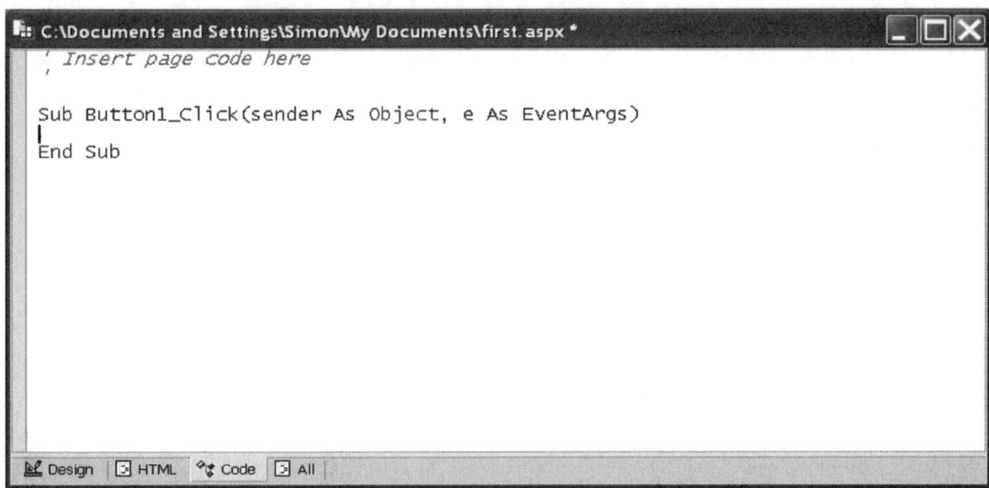

Figure 3.9: Button code

What we see here are a couple of lines of VB.NET code. The two lines of code define the start and end of what is referred to as a subroutine. Don't worry about understanding the details, of what a subroutine is at the moment, we shall consider these later in Chapter 8. What is important is that any VB.NET code that we enter between the *Sub* and *End Sub* lines of code will only be processed when the user clicks the button on the web page. We want the text *"Hello There!"* to be displayed when we click the button. To accomplish this we need to tell the computer to assign the text *"Hello There!"* to our *Label*. Our *Label* has a unique *id*. In fact all controls added to a web page have a unique *id*. In this case the *id* of our *Label* is *Label1* (the Web Matrix tool decided to call it that). Our *Label* has associated with it a large number of what are known as properties. The properties of the *Label* store all the information about the *Label*, such as its size, colour and what text it is currently displaying. The property that is used to store what text a *Label* is currently displaying is called *Text*.

Now we need to formally instruct the computer to set the value of the *Label1 Text* property to *"Hello There!"*. To do this, use the mouse to click on the blank line in between the *Sub* and *End Sub* lines. Then type the following line of code:

```
Label1.Text = "Hello There!"
```

The above line of VB code is the formal way we tell the computer to copy the text *"Hello There!"* to the *Text* property of *Label1*. A professional VB.NET developer would read the line of code as "The *Text* property of *Label1* is assigned the text *Hello There!*", but don't worry about that for the moment. The *Button* code should now look like that shown in Figure 3.10.

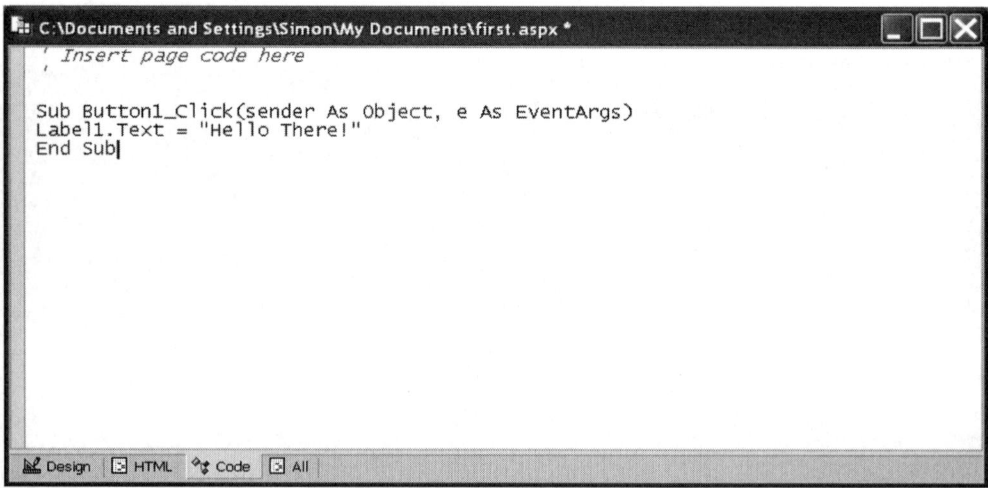

Figure 3.10: Inserted code

Finally, click the Document window Design tab to return to the Design window. We have now completed our first ASP.NET page. It is worth noting that in the Design window it would appear that nothing has happened. Don't worry this is normal. You see all we have done is entered some code which will be processed when the Button control is clicked. Don't bother clicking the Button in the Document window either as this will not cause the Label property to change either. To accomplish this we must view our web page using a web browser. To save the completed script, select the File pull down menu. Then click the Save item from the menu. The next step is to view the output generated by the ASP.NET script in a browser.

3.6   Viewing the script

There are two ways that you can view the output produced by your ASP.NET scripts. The first way is to use the Web Matrix inbuilt web server (the second way is to use the IIS server). The Web Matrix tool will then parse the ASP.NET script and display the results automatically in a web browser. To activate this function select the View pull-down menu and then select the Start menu item, as shown in Figure 3.11. Another quick way of accomplishing this is to press key F5. Whenever there is a shortcut like this available this is noted on the drop-down menu.

Figure 3.11: Launching the Web Matrix server

Selecting the Start menu for the first time will launch the Start Web Application window, shown in Figure 3.12.

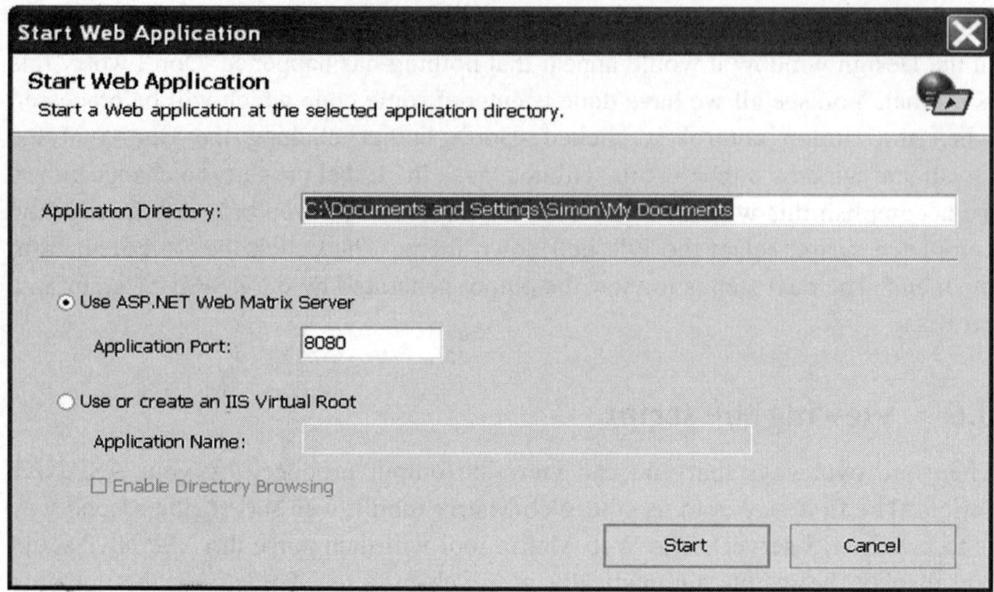

Figure 3.12: Start Web Application window

This window allows you to choose which method you wish to view the results of your ASP.NET script. There are two options from which you can select:

"Use ASP.NET Web Matrix Server". This option allows you to host the web application using the built-in web server that is supplied with Web Matrix. This web server supports only local browser requests and cannot be used to host your pages for others to view.

"Use a new IIS Virtual Root". This option enables you to host the web application using the Microsoft IIS web server.

Note, that this window will only appear the first time you view the ASP.NET script. On subsequent views, Web Matrix will use the web server that was specified the first time you ran the script. Web Matrix will not prompt you to specify a web server again until you close and restart the ASP.NET Web Matrix or stop the Web Matrix server from running by right clicking the mouse on the Web Matrix server icon on the system menu and selecting stop from the menu that appears. Not asking the user which server to use each time allows for more seamless uninterrupted development.

Select the *"Use ASP.NET Web Matrix Server"* and click the Start button. This results in your web browser being launched and your ASP.NET script displayed, as illustrated in Figure 3.13. You should also notice that an icon has appeared on your system tray at the bottom right-hand side of your taskbar to represent the running Web Matrix server. It is worth mentioning that if you wish to stop the Web Matrix server you can by right clicking the mouse on the system tray icon and left clicking the Stop option from the menu which appears. This will force Web Matrix to launch the Start Web Application window shown in Figure 3.12.

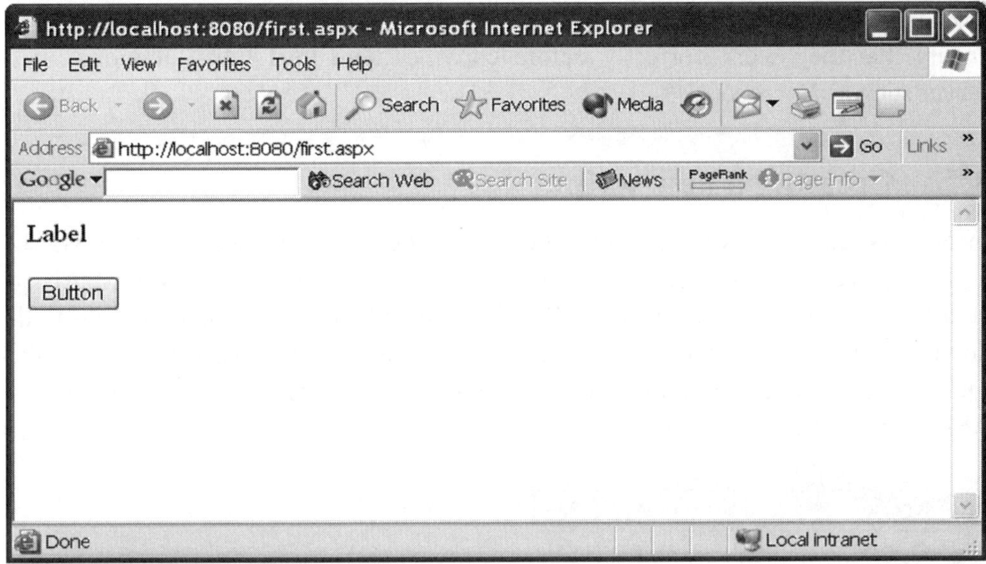

Figure 3.13: Script output

Clicking the button displayed in the browser window will result in the text "*Hello There!*" being displayed on the *Label* replacing the text "*Label*". This is illustrated in Figure 3.14.

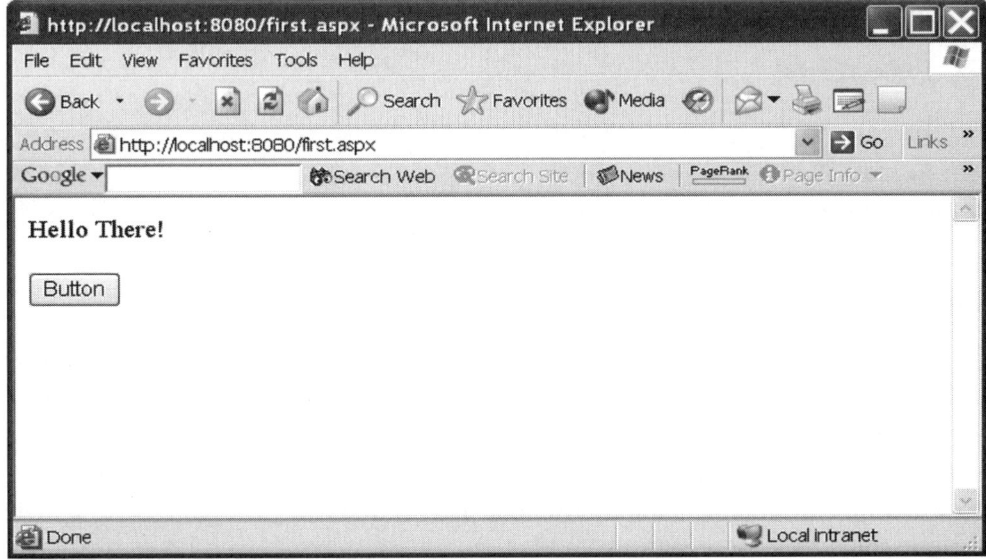

Figure 3.14: Displaying the Hello There label text

While this script is not very interesting it is our first ASP.NET script and it is a very simple one at that. Hopefully, you will have begun to see the potential of what is possible and the ease by which scripts can be created using the Web Matrix tool. Having an in-built web server enables us to more easily test our scripts to ensure that they work correctly before copying them to a fully functional web server such as Microsoft IIS.

3.7   Creating a new script

In our first example we created a new script when we launched the Web Matrix tool. However, once launched you do not need to close and restart Web Matrix to create a new script. Instead like a Word document you can select the File pull-down menu and select the New menu item (see Figure 3.15). This will launch the File creating dialogue window shown in Figure 3.3, enabling you to name a new ASP.NET script.

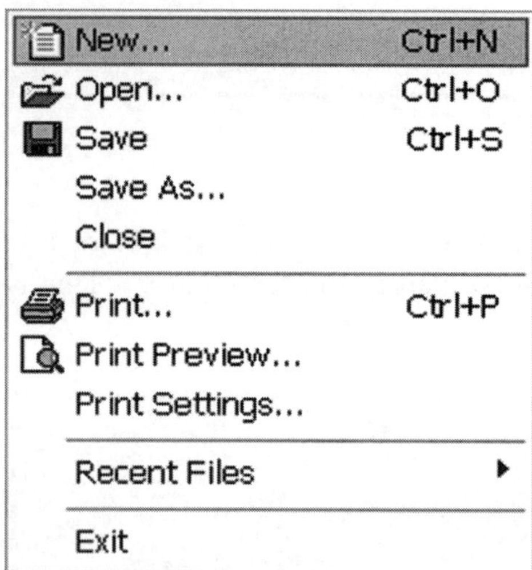

Figure 3.15: Creating a new script

3.8   Creating your second script

Using the New menu option illustrated in Figure 3.15 create a new ASP.NET script called *second.aspx*. Drag and drop onto the Document window a *Label*, a *TextBox* and a *Button* from the Toolbox menu. Don't forget to click the mouse and press enter after dragging each of these controls so that they appear on separate lines. Your Document window should now look like that shown in Figure 3.16, which illustrates the three form controls.

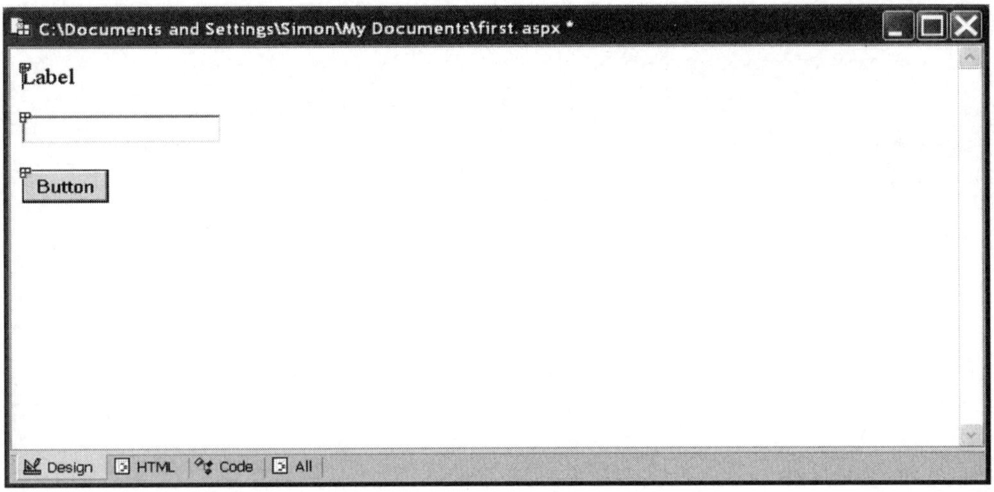

Figure 3:16: Second example

Double click the mouse on the *Button* object to view the code associated with this object. Using the mouse, click on the blank line in between the *Sub* and *End Sub* lines. Then type the following line of code:

```
Label1.Text = TextBox1.Text
```

The above VB script will, when the *Button* is clicked, assign the value of the text stored in TextBox1 and assign this to *Label1*. This will result in whatever you type in the textbox being displayed on the web page after the button is clicked. Save your script by clicking the File pull-down menu. Then from the menu select the Save menu item. Launch the application by selecting the View menu and clicking the Start menu option. Figure 3.17 illustrates what should be displayed.

Type some text into the *Textbox* field and click the button. This text should be displayed on the text *Label*, as shown in Figure 3.18.

Okay, that's it, your second simple ASP.NET script is completed and hopefully working.

One final thought. What happens if you don't type anything into the *TextBox* control and click the button? Well, the VB.NET code does exactly what you have instructed it to do. It copies the contents of the *TextBox1 Text* property (nothing) and assigns this to the *Label1 Text* property. This results in the word "*Label*" disappearing. You see the text "*Label*" is actually the default value of the Text property. This is removed when some new text (or nothing) is assigned to the property.

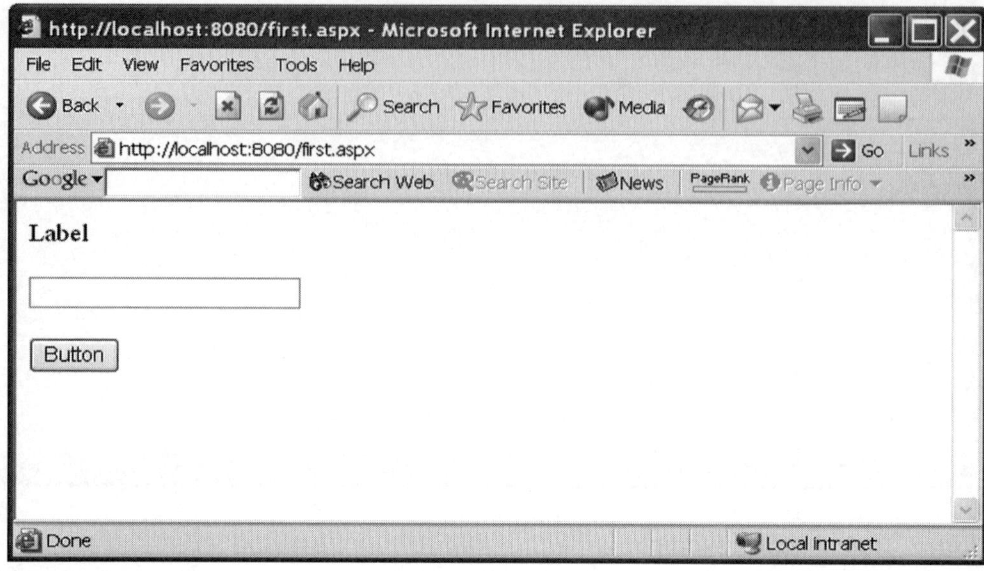

Figure 3.17: Output from second example

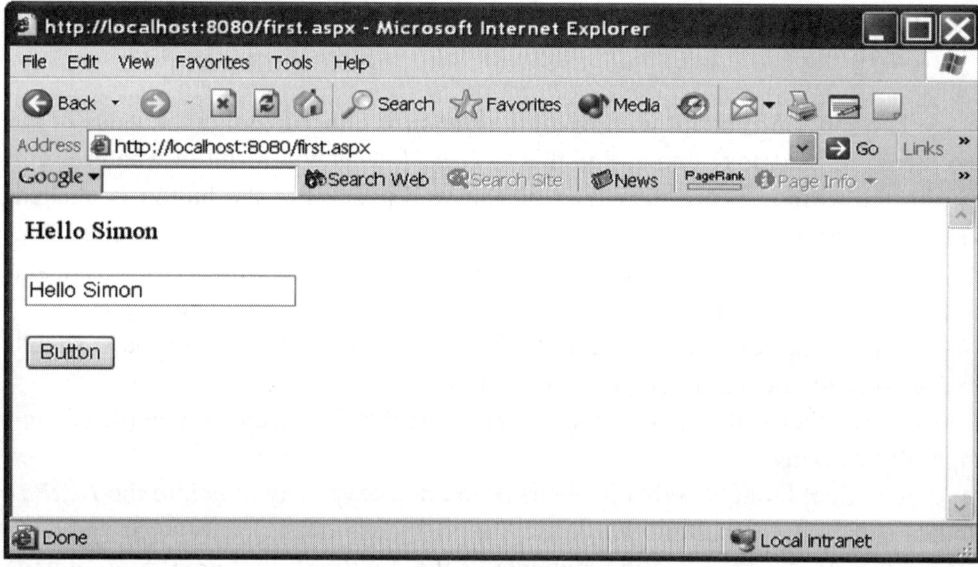

Figure 3.18: Output from second example after user interaction.

3.9　Summary

In this chapter we have introduced the basic workings of the Web Matrix tool. We have shown how to create ASP.NET web pages through dragging and dropping Toolbox web controls onto the Document window and subsequently editing these through the addition of some simple ASP.NET code. We have also shown how the output from your scripts can be viewed using the inbuilt Web Matrix server.

3.10   Exercises

See if you can apply what you have learnt by trying the following exercises:

1. Create a new script called *twoButtons.aspx*. Add one *TextBox* field and two *Button* objects to the Document window. Add code, which enables the text "*You clicked Button One*" and "*You clicked Button Two*" to appear in the label field when each of the corresponding buttons is clicked.

2. Create a new script called *twoLabels.aspx*. Add two *Labels*, two *TextBoxes* and one *Button* to the Document window. Add code which enables the text typed in one *TextBox* to be displayed on one *Label* and the text entered in the other *TextBox* to be displayed on the other *Label*.

4

Finding your way around Web Matrix

4.1   Introduction

In the previous chapter we introduced the Web Matrix tool and illustrated how it can be used to create a simple ASP.NET script. In this chapter we are going to examine the Web Matrix tool in some more detail and illustrate how to use the different components we mentioned briefly in Chapter 3.

4.2   The Toolbox component

We introduced the Toolbox in Chapter 3 and showed that controls can be dragged and dropped from the Toolbox onto the Document. There are a large number of different controls on the Toolbox and while they perform different functions they can all be placed on the Document window in the same way. The Toolbox actually consists of four separate lists of controls. You can access these by clicking on the following tabs to view the separate lists:

- HTML Elements
- Web Controls
- Custom Controls
- My Snippets

Figure 4.1 illustrates the Toolbox Web Controls which are displayed when you select HTML Elements or Web Controls. The HTML Elements list displays controls which are for HTML web page creation while the Web Controls list displays ASP.NET specific controls.

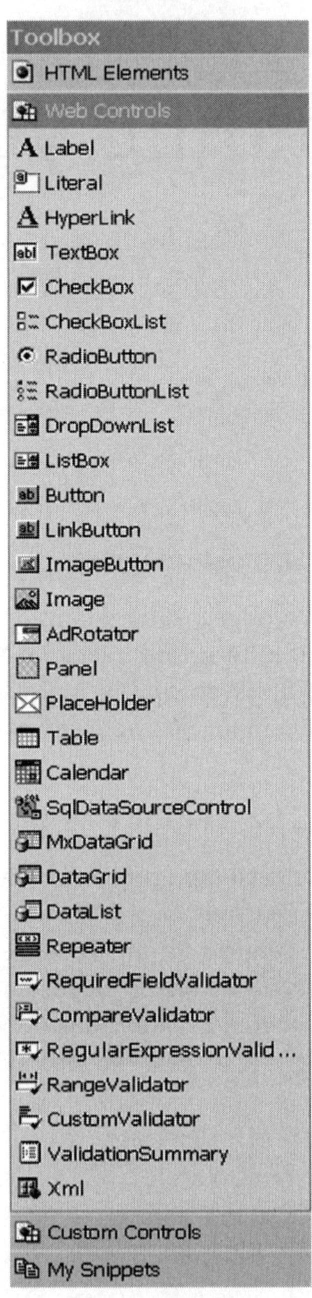

Figure 4.1: Toolbox controls

As a default the Web Controls list is displayed and for now we do not need to change this, as our next example will need to use some of the controls on this list. Custom Controls and My Snippets are blank when you first start using the Web Matrix tool and enable you to add your own controls to these lists to customise your Web Matrix tool. My Snippets is useful for storing any ASP.NET code which you use regularly and do not want to keep retyping. You can add any code to this Toolbar by simply highlighting it with the mouse and then dragging and dropping the code onto the Toolbar component window.

We shall be returning to the Toolbox control in some detail in later chapters. Specifically, in Chapter 5 we shall examine some of the HTML controls in more detail. In Chapter 6 we shall introduce the web controls available for user interaction. Finally, in Chapter 7 we shall examine the web controls which are provided to allow us to validate user input effectively.

4.3   The Document window component

The Document window component is where you view the ASP.NET page that you are creating. To further our knowledge of how this component works let's create a new document called *chapt4.1.aspx* and drag a *Label* and *Calendar* control from the Toolbar onto the Document window as shown in Figure 4.2.

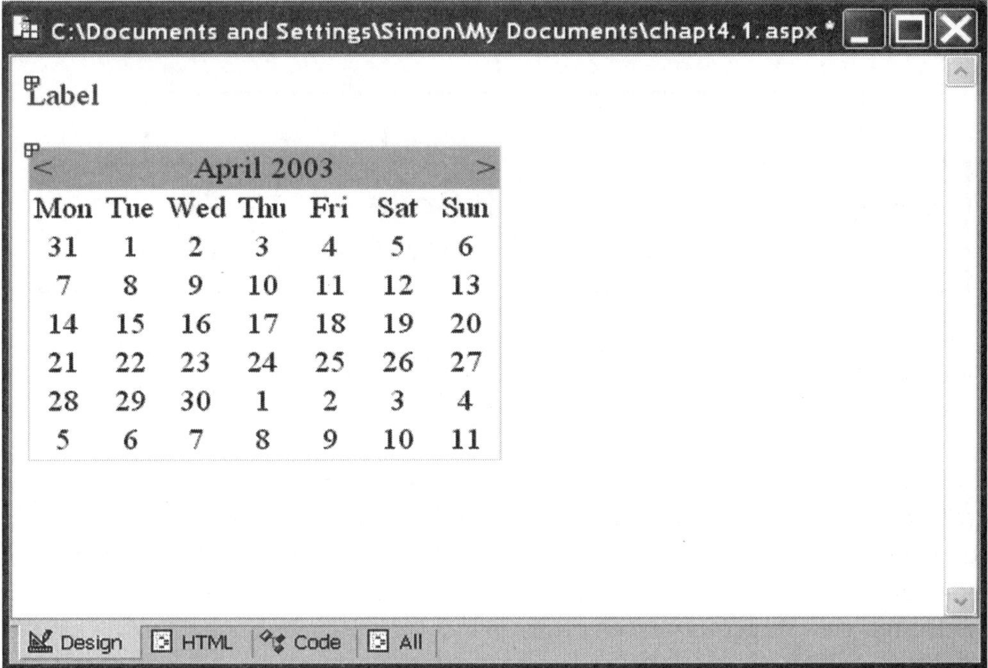

Figure 4.2: Document window component

The Document window component has four different ways of viewing the ASP.NET page that you are designing. These are:

- Design
- HTML
- Code
- All

The different views can be accessed by clicking the tabs at the bottom of the window labelled the same as the list above. Figure 4.3 illustrates that these four different views are simply the Web Matrix tool's way of providing the developer with the means to examine the web page that they are creating in different ways. You will find that different views are more useful to you when you are trying to accomplish different tasks and you will discover this with practice. All that is important to realise now is that you are essentially looking at one web page in four different ways.

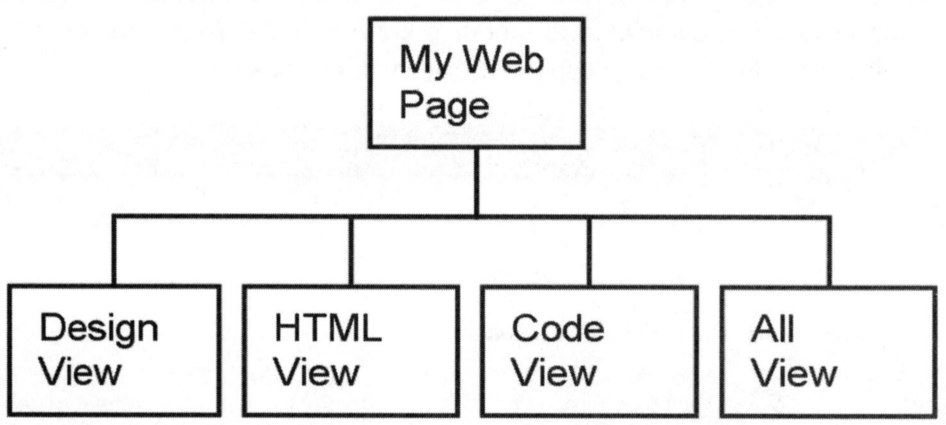

Figure 4.3: Four different views of the same web page

The default view is Design, which is shown in Figure 4.2. The Design view provides us with a drag and drop interface. Different controls and objects which we add to our web page are represented by icons which try and emulate what they will look like when the web page is viewed using a web browser. It is not possible for the Design view to get this exactly right, but at least you get some idea of what the controls are and their relative placement to one another.

Clicking the HTML tab will display the HTML code which has been created for the page. The HTML view of our current web page is shown in Figure 4.4.

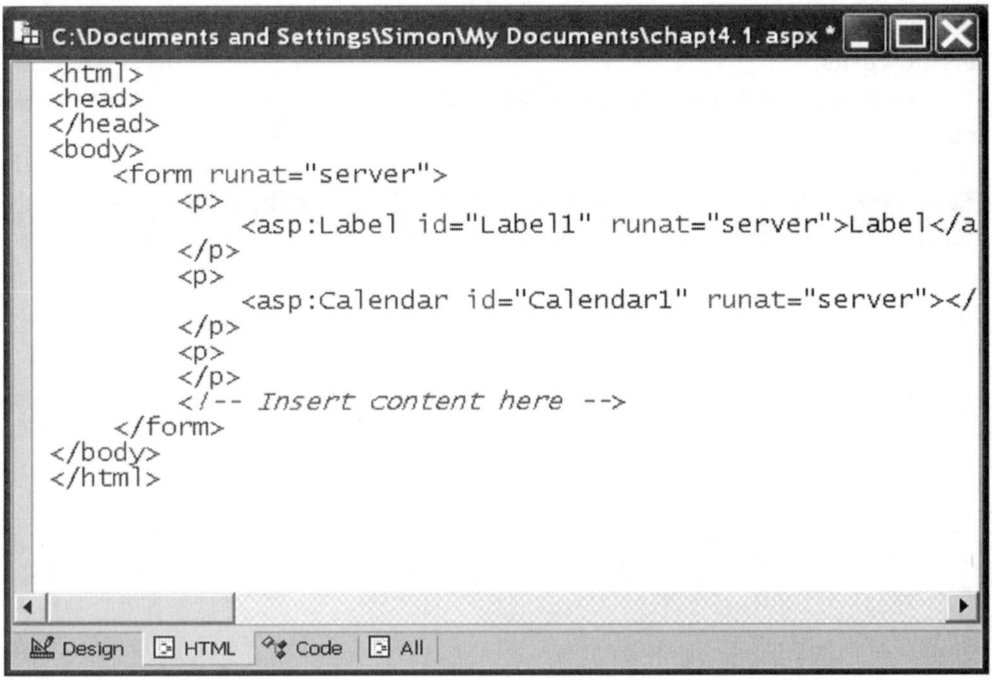

```
<html>
<head>
</head>
<body>
    <form runat="server">
        <p>
            <asp:Label id="Label1" runat="server">Label</a
        </p>
        <p>
            <asp:Calendar id="Calendar1" runat="server"></
        </p>
        <p>
        </p>
        <!-- Insert content here -->
    </form>
</body>
</html>
```

Design   HTML   Code   All

Figure 4.4: HTML Document window view

The HTML view of our web page is a little more complex than the Design view, certainly if you have never seen any HTML syntax before. The first thing to note is that there is no graphical representation of the different components we have added to the Web page, only text. This is because HTML is text-based and consists of nothing else. You should also note that the HTML code is wider than the current Document window and so a scroll-bar has been added to the bottom of the window to allow you to scroll right to view the HTML which is not currently visible. Don't worry that you are not sure that you understand exactly what the HTML code is doing as we shall examine this in the next chapter. However, if you look within the HTML code you should see an HTML line:

```
<asp:Label id="Label1" runat="server" ForeColor="Blue"
BackColor="Yellow">Label</asp:Label>
```

This is the HTML equivalent of the *Label* control which you added to your web page. Likewise the line:

```
<asp:Calendar id="Calendar1" runat="server"
OnSelectionChanged="Calendar1_SelectionChanged"></asp:Calendar>
```

This is the HTML code for the *Calendar* control which you dragged onto the Design window view. It is important to realise that this view and all the others are not simply ways to "look" at our web page. Each and very view is editable so that we can change and modify our web page design no matter which view we are currently using.

Clicking the Code tab will display the ASP.NET code which has been created or entered by you. This is illustrated in Figure 4.5.

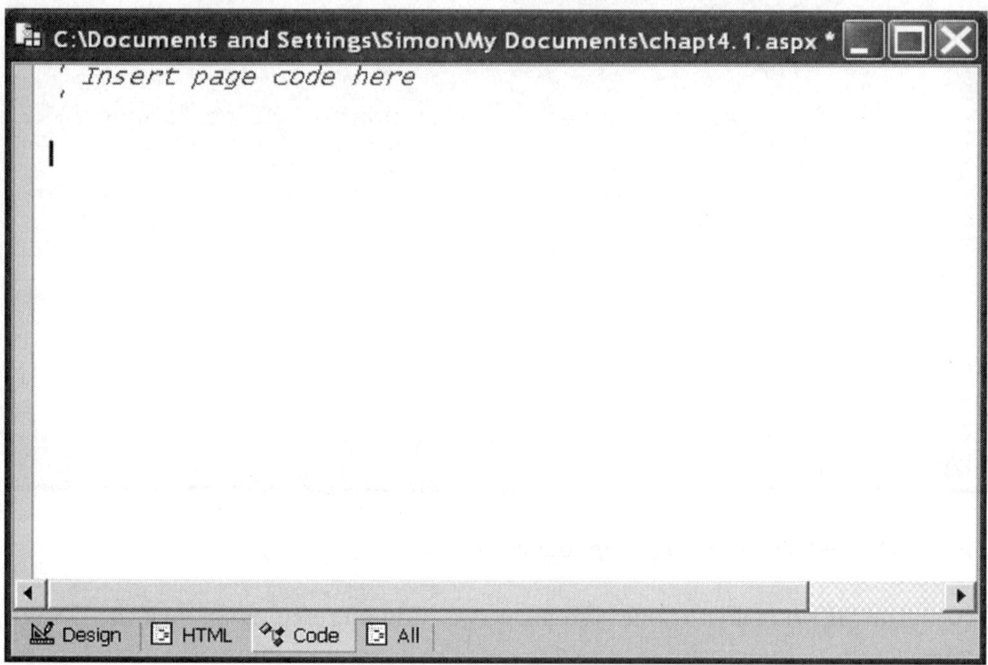

Figure 4.5: Code Document window view

Unfortunately the Code view is quite bare at the moment. All it contains is a comment reading "*Insert page code here*". A comment is simply a note to the developer to remind them of something and does nothing to affect the web page. We shall see later that the Code view is useful for displaying any ASP.NET script which we add to our web page.

Finally clicking the All tab will display both the HTML and the ASP.NET code and is simply a combination of the HTML and Code views. Figure 4.6 illustrates what is displayed by clicking the All tab. In our example the Code extends both off the bottom and off the right of the window and as such two scroll-bars have been added to the window to enable you to view all of the Code and HTML. Note the line at the top of the All view which reads:

```
<%@ Page Language="VB" %>
```

This is an ASP.NET instruction which tells the computer that this ASP.NET page is written using the VB.NET language.

```
1   <%@ Page Language="VB" %>
2   <script runat="server">
3
4       ' Insert page code here
5       '
6
7   </script>
8   <html>
9   <head>
10  </head>
11  <body>
12      <form runat="server">
13          <p>
14              <asp:Label id="Label1" runat="server">L
15          </p>
16          <p>
17              <asp:Calendar id="Calendar1" runat="ser
18          </p>
19          <p>
20          </p>
21          <!-- Insert content here -->
```

Figure 4.6: All Document window view

You will find it useful to switch views when developing your ASP.NET web pages, but for now we shall stick with the Design view. Note that when you do switch between the different document views that the Toolbox control also changes to provide you with the controls which are relevant to the current view mode.

4.4   Workspace component

The Workspace component is located in the top right of the Web Matrix tool and enables access to the directories and files on your computer as well as accessing your Microsoft SQL databases. Figure 4.7 illustrates the default Workspace component.

The Workspace component can be used to access existing ASP.NET scripts which you have created in much the same way as the Windows File Explorer can be used to locate and access documents. By clicking on the + icon next to the "*My Computer*" text in the Workspace window and then clicking the + icon next to the "*C:*" text, results in the Workspace displaying the files and directories available on your computer. This is illustrated in Figure 4.8.

Figure 4.7: Workspace component

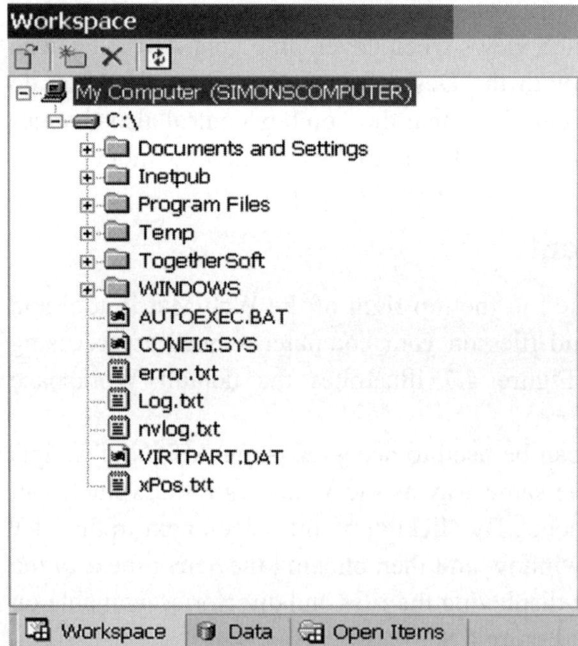

Figure 4.8: Workspace directories on local computer

Using the Workspace component locate the files which you created in Chapter 3. On our computer these are located in:

C:\Documents and Settings\Simon\My Documents\

However, these files could be elsewhere on your computer, depending on exactly how you decided to save these. Figure 4.9 illustrates these files on our computer.

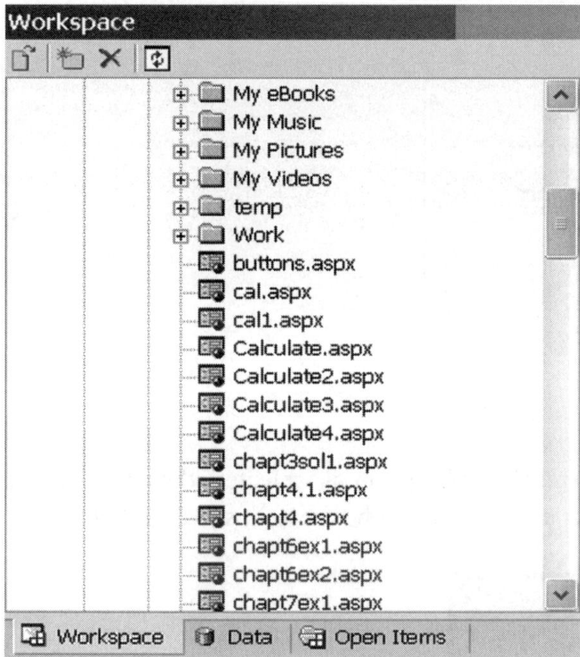

Figure 4.9: My Documents Workspace

The Workspace component allows you to load an existing ASP.NET file into the Web Matrix tool. All ASP.NET files can be identified as they end with the extension .aspx. Simply double click on an .aspx file to load this into Web Matrix.

You can also create new directories from within the Workspace component. Why would you want to do this? Well, you may wish to place your current ASP.NET files in a separate directory from others that you have previously created. Or, you may wish to have a separate directory to store images which will appear on your web pages. Whatever, the reason you can accomplish this task very easily. To do this you select the directory where you would like to create a new directory within. Then right click the mouse button and from the pop-up menu choose the New Workspace menu item and then the Add Folder Shortcut. These pop-up menus are illustrated in Figure 4.10.

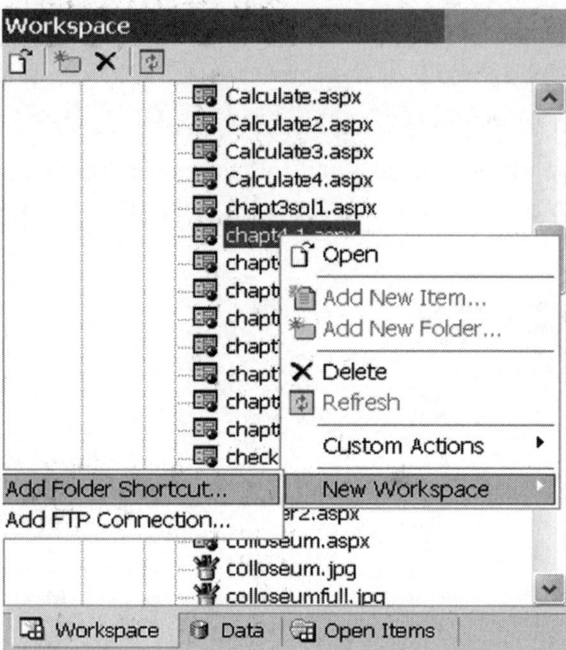

Figure 4.10: Workspace pop-up windows

When the Add Folder Shortcut menu option is selected the Browse for Folder window is launched enabling a new folder to be created, see Figure 4.11.

Figure 4.11: New folder creation

The Workspace component has three different views accessible by clicking on the three tabs at the bottom of the component. These are:

- Workspace
- Data
- Open Items

The Workspace view displays all files and directories on your local computer and this is the view we have been using up until now. The Data view displays the SQL database connections which are present. Finally, the Open Items view displays a list of all files which are currently opened within Document windows. We shall return to the Workspace component in a later chapter when we introduce databases.

4.5   Properties component

The Properties component is located at the bottom right of the Web Matrix tool. The properties component allows you to adjust the properties of your ASP.NET document as well as the properties associated with each control added to your document. To illustrate this make sure that your *chapt4.1.aspx* document is being viewed in Design mode and click the mouse once on the *Label* control that you added to this document earlier in this chapter. The properties window will now display the properties associated with this control. This is illustrated in Figure 4.12.

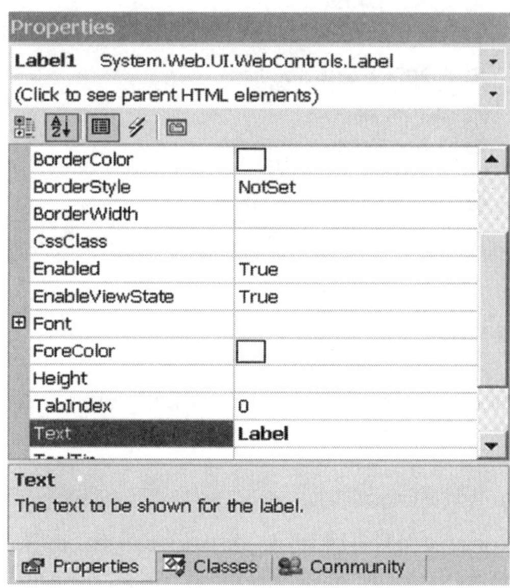

Figure 4.12: Label1 Properties component

In addition to displaying the properties associated with a particular control the Properties component has two other views which can be accessed through the tabs located at the bottom of the component. There are three tabs and they are labelled:

- Properties
- Classes
- Community

While the Properties view is the default there are two other views. The Classes tab displays a list of the ASP.NET classes which form the core of the ASP.NET framework. The Community tab displays a list of web links where further information and tutorials on Web Matrix can be found, see Figure 4.13.

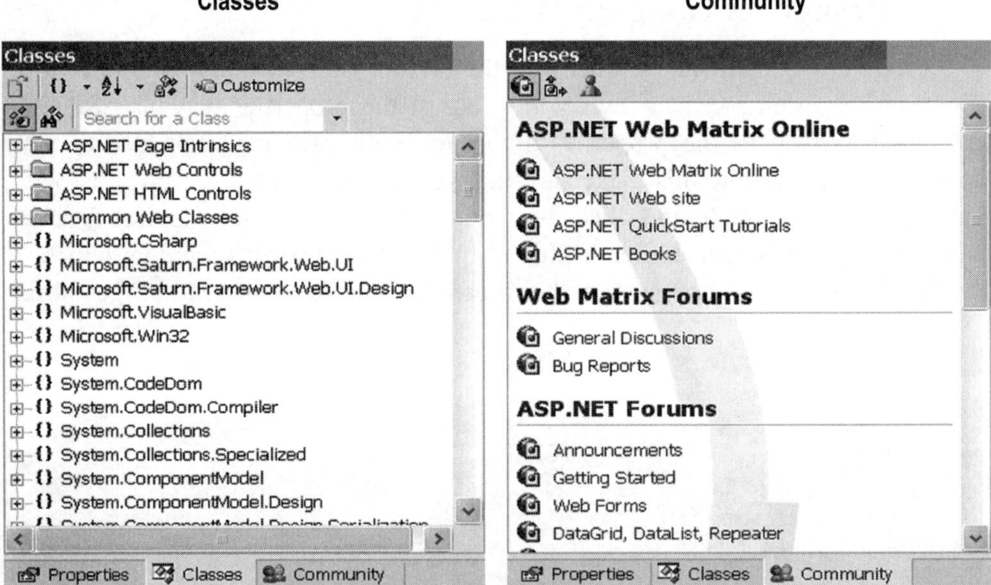

Figure 4.13: Properties component Classes and Community

We came across the concept of Properties in the previous chapter, where we set the *Label* property *Text* with the VB.NET code:

```
Label1.Text = "Hello World!"
```

The above line of code sets the property of a control during run-time. In other words at some point when the ASP.NET web page application is running then the *Text* property will be set to *"Hello Word!"*. If you remember it was because a *Button* control was clicked. The Properties component window allows you to set the control properties before run-time. This means that when the ASP.NET web application is initially viewed in a browser that specific controls properties will be set to certain values without the need to have any ASP.NET code to change them.

Return to the Properties view by clicking on the Properties tab. This should display the properties of the *Label1* control, as shown in Figure 4.12. You can scroll through the different properties using the scroll bar on the right of the control. The properties enable you to specify how your control will appear on the web page. Scroll through the properties list and find the property called *BackColor*. This property allows you to change the background colour of the control. Click the mouse on the *BackColor* property and then click the button to the right of the property to launch the colour selection tool, this is shown in Figure 4.14. Choose the colour yellow from those displayed.

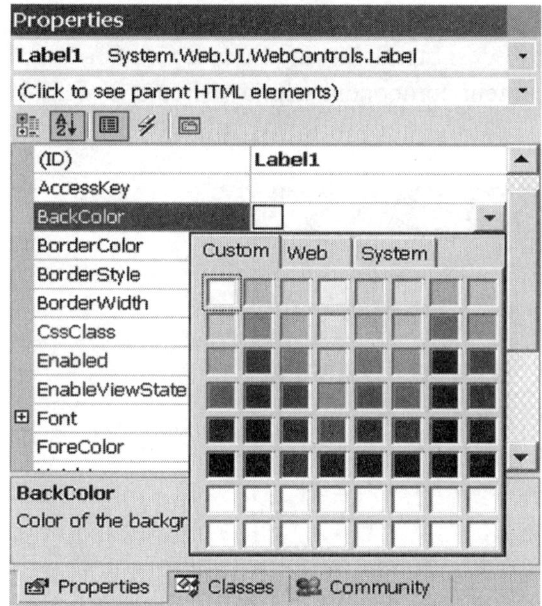

Figure 4.14: BackColor colour selection

Find the *ForeColor* property and select the blue colour. You should notice that the Label in the Documents window will alter how it looks, to reflect the changes to the properties you have made.

If you switch to the HTML view of the Design document window you will see that the properties *BackColor* and *ForeColor* have been added to the HTML code for the *Label* control. This HTML now looks like this:

```
<asp:Label id="Label1" runat="server" ForeColor="Blue"
BackColor="#FFFF80">Label</asp:Label>
```

Note that in the above HTML fragement that the *ForeColor* property was set to Blue while the *BackColor* was set to *"#FFFF80"* and not *"Yellow"*. The reason for this is that HTML uses a Red–Green–Blue (RGB) colour code to represent different colours. To make things easier for the developer some colours such as "Red", "Green", "Blue" etc can be written in name form. In the example above we selected a yellow colour, which wasn't quite standard yellow. You have two choices, you can leave this as it is or using the mouse and keyboard, edit the HTML so that the *BackColor="Yellow"*.

Next click on the *Calendar* control in the Document component and view the properties which are associated with this control. You should note that while some of the properties displayed in the properties component are the same as for the *Label* control there are many others which are different. Also note that below the scrollable list of properties there is now a hyperlink in blue labelled Auto Format. Clicking this link with the mouse will launch the Calendar *Auto Format* window as shown in Figure 4.15. The window allows you to configure the *Calendar* control from a predefined list of designs. Select the Simple form from the list and click the OK button. Your Document component window should now look like that illustrated in Figure 4.16.

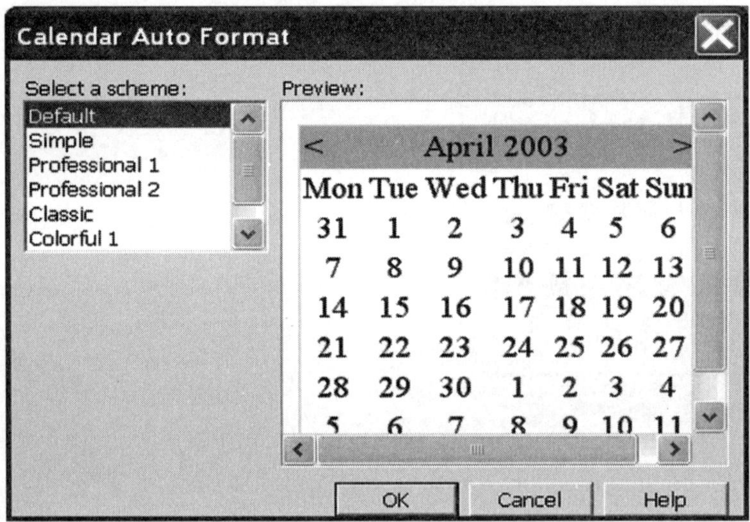

Figure 4.15: Calendar Auto Format window

Before, we continue let us take a quick look at the HTML which has been generated for our revised *Calendar* control. Click on the HTML tab of the Document window component. The following HTML should be displayed for the *Calendar* control:

```
<asp:Calendar id="Calendar1" runat="server" ForeColor="Black"
BackColor="White" CellPadding="4" BorderColor="#999999" Font-
```

```
Names="Verdana" Font-Size="8pt" Height="180px" DayNameFormat="FirstLetter"
Width="200px">
        <TodayDayStyle forecolor="Black"
backcolor="#CCCCCC"></TodayDayStyle>
        <SelectorStyle backcolor="#CCCCCC"></SelectorStyle>
        <NextPrevStyle verticalalign="Bottom"></NextPrevStyle>
        <DayHeaderStyle font-size="7pt" font-bold="True"
backcolor="#CCCCCC"></DayHeaderStyle>
        <SelectedDayStyle font-bold="True" forecolor="White"
backcolor="#666666"></SelectedDayStyle>
        <TitleStyle font-bold="True" bordercolor="Black"
backcolor="#999999"></TitleStyle>
        <WeekendDayStyle backcolor="#FFFFCC"></WeekendDayStyle>
        <OtherMonthDayStyle forecolor="#808080"></OtherMonthDayStyle>
    </asp:Calendar>
```

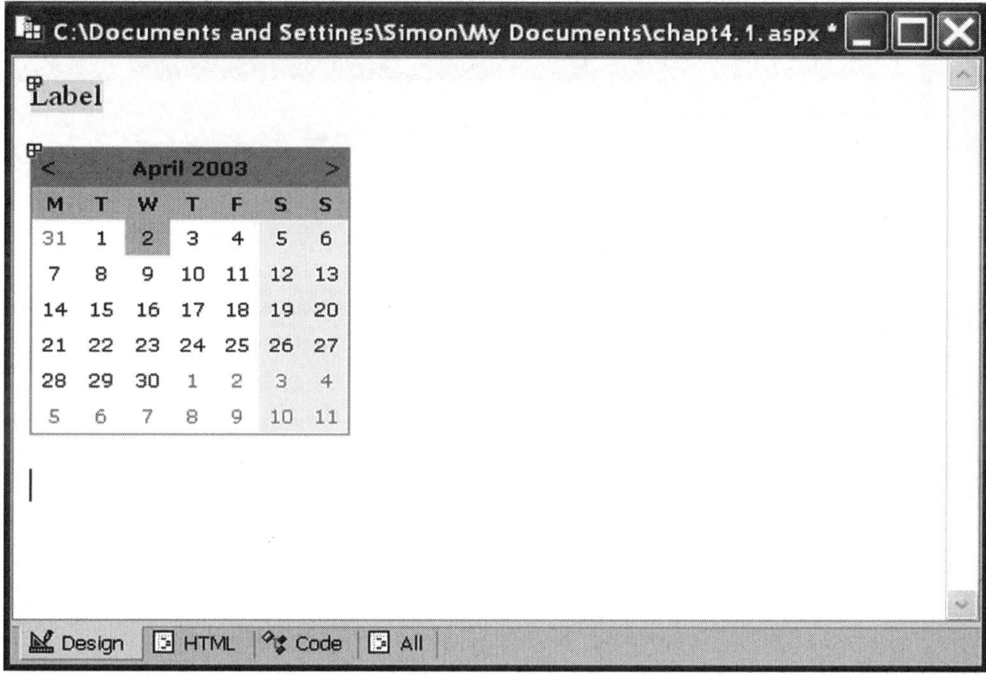

Figure 4.16: Modified controls shown in Document window

We are almost finished configuring this ASP.NET script. The final thing we need to do is to double click on the *Calendar* control in the Document window component. This will display the code associated with this control.

Using the mouse, click on the blank line in between the *Sub* and *End Sub* lines of code. Then type the following line of code:

```
Label1.Text = "The Date you selected is " & Calendar1.SelectedDate
```

The above code will assign the value of the date selected by clicking on the calendar control and assign this to *Label1* which will display this on the web page. The & character is used to join the text *"The Date you selected is"* and the date from the *SelectedDate* property. If you now click on the Code view of the Document window component you will see the following code:

```
' Insert page code here
'


Sub Calendar1_SelectionChanged(sender As Object, e As EventArgs)
Label1.Text = "The Date you selected is " & Calendar1.SelectedDate
End Sub
```

The ASP.NET script is now complete so save it and click Start from the View menu to launch the script. Selecting a date from the *Calendar* control will result in this being displayed on the *Label*. This is illustrated in Figure 4.17.

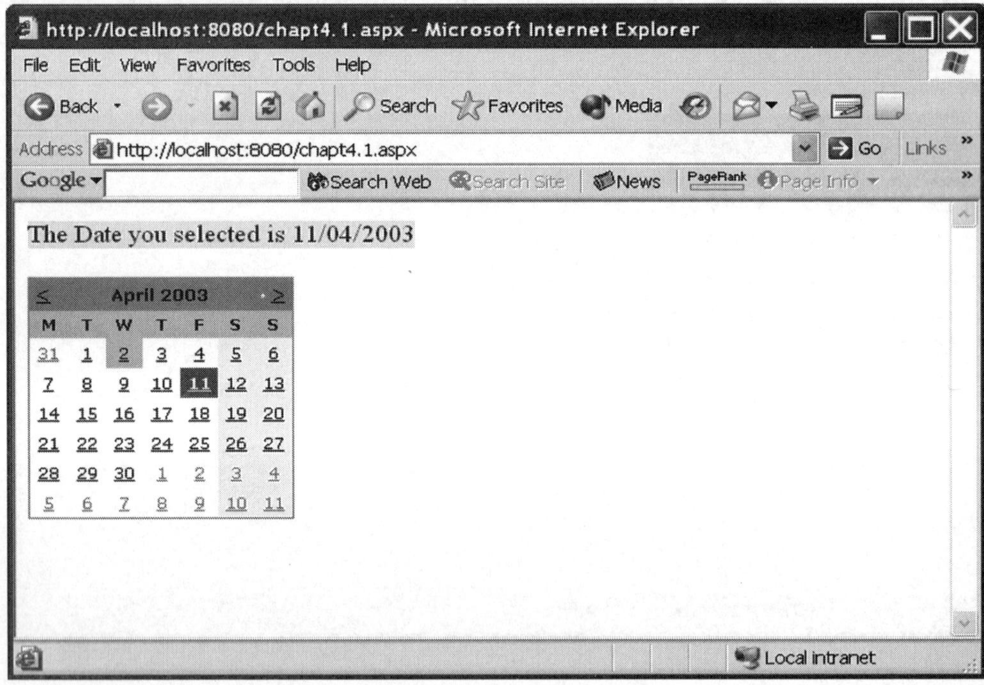

Figure 4.17: Finished Calendar script

4.6   Summary

In this chapter we have examined each of the components that go to make up the Web Matrix tool. We have illustrated how each of these can be used and what functions they perform. We have introduced the Calendar control and illustrated how this can be used to select and access a date, which is displayed on the web page.

4.7   Exercises

See if you can apply what you have learnt by trying the following exercises:

1. Create a New script called *Rule.aspx*. Type the text "*Welcome to my Web page*" onto the document window component. Next select the ToolBox HTML Elements list and drag a *Horizontal Rule* below this text. Click on the *Horizontal Rule* and using the Properties component adjust the rules properties so that it is aligned left, is black has *noShade* and is of *size* 4. Finally, type the text "*This is a horizontal rule.*" below the *Horizontal Rule* you have added.

2. Create a New script called *twoCals.aspx*. Add two *Labels* and two *Calendars* to the Document window. Add code, which enables the date selected from *Calendar* control to be displayed in one *Label* and the date selected in the other *Calendar* control in the other *Label*.

5

Basic HTML elements

5.1 Introduction

In this chapter we shall examine some of the different HyperText Markup Language (HTML) elements that we can use within the Web Matrix tool to construct our web pages. We have decided not to include the HTML elements which are used to create forms in this chapter as these elements have been replaced with ASP.NET form controls and we cover those in Chapter 6.

5.2 HTML document structure

When a new document is created in Web Matrix it already has a number of HTML elements included within it, but in the Design view these are not visible. Create a new document called *html.aspx* and then click the HTML tab of the document window. You will see that although no controls have been added to the document yet there are still some HTML elements which have been automatically created. These HTML elements that have been included are:

```
<html>
<head>
</head>
<body>
   <form runat="server">
      <!-- Insert content here -->
   </form>
</body>
```

```
</html>
```

These HTML elements form a basic skeleton which all HTML documents require. Let us examine what each of these different elements means. The first element is the *<html>* element which consists of a start and end tag:

```
<html>
</html>
```

A start tag is normally exactly the same as its end tag except the end tag has a "/" after the "<" character. This element defines the start and end of an HTML document. All of the rest of the HTML document will appear within these tags. The next HTML element is *<head>* which again consists of two tags which define the start and end of the heading part of the document:

```
<head>
</head>
```

The heading section of a HTML document is used to store information about the document produced. We shall introduce an element which can be included in the heading section when we consider document titles in the following section of this chapter. The next HTML element is *<body>* which again consists of two tags which define the start and end of the body part of the document:

```
<body>
</body>
```

The body of the document is where all the HTML instructions are included. The HTML body is where the majority of the controls and elements we add to our document are inserted. You will note that within the *<body>* section of the document there are already a couple of elements. The first of these is the *<form>* element:

```
<form runat="server">
</form>
```

The form element is used to define the start and end of an ASP.NET form. We will examine form elements in the following chapter. The form element has the *attribute runat="server"*. This defines the form as an ASP.NET form which is to be processed at the web server. Many of our controls which we will add have to be included within the start and end tags of this form element. We shall consider these later when we encounter them. The final element is a comment which looks like this:

```
<!-- Insert content here -->
```

A comment is just a text note which the programmer can leave as a reminder to themselves. The comment is not displayed on the web page. The text *"Insert content here"* can be replaced within any text you like.

5.3   Document title

The *<title>* element is a heading element which should be inserted between the *<head>* and *</head>* tags. The *<title>* element allows you to specify the text which will appear on the blue title bar of the browser. Enter the following *<title>* element between the start and end heading tags:

```
<title>My HTML Example</title>
```

Save the document and then select the Start menu option from the View menu. This should launch a web browser which displays a blank web page. However, if you look closely at the top title bar of the web browser window then you should see the text *"My HTML Example"* displayed. This is illustrated in Figure 5.1.

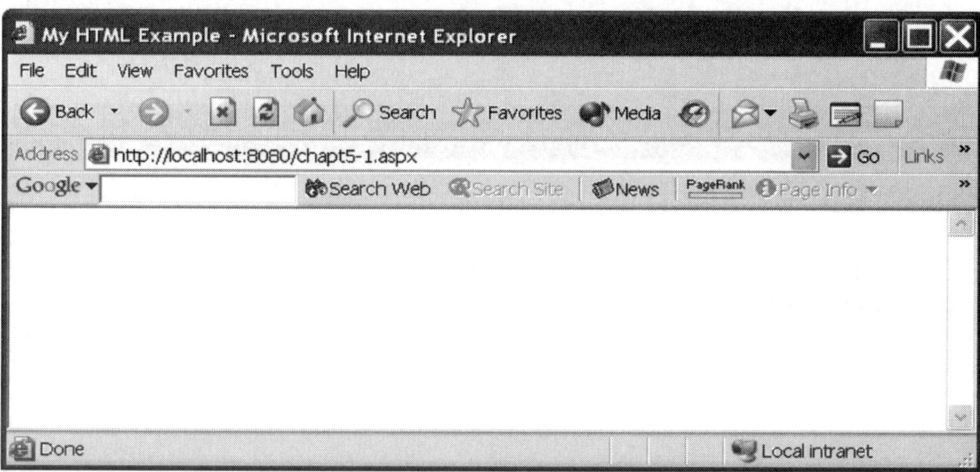

Figure 5.1: Title element

5.4   Text paragraphs

Text can be inserted on a web page. One of the easiest ways of doing this in Web Matrix is to return to the Design view of the document, click the mouse on the Document window and type some text. You can form paragraphs of text by pressing the enter key and continuing typing. An example of this is illustrated in Figure 5.2

Clicking on the HTML tab at the bottom of the document window reveals the generated HTML:

```
<html>
<head>
   <title>My HTML Example</title>
</head>
```

```
<body>
   <form runat="server">
      <p>
         This is some text which I have typed into my document.<!-- Insert content
here -->
      </p>
      <p>
         This is a second line of text which I typed after pressing the enter key at the
end
         of the previous sentence.
      </p>
   </form>
</body>
</html>
```

Note that the tags *<p>* and *</p>* have been inserted around sections of the text. The *<p>* element denotes a paragraph, with a *<p>* tag at the start and the *</p>* tag at the end of a paragraph.

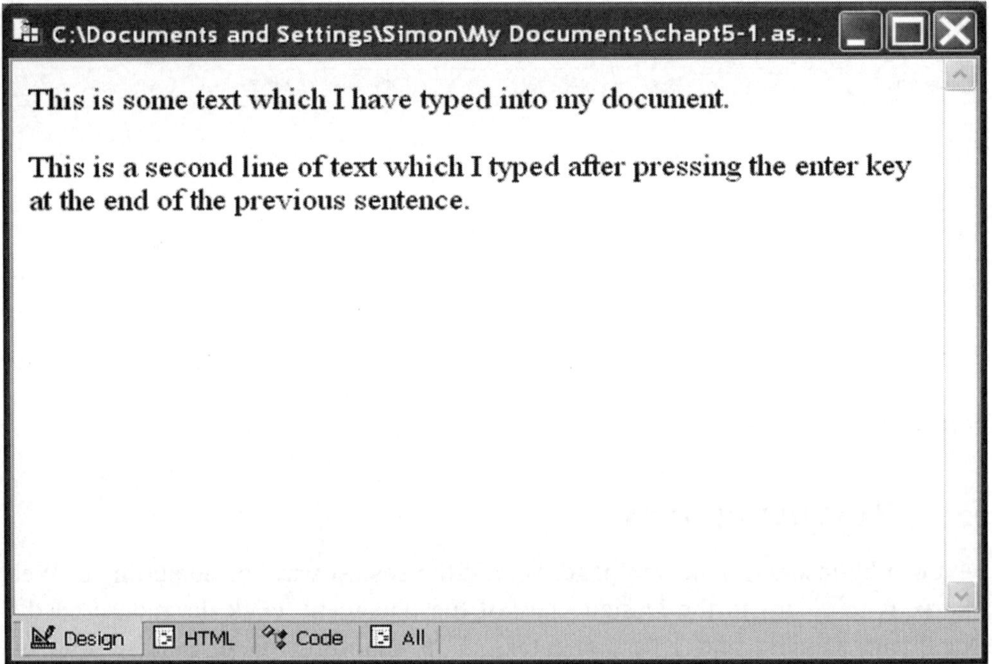

Figure 5.2: Paragraphs of text

Clicking the mouse on one of the paragraphs in the Design view enables the properties of the paragraph to be adjusted in the Properties component of the Matrix tool. Try clicking on the second paragraph of text in the Design view of the document window component. Then, using the properties component find the align property and change this from *Not Set* to *Center* so that the paragraph of text is centered on the page.

5.5   Headings

HTML supports headings. Click the mouse at the end of the second paragraph of your document. Press the enter key and type *"This is a Heading Level 1"*. You may also need to set the Properties of this paragraph so that the text is aligned to the left of the window. All this has achieved is to create a text paragraph that is aligned left. The next stage is to inform Web Matrix that this paragraph is actually a heading. We do this by clicking the mouse on the text we have just entered and then selecting the pull-down menu list just above the Toolbox component. This should read *"Normal"* by default. Click the small arrow button to the right of the text *"Normal"* and from the drop-down list select the option *"Heading 1"*. The text on your third paragraph should then change to a much larger bolder text representing a heading Level 1. This is illustrated in Figure 5.3.

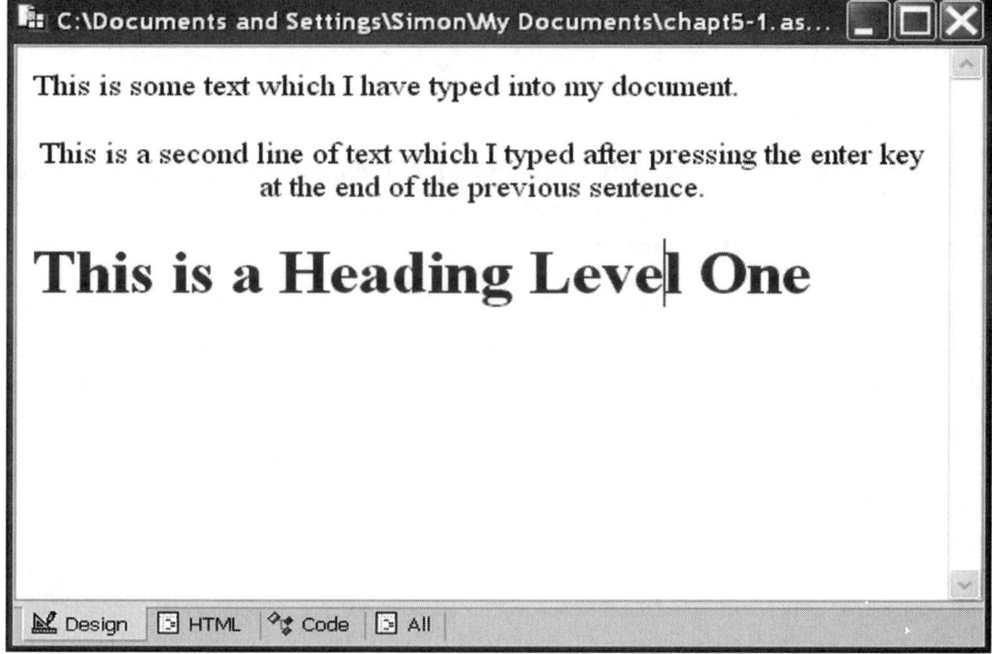

Figure 5.3: Heading Level One

Clicking on the HTML tab of the document component will show you the generated HTML code for this document. Currently this should look like this:

```
<html>
<head>
```

```
    <title>My HTML Example</title>
</head>
<body>
  <form runat="server">
    <p>
       This is some text which I have typed into my document.<!-- Insert content
here -->
    </p>
    <p align="center">
       This is a second line of text which I typed after pressing the enter key at the
end
       of the previous sentence.
    </p>
    <h1 align="left">This is a Heading Level One
    </h1>
  </form>
</body>
</html>
```

Try changing the Heading Level 1 to one of the other heading sizes which are listed in the drop-down menu. To do this, simply return to the Design view and click the mouse on the Heading line. Then select a different heading from the list.

5.6   Line breaks

Sometimes you may wish to start a new line of text without the blank line which is included between paragraphs. The break element enables you to accomplish this. The format of the break element is:

```
<br />
```

The break element is a little different to the two part elements we have come across this far. The break element is a special element which allows the user to declare the start and end elements together. The *
* element consists of only one tag which is an amalgamation of the *
* and *</br>* tags. Click to the HTML view of the document component and type the following below the *</h1>* tag:

```
<br />
Some text
<br />
Some more text on the next line but without a blank line
<br />
And another
```

Returning to the Design view we can see that the text appears on separate lines but without any blank lines between them, as shown in Figure 5.4.

One of the questions that is often raised with beginners learning HTML is what is the difference between: *<p></p>* and *
*? Well, *<p> </p>* defines a paragraph of text with a blank line after the paragraph and before the next. The

*
* element indicates a line break, moving the cursor to the next line. You are allowed to use multiple *
* one after the other to force a number of blank lines but multiple *<p></p>* elements cannot force multiple lines between paragraphs and will be ignored.

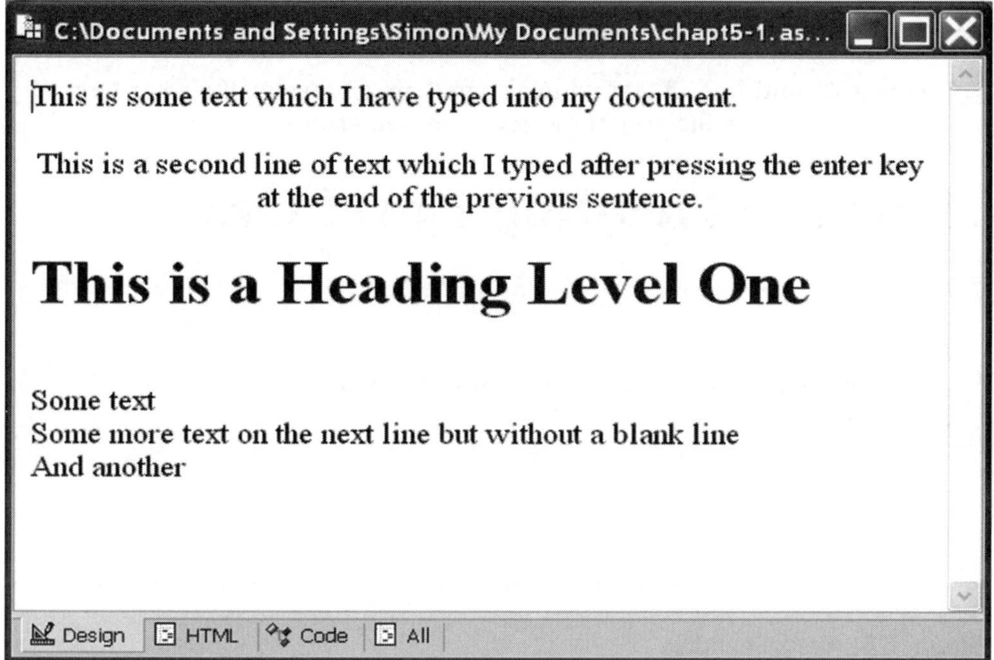

Figure 5.4: Line breaks

5.7   Horizontal rules

Horizontal rules are an element which draws a line across the web page. Properties such as the thickness of the line and its colour can be set. Horizontal rules can be placed in the document by dragging them from the HTML Elements list on the Toolbox. Drag a Horizontal rule from the Toolbox onto your document below the heading you added earlier. Clicking the HTML tab to view the HTML code you will see that the HTML rule element is:

```
<hr />
```

The Horizontal rule element is just like the break element combining both open and close tags in one element.

Returning to the Design view and clicking the mouse onto the Horizontal rule enables you to change the properties using the properties component. We saw how to do this in the previous chapter. However, when you click on the rule you will note that eight small boxes, known as handles are placed at the edges and corners of the rule, see Figure 5.5.

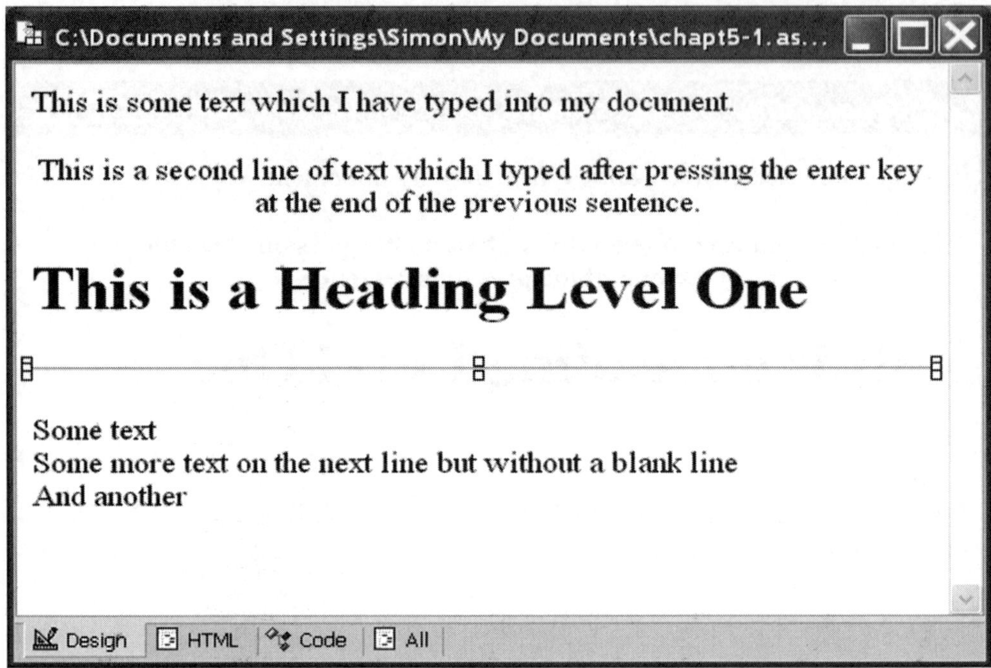

Figure 5.5: Resize handles

If you move the mouse onto one of these handles you will see the mouse pointer change to represent a line with arrow heads at each end. The direction of the arrow, indicates the direction in which the object (in this case the Horizontal rule) can be resized. Move the mouse onto the middle small box on the right of the rule. Click and hold the left button and drag the Horizontal rule to the left of the screen. The Horizontal rule should resize, but remain centred in the middle of the window. Resize the width of the rule so that it is about 5 cm wide. Next click and drag down the bottom handle box in the middle of the Horizontal rule. This will resize the rule thickness. Finally, using the properties component set the *noShade* property to true. Figure 5.6 illustrates what the current Horizontal rule should now look like. The generated code for this web page now looks like this:

```
<html>
<head>
  <title>My HTML Example</title>
</head>
<body>
  <form runat="server">
    <p>
```

```
       This is some text which I have typed into my document.<!-- Insert content
here -->
    </p>
    <p align="center">
       This is a second line of text which I typed after pressing the enter key at the
end of the previous sentence.
    </p>
    <h1 align="left">This is a Heading Level One
    </h1>
    <hr style="WIDTH: 221px; HEIGHT: 27px" noshade="noshade" size="27" />
    Some text
    <br />
    Some more text on the next line but without a blank line
    <br />
    And another
  </form>
</body>
</html>
```

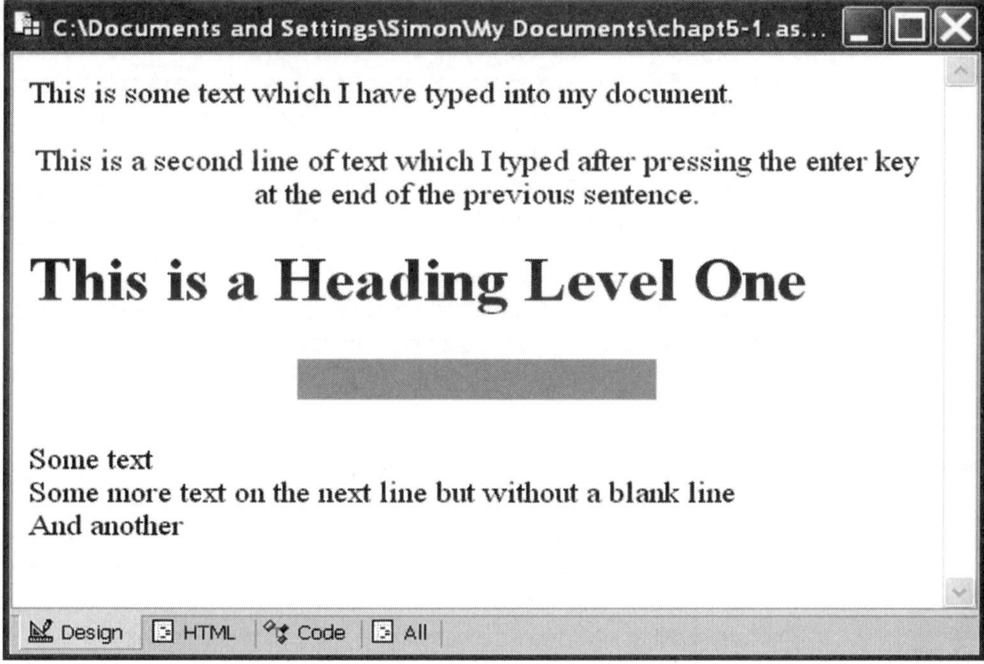

Figure 5.6: Adjusted horizontal rule

5.8   Images

In addition to text HTML allows you to incorporate images into your documents.
To begin using images we must at first have an image. We have taken an image of

one of the authors fishing on holiday in Aruba. It is worth noting at this point that Web pages require images to be in one of a limited choice of formats. The three most commonly used image standards for Web pages are:

- JPEG (JPG)
- GIF
- PNG

Table 5.1 describes each of these image standards. This text was taken from the Paint Shop Pro image editing and creation software tool, available on-line from www.jasc.com. When selecting an image to use on a Web page make sure it is in one of these formats and if not use an image editing tool such as Paint Shop Pro to convert it into one of these supported standards.

Table 5.1: Image formats (taken from Paint Shop Pro V7.0 Help)

Format	Description
JPEG	JPG, or JPEG (Joint Photographic Experts Group), is optimised for photographs and other continuous tone images, but does not do very well with line art, screenshots, cartoons and other high contrast images. It provides variable compression. The compression loses some of the original data, but does so by exploiting the fact that small changes in colour are less noticeable than changes in brightness.
GIF	GIF (Graphics Interchange Format) supports up to 8-bit colour depth images (256 colours), and it is optimised for high contrast images and blocks of colour. GIF89a supports animation as well as single colour transparency. It does not support layers.
PNG	PNG (Portable Network Graphics) is a format used to transmit and store bitmapped images. It was created specifically for the Internet and other networks. It provides alpha transparency, high colour support, and slightly better compression than GIF. The current generation of Netscape Navigator and Internet Explorer may not completely support PNG and previous browsers do not support it at all. While it supports alpha channels and creator information, it does not support layers.

We have saved this image in the following directory:

C:\Documents and Settings\Simon\My Documents\

Using the filename: *fishing.jpg*. The above directory is the default directory where all our ASP.NET scripts have been saved. Having obtained an image the next thing to do is to drag and drop an *Image* control from the Toolbox HTML elements onto the Document window. As our current window is a little full I have created a new document called *image.aspx*. Having added the *Image* control to the Document window we select the Image control and using the properties component type the name of your image you have previously obtained in the property src. In my case the image is called *Fishing.jpg*. Note that there are two similar controls called *Image*. One of these is an HTML image and the other is an ASP image component. While these are similar you select the HTML element image element for this example. When clicking return the *Image* should be displayed in the Document window, as shown in Figure 5.7.

Figure 5.7: Fishing image

The image control has a large number of properties which you can adjust through the Properties component. However, for now click the HTML tab on the document component and examine the generated HTML for the above script. The HTML element for the image is:

```
<img src="fishing.jpg" />
```

Once again the *<img />* element is a single tag element, similar to the horizontal rule element. Note that the element has a single attribute (*src="fishing.jpg"*) which specifies the location and name of the image to display.

5.9   Hyperlinks

A hyperlink is an HTML control which when clicked on by the web user will load a new web page in the browser. Hyperlinks are used to allow navigation from one web page to the next. A hyperlink can be added to the document component by selecting the Anchor control from the list of HTML elements and dragging this onto the Document window. By default the hyperlink anchor has the text anchor as a default. Selecting the HTML tab at the bottom of the document component will display the HTML element which creates a hyperlink. The element is:

```
<a href="">Anchor</a>
```

The element consists of a start and end tag. The start tag has a single attribute which defines the URL of the document to be loaded when the hyperlink is clicked. The start and end tags surround the text which forms the clickable link. Try changing the default "*Anchor*" text to the following:

```
<a href="">Click here to go to a new page</a>
```

Returning to the Design view you should see a hyperlink like that shown in Figure 5.8.

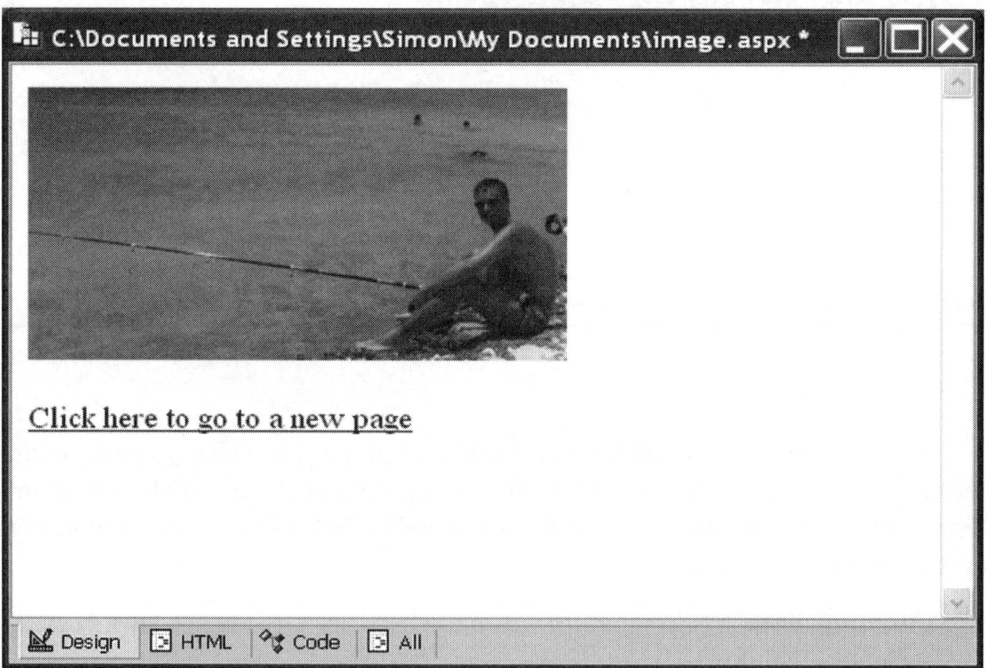

Figure 5.8: Hyperlink

The only thing left to do is to set the hyperlink reference. This tells the browser what web page to load when the hyperlink is clicked. The easiest way to set this is to click the mouse on the hyperlink in the Document window Design view and then enter the name and location of the web page to load in the *href* property of the Property component. If you enter in the name of a script we created earlier, for example *twolabels.aspx* which we created as an answer to one of the exercises in the previous chapter. Clicking the HTML tab at the bottom of the Document component reveals the generated HTML code:

```
<a href="twolabels.aspx">Click here to go to a new page</a>
```

Saving the document and then viewing the output using a web browser will enable you to click the hyperlink and load the *twolabels.aspx* script created before.

5.10   Tables

Tables are used to format how data is displayed on the web page. Tables allow lists of text and numbers to be formatted and displayed into columns and/or allow images and form elements to be neatly formatted on a page. For example, a table would be used if you wanted to create a web page which consisted of three neatly formatted columns of text or which consisted of some text on the left of the web page and an image on the right-hand side. Accessing the HTML elements from the Toolbox menu and dragging a *Table* control onto the Document component results in the Design window illustrated in Figure 5.9.

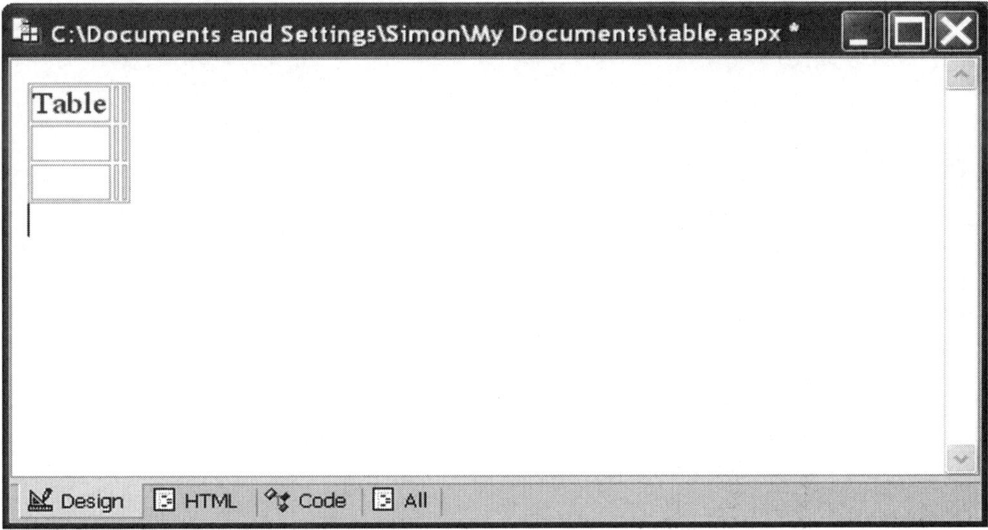

Figure 5.9: Initial table

Clicking on the HTML tab will reveal the HTML elements which are produced by default for the *Table*:

```
<html>
<head>
</head>
<body>
  <form runat="server">
    <table>
      <tbody>
        <tr>
          <td>
             Table</td>
          <td>
          </td>
          <td>
          </td>
        </tr>
        <tr>
          <td>
          </td>
          <td>
          </td>
          <td>
          </td>
        </tr>
        <tr>
          <td>
          </td>
          <td>
          </td>
          <td>
          </td>
        </tr>
      </tbody>
    </table>
    <!-- Insert content here -->
  </form>
</body>
</html>
```

As you can see there is quite a lot of code generated for the *Table*. Don't worry we will examine the elements which have been created one at a time. The first element is *<table>* which consists of start and end tags:

```
<table></table>
```

The *<table>* tag denotes the start of the table and *</table>* the end of the table. All other table related elements will occur within these tags. Next the <tbody> element which also consists of start and end tags:

```
<tbody></tbody>
```

The tags denote the start and end of the body of the table. All structural elements defining the table will be inserted between these tags. The rest of the table consists of row and data elements. Each row has a *<tr>* element which also consists of start and end tags:

```
<tr></tr>
```

There is a table row element for each row of the table. As a default the table is constructed with three rows and three columns. If you want less than three rows then you need to remove the rows you don't need. If you need more then you must add additional rows. Within each row of the table there are individual data cells. These are defined using the <td> element which consists of start and end tags:

```
<td></td>
```

The <td> element surrounds any control or text that you want displayed in the table. By default the table has the text "Table" in the top left cell. Return to the Design view and using the mouse click the cursor into the cell containing the word "Table". Delete this word and replace this with the word "One". Using the right arrow key on the keyboard, move the cursor to the next cell to the right and type the word "Two". Repeat this again and this time type Three. Keep doing this for the remaining cell rows incrementing the number typed in each cell. This will result in a table like that shown in Figure 5.10.

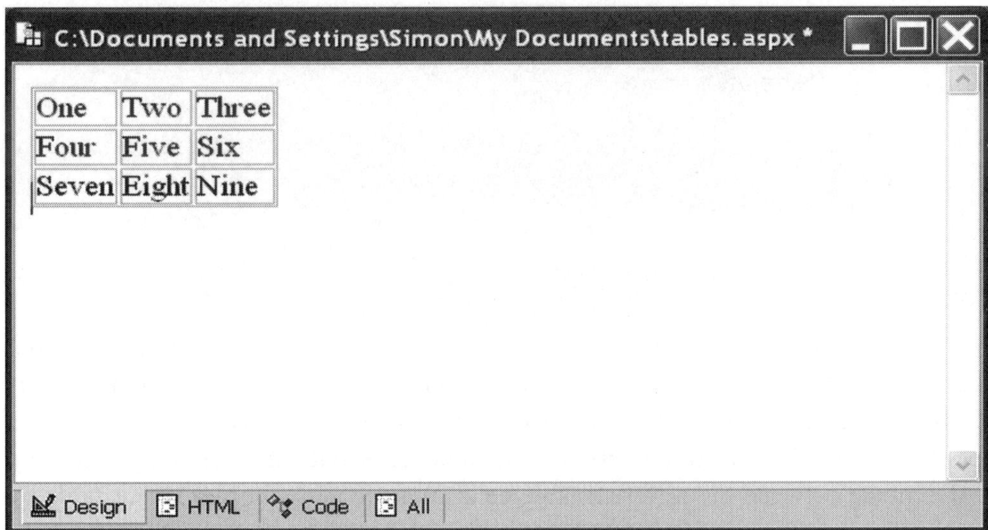

Figure 5.10: Table with data

Clicking on the HTML tab of the Document window control will reveal the HTML for the Table, this is now as follows:

```
<html>
```

```
<head>
</head>
<body>
  <form runat="server">
    <table bordercolor="white" bgcolor="white" border="0">
      <tbody>
        <tr>
          <td>
            One</td>
          <td>
            Two</td>
          <td>
            Three</td>
        </tr>
        <tr>
          <td>
            Four</td>
          <td>
            Five</td>
          <td>
            Six</td>
        </tr>
        <tr>
          <td>
            Seven</td>
          <td>
            Eight</td>
          <td>
            Nine</td>
        </tr>
      </tbody>
    </table>
    <!-- Insert content here -->
  </form>
</body>
</html>
```

When the Table shown in Figure 5.10 is viewed using a browser the output displayed is shown in Figure 5.11. Note that when the table is viewed that there is no border present around the cells. In the Design view shown in Figure 5.10 it looked like we had a border around our table cells but this was simply to help differentiate between the different table cells. We can add a border to our table by firstly clicking the mouse pointer on the table in the document window. Then using the properties component set the border property to the value 2 and the *borderColor* property to a colour of your choice (anything other than white). Saving the code and viewing the resulting output using a browser should result in a table looking similar to that shown in Figure 5.12.

Clicking on the HTML tab at the bottom of the document component window will reveal the generated HTML code for the table border. In my example this HTML is:

```
<table bordercolor="silver" border="2">
```

This defines two attributes for the *<table>* element, specifying the *bordercolor* and border thickness of the table.

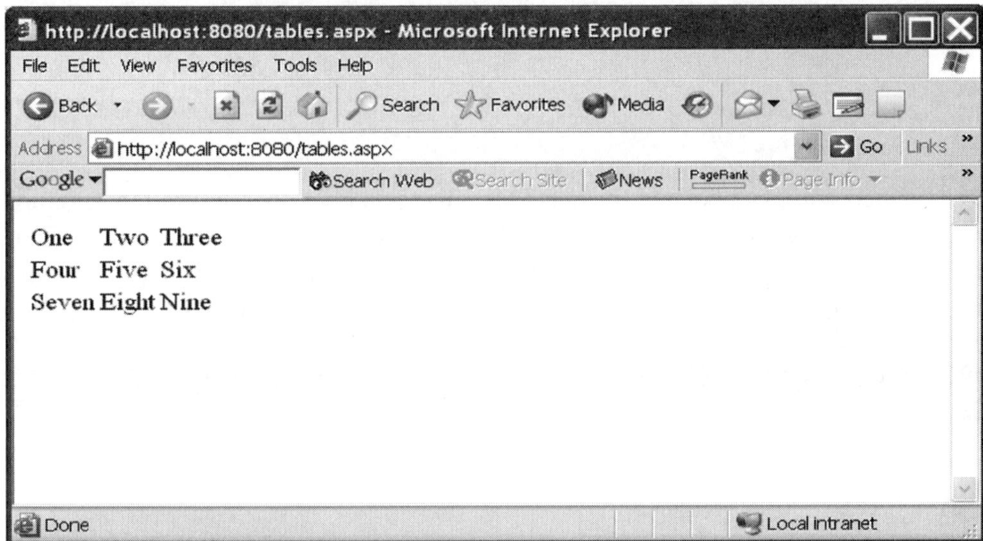

Figure 5.11: Table viewed in browser window

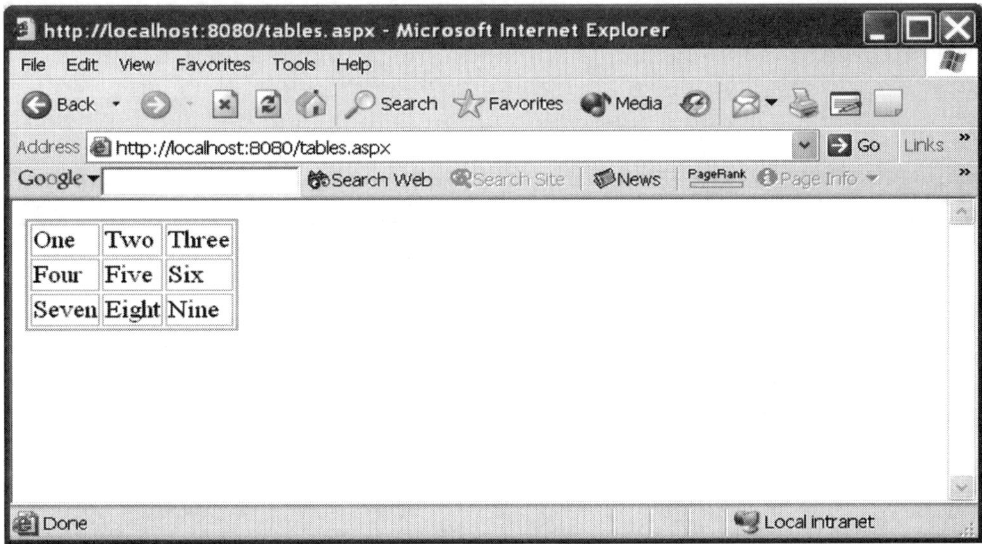

Figure 5.12: Table with border viewed with browser

Tables don't have to be 3 by 3 cells in size. Create a new file called *table2.aspx* and drag and drop an HTML table element from the Toolbox onto the document. Next, click the HTML tab to view the generated HTML code. What we are going to do is to delete one of the three rows of table cells. The code we are going to delete is as follows:

```
<tr>
  <td>
  </td>
  <td>
  </td>
  <td>
  </td>
</tr>
```

When you have deleted these HTML elements click the Design tab to return to the design view. You should note that the table now only consists of two rows of three cells each. In the second row of the table type the letters A, B and C into the three cells. The table should now look like that shown in Figure 5.13.

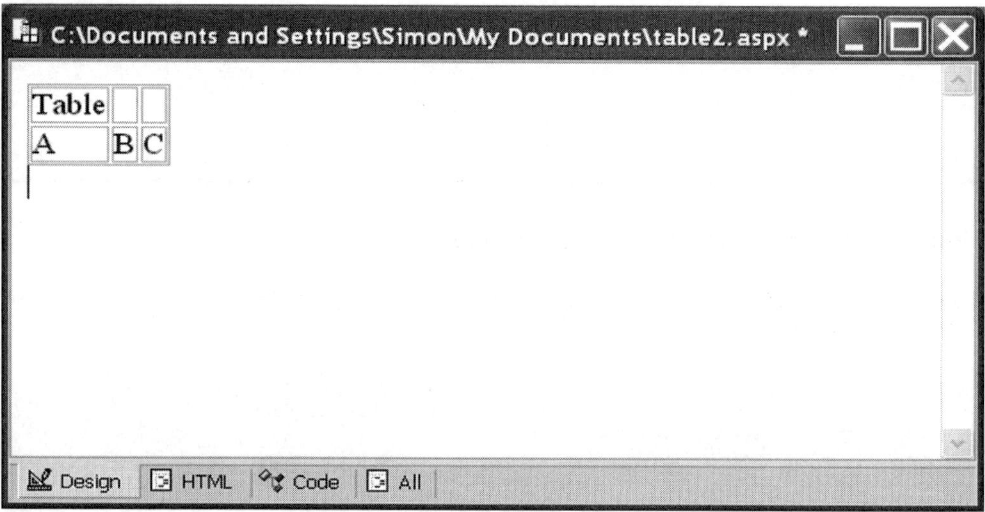

Figure 5.13: Two row table

Cells can be defined to span more than one column (or row). Click the HTML tab and delete the second and third cells of the first row which have no text in them. The HTML you should delete is as follows:

```
<td>
</td>
<td>
</td>
```

Having done that you should return to the Design view and click on the cell with the text Table in it. Select the Properties component and locate the property *colSpan*. Set the value of *colSpan* equal to 3 and press enter. This sets the first cell with the value Table to span three columns of the table. The table should now look like that shown in Figure 5.14.

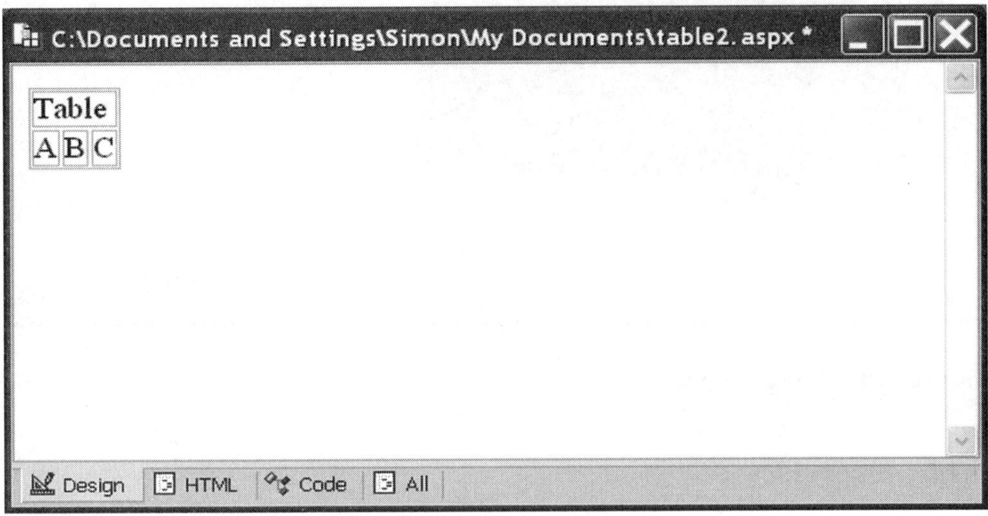

Figure 5.14: Table showing cell colSpan

Tables don't just have to contain text. You can add form elements (described in the following chapter), images and hyperlinks amongst other controls into a table. The table is a convenient receptacle to allow you to format the position of different elements on your web page. Let us try this by firstly deleting the text Table from the first table cell.

Next, drag an HTML image element from the Toolbox into the first cell of the table. Using the Properties component set the name of the image using the *src* property. I have set this to *"fishing.jpg"* which is the image we used previously. The image should appear in the first cell of the table and the cells in the second table row should adjust automatically to the width of the image. This is illustrated in Figure 5.15.

5.11 Summary

In this chapter we have examined some of the elements which together form the HTML language. We have shown how these can be used with the Web Matrix tool and what effects each of these elements have on the design of an ASP.NET web page.

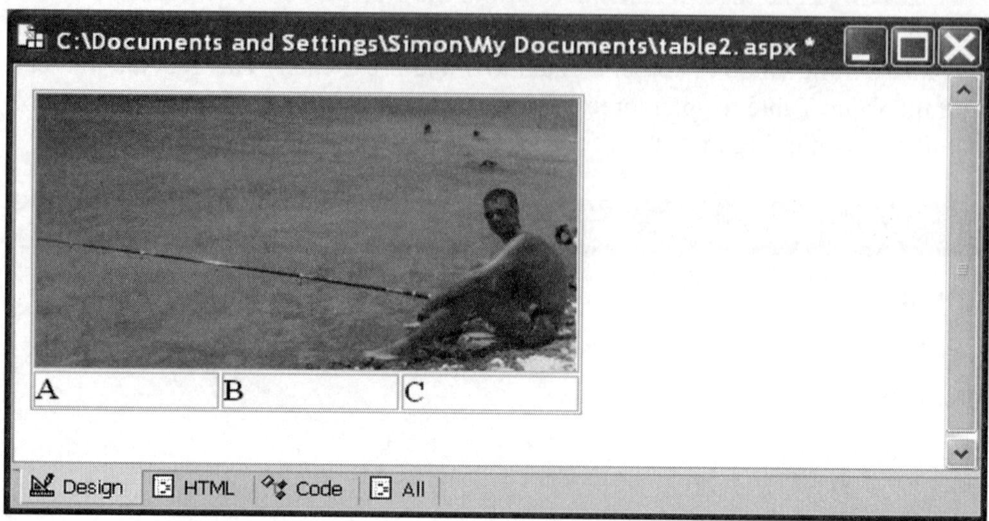

Figure 5.15: Image in a table

5.12   Exercises

See if you can apply what you have learnt by trying the following exercises:

1. Create a web page which includes an image which is centered on the page and has a border of width 5.

2. Create two web pages, each of which has a hyperlink which allows the user to navigate from one page to the other and then back to the original page.

3. Create a table of 2 by 4 cells, with each cell containing a single letter. Using the bgcolor property of each cell change the background colour of each cell to a different colour.

4. Create a table of 3 by 1 cells and insert images into each of the cells.

6

Interacting with the user using ASP.NET forms

6.1 Introduction

Forms have been an integral part of standard HTML development since web pages were first developed. However, while forms could be created using HTML the information entered by the user via the form had to be processed using a third party script operating under the Common Gateway Interface (CGI). With the advent of ASP.NET a new set of form controls have been developed which can enable the processing of form data quickly and easily. We have already seen some examples of these in earlier chapters and include the Button, Label, Textbox and Calendar controls. In this chapter we shall examine these controls again and introduce others that provide a richer ASP.NET form interface for user interaction.

6.2 How ASP forms work

In the introduction above we mention that traditional form data had to be processed using CGI applications. CGI programs were written in a variety of programming languages such as C, C++ and PERL. The CGI programs were completely separate from the web pages which invoked them and there were a number of resource and security issues inherent with their use. With the advent of dynamic web languages such as ASP.NET the ability to process form data was encapsulated together within the same web pages, which displayed the form for the user to complete. This design proved to be far more efficient in terms of computer resources and reduced the security issues, although not totally. The difference between how CGI and ASP.NET forms are processed is illustrated in Figure 6.1.

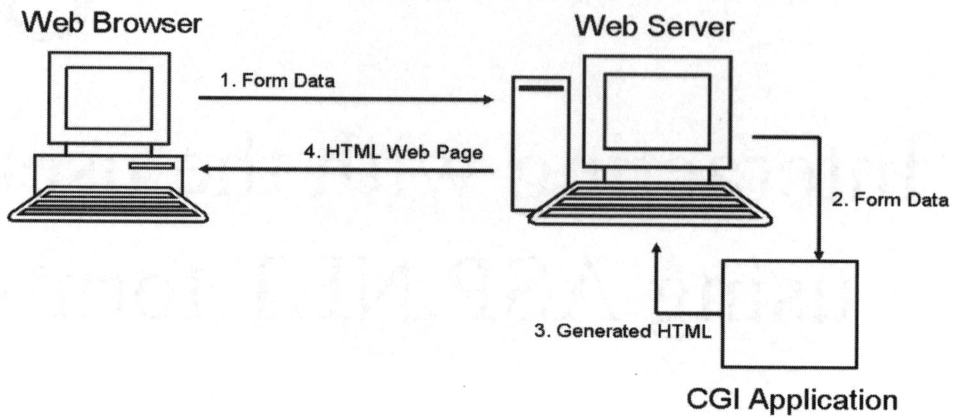

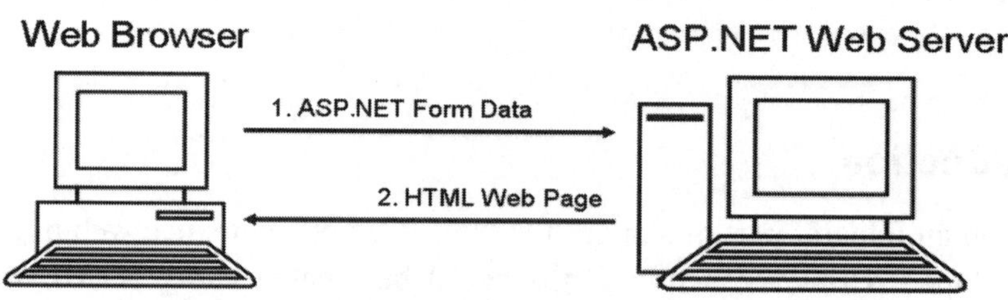

Figure 6.1: CGI and ASP.NET form processing

6.3   Buttons

We first introduced buttons way back in Chapter 4 when we created our first ASP.NET script. Buttons are an important part of forms as they are used by the user to "submit" the form once it has been completed. Dragging and dropping a button control from the Toolbox will generate the following ASP.NET script:

```
<asp:Button id="Button1" runat="server" Text="Button"></asp:Button>
```

Each *Button* is given an *id*. The first *Button id* by default is *"Button1"* and the second button *"Button2"* and so on. Buttons have properties which can be adjusted. We can illustrate this by creating a new script called *buttons.aspx* and dragging two buttons from the Toolbox onto the form. We can select the first *Button* and using the Properties component change the text that appears on the *Button* using the *Text* property. We changed this to *"Submit the form"*. We can also change the text colour using the *ForeColor* property (we chose *DimGray*) and the button colour using the *BackColor* and *BorderColor* properties. We selected a light red colour scheme. The ASP.NET script generated for the button is shown below:

```
<asp:Button id="Button1" onclick="Button1_Click" runat="server" Text="Submit the
form" ForeColor="DimGray" BackColor="#FFC0C0"
BorderColor="#FF8080"></asp:Button>
```

Figure 6.2 illustrates what this button looks like compared to the default.

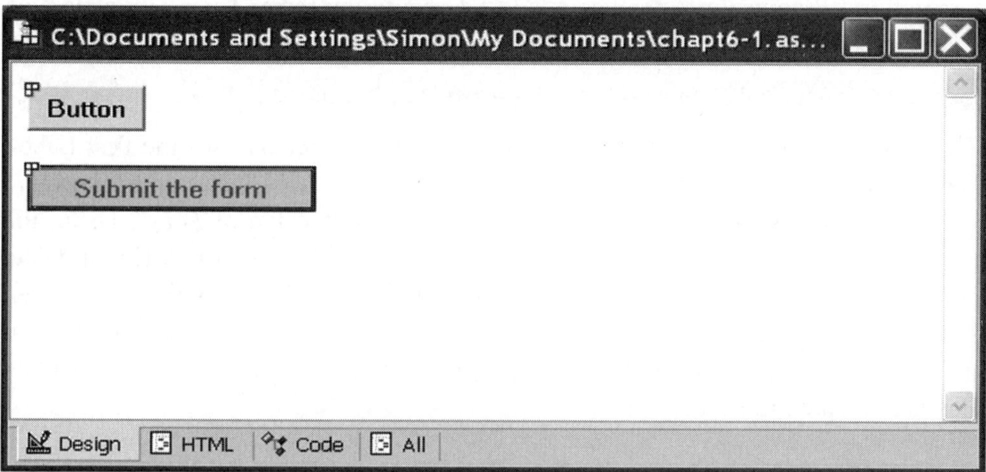

Figure 6.2: Changing a button's properties

Double clicking the mouse on a button will display the ASP.NET code associated with clicking the button. This is illustrated in Figure 6.3. We shall explain later in this chapter how to add some ASP.NET code. However, as we haven't introduced any additional form elements this will have to wait a little while.

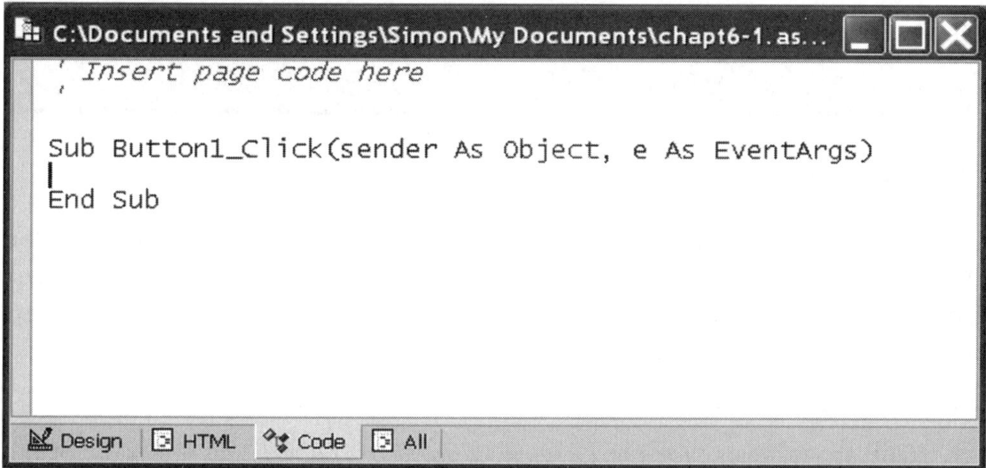

Figure 6.3: Button code

6.4   Labels

Labels were also introduced in Chapter 4. *Labels* are form elements, which can be used to display information on the form. To illustrate what we can do with a *Label* We have removed the second button from the previous form example, but retained the modified *Button*. We have also added a *Label* to the form. The script generated by adding a Label is as follows:

```
<asp:Label id="Label1" runat="server">Label</asp:Label>
```

Each *Label* has a unique *id* which by default is "*Label1*" for the first Label, then "*Label2*" for the next and so on. The colour of the *Label* text and background can be adjusted as can the text. This is given a default value of *Label*. Using the properties component we can change the text displayed by the *Label*. If you delete the text "*Label*" from the *Text* property no text will be displayed by the Label when it is first displayed on the form. Because our *Label* has no text associated with it the Design window displays the *id* of the *Label* instead of the text it will display. This is illustrated in Figure 6.4.

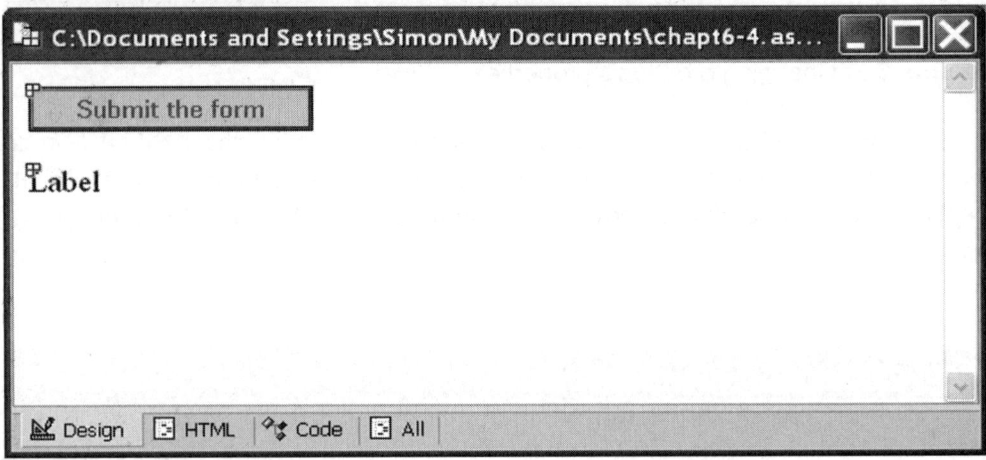

Figure 6.4: Form Label

So far we have changed the text property using the Properties window in the Design view, but we can also change properties using code. The text which is displayed by a *Label* can be changed by setting the value of the *Label* object *Text* property. We do this using the following code:

```
Label1.Text = "The text we wish to display"
```

The above reads "*for the Label with an id of 'Label1' set the value of the Text it should display equal to 'The text we wish to display'*". As our form already has a button control that will enable the user to "submit" the form this would be the best place to insert the above code. Double click the mouse on the button to view the code that will be executed when the button is clicked. The following should be displayed:

```
Sub Button1_Click(sender As Object, e As EventArgs)

End Sub
```

To have the *Label* display some text when the button is clicked we simply insert the *Label1.text* code between the start and end fragments of the subroutine:

```
Sub Button1_Click(sender As Object, e As EventArgs)
Label1.Text = "The text we wish to display"
End Sub
```

Saving the script and viewing the output using a browser will result in the button being displayed and nothing else. Clicking the button will invoke the button subroutine which will assign the text *"The text we wish to display"* to the *Label* control. This is then displayed by the web browser, as shown in Figure 6.5.

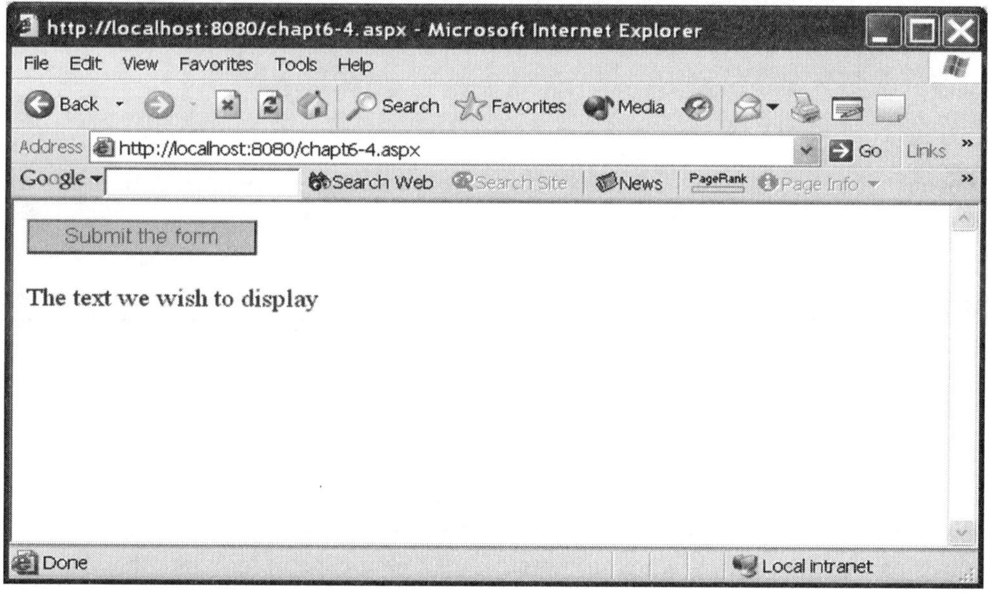

Figure 6.5: Label text

It is worth asking the question at this point "what is the difference between a Label and some text which we simply add to our web page using for example a paragraph <p> </p> element?" Well a Label is a web control which as we have seen has various properties which can be altered by the ASP.NET code which you have also added to your web page. Paragraph text does not have the same kind of properties. For example, we have seen a Label change the text it displays, while text within a paragraph element is generally fixed and cannot be altered. You see a Label component (as are all ASP.NET form components) is processed by the web server and converted into raw HTML code which is then sent to the browser for display. This was illustrated in Figure 6.1 where we see the web server serving an HTML document to the web browser client. However, we can further illustrate this with Figure 6.6, which illustrates the HTML code that is sent to the browser for display from the Label text example we created above illustrated in Figure 6.4 and Figure 6.5. You can view the HTML source code of a web page by right-clicking the mouse on the web browser window and selecting the menu option "View Source".

```
chapt6-4[1] - Notepad
File   Edit   Format   View   Help

<html>
<head>
</head>
<body>
        <form name="_ctl0" method="post" action="chapt6-4.aspx" id="_ctl0">
<input type="hidden" name="__VIEWSTATE" value="dDwtNjI3MTUONjQyO3Q8O2w8aTwxPjs+O2

        <p>
            <input type="submit" name="Button1" value="Submit the form" id="Butto
        </p>
        <p>
            <span id="Label1">The text we wish to display</span>
        </p>
        <!-- Insert content here -->
    </form>
</body>
</html>
```

Figure 6.6: HTML produced by our Label example

6.5   Textboxes

Textboxes are form elements that allow the user to type some text and then submit this as part of the form. We are going to create a new page to look like the example shown in Figure 6.7. To do this we select the File menu and select option "New". We have called this file chapt6-7.aspx. From the Toolbox we dragged a Label onto the document component window. Next we created a new line by clicking the mouse next to the Label control we added and pressed Enter. Then the text "Firstname:" was typed in the window, followed by the addition of a *TextBox* control from the Toolbox component. Another new line was created with the text "Surname:" and a *TextBox* control. Finally, on a new line a button control we added from the Toolbox and its properties changed so that it looks the same as the button in our previous example.

Figure 6.7: TextBox elements on a form

The text entered via a *TextBox* is stored in *TextBox Text* property. This is similar to that of the *Label Text* property and looks like this for TextBox1:

```
TextBox1.Text
```

To display the values entered in each of our textboxes we can assign the values in each of the Text properties to our Label text property, for example:

```
Label1.Text = "Firstname: " & TextBox1.Text & " Surname: " & TextBox2.Text
```

Note the use of the & characters which allow us to join text strings such as *"Firstname:"* and *Text* properties such as *TextBox2.Text* together. Also note the inclusion of an extra space character after the colon at the end of the word Firstname: and Surname:. These are to ensure that when the strings join together that there is a space between the text *"Firstname:"* and the firstname entered on the *TextBox* control. Amend the button subroutine code so that it reads as above. After saving the script and viewing the form in a browser we can enter names in the *TextBoxes* and click the submit button. This is illustrated in Figure 6.8.

The width and height of *TextBox* controls can be adjusted by clicking on the control and then clicking and dragging on the handles, which appear. We have added a third *TextBox* control to our form and resized this as we wish it to allow a user to enter an address on the form. To allow multi-line entry into a textbox we need to change the *TextMode* property so that its reads *"MultiLine"*. In addition some text has been added to indicate that this field expects an address to be entered. A second *Label* control has also been added to the form and the properties adjusted so that it displays no text as a default.

Finally, the button subroutine is also amended as follows so that the text entered into the address textbox is displayed in *Label2*:

```
Sub Button1_Click(sender As Object, e As EventArgs)
```

```
Label1.Text = "Firstname: " & TextBox2.Text & " Surname: " & TextBox1.Text
Label2.text = "Address: " & TextBox3.Text
End Sub
```

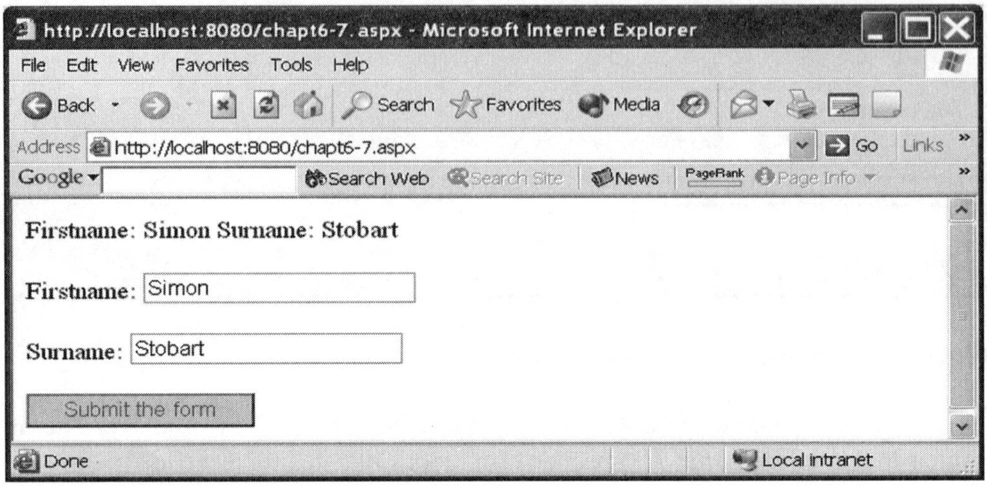

Figure 6.8: Displaying the values of TextBox controls

The design of the form is now shown in Figure 6.9.

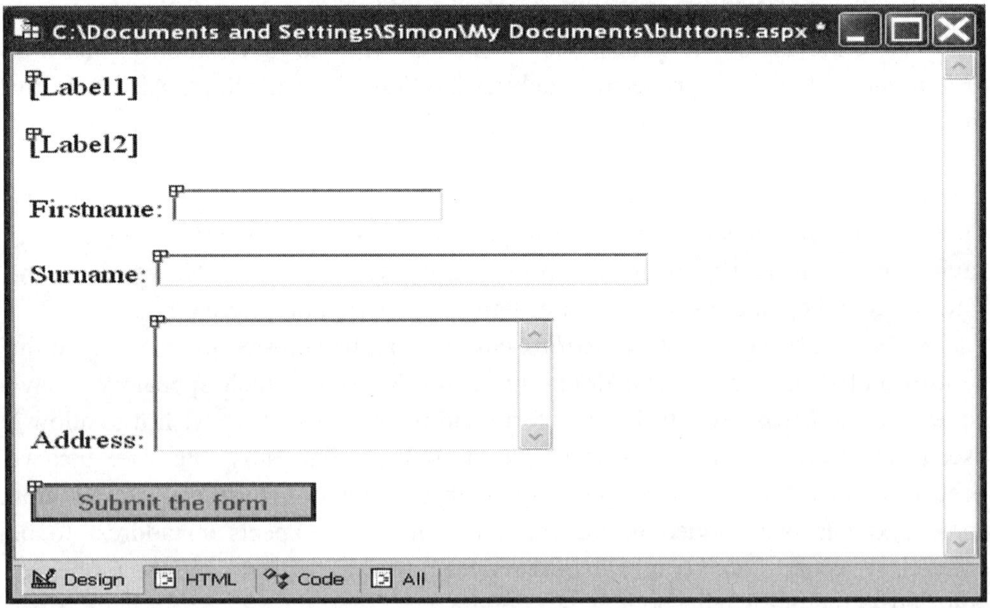

Figure 6.9: A MultiLine TextBox

Figure 6.10 illustrates what the form shown in Figure 6.9 looks like when viewed in a browser before the button is clicked. Note that when entering text into the multi line *TextBox* that a scroll-bar will appear automatically when the number of lines entered is greater that the size of the *TextBox*.

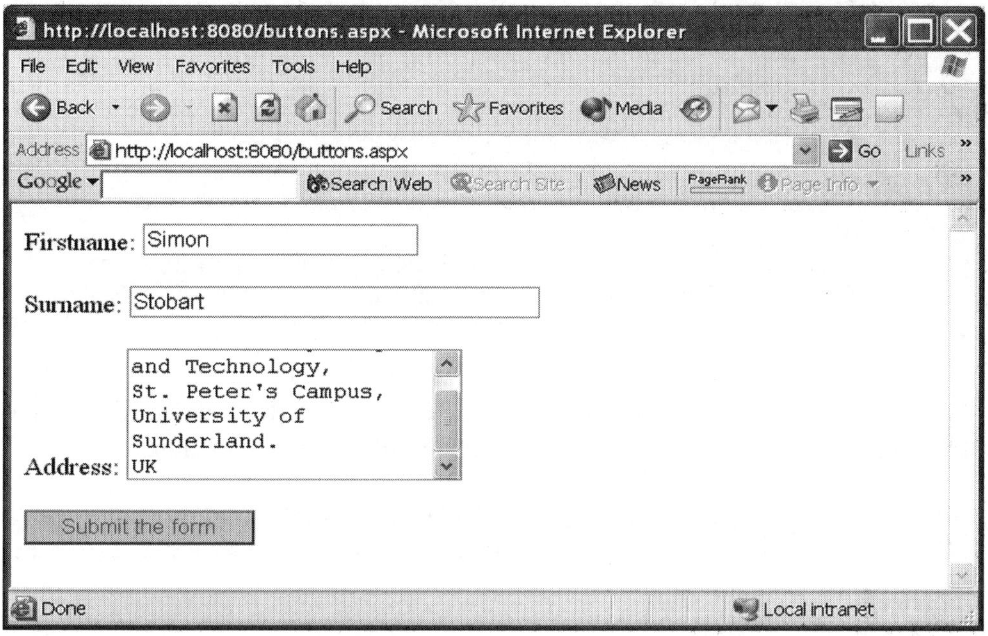

Figure 6.10: Scroll-bar on a MultiLine TextBox

6.6   Calendars

Calendars were introduced in Chapter 5 where we showed how they could be added to a form and enable the Web Matrix user to change the look and feel of the control through the use of the Property component.   Figure 6.11 illustrates a *Calendar* control, *Button* and *Label* which have been added to new form. The button is the same as the one we have used in the previous examples. The Label in Figure 6.11 properties have been altered so that no text is displayed by the *Label* when the web page is first displayed. Between the *Label* and the *Button* is the *Calendar* control. This has been altered using the property components *Auto Format* option described in the previous chapter. The *"Simple"* Calendar style has been selected. The size of the *Calendar* control has been adjusted by clicking on it and using the resize handles to adjust the width of the *Calendar* so that it is the same as the *Button*.

Clicking on the HTML tab of the document component will reveal the HTML code generated for this *Calendar* component. The code is quite complex:

```
        <asp:Calendar id="Calendar1" runat="server" ForeColor="Black"
BackColor="White" BorderColor="#999999" Width="178px"
DayNameFormat="FirstLetter" Height="198px" Font-Size="8pt" Font-
Names="Verdana" CellPadding="4">
        <TodayDayStyle forecolor="Black" backcolor="#CCCCCC">
</TodayDayStyle>
        <SelectorStyle backcolor="#CCCCCC"></SelectorStyle>
        <NextPrevStyle verticalalign="Bottom"></NextPrevStyle>
        <DayHeaderStyle font-size="7pt" font-bold="True"
backcolor="#CCCCCC"> </DayHeaderStyle>
        <SelectedDayStyle font-bold="True" forecolor="White"
backcolor="#666666"> </SelectedDayStyle>
        <TitleStyle font-bold="True" bordercolor="Black" backcolor="#999999">
</TitleStyle>
        <WeekendDayStyle backcolor="#FFFFCC"></WeekendDayStyle>
        <OtherMonthDayStyle forecolor="#808080"></OtherMonthDayStyle>
        </asp:Calendar>
```

Each *Calendar* control has a unique id. By default the first id is *"Calendar1"*, the second *"Calendar2"* etc. The above HTML code consists of the *<asp:calendar>* element and all the associated attributes and elements.

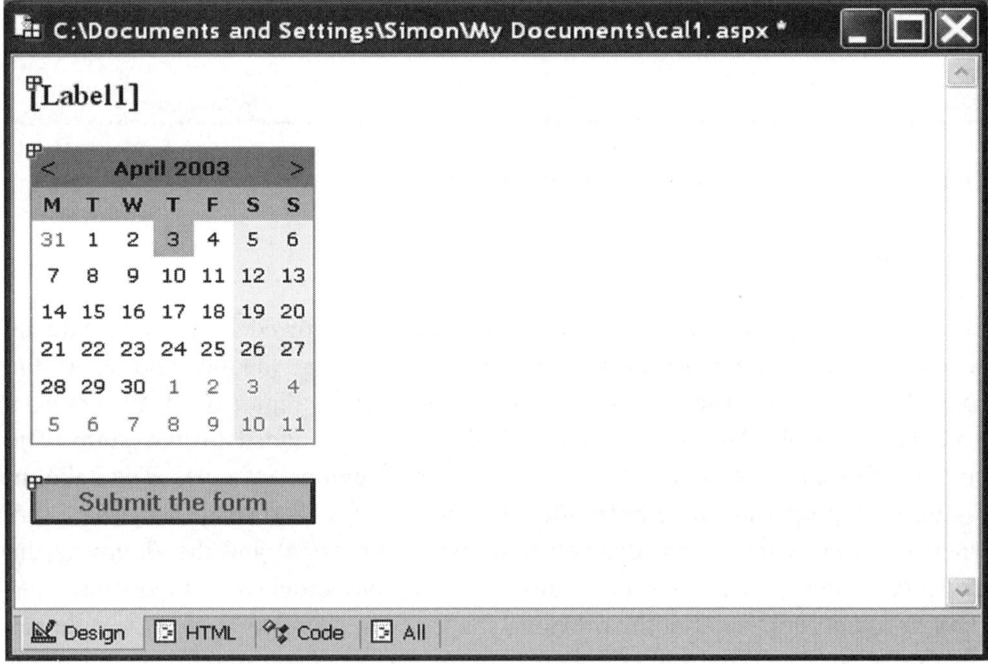

Figure 6.11: Calendar control

The amount and complexity of the code generated above provides an excellent example of why the Web Matrix tool is a real benefit to the ASP.NET developer, as you don't need to manually type this in. The date selected on the *Calendar* control by the user can be accessed through the *SelectedDate* property. This property can be accessed like this for *Calendar1*:

```
Calendar1.SelectedDate
```

This property can be used to display the date selected when the *Button* control is clicked. This requires the following code to be inserted:

```
Sub Button1_Click(sender As Object, e As EventArgs)
Label1.Text = "Submitted Date: " + Calendar1.SelectedDate
End Sub
```

Note that the above code is the same as used in the example in Chapter 5. It is also worth noting that the *Calendar* control like the *Button* has its own subroutine into which code can be added which is processed when a date is clicked on the control. Double clicking the *Calendar* control will reveal its subroutine code, which we can edit as follows:

```
Sub Calendar1_SelectionChanged(sender As Object, e As EventArgs)
Label1.Text = "Selected Date: " + Calendar1.SelectedDate
End Sub
```

The output generated by the above form is illustrated in Figure 6.12.

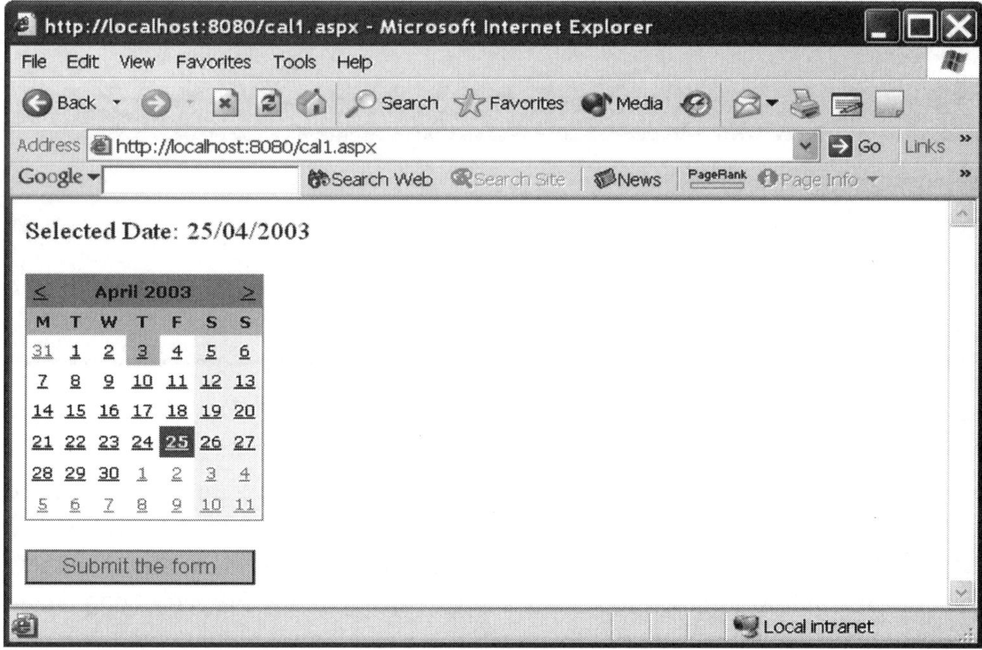

Figure 6.12: Calendar control output

You should note that if you select a date from the *Calendar* control then the message beginning with "*Selected Date*" and ends with the selected date from the Calendar control is displayed on the *Label*. If the *Button* is clicked then the *Label* begins with the text "*Submitted Date*".

6.7   CheckBoxLists

CheckBoxLists are a form control, which allows you to present a number of options to the user and for them to select any or all the options that are presented to them. A *CheckBoxList* is a textual list of items appearing either across or down the web page. Each item in the list has a corresponding checkbox, which as a default is unchecked. The form user is able to select an item from the list by clicking the *Checkbox* icon next to the item causing it to change to a selected item. Clicking the item a second time will reverse the selection.

CheckBoxLists can be created in Web Matrix by selecting the *CheckBoxList* control from the Toolbox component. Dragging this onto a document will result in the following HTML code being generated for the control:

```
<asp:CheckBoxList id="CheckBoxList1" runat="server"></asp:CheckBoxList>
```

Each *CheckBox* control has a unique id. By default the first id is "*CheckBoxList1*", the second "*CheckBoxList2*" etc. Figure 6.13 illustrates what a *CheckBoxList* looks like when dragged onto the document component.

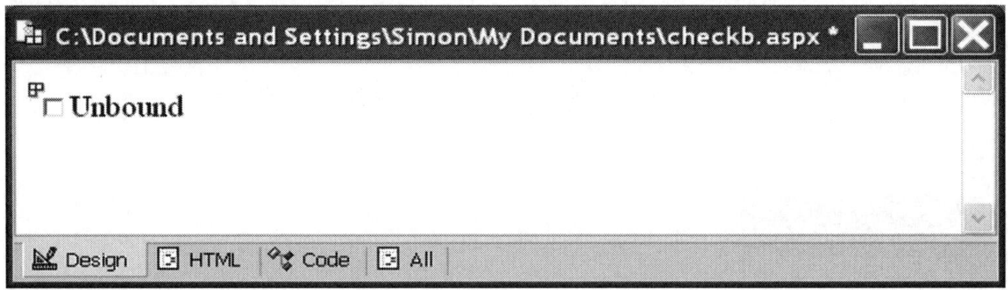

Figure 6.13: Initial CheckBoxList

As a *CheckBoxList* consists of a number of items making up the list we need to specify what they are. The Web Matrix tool provides us with a useful tool to help us do this. To activate the tool simply select the control on the document component window and then locate the Items property in the Property component. You will note that to the right of this property is a small grey button with three dots on it. Clicking this button will launch the *ListItem Collection Editor* as illustrated in Figure 6.14.

The *ListItem Collection Editor* allows you to add and edit items to the *CheckBoxList*. If you click the Add button you will add a new list item to the list. When you do this for the first time you will note that a *CheckBoxList* member appears on the left of the *ListItem Collection Editor* window labelled 0 *ListItem*. On the right of the window are the properties, which affect the list item. The three properties allow you to adjust whether the list item is selected when the list is displayed, the text associated and a value which is associated with the item.

Figure 6.14: ListItem Collection Editor

Having added a ListItem, click on the *Text* property and change this to Oranges. Leave the selected property as false. Then add three more List items and set the *Text* properties to Apples, Bananas and Cherries respectively. The *ListItem Collection Editor* should now look like that shown in Figure 6.15.

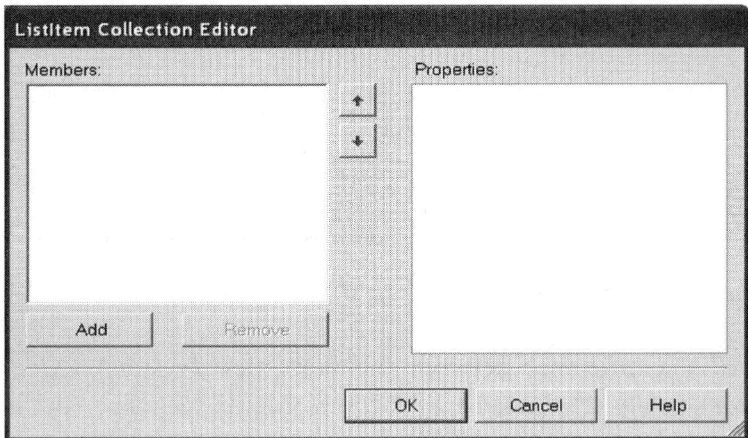

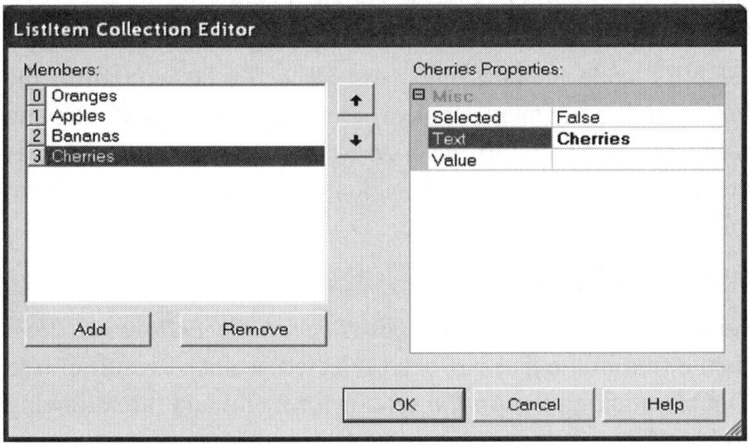

Figure 6.15: Completed ListItem Collection Editor

Clicking the *ListItem Collection Editor* window OK button will result in the document component displaying the completed *CheckBoxList*, as shown in Figure 6.16.

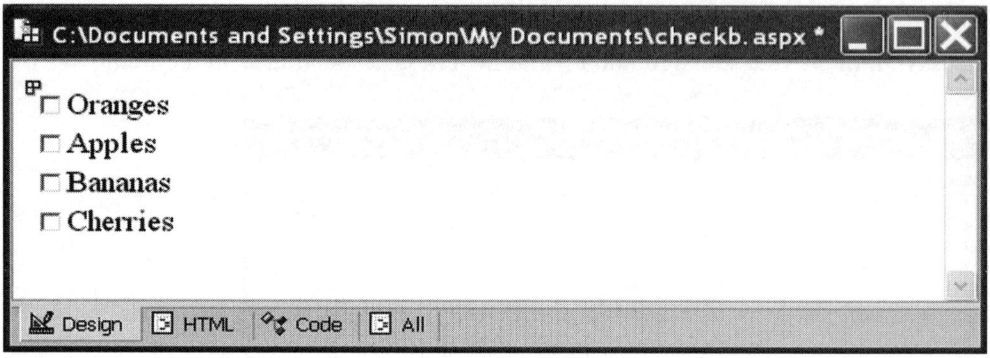

C:\Documents and Settings\Simon\My Documents\checkb.aspx *

Oranges
Apples
Bananas
Cherries

Design   HTML   Code   All

Figure 6.16: Completed CheckBoxList

Note that there is a difference between the properties *Text* and *Value*, although they are automatically set the same by the Web Matrix tool. The *Text* is what is displayed on the web page next to the *CheckBox* symbol, while the *Value* is what information is passed to the server when the item is checked.

Clicking the HTML tab on the document component will display the generated ASP.NET code for this control. This should look like this:

```
<asp:CheckBoxList id="CheckBoxList1" runat="server">
  <asp:ListItem Value="Oranges">Oranges</asp:ListItem>
  <asp:ListItem Value="Apples">Apples</asp:ListItem>
  <asp:ListItem Value="Bananas">Bananas</asp:ListItem>
  <asp:ListItem Value="Cherries">Cherries</asp:ListItem>
</asp:CheckBoxList>
```

The above ASP.NET code includes the *<asp:CheckBoxList>* control, the accompanying attributes and associated control elements. The next step in processing a *CheckBoxList* is to be able to see if an individual item in the list has been selected or not. To determine if an individual checkbox item has been selected we use the following code:

```
CheckBoxList1.Items(0).Selected
```

This code determines whether the *CheckBoxList id CheckBoxList1* Item number zero (which is the first in the list) has been selected or not. A result of true or false is returned. Double click on the *Button* on our form and add the following code into the *Button* subroutine:

```
Sub Button1_Click(sender As Object, e As EventArgs)
Label1.Text = CheckBoxList1.Items(0).Selected
```

```
Label2.Text = CheckBoxList1.Items(1).Selected
Label3.Text = CheckBoxList1.Items(2).Selected
Label4.Text = CheckBoxList1.Items(3).Selected
End Sub
```

The above code will display the values true or false for each *CheckBox* Item in four separate Labels. We will need to drag four Labels onto our form to display these values. In addition we need a button to submit the form data and some text to inform the user what is expected of them. Our form should now look like that shown in Figure 6.17.

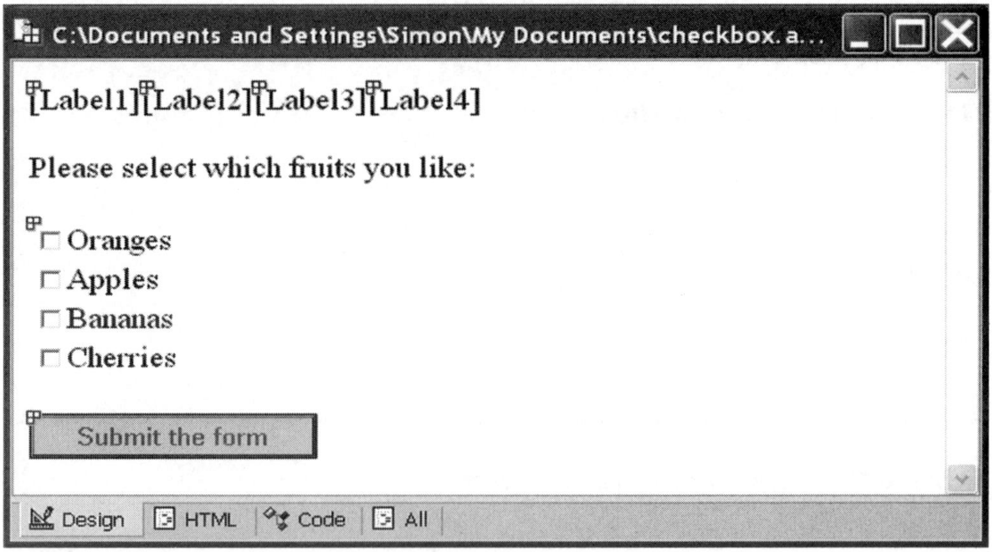

Figure 6.17: Completed CheckBoxForm

Figure 6.18 shows what the *CheckBox* control looks like when viewed with a web browser. Clicking on the *CheckBoxes* and then clicking the Submit Button will display the True and False values representing which Items have been selected.

It is worth noting that the *CheckBoxList* has its own subroutine, in which we can add code. The subroutine looks like this:

```
Sub CheckBoxList1_SelectedIndexChanged(sender As Object, e As EventArgs)

End Sub
```

Any code placed in this subroutine will be processed whenever the *CheckBoxList* is modified, whether or not the Submit Button is clicked. We could add the line:

```
Label1.Text = RadioButtonList1.SelectedItem.Text
```

Between the *Sub* and *End Sub* lines and remove the need for a Submit Button. Why would you want to do this? Well, you may wish to check that a user has done something specific to an individual form control and not wait until they have submitted the complete form.

Figure 6.18: CheckBox control in a browser

6.8   RadioButtonLists

RadioButtonLists are a similar form control to that of the *CheckBoxList* described above. They are created in exactly the same way as *CheckBoxes* and contain individual items which should be created using the *ListItem Collection Editor* also described previously. The only difference between the *RadioButton* control and the *CheckBox* control is in the number of items within the list that can be selected by the user. With a *CheckBox* control we have shown that each and all items can be checked and thus selected. However, with a *RadioButtonList* only one of the items can be selected at any one time.

Create a form that contains a single *Label*, Submit Button and *RadioButtonList* which contains the four fruit items from our previous *CheckBox* example. The HTML code generated by the Web Matrix tool for the *RadioButton* control should look like this:

```
<asp:RadioButtonList id="RadioButtonList1" runat="server"
OnSelectedIndexChanged="RadioButtonList1_SelectedIndexChanged">
    <asp:ListItem Value="Oranges">Oranges</asp:ListItem>
    <asp:ListItem Value="Apples">Apples</asp:ListItem>
```

```
                <asp:ListItem Value="Bananas">Bananas</asp:ListItem>
                <asp:ListItem Value="Cherries">Cherries</asp:ListItem>
            </asp:RadioButtonList>
```

The HTML consists of a *<asp:RadioButtonList>* control and associated attributes. Within this element are the *<asp:ListItem>* elements. Return to the Design view and double click the mouse on the Submit Button. To determine which item from the *RadioButtonList* has been selected we use the following code:

```
RadioButtonList1.SelectedItem.Text
```

This code reads for *RadioButtonList id RadioButtonList1* obtain the text for the selected item. If we amend the *Button* subroutine as below:

```
Sub Button1_Click(sender As Object, e As EventArgs)
Label1.Text = RadioButtonList1.SelectedItem.Text
End Sub
```

The above code will copy the name of the selected *RadioButton* item onto *Label1*. When the Submit Button is clicked the corresponding *RadioButton* selection is displayed on the *Label*. The complete form is shown in Figure 6.19.

Just like *CheckBoxLists RadioButtonLists* have their own subroutine in which code can be placed. This code will be processed whenever a change in the *RadioButtonList* occurs. You can edit the *RadioButton* subroutine by double clicking the mouse on the *RadioButtonList* from the Design view of the form. As with the *CheckBoxList* described previously this subroutine will allow you to execute code whenever a user selects this control.

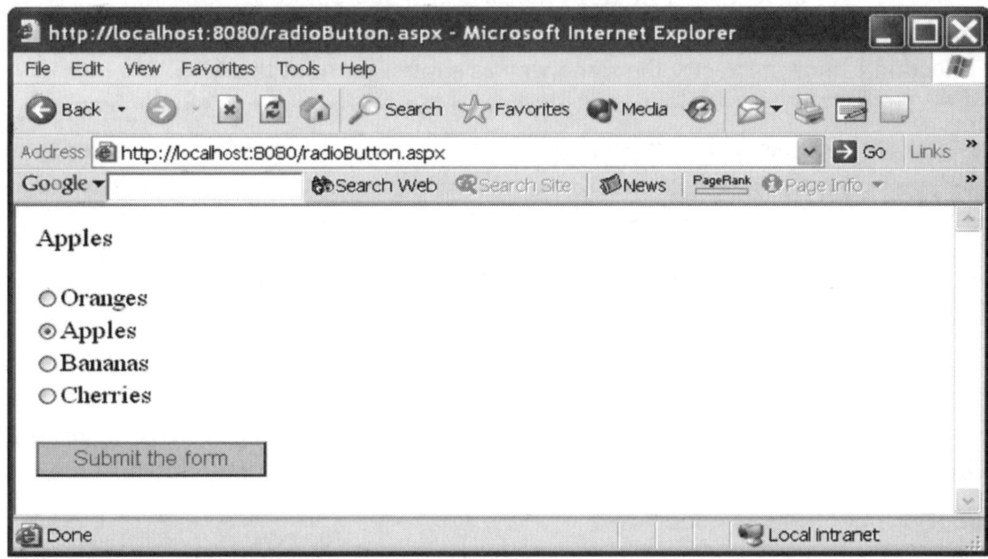

Figure 6.19: RadioButtonList

6.9   DropDown Lists

DropDownLists are, as the name suggests, a form control, which enables a textual list of items to be presented on the form as a menu list. Only one menu item is visible as a default and the user can select their menu item by clicking the button on the right of the list marked "v" to view the list contents and make their selection. This is shown in Figure 6.20.

Figure 6.20: DropDownLists

Create a form, which is identical to the *RadioButtonList* we created previously, but instead of a *RadioButtonList* now includes a *DropDownList*. Note that the menu item contents of the *DropDownList* is populated using the ListItem Collection Editor in exactly the same way as shown for our other lists.

The HTML code generated for the *DropDownList* is shown below:

```
<asp:DropDownList id="DropDownList1" runat="server">
  <asp:ListItem Value="Oranges">Oranges</asp:ListItem>
  <asp:ListItem Value="Apples">Apples</asp:ListItem>
  <asp:ListItem Value="Bananas">Bananas</asp:ListItem>
  <asp:ListItem Value="Cherries">Cherries</asp:ListItem>
</asp:DropDownList>
```

The HTML consists of a *<asp:DropDownList>* control and associated attributes. Within this element are the *<asp:ListItem>* elements. If we return to the Design view and double click the mouse on the Submit Button. To determine which item from the *DropDownList* has been selected we use the following code:

```
DropDownList1.SelectedItem.Text
```

This code reads for *DropDownList id DropDownList1* obtain the text for the selected item. If we amend the *Button* subroutine as below:

```
Sub Button1_Click(sender As Object, e As EventArgs)
Label1.Text = DropDownList1.SelectedItem.Text
End Sub
```

The above code will copy the name of the selected *DropDown* item onto *Label1*. When the Submit Button is clicked the corresponding *DropDown* selection is displayed. The complete form is shown in Figure 6.21.

Figure 6.21: DropDownList

Just like *CheckBoxList* and *RadioButtonLists, DropDownLists* have their own subroutine in which code can be placed. This code will be processed whenever a change in the *DropDownList* occurs. You can edit the *DropDown* subroutine by double clicking the mouse on the *DropDownList* from the Design view of the form.

6.10 Summary

This chapter has introduced the different ASP.NET form controls, which can be used to interact with the web page user. The different controls, which we have at our disposal have been examined and examples of their use illustrated.

6.11 Exercises

See if you can apply what you have learnt by trying the following exercises:

1. Create a form which enables the user to enter their first-name, surname using *TextBoxes* and select their salutation (Mr, Ms, Miss, Mrs, Dr) from a

DropDownList. The form should display the values entered on the form when a Submit Button is clicked.

2. Create a form which consists of a *DropDownList*, a *RadioButtonList*. Each of these lists should consist of the following colour items: Red, Orange, Yellow, Green, Blue, Indigo and Violet. Use a 2 by 3 HTML table to format the different components. Don't forget to include a Submit Button and Labels to display the colours selected from the lists.

7

Validation of user input

7.1 Introduction

In the previous chapter we introduced some of the main elements that can be used to construct forms. Forms enable interaction with the user. Unfortunately, human users are notorious for not providing the information requested either by mistake or deliberate error. To ensure that accurate and valid data is obtained via a form, programmers traditionally wrote Common Gateway Interface (CGI) code to check the data values provided by the user. ASP.NET provides a number of validation controls to check the contents of different form fields. In this chapter we shall examine each of these controls and provide examples of their use using the Web Matrix tool.

7.2 RequiredFieldValidator

The *RequiredFieldValidator* checks to see if a form field has a value or has been left blank. If a form field has been left blank then an error message can be displayed to the user directing them to enter some text or to select, for example, a menu option. Figure 7.1 illustrates a form that has been created. The form consists of *TextBox*. The accompanying text "Surname:" indicates that a surname is expected to be entered in the *TextBox*. The form also contains a Submit Button and a *RequiredFieldValidator* control which you will find on the *ToolBox* Web Control menu.

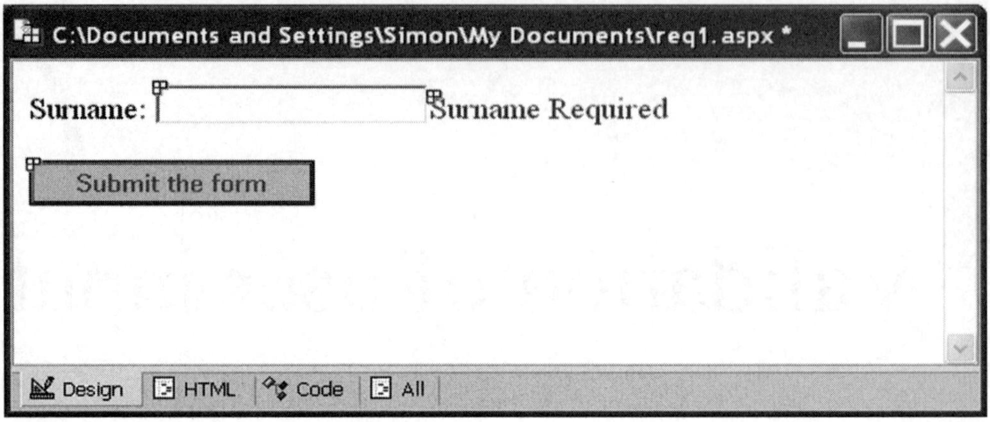

Figure 7.1: RequiredFieldValidator

Clicking the HTML tab of the document component will reveal the RequiredFieldValidator code that has been generated. By default this looks like this:

```
<asp:RequiredFieldValidator id="RequiredFieldValidator1" runat="server"
ErrorMessage="RequiredFieldValidator"></asp:RequiredFieldValidator>
```

Each *RequiredFieldValidator* control must be linked to a Web Control which it is to validate. If your form consists of a number of controls each of which you need to validate then you will need to include separate *RequiredFieldValidator* controls for each control.

To complete our form so that our *RequiredFieldValidator* checks whether our *TextBox* has been completed or not, we need to adjust the properties of the control. Click the mouse on the *RequiredFieldValidator* and then using the Properties component locate the *ErrorMessage* property. Change this property so that it reads "*Surname Required*". You should note that the Document window should update to display the text "*Surname Required*" instead of the text "*RequiredFieldValidator*". Finally, locate the property *ControlToValidate* and from the drop-down menu next to that property select from the list of controls the TextBox1 control. In this example we only have one control to validate and thus this is the only control on the list. However, when you have more than one control that could be validated then this list will contain all possible controls from which you can select.

Our form is now completed. Viewing the form in a web browser will display the *TextBox* field and submit button. Clicking the submit button without typing some text into the *TextBox* field will result in the error message "*Surname Required*" being displayed next to the *Textbox* control. This is illustrated in Figure 7.2. Typing some text into the *TextBox* and clicking the Submit Button will result in no error message being displayed.

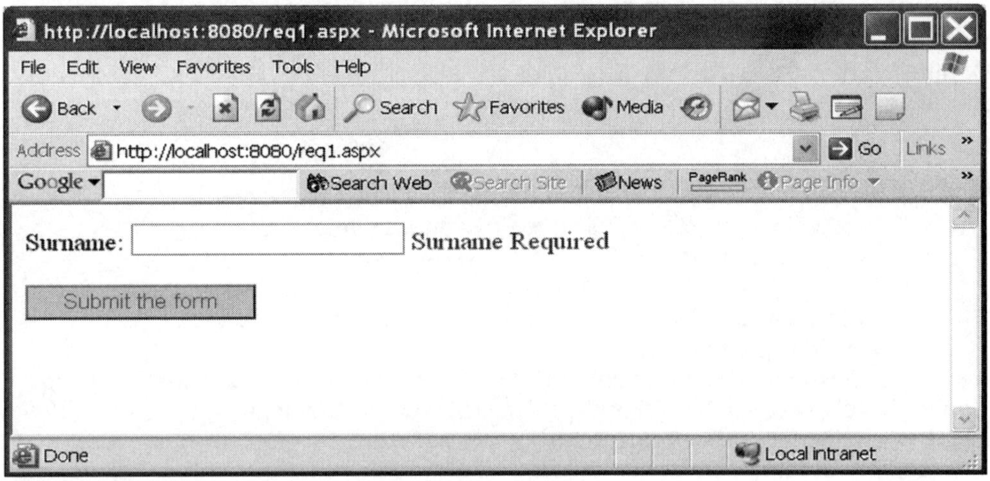

Figure 7.2: RequiredFieldValidator error message

You can use *RequiredFieldValidator* controls with any form control. Let us add a *RadioButtonList* to the above form. We have added the lists of fruits used in the examples in the previous chapter. We have also added a second *RequiredFieldValidator* control. Using the Properties component we have changed the ErrorMessage property to *"Select a Fruit"* and set the *ControlToValidate* property to the *RadioButtonList1*. Our form is illustrated in Figure 7.3.

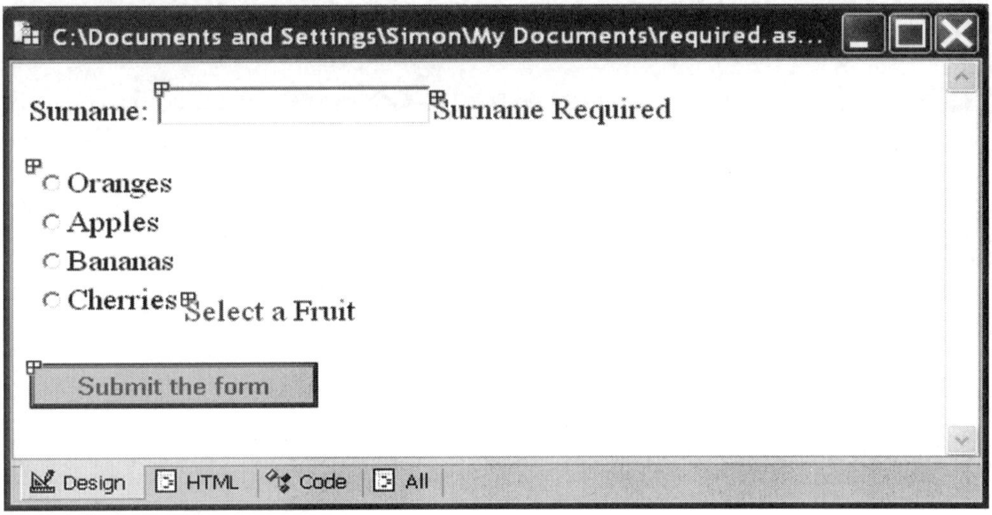

Figure 7.3: Two RequiredFieldValidator error messages

The HTML generated for the form shown in Figure 7.3 is as follows:

```
        Surname:
        <asp:TextBox id="TextBox1" runat="server"></asp:TextBox>
        <asp:RequiredFieldValidator id="RequiredFieldValidator1" runat="server"
ControlToValidate="TextBox1" ErrorMessage="Surname
Required"></asp:RequiredFieldValidator>
    </p>
    <p>
        <asp:RadioButtonList id="RadioButtonList1" runat="server">
            <asp:ListItem Value="Oranges">Oranges</asp:ListItem>
            <asp:ListItem Value="Apples">Apples</asp:ListItem>
            <asp:ListItem Value="Bananas">Bananas</asp:ListItem>
            <asp:ListItem Value="Cherries">Cherries</asp:ListItem>
        </asp:RadioButtonList>
        <asp:RequiredFieldValidator id="RequiredFieldValidator2" runat="server"
ControlToValidate="RadioButtonList1" ErrorMessage="Select a
Fruit"></asp:RequiredFieldValidator>
    </p>
    <p>
        <asp:Button id="Button1" onclick="Button1_Click" runat="server"
BorderColor="#FF8080" BackColor="#FFC0C0" ForeColor="DimGray"
Text="Submit the form"></asp:Button>
        <!-- Insert content here -->
    </p>
```

Viewing this form in a browser and either not entering a surname in the *TextBox* or not selecting an item from the *RadioButtonList* will result in one or both of the errors messages being displayed. These are illustrated in Figure 7.4.

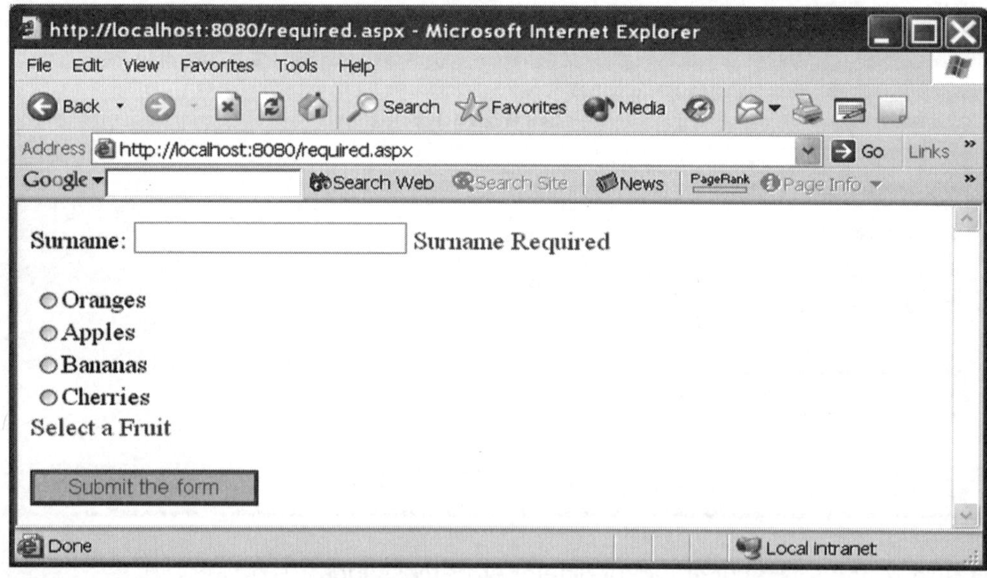

Figure 7.4: Two error messages

7.3   CompareValidator

Sometimes simply being able to determine if a control value has been entered is not enough. What you want to be able to do is to determine if a control has a certain value. The *CompareValidator* allows you to compare the value of a control to another control or to another value.

Let us consider an example of the use of this control. If we assume that we have a form where we want the user to enter a password in a *TextBox* control. To make sure the user has correctly entered the password we shall ask them to enter the password again in a second *TextBox*. We will then use the *CompareValidator* to ensure that the values entered in these two *TextBox* controls are the same.

We begin by creating a form consisting of two *TextBox* controls, some accompanying text informing the user to type and retype a password and a Submit Button to submit the form data. Using the Properties component we adjust the *TextBox* property *TextMode* to *Password*. This will ensure that the passwords that are typed into the control are not displayed, but instead a series of dots is shown. A *CompareValidator* control is also dragged onto the form from the Toolbox Web Control menu. The properties of this control are adjusted so that the *ErrorMessage* reads "Passwords not the same". The property *ControlToValidate* is set to *TextBox2*. This is the *TextBox* that the *CompareValidator* control is linked to. Next, the *ControlToCompare* property is set to *TextBox1*. This is the name of the control which we wish to compare the contents of *TextBox1* against. Figure 7.5 illustrates what the form design now looks like.

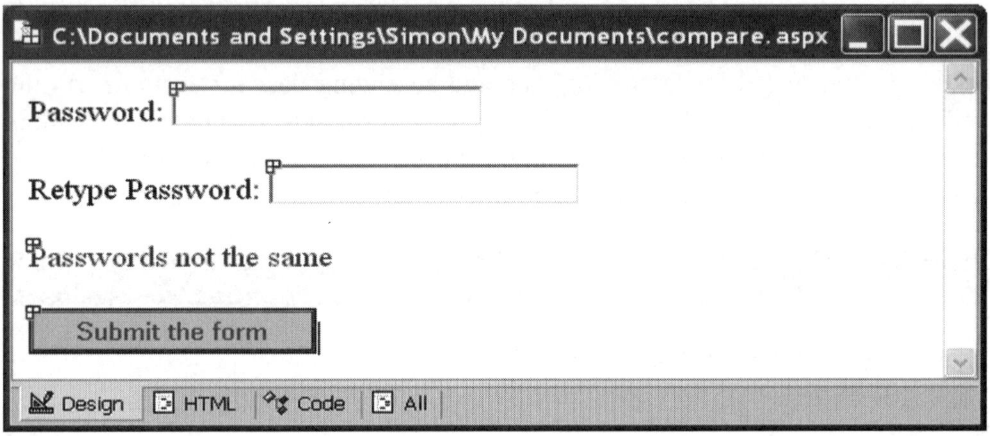

Figure 7.5: CompareValidator form

Clicking the HTML tab will reveal that the generated HTML *CompareValidator* code looks like:

```
<asp:CompareValidator id="CompareValidator1" runat="server"
ControlToCompare="TextBox1" ControlToValidate="TextBox2"
ErrorMessage="Passwords not the same"></asp:CompareValidator>
```

Viewing the form in a browser will result in the error message *"Passwords not the same"* being displayed if the two password fields do not contain the same values. This is illustrated in Figure 7.6.

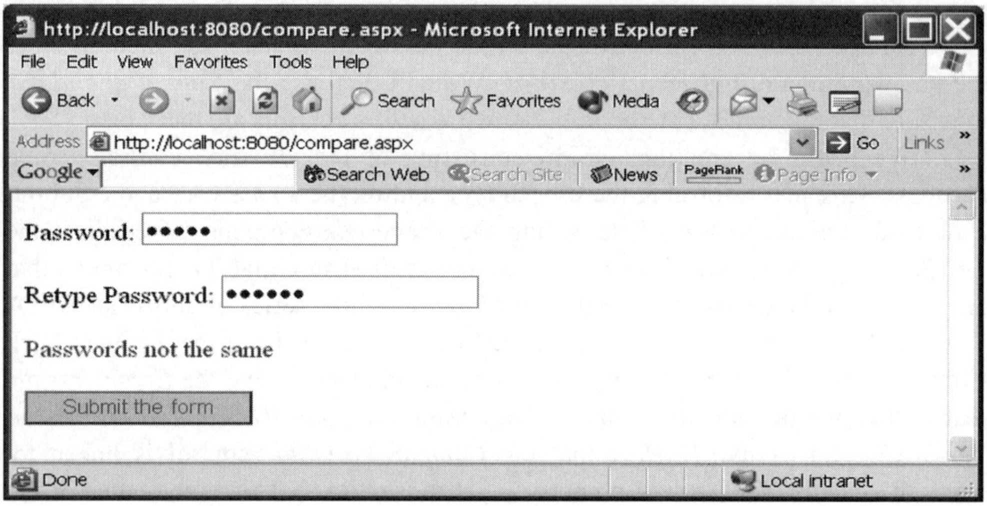

Figure 7.6: CompareValidator error message

The *CompareValidator* control can do more than compare two form controls to see if they contain the same values. Consider an example form where the user is asked to enter two dates, a starting date and an ending date for example. As the ending date comes after the starting date then the form must ensure that the ending date is the same or larger than the starting date. Figure 7.7 illustrates a form we have created consisting of two *DropDownLists* consisting of start and end dates.

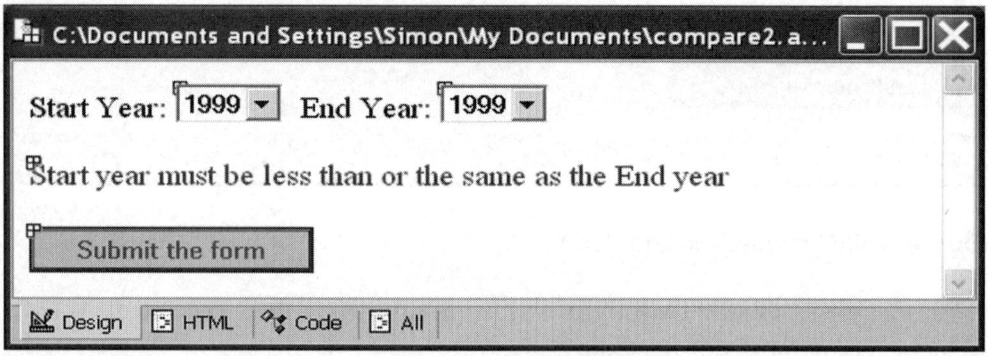

Figure 7.7: CompareValidator less than or equal to form

The *DropDownLists* have list items consisting of years from 1999 until 2004. The form also has a *CompareValidator* with an *ErrorMessage* property which has been set to *"Start year must be less than or the same as the End year"*. The property *ControlToValidate* has been set to *DropDownList1* and the *ControlToCompare* has been set to *DropDownList2*.

Finally, the property *Operator* has been set to *"LessThanEqual"*. This means that the value selected in *DropDownList1* must be less than or equal to that selected in *DropDownList2*. The generated HTML code for this control is as follows:

```
<asp:CompareValidator id="CompareValidator1" runat="server"
ErrorMessage="Start year must be less than or the same as the End year"
ControlToCompare="DropDownList2" ControlToValidate="DropDownList1"
Operator="LessThanEqual"></asp:CompareValidator>
```

Figure 7.8 illustrates the error message which is generated when the year date selected from the second *DropDownList* is less than that of the first.

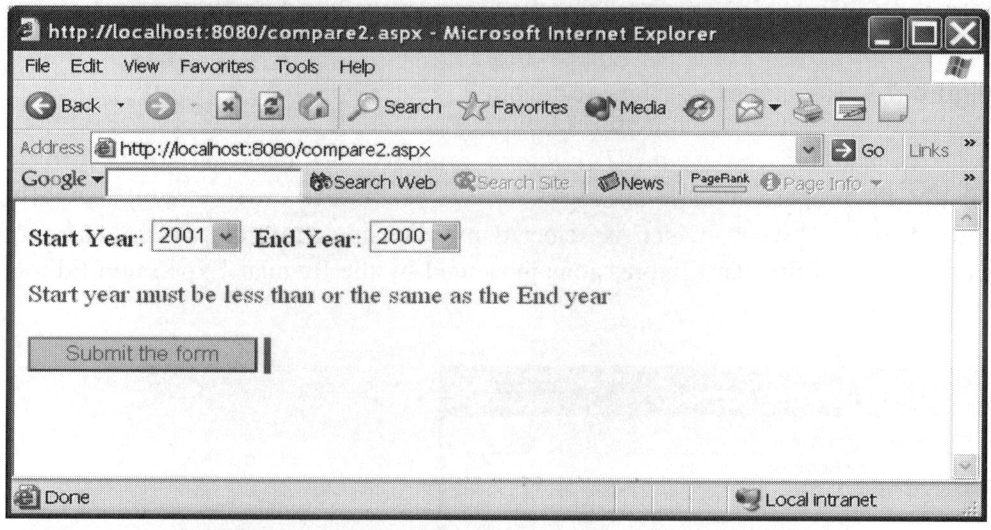

Figure 7.8: CompareValidator less than or equal to error message

7.4   Regular expression validation

The *RegularExpressionValidator* is a form control that uses an expression to check the validity of a control value. Regular expressions can be quite complex and difficult for the beginner to get to grips with. For example a regular expression to validate an email address looks like this:

```
\w+([-+.]\w+)*@\w+([-.]\w+)*\.\w+([-.]\w+)*
```

Luckily, the Web Matrix has some regular expressions built into the tool that we can use without having to understand how to create them from scratch. Figure 7.9 illustrates a form consisting of a *TextBox*, the associated text *"Email"*, a *RegularExpressionValidator* and a submit *Button*. The *ErrorMessage* property of the *RegularExpressionValidator* control has been changed to "Invalid Email Address".

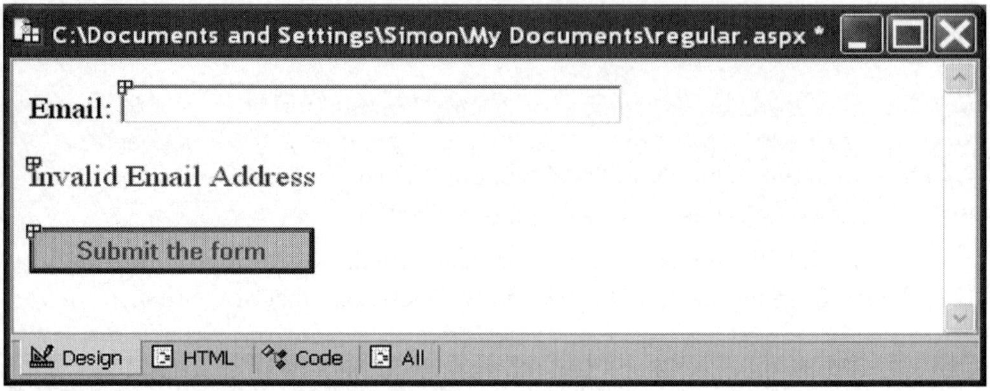

Figure 7.9: Regular expression validation

In addition the *ControlToValidate* property has been set to TextBox1. Finally, the property *ValidationExpression* has been set to \w+([-+.]\w+)*@\w+([-.]\w+)*\.\w+([-.]\w+)*, which is selected by choosing *"Internet Email Address"* from the list of Standard Expressions presented by the Regular Expression Editor, shown in Figure 7.10.

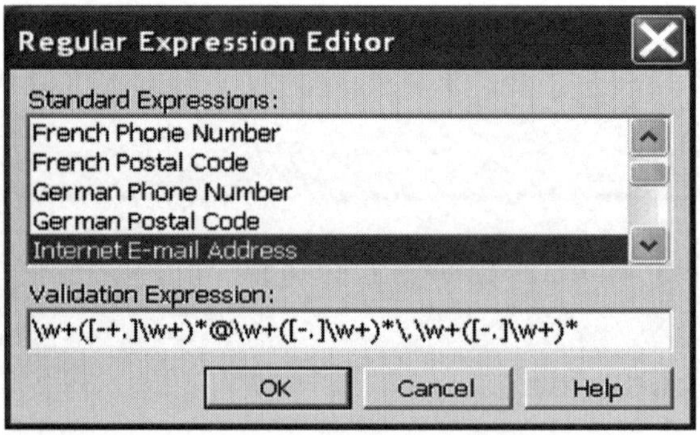

Figure 7.10: Regular Expression Editor

The HTML code generated for the *RegularExpressionValidator* control in Figure 7.9 is as follows:

```
<asp:RegularExpressionValidator id="RegularExpressionValidator1"
runat="server" ErrorMessage="Invalid Email Address"
ValidationExpression="\w+([-+.]\w+)*@\w+([-.]\w+)*\.\w+([-.]\w+)*"
ControlToValidate="TextBox1"></asp:RegularExpressionValidator>
```

Figure 7.11 illustrates the error message generated by the above control when an invalid email address is entered into the *TextBox* control.

Figure 7.11: RegularExpressionValidator error message

Note that regular expressions are not perfect. While, for example, they can tell us in this case if an entered string looks like an email address is supposed to look like, they cannot tell if the email address actually exists. So, for example the following email address would be accepted as being valid even though this email does not exist: simon.stoddart@sunderland.ac.uk

7.5   RangeValidator

The *RangeValidator* control provides a means by which the value (normally numeric) can be checked to see that it lies between defined minimum and maximum values. Figure 7.12 illustrates a form which has a single *TextBox* where an age is expected to be entered. The form has Submit Button and a *RangeValidator* control.

The Properties of the *RangeValidator* control have been set as follows. Firstly, the *ControlToValidate* has been set to *TextBox1*. The *ErrorMessage* has been set to "*Age between 18 and 70*". Finally, *MaximumValue* and *MinimumValue* have been set to 70 and 18 respectively.

The HTML code generated for the above *RangeValidator* control is as follows:

```
<asp:RangeValidator id="RangeValidator1" runat="server" ErrorMessage="Age
between 18 and 70" ControlToValidate="TextBox1" MaximumValue="70"
MinimumValue="18"></asp:RangeValidator>
```

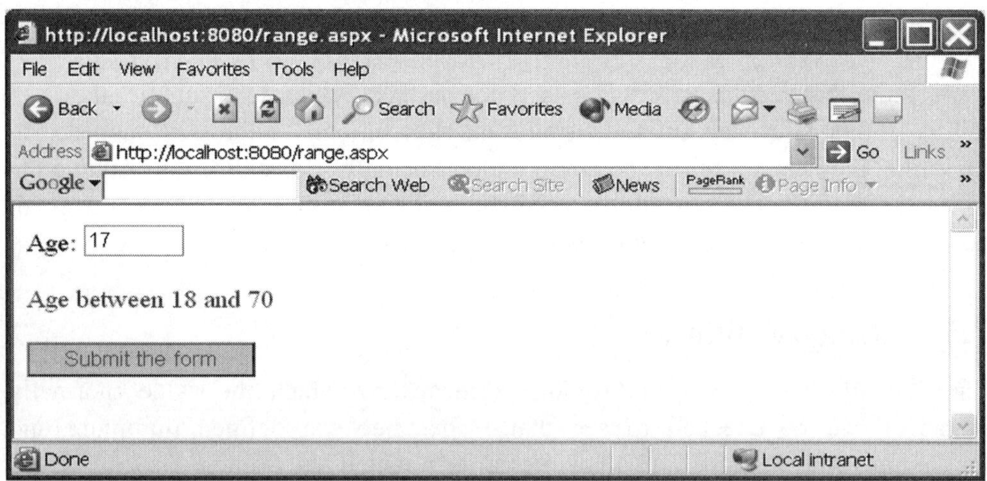

Figure 7.12: RangeValidator form

Figure 7.13 illustrates the error message generated by the control when an age is entered outside the 18 to 70 range.

Figure 7.13: RangeValidator error message

7.6   Multiple Validations

You don't have to only apply one validation control to a form control. You can in fact apply multiple validations. Consider the example form illustrated in Figure 7.14. This illustrates a form which employs two different validations on the same control. The two date *TextBoxes* have *RangeValidator* controls which ensure that the dates are between 1990 and 2003. If the dates are outside this range then the message *"Between 1990 and 2003"* will be displayed next to each of the *TextBoxes*. In addition a *CompareValidator* ensures that the start date is always earlier than the end date. If this is not true then the message *"End date must be greater than start date"* is displayed.

http://localhost:8080/multiple.aspx - Microsoft Internet Explorer

File   Edit   View   Favorites   Tools   Help

Back   Search   Favorites   Media

Address   http://localhost:8080/multiple.aspx   Go   Links

Google   Search Web   Search Site   News   PageRank   Page Info

Start Date: 2005   Between 1990 and 2003

End Date: 1999

End date must be greater than start date

Submit the form

Done   Local intranet

Figure 7.14: Multiple validation

The HTML code generated for the form illustrated in Figure 7.14 is as follows:

```
<form runat="server">
  <p>
    Start Date:
    <asp:TextBox id="TextBox1" runat="server"
Width="103px"></asp:TextBox>
    <asp:RangeValidator id="RangeValidator1" runat="server"
MinimumValue="1990" MaximumValue="2003" ControlToValidate="TextBox1"
ErrorMessage="Between 1990 and 2003 "></asp:RangeValidator>
  </p>
  <p>
    End Date:
    <asp:TextBox id="TextBox2" runat="server"
Width="103px"></asp:TextBox>
    <asp:RangeValidator id="RangeValidator2" runat="server"
MinimumValue="1990" MaximumValue="2003" ControlToValidate="TextBox2"
ErrorMessage="Between 1990 and 2003"></asp:RangeValidator>
  </p>
  <p>
```

```
      <asp:CompareValidator id="CompareValidator1" runat="server"
ControlToValidate="TextBox2" ErrorMessage="End date must be greater than start
date" Operator="GreaterThanEqual"
ControlToCompare="TextBox1"></asp:CompareValidator>
    </p>
    <p>
      <asp:Button id="Button1" onclick="Button1_Click" runat="server"
Text="Submit the form" ForeColor="DimGray" BackColor="#FFC0C0"
BorderColor="#FF8080"></asp:Button>
      <!-- Insert content here -->
    </p>
  </form>
```

7.7   Summary

Form validation is of key importance. You cannot assume that the information you ask a user to enter on a form will be the data that they do enter. To ensure the integrity of your applications and to verify your data you should always validate the data entered before you assume that it is what you expected. This chapter has introduced the various validation controls that ASP.NET provides in order to ensure that the data you expect to be entered by a user on a form is actually what you wanted.

7.8   Exercises

See if you can apply what you have learnt by trying the following exercises:

1. Create a form which consists of three *TextBox* controls. These controls are to be used to obtain the users first-name, surname and address. The form should incorporate three *RequiredFieldValidator* controls to ensure that data is entered in each *TextBox* control. You should also make use of a HTML table to format your form so that the *TextBox* controls, accompanying text and *RequiredFieldValidator* error messages are displayed as follows:

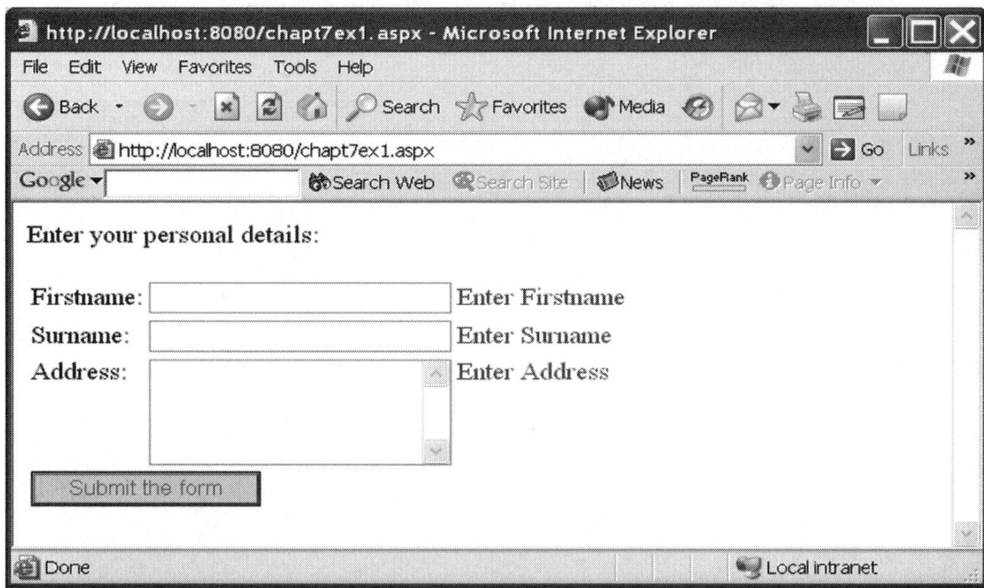

2. Create a form which consists of two *DropDownLists* consisting of music types: Pop, Rock, Classical, Punk and Country. A *CompareValidator* should ensure that the first and second choices are not the same. The completed form should look like this:

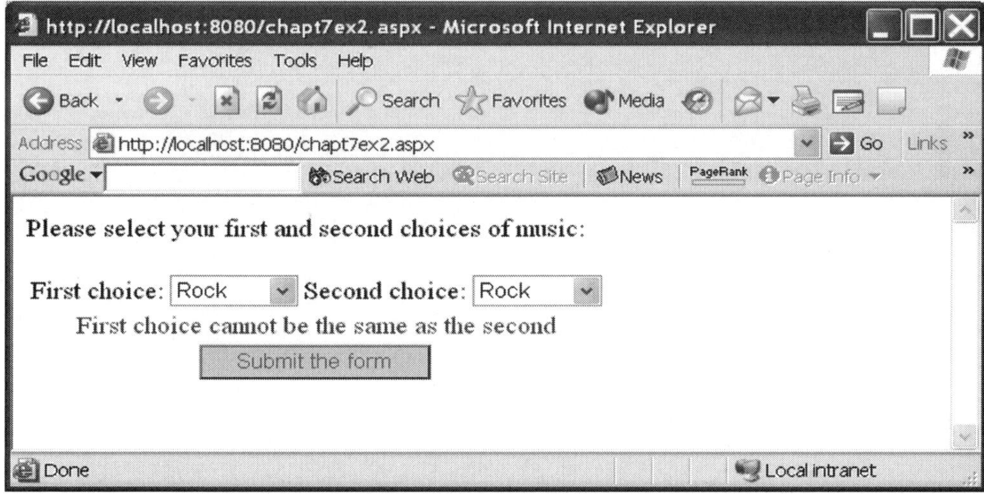

8

Introduction to VB.NET

8.1　Introduction

As you know the programming language used within this book is VB.NET. This variant of Visual Basic (VB) allows developers with experience in VB to migrate to the development of dynamic web pages within ASP.NET. Furthermore, of the languages supported by .NET Framework VB.NET is probably the most approachable to novice programmers and it is for this reason that it is being used. While in previous chapters we have introduced some elements of the VB.NET programming syntax we have not examined the language in any great detail. In this chapter we begin to rectify this while we will not teach you how to program from scratch in VB.NET we will introduce VB.NET programming syntax where it is needed in order to achieve some particular functionality. Examples are also introduced that explain how and where to apply program code.

8.2　ASP.NET and code

You are aware that, by default, Web Matrix creates web pages based on forms, and as a result, when you created objects on that form, you also came across ASP.NET delimiters.

```
<%     %>
```

All embedded ASP.NET statements used on the form, whether they are server controls or VB.NET statements must be framed by these delimiters. These can be single or multi-line statements such as:

```
<% output.text = "ABC"  %>
```

8.3   Assigning values to objects

The following is a simple *assign* statement that assigns the value that is on the right-hand side of the assignment (=) operator to, in this case, the *text* property of the object called *output*:

```
<% output.text = "ABC"  %>
```

In Visual Basic, assuming that the *output* object exists on the current form, this operation will perform effectively.

Given the above you would assume that the following code would work using VB.NET:

```
<%@Page Language="VB" Explicit="True" Debug="True"%>
<html>
<head>
</head>
<body>
  <form runat="server">
    <asp:TextBox id="output" runat="server"></asp:TextBox>
    <%
    output.text = "ABC"
    %>
  </form>
</body>
</html>
```

You can enter the above code using the Document component window using the 'All' view. The *textbox* server control is first created and then a string is assigned to it. This makes logical sense but it doesn't work, why? The problem is that VB.NET operates working within a web-based environment and the code is compiled and run on the server and it needs some event to make that code interact with the web page. Let's look at the code again:

```
<asp:TextBox id="output" runat="server"></asp:TextBox>
```

TextBox is a VB.NET method for creating a *TextBox*. It is given the *id* "*output*" which is a name that uniquely identifies its function. *runat="server"* ensures the ASP.NET code is run on the server. Once the method has run it creates the following as line of HTML within the form:

```
<input name="output" type="text" id="output" />
```

In the following line of ASP.NET the assign statement runs on the server.

```
output.text = "ABC"
```

The *TextBox* does not exist on the server only the code that created it in HTML. The server therefore does not understand what *output.text* is but this does not result in an error message. VB.NET remembers the object and its value and should a method be run subsequently that creates the *TextBox* then the *Text* property of that object will be assigned the appropriate value in HTML. Since this does not occur nothing appears to happen. To make this work the lines need to be reversed as follows:

```
<%@Page Language="VB" Explicit="True" Debug="True"%>
<html>
<head>
</head>
<body>
  <form runat="server">
    <%
    output.text = "ABC"
    %>
      <asp:TextBox id="output" runat="server"></asp:TextBox>
  </form>
</body>
</html>
```

This results in the following HTML output:

```
<input name="output" type="text" value="ABC" id="output" />
```

Figure 8.1 illustrates the output from the script when viewed in a browser.

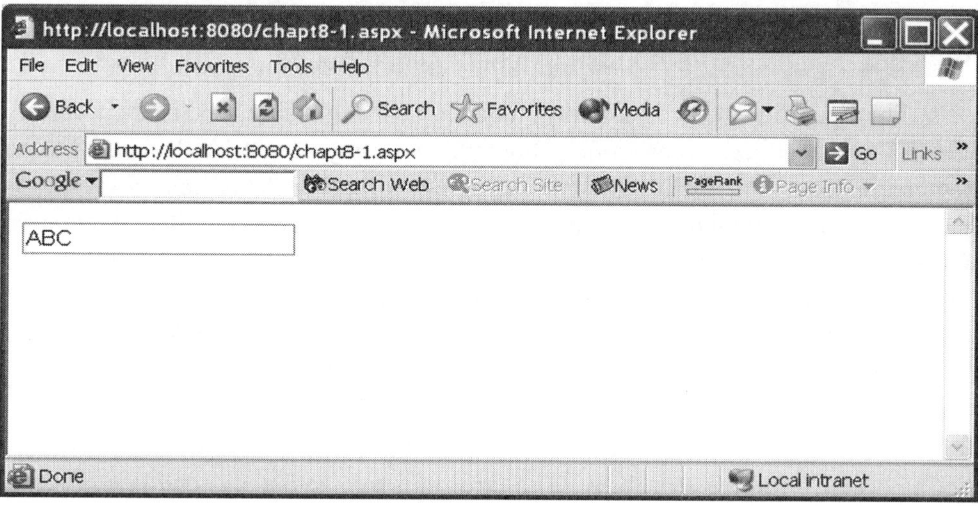

Figure 8.1: Simple form output

8.4   Reading values from objects

That deals with assigning values to objects, but what about reading values from objects? Let's assume that we have created a *TextBox* on a form and we want the user to enter a value and then be able to use what they type in our code. Consider the following:

```
<%@Page Language="VB" Explicit="True" Debug="True"%>
<html>
<head>
</head>
<body>
<form runat="server">
        <%
        Dim Input as Integer
        Input = txtInput.text
        %>
        <asp:TextBox id="txtInput" runat="server"></asp:TextBox>
  </form>
</body>
</html>
```

There are several new things here but before we examine them we should tell you that should you run this page it will result in the following error whether the code comes before or after the text box is created:

```
[InvalidCastException: Cast from string "" to type 'Integer' is not valid.]
```

8.4.1   ASP.NET header

So, what is new? The first line of this and subsequent ASP.NET pages looks like this:

```
<%@Page Language="VB" Explicit="True" Debug="True"%>
```

This specifies the programming language used as being VB (more precisely VB.NET), that all *variables* (more about them shortly) must be declared before they can be used and finally, that the *Debug* is set to *True*. This final point means that if an error occurs when the code is compiled you receive a detailed breakdown of what the error is and where it occurred. Unfortunately, it tends to provide too much information and you have to have a reasonable level of technical knowledge before you can decipher the real cause of the error. In addition it will only display the first error it comes to. Fixing that may only provide you with another error to solve.

Nevertheless, having set the Debugger to true it does provide you with a starting point in solving a problem. The error message above was one line of a full screen explanation.

8.4.2   Variables

As mentioned, this line also ensures that all variables are declared. So what are variables? When a program is running you often want the system to remember things. You could store values in objects such as text boxes; soon the screen would become cluttered, particularly if you only want the system to remember a value temporarily. The other way is by means of variables. Variables are areas in memory that are set aside to store data of specific types, in the example used here we needed to store a whole number which is a specific data type called an *Integer*:

```
Dim Input as Integer
```

A *Dim* (short for dimension) statement declares/creates a variable. All variables must have a name not used anywhere else on the page. This name should be meaningful and shouldn't include spaces e.g. *Input* as in the example above. Following this is the key word *as* and then the data type that the variable should store. The most commonly used data types supported by VB.NET are shown in Table 8.1.

Type	Description
Integer	Whole number
Long	Large whole number
Single	Decimal number
Double	Large decimal number
Boolean	Yes/No, True/False, 1/0
Date	Date
String	Text

Table 8.1: Commonly supported data types

You should refer to a text on VB.NET or the Microsoft web site to find out the full list of data types and their precise characteristics.

So how do you use variables? Once created, the major characteristics of a variable are that they can store values and that those values can change, hence the name variable. Values are assigned to variables in exactly the same way as we did earlier to assign values to the *Text* property of a *TextBox*:

```
Variable = Value
```

Remember that in the first line there was the statement:

```
Explicit="True"
```

As mentioned this forces you to create variables using the *Dim* statement prior to their use. It is possible to create variables without the use of the *Dim* statement merely by assigning a value to a previously unused name. The system assumes that the name on the left of the assign statement is a variable and will check the data type of the value passed to it and from that point on will treat the name as though it was a variable of that type. There are major problems with this casual approach to creating variables. Firstly the previously unused name may simply be a typing error for example; you might mistype a valid variable such as *"input"* as *"inpit"*. If you do not notice this, the system is not clever enough to recognise your error, it will assume this is a new variable and set its value accordingly. The result is that the page will not run as expected despite all of the code being syntactically correct. The second reason is that with explicit declarations you are stating the precise data type, this is important particularly if you are intending to perform mathematical operations on variables. If you used the casual approach it may appear that the data is stored as the correct type but you are never sure. If they are then used in mathematical calculations it may result in unexpected solutions. The other reason for having explicit declarations is that they are clearly visible within your code and that makes it easier to modify.

8.4.3   More on server-side code

At the beginning of this section we said that the following code will result in an error when run:

```
<%@Page Language="VB" Explicit="True" Debug="True"%>
<html>
<head>
</head>
<body>
<form runat="server">
        <%
        Dim Input as Integer
        Input = txtInput.text
        %>
        <asp:TextBox id="txtInput" runat="server"></asp:TextBox>
  </form>
</body>
</html>
```

The error message generated is as follows:

```
[InvalidCastException: Cast from string "" to type 'Integer' is not valid.]
```

So what does the error message from our program mean? What it says is that you cannot convert (*cast*) an empty string ("") to an *Integer*. What this means is that the code is compiled and run before the page is loaded and so the textbox *txtInput* has no value. But wait a minute! Earlier we said that you can not assign a value to an object unless there was an event to cause it to happen and that is true no event has occurred but we are not trying to assign a value. Whilst you cannot assign values you can read values without an event and so when the code is compiled it attempts to get the current value of the *TextBox* before there is anything in it, hence an empty string. The line that causes the problem is as follows:

```
Input = txtInput.text
```

But the error message seems to imply that whilst you cannot convert from an empty string to an integer it is possible to cast other data types. This is true, in many cases it is possible to cast one type into another as long as they are fundamentally the same, for example any text in a *TextBox* is of data type *String* whether or not the characters are letters, numbers or symbols. If the value stored in the *TextBox* is a number such as "*10*" then it can be assigned to an *Integer* variable. By so doing the value is cast from a *String* to an *Integer* before the variable is updated and so the new value of the variable would be *10*.

Later we will look at a more detailed example where an attempt to convert a number formatted as currency that includes the currency symbol fails to be cast back into a number because the characters that make it up include both numbers (e.g. *10*) and *String* characters (e.g. £).

So how do we get around the problem that we need data from the user but all the code is compiled before the web page is displayed? The answer is to keep separate the code for a particular event from that which is needed when the page is run. So where do you put it? This is discussed in the next section.

8.5   Subroutines – what are they?

A long time ago, or so it seems, there was a programming language called Basic. Basic was designed for the PC market rather than for professional programmers. It had its critics and one of the areas of criticism was the way in which it handled subroutines. A subroutine is a way of breaking a program down into blocks that could be called from another part of the program. The intention was, and still is, to break down code into blocks, each of which has a particular functionality for example, generating a report, accepting input from the user, calculating a particular value. The benefit of this approach is that the code becomes more structured, easier to correct and more understandable. In addition it means that a particular block of code may be used numerous times within a program without the need to type it in again. This should improve the efficiency of the code and cut down on errors in coding.

However, the way in which Basic and other similar languages achieved this was criticised. It allowed for code that became highly fragmented, complex and prone to error, with subroutines calling other subroutines until it could become impossible to track the flow of the program (hence "spaghetti code"). When Visual

Basic was introduced, subroutines were largely replaced with Procedures (blocks of code that perform specific functionality) and Functions (blocks of code that perform specific functionality but return a single value back to the part of the program that called it and are therefore ideal for calculations); subroutines were still supported and could be used within a procedure or function but they were rarely mentioned.

But now the concept of a subroutine is back in VB.NET, presumably because enough time has passed that it no longer has such negative associations. It replaces the term Procedure since, apart from the mechanics of writing them, procedures and subroutines perform the same activity. Functions still exist and how to use them will be discussed later.

8.6   How are subroutines used?

As noted above there are clear benefits to breaking up your code into meaningful blocks, but in addition, in ASP.NET, they also stand separate from the page to be loaded and are called from within the page when required.

For example, you could associate a subroutine with a button and the event of clicking that button triggers a method. This method calls a subroutine to assign or read a value from an object. How to achieve this will be discussed shortly.

But the user clicking a button on the form is an event that occurs after the page has loaded and so we need some way of monitoring an object to see if a particular event occurs. For objects such as buttons the system assumes that they have been used to be clicked and so all that is required to call a subroutine from a button is to include the *OnClick* method in its definition, for example:

```
<asp:Button id="cmdCalculate" onclick="calculate" runat="server"
Text="Calculate"></asp:Button>
```

Here the *OnClick* method is included in the definition of the button and only when the user clicks this button will the *OnClick* method be invoked and the *calculate* subroutine be called. In the next section we will examine the example this line of code is taken from.

The line of code above should appear on a single line but is actually too long to be viewed all on one line. This can also occur in the development environment but there the code scrolls off the screen. This can be very frustrating when you are trying to make sense of your code and need to see it all. You cannot just hit Return and divide it as the compiler will then see it as two separate commands and is likely to result in an error. It is possible to split lines, as done here, by means of a continuation character (an underscore _).

Make sure the underscore is not part-way through a string otherwise it will be just seen as another character, and always leave a single space between the last character on the line and the continuation character.

8.7   Multiplication table

8.7.1   Introduction

What we want to create is a simple calculation tool that requests the user to enter a number between 2 and 12 and then the multiplication table (1 to 12 times) for that number will be displayed. The interface is shown in Figure 8.2 and Figure 8.3.

Before we launch into the code, the first thing we need to consider is the design of the interface. Here we are not talking about web design but rather what you want the user to do and in what order. In addition you also need to consider what they might do differently and how the interface should react.

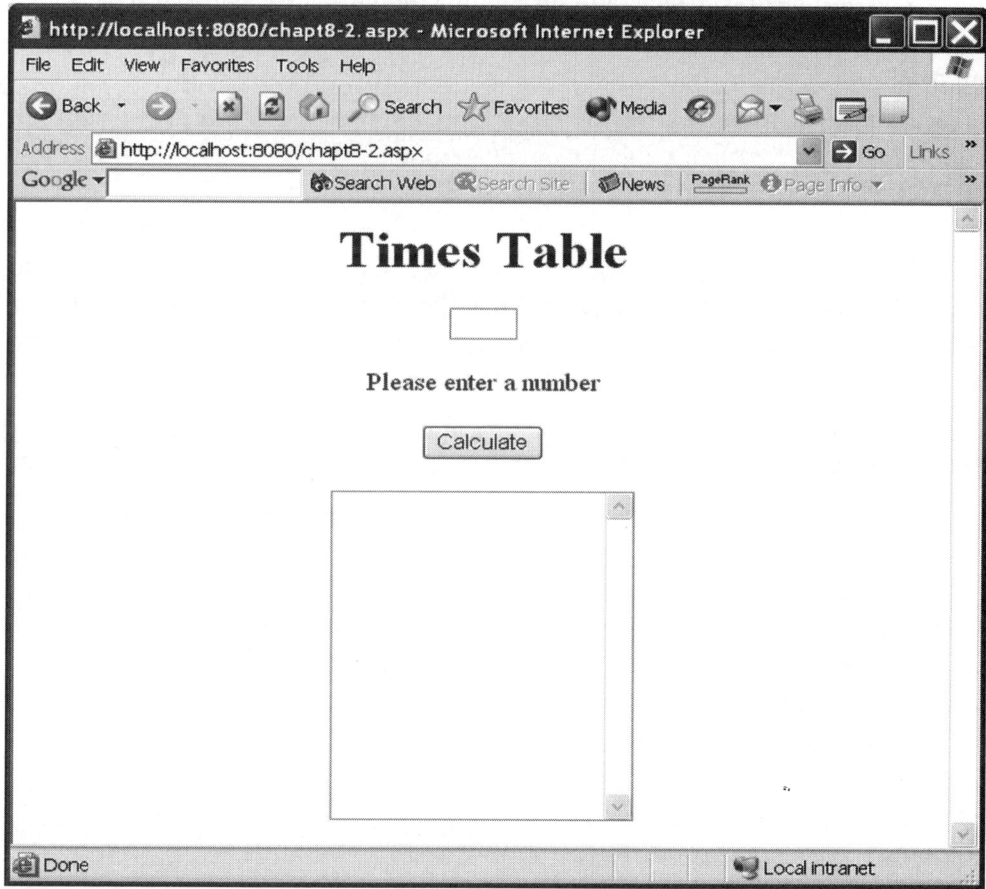

Figure 8.2: Times Table interface

A heading is important to identify the purpose of this screen. You need some form of instruction to tell the user what to do:

```
<h1 align="center">Times Table</h1>
```

You also need some way for the user to enter a number, this could be achieved in a number of ways but to keep it simple we will use a *TextBox*:

```
<p align="center">
<asp:TextBox id="txtInput" runat="server" Width="50px" autopostback="true"
ontextchanged="calculate"></asp:TextBox>
</p>
```

Since this *TextBox* will be referred to within the code we have changed the default **Id** to make it more meaningful. Other changes such as *autopostback* and *ontextchanged* will be explained later.

You also need somewhere to display the output, once again I have chosen a *TextBox* but this time made it *MultiLine* and made it large enough to display the full result:

```
<p align="center">
<asp:TextBox id="txtOutput" runat="server" ReadOnly="True"
TextMode="MultiLine" Rows="13"></asp:TextBox>
</p>
```

Assuming that the user enters a number, there needs to be some way to trigger the calculation. We have decided that the most appropriate way to do this is by means of a *Button* and when this is clicked it will trigger the calculation and display the output, hence the *Button* labeled *Calculate*.

```
<asp:Button id="cmdCalculate" onclick="calculate" runat="server" Width="90px"
Text="Calculate"></asp:Button>
```

This line creates the *Button*. Its *id* I have given a meaningful name that identifies that it is a command button (*cmd*) and its function (*calculate*). You should always rename objects that are going to be manipulated by the code as this will make the relationship between the web page and the code more obvious. The following *onclick="calculate"* states that when the button is clicked this calls the subroutine named *calculate*.

What follows is the code generated from the design:

```
<form runat="server">
    <h1 align="center">Times Table
    </h1>
    <p align="center">
        <asp:TextBox id="txtInput" runat="server" Width="50px"
autopostback="true" ontextchanged="calculate"></asp:TextBox>
    </p>
        <p align="center">
```

```
        <asp:Label id="lblMessage" runat="server">Please enter a
number</asp:Label>
    </p>
    <p align="center">
        <asp:Button id="cmdCalculate" onclick="calculate" runat="server"
Width="90px" Text="Calculate"></asp:Button>
        <asp:Button id="cmdAgain" onclick="cancel" runat="server" Width="90px"
Text="Again" Visible="False"></asp:Button>
    </p>
    <p align="center">
    </p>
    <p align="center">
        <asp:TextBox id="txtOutput" runat="server" ReadOnly="True"
TextMode="MultiLine" Rows="13"></asp:TextBox>
    </p>
  </form>
```

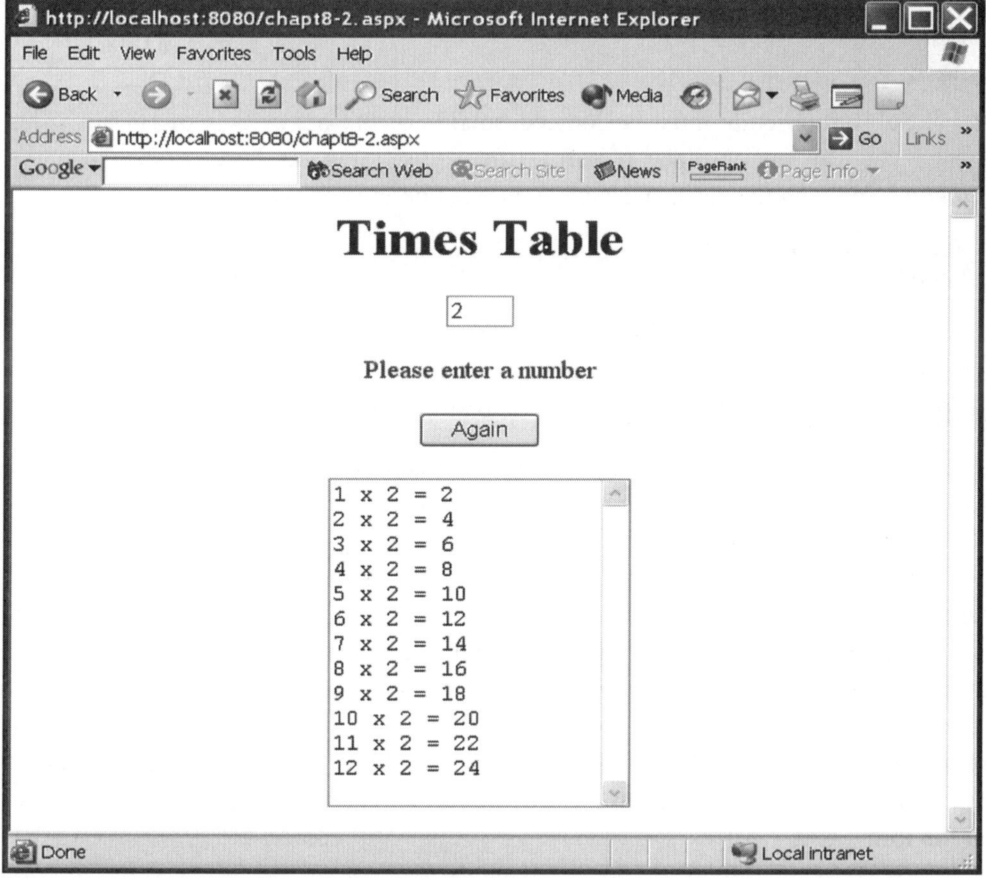

Figure 8.3: Times Table required output

What follows is the code for the *calculate* subroutine:

```
<%@ Page Language="VB" Explicit="True" Debug="True" %>

<script runat="server">

  sub calculate(Sender As Object, E As System.EventArgs)
     dim count as integer
     dim value as double

     value = txtInput.text
     for count = 1 to 12
        txtOutput.text = txtOutput.text & chr(13) & count _
           & " x " & value & " = " & count * value
     next count
  end sub
</script>


<html>
<head>
</head>
```

Subroutine code must be located outside of the major tags of HTML. This means you can either place it before the *<html>* tag, as here, or between the *</head>* and *<body>* tags. All such code must be written within a *script* tag.

```
<script runat="server">
</script>
```

A subroutine always begins with the *sub* key word and ends with *end sub*. The first line of the *calculate* subroutine is as follows:

```
sub calculate(Sender As Object, E As System.EventArgs)
```

To use a subroutine outside of the form code requires that you immediately follow the name of the subroutine with *(Sender As Object, E As System.EventArgs)*. All subroutines will have their name followed by a pair of parentheses as this allows data to be passed into the subroutine from outside (arguments, also called parameters).

All arguments must be given a name and a type and be separated by commas. Outside form code these arguments are required as they allow code to interact with the form. It is possible to write subroutines inside the form, but remember in this case we need the code to interact with form objects as a result of events that occur once the form is loaded and that cannot be done by a subroutine in the form code.

Next, two variables are declared and the current value of the text property of the *txtInput* textbox is assigned to the variable *value*:

```
dim count as integer
dim value as doublce
```

```
value = txtInput.text
```

Whilst the user of a times table is likely to be young and probably use small whole numbers you cannot be sure of that and so we have allowed for the worst case scenario, that the user will enter a very large decimal number by making the variable that will store the result a *Double*.

8.7.2   For Next loop

Now we need to calculate the output using a For Next loop as follows:

```
for count = 1 to 12
    txtOutput.text = txtOutput.text & chr(13) & count _
      & " x " & value & " = " & count * value
next count
```

Since we know that there will be twelve calculations, one for each of the multiplications we could write twelve separate lines of code but the only thing that would differ between each line would be the value of the multiplier and that increments by one every time. So why write twelve lines of code when we could run the same line twelve times changing the multiplier each time. That is one of the main reasons for using a loop. There are two types of loop a *For Next* loop and a *Do* loop. A *For Next* loop is ideal if there are a fixed number of times that you want a particular block of code to be repeated as is the case here. The basic syntax of a *For Next* loop is:

```
FOR variable = start number TO end number
    Code to be iterated
NEXT variable
```

Basically you use a variable as a counter. The first line sets the initial value of the variable and the maximum number of times the code is to be run. The last line of the *For Next* loop increments the counter. The code will continue to repeat until that value is reached at which point the program drops out of the loop.

In our example, the code within the loop is a single statement that assigns a value to the text property of the *textbox (txtOutput)*. If you look at the output from this code you will see that the text box is to contain twelve lines, each line has the following format e.g.:

```
9 x 10 = 90
```

If the multiplication starts at 1 and ends at 12 and the variable counter does the same in the loop, then the first character in the output can be the current value of the variable *count*. The *x* is merely a keyboard character. The next character is the value that the user typed in, currently stored in the variable *value*. The = is a keyboard character, whilst the last character is the product of multiplying *value* with *count*.

8.7.3 Concatenation

However, the value currently stored in the text property of *txtOutput* acts like a variable so every time we go through the loop it overwrites the previous value, which is not what we want. What we need to do in every loop is take the current value of the text property and "glue" it to the previous value. Regardless of type(s) on the right-hand side of the assign statement, everything assigned to the left-hand side is treated as a *string*. In VB.NET one string can be glued to another by means of the *concatenation* character (&). So the assignment becomes:

```
txtOutput.text = txtOutput.text & count _
& " x " & value & " = " & count * value
```

But we still have a problem because all of this will appear on one line that will word wrap as the 2 times table shown in Figure 8.4.

To overcome this we need to insert a line break after each line. This can be achieved by using the character value that represents the pressing of the *Enter/Return* key.

```
Chr(13)
```

Put it all together and we get:

```
for count = 1 to 12
        txtOutput.text = txtOutput.text & chr(13) & count _
        & " x " & value & " = " & count * value
next count
```

This works and will calculate and display the times table for any number that the user types in. But what happens if the user doesn't type in a value at all?

The answer is that an error occurs because we would be attempting to assign an empty string to a variable, which we know from earlier in the chapter is not allowed. So how do we protect the user from this?

8.7.4 If statement

The simplest solution to the problem is that the code is only allowed to run if a valid number has been entered. So we need a test. The most common way of testing values is by means of an *If* statement. The syntax for an *If* statement can become quite complicated but a simple form is below:

```
IF test THEN
        code
END IF
```

The test is a test of *truth*, in our case if the *Text* property of *txtInput* is not equal to (<>) an empty string ("") then do our code. Consequently, if we put such a test around the code then it will not run unless the test is true. Here is the test:

```
If txtInput.text <> ""
```

So the subroutine code becomes:

```
sub calculate(Sender As Object, E As System.EventArgs)
   dim count as integer
   dim value as double

   if txtInput.text <> ""
     value = txtInput.text
     for count = 1 to 12
       txtOutput.text = txtOutput.text & count _
         & " x " & value & " = " & count * value
     next count
   end if
end sub
```

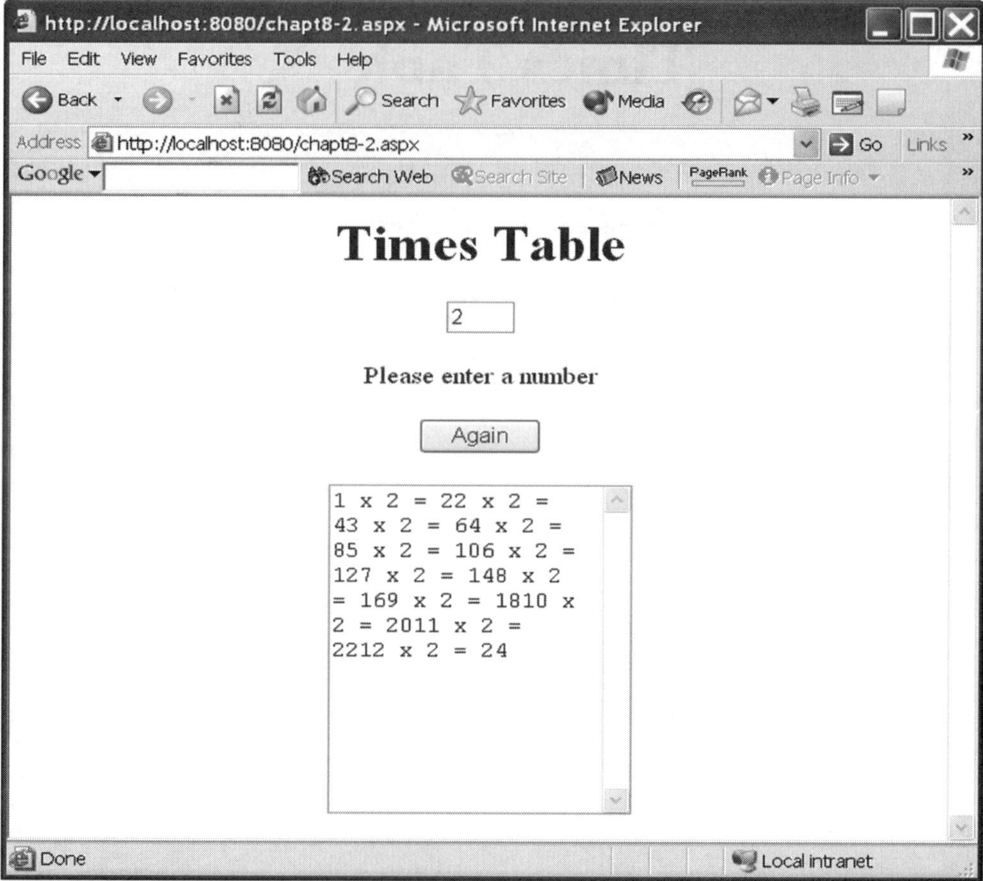

Figure 8.4: Times Table word wrap

The next question is what if the user, having run the calculation once wants to type in another number? The way we have structured the program means that the user can remove the original input number, type in another and click the button again. Since our code uses the *For Next* loop to glue any values to any preceding values the new times table will be added to the end of the previous one. In addition, because the output *TextBox* is read only they are unable to manually remove the old calculation as they did with the input. So how do we resolve this problem? For that we need to go back to the design.

8.7.5   Property manipulation at design time

Figure 8.5 illustrates the Time Table design, as viewed from Web Matrix document Design window.

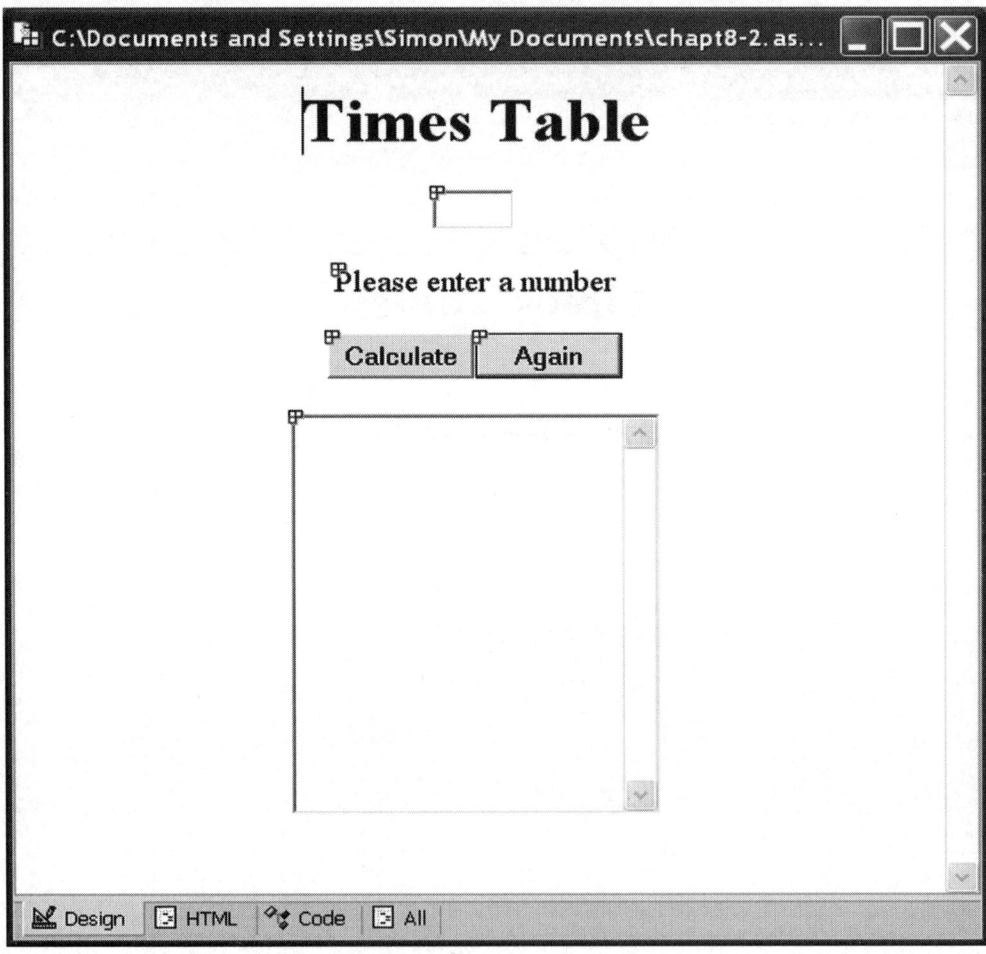

Figure 8.5: Times Table design

When you examine the design of this web page the first thing you should recognise is that all the objects are centred. The next thing to notice is that there are two buttons *Calculate* and *Again*. We have done the code for the *Calculate Button*; the *Again Button* will clear both of the text boxes ready for the next calculation.

But before we get to that, we also wanted to design this page so that the interface was as simple as possible so we only wanted the appropriate *Button* to be visible at any one time. So when the web page first opens the *Calculate Button* is the only one seen. We did this by setting the *Visible* property of the *Again Button* to *False* in the Design View in Web Matrix. This is illustrated in Figure 8.6.

Properties	
cmdAgain System.Web.UI.WebControls.Button	
(Click to see parent HTML elements)	
(DataBindings)	
(ID)	**cmdAgain**
AccessKey	
BackColor	
BorderColor	
BorderStyle	NotSet
BorderWidth	
CausesValidation	True
CommandArgument	
CommandName	
CssClass	
Enabled	True
EnableViewState	True
⊞ Font	
ForeColor	
Height	
TabIndex	0
Text	**Again**
ToolTip	
Visible	**False**
Width	**90px**

Text
The text to be shown on the button.

Properties | Classes | Community

Figure 8.6: Properties of the Again button

When the web page is opened, because all of the objects are centred the Calculate button centres on the screen. If we then reversed the *Visible* properties of the buttons the *Again Button* replaces it in exactly the same position. But how and where do we change these properties?

8.7.6   Property manipulation at run time

What we want is that when the user clicks on the *Calculate Button* the calculation occurs, the output is displayed and the button changes to the *Again Button*. Remember that code runs so fast that it appears as though these actions appear simultaneously. Consequently, we need to amend the code we have just written to add the button change. Since we already know how to assign new values to the properties of objects the following code should make sense:

```
cmdCalculate.visible="false"
cmdAgain.visible="true"
```

Now for the Again button. When the user clicks on it should empty two *TextBoxes* and swap the *Buttons* so that the *Calculate Button* is visible again. We are therefore going to create a subroutine called *cancel* that will be called when the *Again Button* is clicked. The *Button* definition is as follows:

```
<asp:Button id="cmdAgain" onclick="cancel" runat="server" _
Width="90px" Text="Again" Visible="False"></asp:Button>
```

The code for the subroutine *cancel* is below and follows the same structure as the previous subroutine:

```
sub cancel(Sender As Object, E As System.EventArgs)
    txtInput.text = ""
    txtOutput.text = ""
    cmdCalculate.visible="true"
    cmdAgain.visible="false"
end sub
```

One final thing before we finish with this example. Users are renowned for doing what they want and not what you want. So we made an assumption that the user may ignore the *Calculate Button* and press the Enter/Return key once they had entered their number. Therefore we needed some mechanism that would monitor the *TextBox* and react accordingly.

8.7.7   AutoPostBack

Buttons automatically assume that someone is going to click them and so require the services of a subroutine, but objects such as *TextBoxes* are somewhat passive and require an additional method to be added to its definition to monitor events. This is called the *AutoPostBack* method and needs to be set to true. However, we also need to tell it which event to look for and this is done by the *ontextchanged* method. Consequently, the definition of the *txtInput TextBox* needs to be modified as follows:

```
<asp:TextBox id="txtInput" runat="server" ontextchanged="calculate" _
autopostback="true" Width="50px"></asp:TextBox>
```

It should be apparent now that using subroutines for this webpage has the benefit of not only associating code with events on objects but also that the same subroutine can be used for two or more separate events.

8.7.8   Code for multiplication table

The completed code is as follows:

```
<%@ Page Language="VB" Explicit="True" Debug="True" %>
<script runat="server">

  sub calculate(Sender As Object, E As System.EventArgs)
     dim count as integer
     dim value as double

     if txtInput.text <> ""
        value = txtInput.text
        for count = 1 to 12
           txtOutput.text = txtOutput.text & chr(13) & count _
              & " x " & value & " = " & count * value
        next count
        cmdCalculate.visible="false"
        cmdAgain.visible="true"
     end if
  end sub

  sub cancel(Sender As Object, E As System.EventArgs)
     txtInput.text = ""
     txtOutput.text = ""
     cmdCalculate.visible="true"
     cmdAgain.visible="false"
  end sub

</script>
<html>
<head>
</head>
<body>
  <form runat="server">
    <h1 align="center">Times Table
    </h1>
    <p align="center">
       <asp:TextBox id="txtInput" runat="server" ontextchanged="calculate"
autopostback="true" Width="50px"></asp:TextBox>
    </p>
    <p align="center">
```

```
        <asp:Label id="lblMessage" runat="server">Please enter a
number</asp:Label>
    </p>
    <p align="center">
        <asp:Button id="cmdCalculate" onclick="calculate" runat="server"
Width="90px" Text="Calculate"></asp:Button>
        <asp:Button id="cmdAgain" onclick="cancel" runat="server" Width="90px"
Text="Again" Visible="False"></asp:Button>
    </p>
    <p align="center">
    </p>
    <p align="center">
        <asp:TextBox id="txtOutput" runat="server" Rows="13"
TextMode="MultiLine" ReadOnly="True"></asp:TextBox>
    </p>
  </form>
</body>
</html>
```

8.8   Image use

8.8.1   Introduction

In this next example we are going to examine how we can use ASP.NET to provide interest to a web page by making it slightly different every time it is visited. In addition, we have seen how Web Matrix can automatically generate ASP.NET code for the objects we select; well we will also examine how to write code that creates objects to meet our needs.

The web page to be created uses images to add richness to the environment. Care should be taken when using images as they invariably make the page slower to load. Consequently be sure that using images is the best way forward. Where they must be used try and keep them small, use thumbnails where appropriate.

Figure 8.7 and Figure 8.8 demonstrate the same interface but every time the user visits the site or refreshes the page it will be subtly different. This can be enough to get the interest of the user and you want to attract users. There are three rows of images. The top row consists of two images that each randomly displays one of four photographs of Italy. The second row consists of between one and four unique photographs. The bottom row also contains four photographs but the difference here is that if the user clicks on one then it will open a full-size version of that photograph in a new web page. We would not expect you to use all of these on any one page but they are introduced here to start you thinking what could be achieved on your own sites. We are going to use *Arrays* to store the images for this site, but before we discuss this it is useful to examine in more detail the nature of data storage. You need to decide what data you need to store, how long it is to be stored and how it can be changed.

Figure 8.7: Visit Italy interface

8.8.2   Literals

The least flexible form of data manipulation is through the use of values that are "hard-wired" into your code. For example in the following assign statement the expression on the right of the assignment operator is what is termed a *string literal*. A *string literal* is any expression that consists of a sequence of contiguous characters surrounded by quotation marks that is *literally* interpreted as the characters within the quotation marks.

```
<%
        txtOutput.text = "This is a string literal"
%>
```

The value of that literal is fixed and cannot be influenced either by the user of the program or by the code. The only way to change the value is to change what appears between the double quotes in the code.

Figure 8.8: Visit Italy interface…again?

8.8.3 Constants

The use of literals is similar in certain respects to that of constants in that once a constant is set it cannot be modified at runtime:

```
<%
        Const FixedValue as String = "This is a constant value"

        txtOutput.text = FixedValue
%>
```

However, a constant has the benefit that if you need to use it more than once in your code and you want to change its value, then changing the declaration of the constant will change all instances of its use. This has benefits not only in terms of avoiding typographic coding errors through duplication but also means that values used in your code are clearly identifiable as you can keep all declarations together.

8.8.4   Variables

We have dealt with variables quite extensively so far so it only needs to be stated that a variable stores a single value of a particular data type. Assigning a value to a variable overwrites whatever was stored inside it:

```
<%
        Dim VariableValue as String

        VariableValue = "This is a variable value"

        txtOutput.text = VariableValue
%>
```

One thing to consider is that if you are going to perform any calculations or data manipulation with the values stored in your variables then it is probably best to *initialise* the variables. Declaring a variable creates a space in memory of a specific data type but there is a minimal risk that that space will not empty. If there is anything there it will not be data that is of any importance but it may affect your program. Therefore you should consider setting the variables to default values before you use them:

```
<%
        Dim VariableData as Integer

        VariableData = 0
%>
```

8.8.5   Arrays

There are times when you would like to store a collection of the same type of values; this is the job of an *array*. When an *array* is created instead of setting aside one area of memory of a particular type it will generate as many as are required. Each of these areas will be known by the same name but will be distinguished from one another by an *index value* stored in a *sub-script*. Probably the best way to explain this is through an example:

```
<%
        Dim ArrayData(3) as Integer
%>
```

This declaration creates a one dimensional *Integer array* of four elements. This statement needs some explanation. An *array* can have one or more dimensions. The concept of multiple dimensions is a difficult one to explain beyond two dimensions, but that is enough to explain the principle. Below is a representation of the single dimension array *ArrayData*. The index for an *array* in VB.NET always starts from zero and so *ArrayData(3)* is an *array* of four indexed elements each of which can store an *Integer* value, see Figure 8.9.

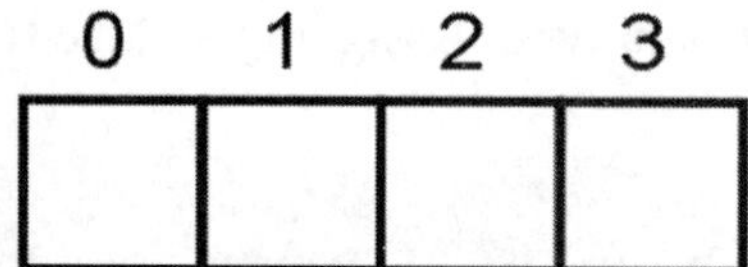

Figure 8.9: Four element array

To assign a value to an element of an *array* is similar to doing it for a variable:

```
<%
        Dim ArrayData(3) as Integer

        ArrayData(1) = 10
%>
```

This will assign the *Integer* value of *10* to the second element of the *array*, as illustrated in Figure 8.10.

Figure 8.10: Value 10 assigned to the second array element

A two dimensional *array* has two sub-scripts and a graphical representation of one is like a spreadsheet in appearance:

```
<%
        Dim ArrayData(3, 3) as Integer
%>
```

This declaration creates a 4 x 4 matrix. The first sub-script can be said to refer to the rows whilst the second deals with the columns. This is illustrated in Figure 8.11.

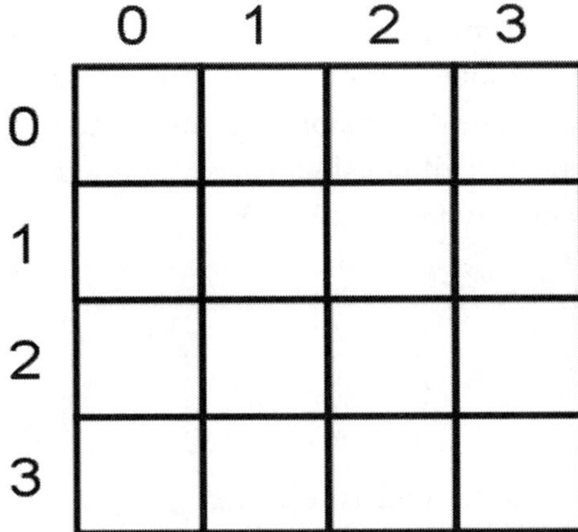

Figure 8.11: Two dimensional array

To assign a value to a particular cell within the matrix you need to specify not only the row index but also the column. For example:

```
<%
    Dim ArrayData(3, 3) as Integer

    ArrayData(1, 2) = 10
%>
```

This assigns the *Integer* value to the cell located in the third column and the second row and is illustrated in Figure 8.12.

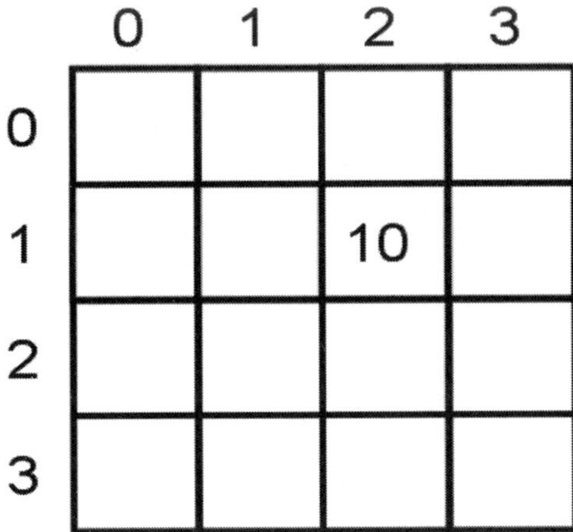

Figure 8.12: Value assigned in third column and second row

Whilst it is useful to initially think in terms of grids in order to understand the concept of *arrays* you can run into problems the greater the number of dimensions, three would be a cube but what about four or more? Probably a better and more accurate way of describing a multi-dimensional *array* is that each indexed item within a sub-script contains a single dimensional *array* defined by the sub-script next to it. This is illustrated graphically in Figure 8.13.

```
<%
        Dim ArrayData(3, 2, 1) as Integer

        ArrayData(1, 2, 0) = 10
%>
```

Consequently the code above could be described as follows:

- Sub-script 1 – A single dimensional array of four indexed elements. Each indexed value is a single dimensional array.
- Sub-script 2 – A single dimensional array of three indexed elements. Each indexed value is a single dimensional array.
- Sub-script 3 – A single dimensional array of two indexed integer values.

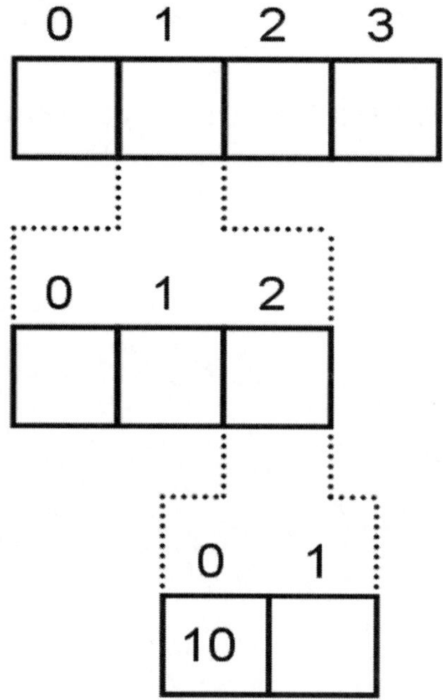

Figure 8.13: Multi-dimensional array

So far we have used literals to control the assignment of values to elements of an *array*, but there is no reason why variables could not perform that purpose.

The benefit of this is that as with variables it is possible to place *arrays* under programmable control.

One of the major benefits of *arrays* is that they allow a simple and elegant mechanism for performing control (e.g. adding or removing values), manipulation (e.g. sorting items) and examination (e.g. finding items) activities on potentially large numbers of similar objects. We will not be able to pursue all of these within this book. In this chapter we will use an array to store references to the images of Italy.

8.8.6   Creating Part 1 of the interface

As noted earlier there are three main elements to the interface. The first of these are the two images at the top of the screen. In order to space objects horizontally on a web page the most common method is to use a *table*:

```
<asp:Table id="Table1" runat="server" Width="100%">
    <asp:TableRow>
        <asp:TableCell HorizontalAlign="Left">
            <asp:Image runat="server" ID="photo1" Height="125px"></asp:Image>
        </asp:TableCell>
        <asp:TableCell HorizontalAlign="Right">
            <asp:Image runat="server" ID="photo2" Height="125px"></asp:Image>
        </asp:TableCell>
    </asp:TableRow>
</asp:Table>

<h1 align="center">Visit Italy
</h1>
<h1 align="center">
</h1>
```

This creates a *table* that fills the width of the web page. It consists of a single row that has two cells. The first of these cells is left-aligned whilst the other is right-aligned. Each cell contains an image but there is no reference to the source of that image, this is to be supplied through code. The last four lines provide the heading for the web page.

As we have discussed, it is not possible to use code to assign values to objects unless the code comes first. The images are selected randomly from an array of images. To store the references to these images we need to create a single dimensional array of string elements and then assign the path to each of the images to the indexed element of the array. Since the images are stored in the same folder/directory as the page only the file name is required.

```
<%
    Dim picture(3) as string

    picture(0)="colloseum.jpg"
```

```
    picture(1)="david.jpg"
    picture(2)="trevi.jpg"
    picture(3)="pisa.jpg"

%>
```

In order to use the elements of the array a value needs to be assigned to the *ImageUrl* property of the image object. If we were using literals then the code might be as follows:

```
photo1.ImageUrl=picture(2)
photo2.ImageUrl=picture(1)
```

However, we want to use code to randomly select one of the values. To do that we need to use the *rnd()* function. This function returns a random fractional number that is equal to or greater than zero but less than one. If we multiply this fractional number by the number of elements in our array then we will get a fractional number that is less than the number of elements. We can then use the *int()* function to convert this fraction to an integer. The function does this by checking the data type of the item within the parentheses and if it is fractional then it will round the value to a whole number. For example:

- If rnd() generates 0.85
- 4 x 0.85 = 3.4
- The int() function rounds this value to 3

In our example we need to use this within the index of the array for each of the images:

```
photo1.ImageUrl=picture(int(4 * rnd()))
photo2.ImageUrl=picture(int(4 * rnd()))
```

The outcome of this is that every time the page is opened or refreshed each of the images will randomly display one of the four photographs. This means that it is not possible to predict the combination of photographs displayed.

8.8.7   Creating Part 2 of the interface

In the next part of the interface we want to display a random number of images taken from the *array*. These images are to be centred on the web page and placed side by side as such they do not require a table.

```
<p align="center">
    <asp:Image id="photos" runat="server" Height="125px"></asp:Image>
</p>
```

We are going to use a *For Next* loop to create the image and display its appropriate photograph. The loop test determines how many images are going to be displayed and since we want this to be random the *rnd()* function will be used.

```
<%
   for count = (1 + int(4 * rnd())) to 4


   next count
%>
</p>
```

The test will return a value between one and four. If the value is, for example, two the loop will iterate three times and the value of the variable *count* will be *2, 3* and *4* respectively. If the value is four then the loop will only iterate once.

We mention the value of *count* because we are also going to use this to determine the photograph for each picture:

```
<%
    photos.ImageUrl=picture(count - 1)
%>
<asp:Image id="photos" runat="server" Height="125px"></asp:Image>
```

Note we use (*count − 1*) because the array indices are 0 − 3 whilst the loop is 1 − 4. Putting the elements together results in the following:

```
<p align="center">
   <%
    for count = (1 + int(4 * rnd())) to 4
       photos.ImageUrl=picture(count - 1)
   %>
   <asp:Image id="photos" runat="server" Height="125px"></asp:Image>
   <%
     next count
   %>
</p>
```

8.8.8   Creating Part 3 of the interface

The final part of the interface consists of the four photographs displayed side by side in a table across the width of the web page:

```
<asp:Table id="Table2" runat="server" Width="100%">
<asp:TableRow HorizontalAlign="Center">
    <asp:TableCell>
        <asp:ImageButton runat="server" Height="125px"
        ID="imgbtncolloseum" onclick="colloseum"></asp:ImageButton>
    </asp:TableCell>
    <asp:TableCell>
        <asp:ImageButton runat="server" Height="125px" ID="imgbtndavid"
```

```
            onclick="david"></asp:ImageButton>
        </asp:TableCell>
        <asp:TableCell>
            <asp:ImageButton runat="server" Height="125px" ID="imgbtntrevi"
            onclick="trevi"></asp:ImageButton>
        </asp:TableCell>
        <asp:TableCell>
            <asp:ImageButton runat="server" Height="125px" ID="imgbtnpisa"
            onclick="pisa"></asp:ImageButton>
        </asp:TableCell>
    </asp:TableRow>
</asp:Table>
```

You will notice from the definition of each of the images there is an *onclick* method. This means that when the object is clicked the associated subroutine will be called. ASP.NET Image objects do not allow for this method and so we have used *ImageButtons*.

We are going to use code to assign the photograph to the *ImageButton*. In this case we are doing it to keep all of the paths together so that it makes them easier to find if the webpage needs to be updated:

```
<%
    imgbtncolloseum.ImageUrl="colloseum.jpg"
    imgbtntrevi.ImageUrl="trevi.jpg"
    imgbtndavid.ImageUrl="david.jpg"
    imgbtnpisa.ImageUrl="pisa.jpg"
%>
```

As there are four images we need four subroutines:

```
sub colloseum(Sender as Object, E as System.Web.UI.ImageClickEventArgs)
    dim path as string
        path="colloseum.aspx"
        response.redirect(path)
end sub

sub david(Sender as Object, E as System.Web.UI.ImageClickEventArgs)
    dim path as string
        path="david.aspx"
        response.redirect(path)
end sub

sub pisa(Sender as Object, E as System.Web.UI.ImageClickEventArgs)
    dim path as string
        path="pisa.aspx"
        response.redirect(path)
end sub

sub trevi(Sender as Object, E as System.Web.UI.ImageClickEventArgs)
    dim path as string
        path="trevi.aspx"
```

```
    response.redirect(path)
end sub
```

You will note that since the event is to click an image the arguments of each subroutine are slightly different from what has been defined before. We do not expect you to remember the different versions of the arguments as provided you have *Debug* set to *True* then the error messages provided should tell you what to use.

Each subroutine declares a local *string* variable called *path*. This is assigned the path to the page to be opened. *Response.redirect(path)* uses the value of the variable and redirects the browser to open that page.

8.8.9   Code for image use

The completed code is as follows:

```
<%@ Page Language="VB" Explicit="True" Debug="True" %>
<script runat="server">

  sub colloseum(Sender as Object, E as System.Web.UI.ImageClickEventArgs)
    dim path as string
      path="colloseum.aspx"
      response.redirect(path)
  end sub

  sub david(Sender as Object, E as System.Web.UI.ImageClickEventArgs)
    dim path as string
      path="david.aspx"
      response.redirect(path)
  end sub

  sub pisa(Sender as Object, E as System.Web.UI.ImageClickEventArgs)
    dim path as string
      path="pisa.aspx"
      response.redirect(path)
  end sub

  sub trevi(Sender as Object, E as System.Web.UI.ImageClickEventArgs)
    dim path as string
      path="trevi.aspx"
      response.redirect(path)
  end sub

</script>
<html>
<head>
</head>
<body>
  <form runat="server">
```

```
<%
dim picture(3) as string
dim count as integer

picture(0)="colloseum.jpg"
picture(1)="david.jpg"
picture(2)="trevi.jpg"
picture(3)="pisa.jpg"

photo1.ImageUrl=picture(int(4 * rnd()))
photo2.ImageUrl=picture(int(4 * rnd()))
%>
<asp:Table id="Table1" runat="server" Width="100%">
  <asp:TableRow>
    <asp:TableCell HorizontalAlign="Left">
      <asp:Image runat="server" ID="photo1"
       Height="125px"></asp:Image>
    </asp:TableCell>
    <asp:TableCell HorizontalAlign="Right">
      <asp:Image runat="server" ID="photo2"
       Height="125px"></asp:Image>
    </asp:TableCell>
  </asp:TableRow>
</asp:Table>
<h1 align="center">Visit Italy
</h1>
<h1 align="center">
</h1>
<p align="center">
  <%
for count = (1 + int(4 * rnd())) to 4
  photos.ImageUrl=picture(count - 1)
%>
  <asp:Image id="photos" runat="server" Height="125px"></asp:Image>
  <%
next count
%>
</p>
<%
imgbtncolloseum.ImageUrl="colloseum.jpg"
imgbtntrevi.ImageUrl="trevi.jpg"
imgbtndavid.ImageUrl="david.jpg"
imgbtnpisa.ImageUrl="pisa.jpg"
%>
<div align="center">
  <asp:Table id="Table2" runat="server" Width="100%">
    <asp:TableRow HorizontalAlign="Center">
      <asp:TableCell>
        <asp:ImageButton runat="server" Height="125px"
        ID="imgbtncolloseum" onclick="colloseum"></asp:ImageButton>
```

```
        </asp:TableCell>
        <asp:TableCell>
          <asp:ImageButton runat="server" Height="125px" ID="imgbtndavid"
          onclick="david"></asp:ImageButton>
        </asp:TableCell>
        <asp:TableCell>
          <asp:ImageButton runat="server" Height="125px" ID="imgbtntrevi"
          onclick="trevi"></asp:ImageButton>
        </asp:TableCell>
        <asp:TableCell>
          <asp:ImageButton runat="server" Height="125px" ID="imgbtnpisa"
          onclick="pisa"></asp:ImageButton>
        </asp:TableCell>
      </asp:TableRow>
    </asp:Table>
  </div>
  </form>
</body>
</html>
```

8.9   Summary

In this chapter we have examined how code may be used to enrich a web page as well as to allow interaction between the user and the system. The key issues to remember are:

- ASP.NET code is run on the server whilst a web page is interpreted in the client browser of the user
- Values assigned in code to objects on the web page must be done before the object is created
- Objects should contain values before you can use them
- Subroutines should be used to write object-specific code
- Iteration statements such as the For Next loop are used to allow the same piece of code to be repeated in a controlled way
- Selection statements such as If are controlled by tests of truth
- Properties can be manipulated at design or runtime and you need to decide which is most appropriate
- You should decide how you need to store data and decide how and if you want it to change

8.10   Exercises

See if you can apply what you have learnt by trying the following exercises:

1. The aim is to develop an interface that tests user input. It should allow the user to enter their name. The user would then click on an appropriate *Button* that will test if the name is stored in the system. If the name entered matches the one stored by the system (*"Fred"*) a second web page should be displayed that welcomes the user. If the name is not recognised by the system then the web page should then hide the test *Button* replacing it with another that allows the user to try again. In addition the interface should display a personalised message. Below are interfaces you should aim at:

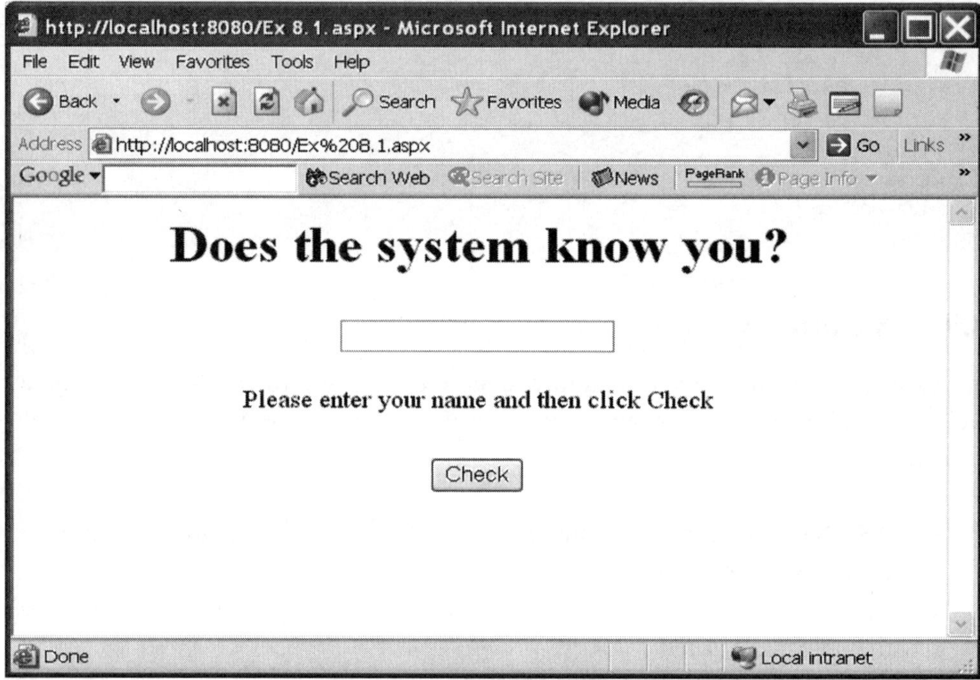

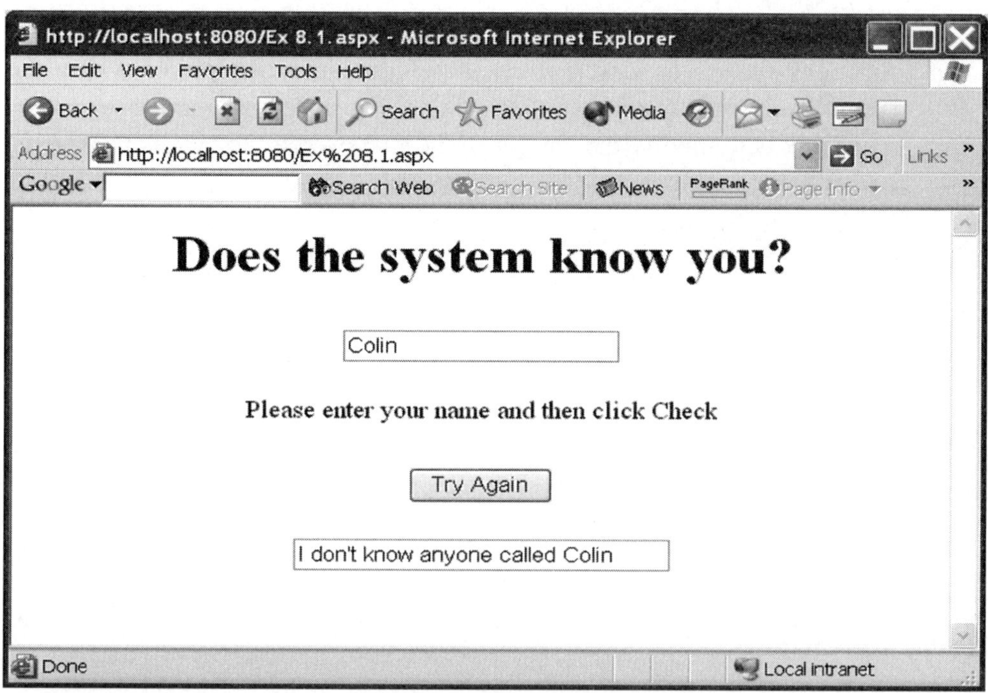

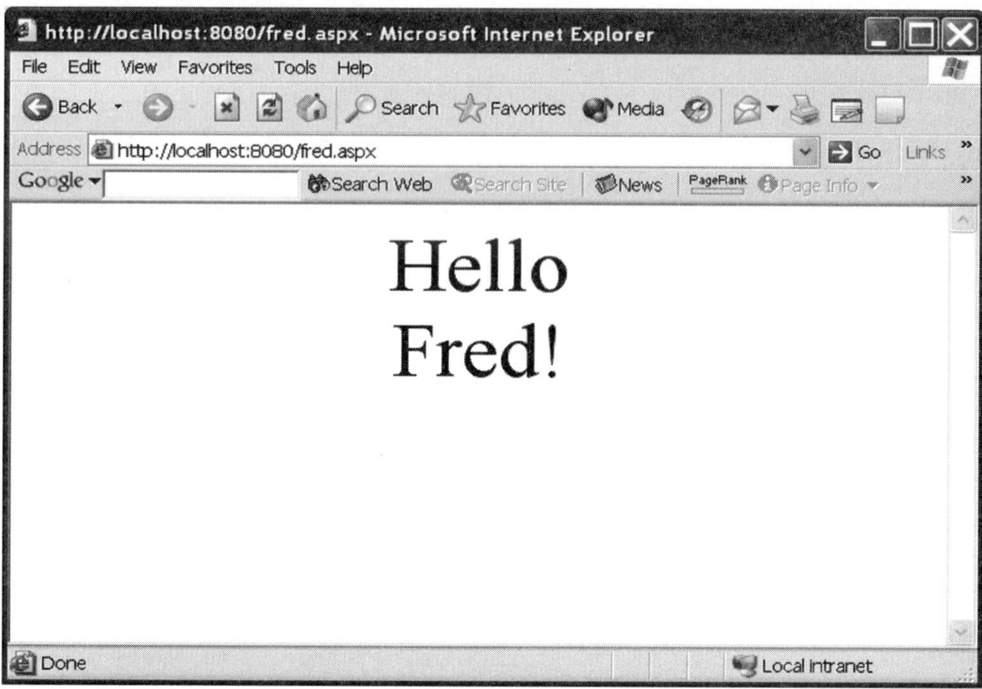

2. You may have noticed that when you are testing strings VB.NET is very case sensitive, for example "*fred*" is not the same as "*Fred*". One way to get around the problem of ensuring the user types in the correct word in the

appropriate case combination is to use one of the VB.NET built-in functions *ucase()* or *lcase()*. *Ucase()* returns any string placed within the parentheses as all upper case. *Lcase()* does the same but returns lower case. Your task is to modify the answer to the first exercise to take advantage of one of these functions.

9

Further programming

9.1 Introduction

In this chapter we are going to look at two slightly more complex, but probably more realistic examples of dynamic web pages. In the first of these we are going to develop an order screen where the user should be able to select items, specify the quantity of each item and the web page will calculate sub-totals and an overall total. In addition, the user should be able to change their mind and the calculations should respond accordingly. In the second we are going to develop a basic on-line quiz where the user is required to answer multiple choice questions and can then check to see how many are correct.

9.2 Milkshake ordering system

In the first example the web page is aimed at a company that deals with the ordering of milkshakes. The interface is driven by the initial selection of the user. Users can select/de-select a particular flavour of milkshake. By selecting a flavour this allows the user to specify the quantity required. The system will then calculate the individual cost of that flavour as well as the overall cost of the order. The completed interface is shown in Figure 9.1. The remainder of this chapter will examine an example that introduces additional VB.NET constructs.

9.3   The interface

The Milk Shakes interface has three major elements. These are a logo (*Image*) of a cow, a heading (*H1* centred) *"The Milk Shakes!"* and a 3 x 3 table which displays the different milk shakes available, the quantity to be ordered and the price to purchase.

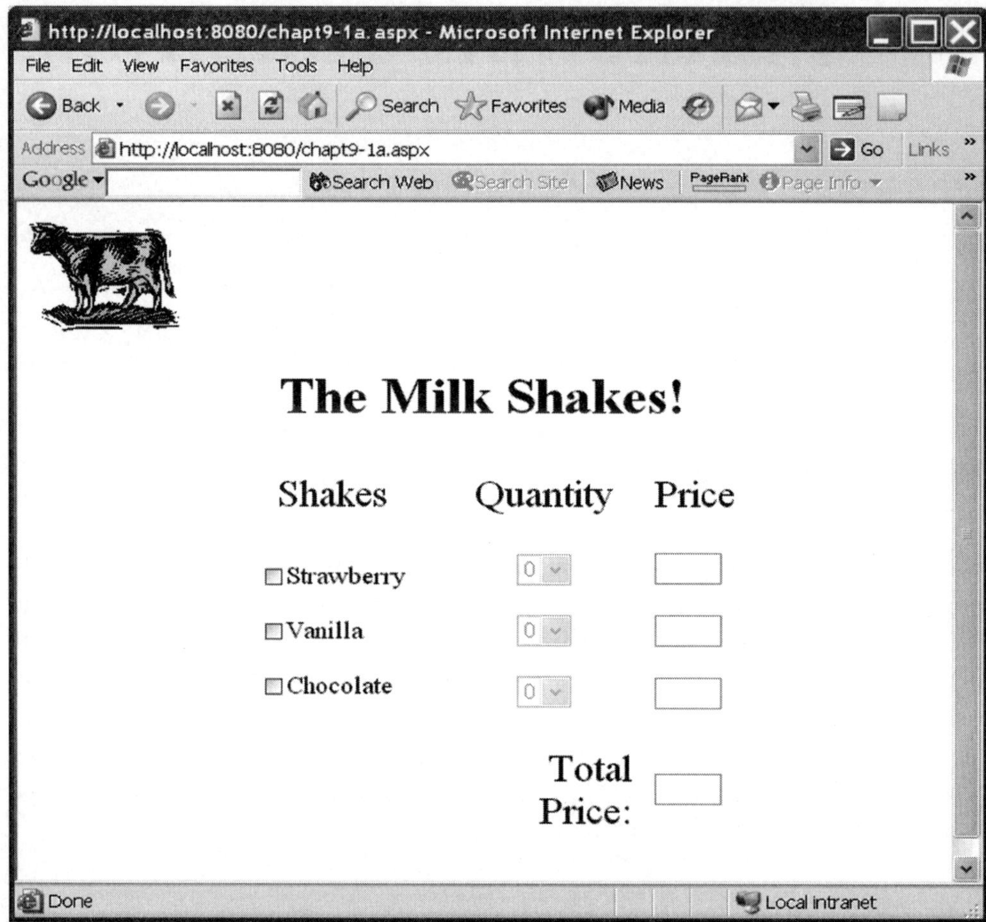

Figure 9.1: The Milk Shakes interface

Figure 9.2 illustrates what the interface looks like when created in Web Matrix. While the graphic logo and the heading are useful in providing an informative and more interesting web page the key to this script is the table with its form elements. Let's examine the table in some more detail.

The table is aligned center with *cellspacing* set to 15, this stops the items from becoming too crowded on the screen. The cells with *Shakes, Quantity, Price* and *Total Price* are text and will not change.

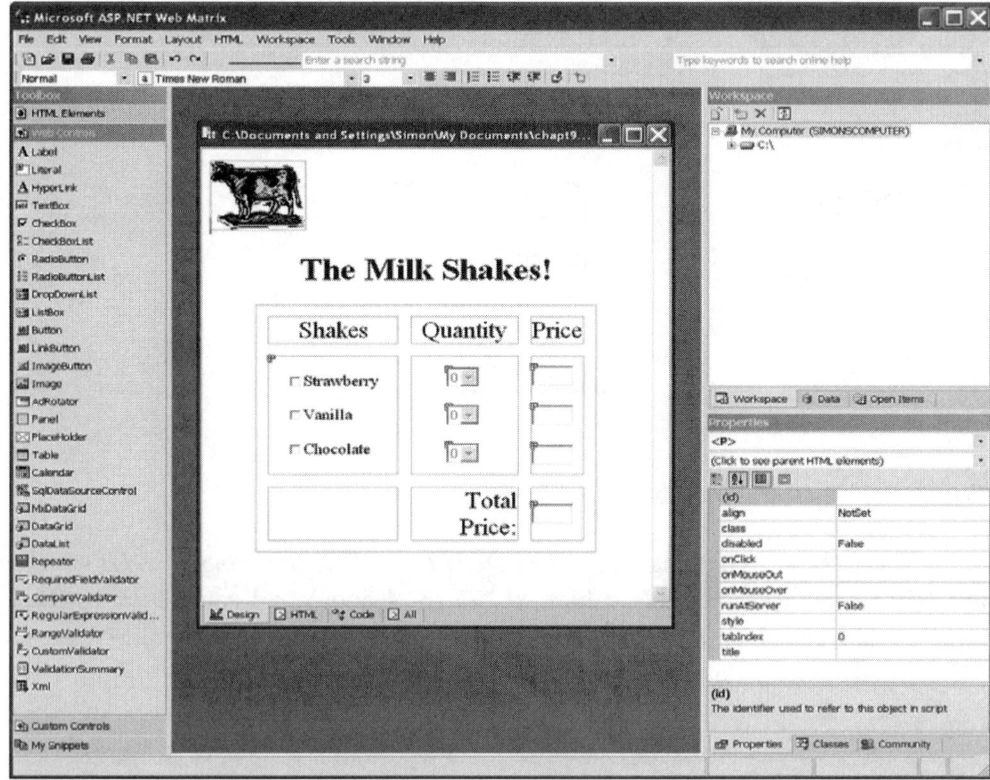

Figure 9.2: The interface viewed in Web Matrix

The basic table structure is shown in Figure 9.3. The table consists of three columns and three rows. The first of the rows is merely for headings and as such will not be discussed. The first of the three columns is a *CheckBoxList* that has the *Id chkFlavours*. Its *AutoPostBack* value should be set to *True*. The code for this *CheckBoxList* is as follows:

```
<asp:CheckBoxList id="chkFlavours" runat="server"
  AutoPostBack="True" onselectedindexchanged="chkFlavoursProcess"
  CellSpacing="20">
  <asp:ListItem Value="Strawberry">Strawberry</asp:ListItem>
  <asp:ListItem Value="Vanilla">Vanilla</asp:ListItem>
  <asp:ListItem Value="Chocolate">Chocolate</asp:ListItem>
</asp:CheckBoxList>
```

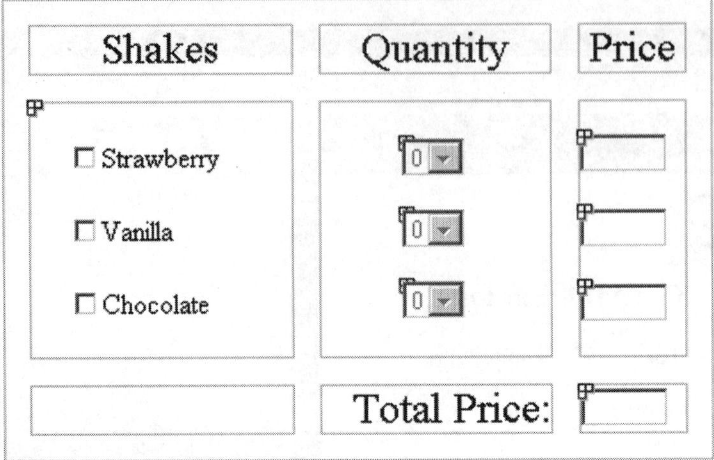

Figure 9.3: The table interface

The next cell contains three *DropDownLists*, *DDLStrawberry*, *DDLVanilla* and *DDLChocolate*. Each has values of 1, 2, 3, 4 and 5 and each *AutoPostBack* value should be set to *True*. In addition, their enabled property should be set to *False*. The HTML code for the *DropDownLists* is as follows:

```
<p align="center">
  <asp:DropDownList id="DDLStrawberry" runat="server"
    AutoPostBack="True" onselectedindexchanged="DDLStrawberryProcess"
    Enabled="False">
    <asp:ListItem Value="0" Selected="True">0</asp:ListItem>
    <asp:ListItem Value="1">1</asp:ListItem>
    <asp:ListItem Value="2">2</asp:ListItem>
    <asp:ListItem Value="3">3</asp:ListItem>
    <asp:ListItem Value="4">4</asp:ListItem>
    <asp:ListItem Value="5">5</asp:ListItem>
  </asp:DropDownList>
</p>
<p align="center">
  <asp:DropDownList id="DDLVanilla" runat="server"
    AutoPostBack="True" onselectedindexchanged="DDLVanillaProcess"
    Enabled="False">
    <asp:ListItem Value="0" Selected="True">0</asp:ListItem>
    <asp:ListItem Value="1">1</asp:ListItem>
    <asp:ListItem Value="2">2</asp:ListItem>
    <asp:ListItem Value="3">3</asp:ListItem>
    <asp:ListItem Value="4">4</asp:ListItem>
    <asp:ListItem Value="5">5</asp:ListItem>
  </asp:DropDownList>
</p>
<p align="center">
  <asp:DropDownList id="DDLChocolate" runat="server"
```

.e news

free and exclusive features, offers and news for you

Register for eNews, the email service from Elsevier Science, Technology and Business Books, to receive:

- **specially written author articles**
- **free sample chapters**
- **advance news of our latest publications**
- **regular discounts**
- **related event information**

...and more

Go to **www.bh.com**, select a subject, register and the eNews Bulletin will soon be arriving on your desktop!

Alternatively, flip this card over for other options....

 Architectural Press

ComputerWeekly PROFESSIONAL SERIES

 Focal Press

Pergamon Flexible Learning for tomorrow's managers

MADE SIMPLE BOOKS

Newnes

 ELSEVIER

BUTTERWORTH HEINEMANN

dp Digital Press

G|P P|W Gulf Professional Publishing

IMPRINTS OF ELSEVIER

Return this card today and enter £100 book draw

Select the subjects you'd like to receive information about, enter your email and mail address and freepost it back to us.

TECHNOLOGY

- **Architecture and Design:**
  - History of architecture ○
  - Landscape ○
  - Urban design ○
  - Sustainable architecture ○
  - Planning and design ○
- **Building and Construction**
- **Computing: Professional:**
  - Communications ○
  - Data Management ○
  - Enterprise Computing ○
  - IT Management ○
  - Operating Systems ○
- **Computing: Beginner:**
  - Computing ○
  - Programming ○
- **Conservation and Museology**
- **Engineering:**
  - Aeronautical Engineering ○
  - Automotive Engineering ○
  - Chemical Engineering ○

- Health & Safety ○
- Environmental Engineering ○
- Plant / Maintenance / Manufacturing ○
- Marine Engineering ○
- Materials Science & Engineering ○
- Mechanical Engineering ○
- Petroleum Engineering ○
- Quality ○
- **Electronics and Electrical Engineering:**
  - Electrical Engineering ○
  - Electronic Engineering ○
  - Radio, Audio and TV Technology ○
  - Computer Technology ○
- **Film, Television, Video & Audio:**
  - Audio/Radio ○
  - Post Production ○
  - Lighting ○
  - Theatre Performance ○
  - Photography/Imaging ○
  - Radio ○

- TV ○
- Film/TV/Video Production ○
- Journalism ○
- Multimedia ○
- Computer Graphics/ Animation ○
- Broadcast Management & Theory ○
- Broadcast & Communications Technology ○
- Security

MANAGEMENT

- Finance and Accounting
- Hospitality, Leisure and Tourism
- HR and Training
- Pergamon Flexible Learning
- Knowledge Management
- Management
- Marketing
- IT Management

Name: _______________________

Email address: _______________________

Mail address: _______________________

Postcode _______________________   Date _______________________

Please keep me up to date by ☐ email ☐ post ☐ both

Science & Technology Books, Elsevier Ltd., Registered Office: The Boulevard, Langford Lane, Kidlington, Oxon OX5 1GB. Registered number: 1982084

Jo Blackford

Data Co-ordinator

Elsevier

FREEPOST - SCE5435

Oxford

Oxon

OX2 8BR

```
        AutoPostBack="True" onselectedindexchanged="DDLChocolateProcess"
        Enabled="False">
        <asp:ListItem Value="0" Selected="True">0</asp:ListItem>
        <asp:ListItem Value="1">1</asp:ListItem>
        <asp:ListItem Value="2">2</asp:ListItem>
        <asp:ListItem Value="3">3</asp:ListItem>
        <asp:ListItem Value="4">4</asp:ListItem>
        <asp:ListItem Value="5">5</asp:ListItem>
    </asp:DropDownList>
</p>
```

Finally, the last column contains the *TextBoxes txtPriceStrawberry, txtPriceVanilla, txtPriceChocolate* and *txtTotalPrice*. Their *Readonly* value should be set to *False*. The HTML for these *TextBoxes* is as follows:

```
<td>
    <p>
        <asp:TextBox id="txtPriceStrawberry" runat="server" Width="50px"
            readonly="true"></asp:TextBox>
    </p>
    <p>
        <asp:TextBox id="txtPriceVanilla" runat="server" Width="50px"
            readonly="true"></asp:TextBox>
    </p>
    <p>
        <asp:TextBox id="txtPriceChocolate" runat="server" Width="50px"
            readonly="true"></asp:TextBox>
    </p>
</td>
</tr><tr>
    <td></td>
    <td>
        <p align="right">
            <font size="5">Total Price:</font>
        </p>
    </td>
    <td>
        <asp:TextBox id="txtTotalPrice" runat="server" Width="50px"
            readonly="true"></asp:TextBox>
    </td>
</tr>
```

9.4   Adding functionality

9.4.1   Introduction

VB.NET is an event driven language. What that means is that you write code that will run if particular events occur. With a graphical user interface there are potentially many objects on the page and the user can interact with them in a variety of ways and in an unpredictable order. Therefore, what you need to do is to think carefully about the sorts of objects you require on the page, how you expect the user to interact with them and write the code that does that. But in addition you need to control the interface to ensure as much as possible that the user does these things when you want them to and in the required order. Conversely you do not want the interface to be too rigid thereby removing all control from the user. Therefore you have to think of all the possible actions the user could do that differ from the expected and control for those too through code. It is often this type of error trapping code that dominates this type of programming. Unfortunately you cannot avoid the need to protect users from themselves.

Now the first thing we need to do is to set the price for the shakes. In this case all of the shakes are going to be the same price. In VB.NET there isn't a data type called currency, nor will any of the data types automatically add the currency symbol. This will cause us problems later on, but at the moment we are going to create a *constant* to store the price. We will use the same price for all shakes:

```
<script runat="server">
   const price as single = 1.5
</script>
```

9.4.2   Local and global variables

So far when we have created variables they have been declared within the *Sub* and *End Sub* of a subroutine. What happens when we do this is that the area of memory created by the *Dim* statement will remain active from the declaration until the end of the subroutine, at which point it will be destroyed along with its contents. This means that variables can be created and used when they are required and when that time is over they are removed thereby freeing system resources. Variables created within a subroutine are *local* to that sub routine and therefore any attempt to use that variable by another subroutine will result in an error. It is possible to create a variable with the same name in another subroutine but as far as the system is concerned this is a different variable and will not recover the value of the earlier version.

So how can you pass values from one subroutine to another? What we need to do is to make a variable *Global*. If a variable declared in a subroutine is local to that subroutine then a global variable must be declared outside of a subroutine. As long as the declaration is within the *script* tags it will be recognised and its value used by all other code on that page, whether or not it is in a subroutine. So why not create all variables as global. We have already mentioned one reason, in that it is wasteful of system resources. Another reason is that it is very easy to make mistakes with global variables and forget where they are used and for what purpose. The result might be that the variable is used for more than one purpose resulting in wrong values.

Variables are useful if you have values that you want to be able to vary, but sometimes in your programming you want to be able to store values that are not allowed to vary. I suppose you could use a variable, but there is always the risk that you will forget that it shouldn't vary and change it. VB.NET provides Constants to store values that are not allowed to change. As was discussed in Chapter 8 a constant is declared in a similar manner to variables using the keyword *const*. The difference is that when declaring a constant you also assign its permanent value.

Consequently, the line of code declares a constant called *price* with the data type *single* and assigns it 1.5:

```
const price as single = 1.5
```

9.4.3   Handling DropDownLists

One of the key things we want the interface to do is that if the user selects a flavour the appropriate quantity *DropDownList* becomes enabled. What follows is the subroutine *chkFlavoursProcess* that achieves this:

```
Sub chkFlavoursProcess(Sender as Object, E as EventArgs)
    if chkFlavours.items(0).selected = true then
        DDLStrawberry.enabled = true
    else
        DDLStrawberry.selectedindex = 0
        DDLStrawberry.enabled = false
    end if
    if chkFlavours.items(1).selected = true then
        DDLVanilla.enabled = true
    else
        DDLVanilla.selectedindex = 0
        DDLVanilla.enabled = false
    end if
    if chkFlavours.items(2).selected = true then
        DDLChocolate.enabled = true
    else
        DDLChocolate.selectedindex = 0
        DDLChocolate.enabled = false
    end if
End Sub
```

There are three *If* statements in this subroutine and they all have a very similar structure. Therefore we will talk you through the first one and the meaning of the others should become apparent.

9.4.4   Handling CheckBoxes

Since *chkFlavours* is a *CheckBoxList* it is a list of things and as such is an object that has objects inside it, therefore we are dealing with a number of levels of objects. Each object within a level has its own properties. One of the properties of the object at the highest level, the list itself, is the objects inside it.

```
chkFlavours.items(0)
```

A *CheckBoxList* is an array of checkboxes. Since an element of an array is referred to by its index, *items(0)* refers to the first *checkbox* (Strawberry). The test examines if the *selected* property of that item is set to *true* (that is if there is a cross/check in the box). If this is the case then the *enabled* property of the *DropDownList DDLStrawberry* is set to *true*. So what that means is if the user has selected strawberry then the *DropDownList* for strawberry is enabled:

```
if chkFlavours.items(0).selected = true then
    DDLStrawberry.enabled = true
```

The *Else* statement runs if the checkbox item is not selected:

```
else
    DDLStrawberry.selectedindex = 0
    DDLStrawberry.enabled = false
end if
```

If in the past the user has selected this item from the checkbox and then selected a value from its *DropDownList* then if the check is removed the list would still display that value. What we want is for the list to re-set to zero as well as becoming disabled. Therefore, the first line resets the *DropDownList* to zero. The second line disables the *DropDownList*.

It may have occurred to you that the user may not have clicked on strawberry but may have clicked on one of the other flavours as such they may not have used this *DropDownList* before. If this is the case then its index value would still be zero and it would be disabled. Therefore the code for strawberry is redundant and there is no reason for it to run, but it does run. Unfortunately, there is no way around this. The event that triggers this subroutine is based on the *CheckBoxList*; as such it does not know whether any of the checkbox items are checked, also it does not know whether the event that triggered it was one that checked an item or unchecked it. Consequently, this subroutine has to act on all three checkboxes and it is for this reason that there are three *If* statements rather than one and that every click will result in code being run that has no effect.

9.4.5   Calculating the price

Assuming the user has selected a flavour and a quantity, the next thing we need to do is to take the quantity, multiply it by the individual price and display it in the appropriate textbox. The subroutine for Strawberry is below:

```
Sub DDLStrawberryProcess(Sender as Object, E as EventArgs)
    txtPriceStrawberry.text = _
DDLStrawberry.items(DDLStrawberry.selectedindex).value * price
```

```
        End Sub
```

This subroutine is called when the user selects a quantity. We know that *DDLStrawberry.items()* is an array and that *DDLStrawberry.selectedindex* is the current index of that array. So the single line of code takes the value of that selected item, multiplies it by the constant *price* and assigns the result to the text property of *txtPriceStrawberry*. We could have made this line simpler:

```
        txtPriceStrawberry.text = DDLStrawberry.selectedindex * price
```

For this program the value stored in each of the index items has the same value as the index itself, see Table 9.1.

Index	Value
0	0
1	1
2	2
3	3
4	4
5	5

Table 9.1: Program value index

But this is not often the case, as the following example demonstrates, illustrated in Table 9.2.

Index	Value
0	Peter
1	John
2	David
3	Paul
4	Ann
5	Mary

Table 9.2: Program name index

Consequently, we are using the longer variant to ensure that we are getting exactly what we want.

The value of the index is a string whilst the index is a number. Therefore we are now multiplying a string with a single. VB.NET casts the value into a single, performs the multiplication and then casts the result into text so that it can be assigned to the text property of *txtPriceStrawberry*. I have gone into this detail because shortly we will be having problems with casting.

Since there are three flavours there needs to be three subroutines. This is code:

```
Sub DDLStrawberryProcess(Sender as Object, E as EventArgs)
    txtPriceStrawberry.text = _
    DDLStrawberry.items(DDLStrawberry.selectedindex).value * price
End Sub

Sub DDLVanillaProcess(Sender as Object, E as EventArgs)
    txtPriceVanilla.text = _
    DDLVanilla.items(DDLVanilla.selectedindex).value * price
End Sub

Sub DDLChocolateProcess(Sender as Object, E as EventArgs)
    txtPriceChocolate.text = _
    DDLChocolate.items(DDLChocolate.selectedindex).value * price
End Sub
```

9.4.6   Calculating the total price

If the user has selected one or more shakes we now need to calculate the total price. What follows is the code for Strawberry:

```
Sub DDLStrawberryProcess(Sender as Object, E as EventArgs)
    txtPriceStrawberry.text = _
    DDLStrawberry.items(DDLStrawberry.selectedindex).value * price
    txtTotalPrice.text = val(txtPriceStrawberry.text) + val(txtPriceVanilla.text) _
    + val(txtPriceChocolate.text)
End Sub
```

This line is included in each of the three subroutines and as such it occurs at the same time as the individual price is calculated. It introduces *val()* which is an in-built function of VB.NET, but why do we need it? In the last chapter we used the concatenation character & which allows us to 'glue' strings together. Unfortunately the plus symbol (+) is both a mathematical operator and a concatenation character. Therefore, if we just used the following it would not give us the output we desire:

```
txtTotalPrice.text = txtPriceStrawberry.text + txtPriceVanilla.text _
+ txtPriceChocolate.text
```

e.g. *"1.533" = "1.5" + "3" + "3"* rather than *"7.5" = 1.5 + 3 + 3*

The *val()* function returns the numeric value of the text within the parentheses. These can then be added together and the result cast back into text to be assigned to the text property of *txtTotalPrice*. The completed subroutines are as follows:

```
    Sub DDLStrawberryProcess(Sender as Object, E as EventArgs)
      txtPriceStrawberry.text = _
      DLStrawberry.items(DDLStrawberry.selectedindex).value * price
      txtTotalPrice.text = val(txtPriceStrawberry.text) + val(txtPriceVanilla.text) _
      + val(txtPriceChocolate.text)
    End Sub

    Sub DDLVanillaProcess(Sender as Object, E as EventArgs)
      txtPriceVanilla.text = _
      DDLVanilla.items(DDLVanilla.selectedindex).value * price
      txtTotalPrice.text = val(txtPriceStrawberry.text) + val(txtPriceVanilla.text) _
      + val(txtPriceChocolate.text)
    End Sub

    Sub DDLChocolateProcess(Sender as Object, E as EventArgs)
      txtPriceChocolate.text = _
      DDLChocolate.items(DDLChocolate.selectedindex).value * price
      txtTotalPrice.text = val(txtPriceStrawberry.text) + val(txtPriceVanilla.text) _
      + val(txtPriceChocolate.text)
    End Sub
```

This works well as long as the user doesn't change their mind and cancel their order of one flavour by de-selecting the checkbox. To allow for this possibility we need to add two lines to each of the Else clauses in the subroutine *chkFlavoursProcess* as follows for Strawberry:

```
    else
        DDLStrawberry.selectedindex = 0
        DDLStrawberry.enabled = false
        txtTotalPrice.text = val(txtTotalPrice.text) - val(txtPriceStrawberry.text)
        txtPriceStrawberry.text = ""
    end if
```

The first of these lines (line 3 of the Else statement) takes the value of the strawberry shakes away from the total price and then assigns the result to the text property of txtTotalPrice. The second line removes the value of strawberry shakes. Simple enough, but this highlights that you have to think about the order in which things need to happen. If these two lines were reversed we would not get an error, because the *val()* function would convert the empty string to a zero, but whilst the value of strawberry would disappear nothing would be taken from the total price.

9.4.7 Calling subroutines

Before we extend this code any further we need to examine how the subroutines are called. Each of the calls uses the method *onselectedindexchanged* since all are lists and we want to monitor when changes occur to their indexes. In addition, since the *checkboxes* fill a single cell in the table I have used *cellspacing* to spread them out. However, this cannot be used for the *DropDownLists* as these are three separate objects and so in the design they are separated by a line break, this is also the case for the textbox prices:

```
<asp:CheckBoxList id="chkFlavours" runat="server" AutoPostBack="True" _
onselectedindexchanged="chkFlavoursProcess" CellSpacing="20">

<asp:DropDownList id="DDLStrawberry" runat="server" AutoPostBack="True" _
onselectedindexchanged="DDLStrawberryProcess" Enabled="False">

<asp:DropDownList id="DDLVanilla" runat="server" AutoPostBack="True" _
onselectedindexchanged="DDLVanillaProcess" Enabled="False">

<asp:DropDownList id="DDLChocolate" runat="server" AutoPostBack="True" _
onselectedindexchanged="DDLChocolateProcess" Enabled="False">
```

9.4.8   Handling currency

So far we have a working system but the shake prices and the total price are displayed as numbers not currency. Consequently the final stage is how we handle this issue given that VB.NET does not handle it itself. This is not straightforward, because we need to format the output as currency, including the currency symbol. In addition, as you are aware, at various points we are dealing with text as output which needs to be converted to numbers to perform calculations. Where we are dealing with numbers in the form of text these can be converted for calculation using *val()*. Where there is a value that contains characters other than a number, e.g. £ character, this cannot be converted using the *val()* function. Therefore we have two tasks: how to format the output as currency and how to un-format currency back into a number.

VB.NET has an in-built function called *format()*. There are a number of different variations of this but there is one specifically for currency:

```
Format(value to be formatted, "currency")
```

e.g.

```
format(DDLStrawberry.items(DDLStrawberry.selectedindex).value _
   * price, "currency")
```

This example takes the price of strawberry shakes which is stored as a single and converts them into a string formatted to look like currency e.g. the output from format(1.5, "currency") is "£1.50". The currency format displayed is determined by the Region and Language options in your operating system. But remember the operating system is the one on the server not the client. This means the user will not necessarily see the prices in currency of their own country.

Now everywhere we display output we need *format()* around the value before it is assigned to the text property of the object. This presents the results in an appropriate way but it no longer calculates correctly since the currency symbol confuses either the output from *val()* or where casting occurs. What we need is a mechanism to strip currency formatting away from values before calculation and then put it back on the result.

The *mid()* function returns part of a string. Given a string you can specify which character the sub-string starts, you can also specify the length of the sub-string but we do not need that here.

e.g. *mid("apple", 3)* will return *"ple"*

What we need to do is to remove the first character. Therefore we need to modify all sections of the code that performs calculations using *mid(string, 2)*, where *string* is the value displayed as currency.

Unfortunately the adding and removal of formatting makes individual lines of code complex and hard to read, they can also make the code run more slowly since each line can call upon a number of functions. But that is the price you pay for usability.

9.4.9   Code for the milkshake ordering system

The finished code is below; we have placed line spaces between lines so that it is clear where there are long lines that go over a single line:

```
<%@ Page Language="VB" Debug="true" %>
<script runat="server">
  const price as single = 1.5

    Sub DDLStrawberryProcess(Sender as Object, E as EventArgs)
      txtPriceStrawberry.text =
format(DDLStrawberry.items(DDLStrawberry.selectedindex).value * price,
"currency")

      txtTotalPrice.text = format(val(mid(txtPriceStrawberry.text, 2)) +
val(mid(txtPriceVanilla.text, 2)) + val(mid(txtPriceChocolate.text, 2)), "currency")
    End Sub

    Sub DDLVanillaProcess(Sender as Object, E as EventArgs)
      txtPriceVanilla.text =
format(DDLVanilla.items(DDLVanilla.selectedindex).value * price, "currency")

      txtTotalPrice.text = format(val(mid(txtPriceStrawberry.text, 2)) +
val(mid(txtPriceVanilla.text, 2)) + val(mid(txtPriceChocolate.text, 2)), "currency")
    End Sub

    Sub DDLChocolateProcess(Sender as Object, E as EventArgs)
      txtPriceChocolate.text =
format(DDLChocolate.items(DDLChocolate.selectedindex).value * price,
"currency")
      txtTotalPrice.text = format(val(mid(txtPriceStrawberry.text, 2)) +
val(mid(txtPriceVanilla.text, 2)) + val(mid(txtPriceChocolate.text, 2)), "currency")
```

```
      End Sub

      Sub chkFlavoursProcess(Sender as Object, E as EventArgs)
        if chkFlavours.items(0).selected = true then
           DDLStrawberry.enabled = true
        else
           DDLStrawberry.selectedindex = 0
           DDLStrawberry.enabled = false
           txtTotalPrice.text = format(val(mid(txtTotalPrice.text, 2)) -
val(mid(txtPriceStrawberry.text, 2)), "currency")
           txtPriceStrawberry.text = ""
        end if
        if chkFlavours.items(1).selected = true then
           DDLVanilla.enabled = true
        else
           DDLVanilla.selectedindex = 0
           DDLVanilla.enabled = false
           txtTotalPrice.text = format(val(mid(txtTotalPrice.text, 2)) -
val(mid(txtPriceVanilla.text, 2)), "currency")
           txtPriceVanilla.text = ""
        end if
        if chkFlavours.items(2).selected = true then
           DDLChocolate.enabled = true
        else
           DDLChocolate.selectedindex = 0
           DDLChocolate.enabled = false
           txtTotalPrice.text = format(val(mid(txtTotalPrice.text, 2)) -
val(mid(txtPriceChocolate.text, 2)), "currency")
           txtPriceChocolate.text = ""
        end if
      End Sub
</script>
<html>
<head>
</head>
<body>
  <form runat="server">
    <p>
      <img height="90" src="J0149627.wmf" width="114" />
    </p>
    <h1 align="center">The Milk Shakes!
    </h1>
    <h1 align="center">
    </h1>
    <table style="WIDTH: 407px; HEIGHT: 168px" cellspacing="15"
align="center">
        <tbody>
          <tr>
            <td>
               <p align="center">
```

```
                        <font size="5">Shakes</font>
                    </p>
                </td>
                <td>
                    <p align="center">
                        <font size="5">Quantity</font>
                    </p>
                </td>
                <td>
                    <p align="center">
                        <font size="5">Price</font>
                    </p>
                </td>
            </tr>
            <tr>
                <td>
                    <p align="left">
                        <asp:CheckBoxList id="chkFlavours" runat="server"
AutoPostBack="True" onselectedindexchanged="chkFlavoursProcess"
CellSpacing="20">
                            <asp:ListItem Value="Strawberry">Strawberry</asp:ListItem>
                            <asp:ListItem Value="Vanilla">Vanilla</asp:ListItem>
                            <asp:ListItem Value="Chocolate">Chocolate</asp:ListItem>
                        </asp:CheckBoxList>
                    </p>
                </td>
                <td>
                    <p align="center">
                        <asp:DropDownList id="DDLStrawberry" runat="server"
AutoPostBack="True" onselectedindexchanged="DDLStrawberryProcess"
Enabled="False">
                            <asp:ListItem Value="0" Selected="True">0</asp:ListItem>
                            <asp:ListItem Value="1">1</asp:ListItem>
                            <asp:ListItem Value="2">2</asp:ListItem>
                            <asp:ListItem Value="3">3</asp:ListItem>
                            <asp:ListItem Value="4">4</asp:ListItem>
                            <asp:ListItem Value="5">5</asp:ListItem>
                        </asp:DropDownList>
                    </p>
                    <p align="center">
                        <asp:DropDownList id="DDLVanilla" runat="server"
AutoPostBack="True" onselectedindexchanged="DDLVanillaProcess"
Enabled="False">
                            <asp:ListItem Value="0" Selected="True">0</asp:ListItem>
                            <asp:ListItem Value="1">1</asp:ListItem>
                            <asp:ListItem Value="2">2</asp:ListItem>
                            <asp:ListItem Value="3">3</asp:ListItem>
                            <asp:ListItem Value="4">4</asp:ListItem>
                            <asp:ListItem Value="5">5</asp:ListItem>
                        </asp:DropDownList>
```

```
                </p>
                <p align="center">
                    <asp:DropDownList id="DDLChocolate" runat="server"
AutoPostBack="True" onselectedindexchanged="DDLChocolateProcess"
Enabled="False">
                        <asp:ListItem Value="0" Selected="True">0</asp:ListItem>
                        <asp:ListItem Value="1">1</asp:ListItem>
                        <asp:ListItem Value="2">2</asp:ListItem>
                        <asp:ListItem Value="3">3</asp:ListItem>
                        <asp:ListItem Value="4">4</asp:ListItem>
                        <asp:ListItem Value="5">5</asp:ListItem>
                    </asp:DropDownList>
                </p>
            </td>
            <td>
                <p>
                    <asp:TextBox id="txtPriceStrawberry" runat="server"
Width="50px" readonly="true"></asp:TextBox>
                </p>
                <p>
                    <asp:TextBox id="txtPriceVanilla" runat="server" Width="50px"
readonly="true"></asp:TextBox>
                </p>
                <p>
                    <asp:TextBox id="txtPriceChocolate" runat="server"
Width="50px" readonly="true"></asp:TextBox>
                </p>
            </td>
          </tr>
          <tr>
            <td></td>
            <td>
              <p align="right">
                 <font size="5">Total Price:</font>
              </p>
            </td>
            <td>
                <asp:TextBox id="txtTotalPrice" runat="server" Width="50px"
readonly="true"></asp:TextBox>
            </td>
          </tr>
        </tbody>
      </table>
      <p></p>
   </form>
   <p></p>
   <p align="center">
   </p>
 </body>
 </html>
```

9.5   On-line quiz

In this example we are going to create a basic on-line quiz. It is common for web sites to include some form of questionnaire. It does not have to be in the form of a quiz but data collection should be purposeful. This example should be used as something to stimulate your thoughts as to how data can be collated.

The on-line quiz has four multiple answer questions, see Figure 9.4.

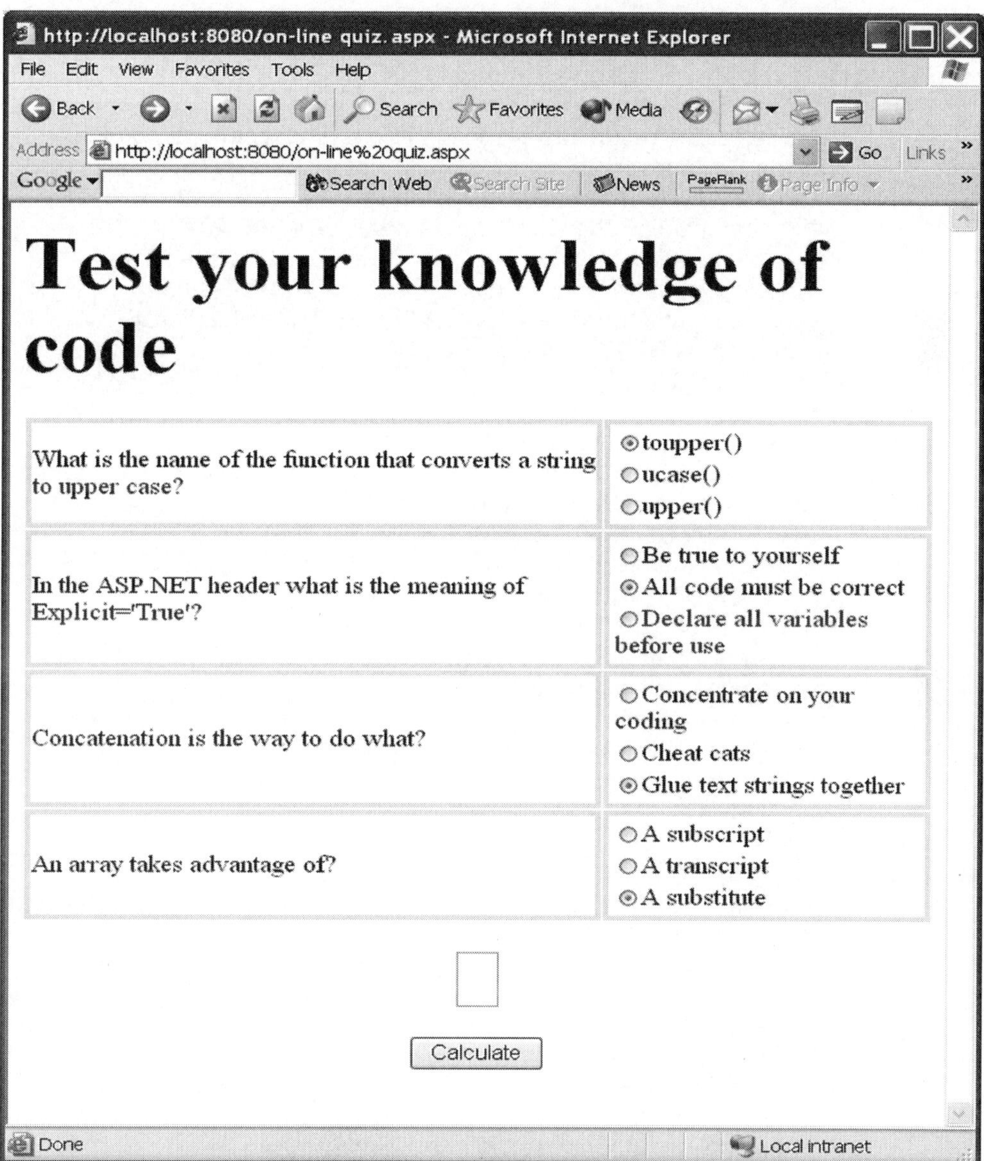

Figure 9.4: On-line quiz interface

9.5.1 Creating the interface

The interface has been designed to be as simple and self-explanatory as possible. It consists of a four-row and two-column table. This contains the questions in the left-hand column and the optional answers in the right column. The optional answers associated with a question are a *RadioButtonList*. Below the table is a *TextBox* centred on the screen. This will display the result. Calculation of the result is carried out when the user clicks on the Calculate button. The ASP.NET code for the table is as follows:

```
<asp:Table id="Table1" runat="server" width="100%">
    <asp:TableRow BorderStyle="Solid">
        <asp:TableCell BorderStyle="Solid" Text="What is the name of the
        function that converts a string to upper case?"></asp:TableCell>
        <asp:TableCell BorderStyle="Solid">
            <asp:RadioButtonList runat="server" ID="RBList1">
            <asp:ListItem Value="toupper()">toupper()</asp:ListItem>
            <asp:ListItem Value="ucase()">ucase()</asp:ListItem>
            <asp:ListItem Value="upper()">upper()</asp:ListItem>
            </asp:RadioButtonList>
        </asp:TableCell>
    </asp:TableRow>
    <asp:TableRow BorderStyle="Solid">
        <asp:TableCell BorderStyle="Solid" Text="In the ASP.NET header
        what is the meaning of Explicit='True'?"></asp:TableCell>
        <asp:TableCell BorderStyle="Solid">
            <asp:RadioButtonList runat="server" ID="RBList2">
            <asp:ListItem Value="Be true to yourself">Be true to
            yourself</asp:ListItem>
            <asp:ListItem Value="All code must be correct">All code must
            be correct</asp:ListItem>
            <asp:ListItem Value="Declare all variables before use">Declare
            all variables before use</asp:ListItem>
            </asp:RadioButtonList>
        </asp:TableCell>
    </asp:TableRow>
    <asp:TableRow BorderStyle="Solid">
        <asp:TableCell BorderStyle="Solid" Text="Concatenation is the way
        to do what?"></asp:TableCell>
        <asp:TableCell BorderStyle="Solid">
            <asp:RadioButtonList runat="server" ID="RBList3">
            <asp:ListItem Value="Concentrate on your
            coding">Concentrate on your coding</asp:ListItem>
            <asp:ListItem Value="Cheat cats">Cheat cats</asp:ListItem>
            <asp:ListItem Value="Glue text strings together">Glue text
            strings together</asp:ListItem>
            </asp:RadioButtonList>
        </asp:TableCell>
    </asp:TableRow>
```

```
        <asp:TableRow BorderStyle="Solid">
            <asp:TableCell BorderStyle="Solid" Text="An array takes
            advantage of?"></asp:TableCell>
            <asp:TableCell BorderStyle="Solid">
                <asp:RadioButtonList runat="server" ID="RBList4">
                <asp:ListItem Value="A subscript">A subscript</asp:ListItem>
                <asp:ListItem Value="A transcript">A transcript</asp:ListItem>
                <asp:ListItem Value="A substitute">A substitute</asp:ListItem>
                </asp:RadioButtonList>
            </asp:TableCell>
        </asp:TableRow>
</asp:Table>
```

Inside a *TableRow* are two cells. The first of these has the question as its Text parameter for example:

```
<asp:TableCell BorderStyle="Solid" Text="What is the name of the function that
converts a string to upper case?"></asp:TableCell>
```

The second contains the definition and values of the *RadioButtonList* for example:

```
<asp:TableCell BorderStyle="Solid">
    <asp:RadioButtonList runat="server" ID="RBList1">
        <asp:ListItem Value="toupper()">toupper()</asp:ListItem>
        <asp:ListItem Value="ucase()">ucase()</asp:ListItem>
        <asp:ListItem Value="upper()">upper()</asp:ListItem>
    </asp:RadioButtonList>
</asp:TableCell>
```

9.5.2 Adding functionality

In order to calculate the score you need to determine whether a particular radio button has been selected. *RadioButtonLists* are treated as though they are arrays of values with each indexed element having a value of *True* or *False* where True is a selected option and False is not selected. We are going to use an *If* statement to test if an element of the list is selected, remembering that like an array the sub-script starts at 0. To do this you need to refer to the *selectedindex* element of the *RadioButtonList* as follows:

```
If RBList1.selectedindex = 1 Then
```

Here *RBList* is the *id* of one of the *RadioRuttonLists* and the test is if the second element is selected. You also need to increment values in order to calculate the total. The simplest way to do this is by adding one to a variable and then assigning the result to itself as follows:

```
Variable = Variable + 1
```

The variable obviously is something that is used for every test of an individual *RadioButtonList* and that there must be an *If* statement for every list. These *If* statements are triggered by the user clicking the Calculate *Button* and so the definition for the button contains a call to a subroutine called *calculate*:

```
<asp:Button id="Button1" onclick="calculate" runat="server" Text="Calculate">
</asp:Button>
```

The completed subroutine is as follows:

```
Sub calculate(Sender as Object, E as EventArgs)
    Dim total as Integer
    total = 0

    If RBList1.selectedindex = 1 Then
       total = total + 1
    End If

    If RBList2.selectedindex = 2 Then
       total = total + 1
    End If

    If RBList3.selectedindex = 2 Then
       total = total + 1
    End If

    If RBList4.selectedindex = 0 Then
       total = total + 1
    End If

    textbox1.text = total

End Sub
```

Assume that the user has selected only correct answers. Since lines of code are run in sequence the variable *total* is initially zero RBList1 does have a value of 1 so *total* is assigned $0 + 1$, so now *total* has a value of 1. With the next *If* statement *total* is assigned $1 + 1$ and so on. Ultimately *total* has a value of 4 and this is assigned to the text property of the textbox textbox1.

9.5.3   Code for the on-line quiz

The complete code for the on-line quiz web page is as follows:

```
<%@ Page Language="VB" Explicit="True" Debug="True" %>
<script runat="server">
   sub calculate(Sender as Object, E as EventArgs)
      dim total as integer
      total = 0
```

```
      if RBList1.selectedindex = 1 then
         total = total + 1
      end if
      if RBList2.selectedindex = 2 then
         total = total + 1
      end if
      if RBList3.selectedindex = 2 then
         total = total + 1
      end if
      if RBList4.selectedindex = 0 then
         total = total + 1
      end if

   textbox1.text = total
   end sub
</script>

<html>
<head>
</head>
<body>
   <form runat="server">
      <p align="left">
         <asp:Label id="Label1" runat="server" Font-Size="XX-Large" Font-
         Bold="True">Test your knowledge of code</asp:Label>
      </p>
      <p>
         <asp:Table id="Table1" runat="server" width="100%">
            <asp:TableRow BorderStyle="Solid">
               <asp:TableCell BorderStyle="Solid" Text="What is the name of the
               function that converts a string to upper case?"></asp:TableCell>
               <asp:TableCell BorderStyle="Solid">
                  <asp:RadioButtonList runat="server" ID="RBList1">
                     <asp:ListItem Value="toupper()">toupper()</asp:ListItem>
                     <asp:ListItem Value="ucase()">ucase()</asp:ListItem>
                     <asp:ListItem Value="upper()">upper()</asp:ListItem>
                  </asp:RadioButtonList>
               </asp:TableCell>
            </asp:TableRow>
            <asp:TableRow BorderStyle="Solid">
               <asp:TableCell BorderStyle="Solid" Text="In the ASP.NET header
               what is the meaning of Explicit='True'?"></asp:TableCell>
               <asp:TableCell BorderStyle="Solid">
                  <asp:RadioButtonList runat="server" ID="RBList2">
                     <asp:ListItem Value="Be true to yourself">Be true to
                     yourself</asp:ListItem>
                     <asp:ListItem Value="All code must be correct">All code must be
                     correct</asp:ListItem>
                     <asp:ListItem Value="Declare all variables before use">Declare
                     all variables before use</asp:ListItem>
```

```
                  </asp:RadioButtonList>
                </asp:TableCell>
              </asp:TableRow>
              <asp:TableRow BorderStyle="Solid">
                <asp:TableCell BorderStyle="Solid" Text="Concatenation is the way to
                do what?"></asp:TableCell>
                <asp:TableCell BorderStyle="Solid">
                  <asp:RadioButtonList runat="server" ID="RBList3">
                    <asp:ListItem Value="Concentrate on your coding">Concentrate
                    on your coding</asp:ListItem>
                    <asp:ListItem Value="Cheat cats">Cheat cats</asp:ListItem>
                    <asp:ListItem Value="Glue text strings together">Glue text
                    strings together</asp:ListItem>
                  </asp:RadioButtonList>
                </asp:TableCell>
              </asp:TableRow>
              <asp:TableRow BorderStyle="Solid">
                <asp:TableCell BorderStyle="Solid" Text="An array takes advantage
                of?"></asp:TableCell>
                <asp:TableCell BorderStyle="Solid">
                  <asp:RadioButtonList runat="server" ID="RBList4">
                    <asp:ListItem Value="A subscript">A subscript</asp:ListItem>
                    <asp:ListItem Value="A transcript">A transcript</asp:ListItem>
                    <asp:ListItem Value="A substitute">A substitute</asp:ListItem>
                  </asp:RadioButtonList>
                </asp:TableCell>
              </asp:TableRow>
          </asp:Table>
      </p>
      <p align="center">
      </p>
      <p align="center">
        <asp:TextBox id="TextBox1" runat="server" Font-Size="X-Large"
        Width="31px" Height="45px"></asp:TextBox>
      </p>
      <p align="center">
        <asp:Button id="Button1" onclick="calculate" runat="server"
        Text="Calculate"></asp:Button>
      </p>
      <p align="center">
      </p>
    </form>
</body>
</html>
```

9.6 Summary

In this chapter we have used a number of code examples to demonstrate how programming in VB.NET can add functionality and richness to your web sites. In addition we have introduced simple examples of common interactive web sites. These can obviously form the basis of your own developments.

9.7   Exercises

See if you can apply what you have learnt by trying the following exercises:

1.   In the on-line quiz example we used multiple-choice answers. Multiple-choice takes advantage of user recognition rather than recall. In psychological terms recognition is faster and often more reliable. But that assumes the user knows the answer to start off with. In our example the user can have as many attempts as they like but there is no indication from the system which answers are correct. That means if guesswork alone is employed the activity could continue for some significant time. However, with some minor changes to the code you can provide feedback to the user as to which answers continue to be incorrect and also to limit the number of attempts. To do this you need to provide Id values for each row, and then you can set the *Visible* property of a correct row to False. Modify the code for the on-line quiz so that when a user gets a question correct it disappears.

2.   So far we have only used colour in the design of web pages, but it is also possible to influence colour of objects at run time. To do this we need to add a new line to the ASP.NET header:

```
<%@ import Namespace="system.drawing" %>
```

This allows us to assign colour values to objects using the **color** method. In design view select an object such as a label. Examine its *BackColor* properties. Under the web tab you will find a large selection of colours each of which has a name. You can refer to a colour by its name:

```
row1.backcolor = color.red
```

Modify the on-line quiz to change the *BackColor* of a row to red if the answer is wrong and green if the answer is correct.

10

Installing and creating a database

10.1 Introduction

At the heart of most dynamic web sites is a database that stores the details to be displayed to the user as they require them. In much the same way as a traditional database, databases that sit behind websites require tables to store the data and queries to interrogate and update the data. In this chapter and the following two chapters we will show how you can use Web Matrix to develop and then utilise databases within the ASP.NET environment. In this chapter we will be examining the tools provided to create databases and the facilities offered by Web Matrix to allow the user to interface with the database. One of the most common reasons for developing a database for use on the web is to allow for products to be bought by users. In these chapters we will develop such a site.

10.2 How to create a database

Web Matrix supports SQL databases, principally the one created by Microsoft, SQL Server. If you do not have SQL Server this is not a problem as a cut-down version of it called MSDE is available from the ASP.NET web site. MSDE is a free to download from the Web Matrix download page.

Both Microsoft SQL Server and MSDE are not databases in their own right but rather are environments that allow you to create databases. Web Matrix allows you to create and use SQL databases. Before we start to create a database, let's have a look at the area of Web Matrix that handles databases. Using Web Matrix examine the Workspace window component in the top right-hand section of interface. This displays information about the environment in which you are working. There are three tabs at the bottom and by default Workspace is selected. The Data tab deals with access to databases, see Figure 10.1.

Figure 10.1: Data tab window

At this time you are not connected to any databases. To do so, you need to click **New Connection** which is the only icon enabled. This displays the dialog box illustrated in Figure 10.2.

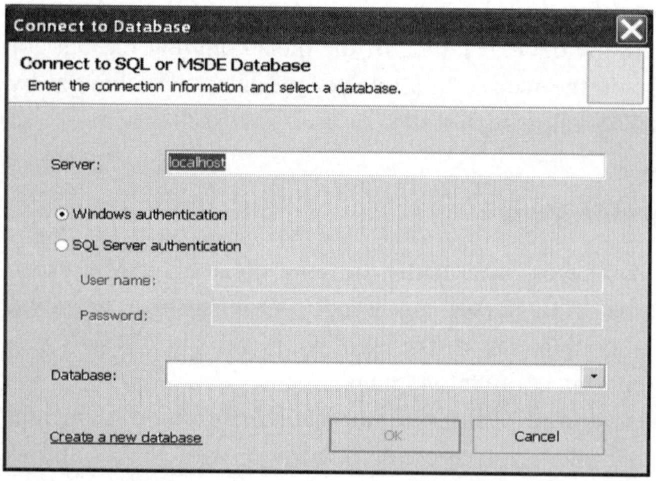

Figure 10.2: New connection dialog

The server is by default localhost and should not be changed since you are using MSDE on your local computer. Windows authentication is selected from the option buttons as this supports the use of MSDE. Then you have two choices, either to select an existing database by means of the drop-down list or to create a new database by clicking the hyper-link. Since you have not created a database yet we are going to click the link. This opens the following dialog box where you are required to enter a unique name for your database, see Figure 10.3. This should have no spaces but be meaningful to what you are wanting the database to do.

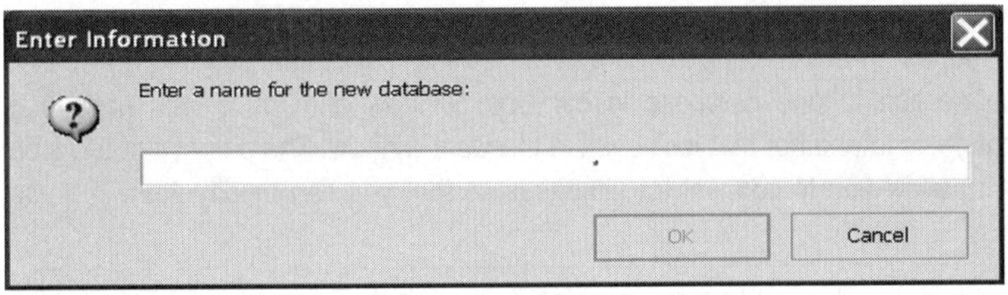

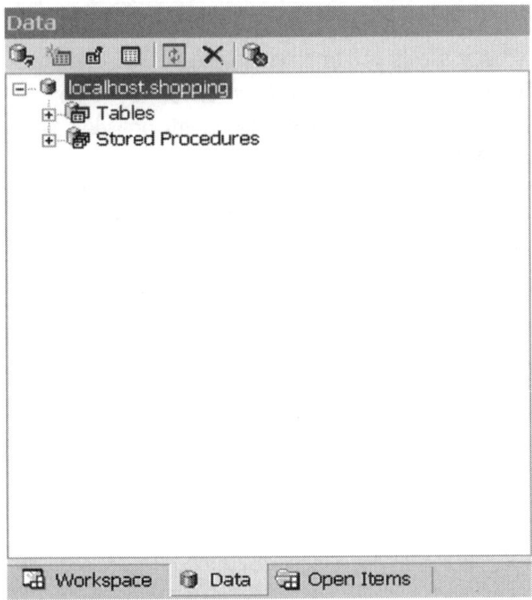

Figure 10.3:Database name dialog

For the purposes of this development we are going to create a database called **shopping**. Having entered the name of the new database and clicking OK the Data window is now modified to show the newly created database, as shown in Figure 10.4.

Figure 10.4: Updated Data window

You will notice that now we have connected to a database a number of the disabled icons are now enabled, see Table 10.1. Their enabled state changes depending on which object we click on in the data window.

Table 10.1: Data window icons

Icon	Description
	New Connection – We have already mentioned this icon, but one thing you do need to be aware of is creating or opening a connection with a database has no influence on any web page you may be editing. Consequently you may open a connection to one database in the Data window and run a web page that connects to another that isn't even in the Data window. The purpose of this icon is to allow you to connect to databases so that you can modify them in some way.
	New Item – This will become enabled if you select either of the folders (Tables or Stored Procedures). Clicking on the New Item icon will allow you to create a new instance of the selected object. In this book we will only be looking at New Tables.
	Edit – This allows you to edit either the database or tables you may have already created. If you click Edit when the database is selected then a dialog will be displayed that provides details of the current database and provides limited management over its size. We will look at editing tables later.
	Query Tool – This option can be used at any time but we think that it currently offers limited functionality. What it allows you to do is to write an SQL statement and then test if it works. The problem is that there is no direct way to save or copy the query once you have tested it. In addition, Web Matrix provides better SQL tools elsewhere, more of that later.
	Refresh – This allows you to refresh the display for the tables that you have created. This is rarely needed.
	Delete – This allows you to delete tables but does not allow you to delete databases. Any Web Matrix will allow you to click on Delete when the database is selected but this will only result in an error message.
	Close Connection – This removes the database from the Data window but does not delete it.

10.3   Database design

A database is of little use unless you create tables to store the data. In this book we will assume that you do not have detailed experience of database design. So we will initially discuss the principles of database development, how to consider the design of a database and why this is important. This is important for a number of reasons; the most obvious of these is to ensure the efficiency and effectiveness of the database.

10.4   The video store

The following sections of this chapter are based around the design of a simple example of a system. An organisation that sells DVDs and videos requires a web-based system that will allow the store to add, remove and modify items displayed to users. It also should allow users to select purchases from either DVDs or videos or both. At this stage it is not important how this is to be achieved only that these are the high level requirements.

10.5   Data storage

10.5.1   Flat file structure

Many early databases and some poorly designed modern databases are treated as a flat file. It is called a flat file because like a piece of paper it is only in two dimensions that consist of rows and columns of data. A file stores the values that the system needs to hold, it does not store or understand the labels and instructions that explain to the user what to enter. Consequently, looking at a flat file is meaningless unless you understand what the data is and how it has been stored. In a database additional information is stored such as a label to indicate what a particular item represents and a data type that determines what sort of value is stored. Regardless, it is possible to store all *transactions* within a single file or table.

10.5.2   Rows

Each item would represent one *row/record* within the *file*. However, there is a problem with having one record per row representing any transaction in that it can lead to duplication of data. If there is only one thing in your system that you wish to store data about then a flat file structure is appropriate. But in most systems you will want to store details about a number of things. For example in the current example we will need to store data about our customers and our products.

10.5.3   Columns

Each item in a record is made up of a number of pieces of data (**fields**) that are of interest to the user of the system. The data items in each row are always in the same order. If our system just held data about customers then it might have the following fields, illustrated in Table 10.2.

Table 10.2: Customer fields

First Name	Family Name

Why not have a single field called Name? If the customer's name is relatively unimportant then there is no reason why not. But names are normally important fields as you may wish to find items belonging to a particular person. Don't make work for yourself; if a field is not important, but is required, keep its name simple. If you do wish to carry out actions that require a detailed specification then create fields that correspond to your requirements. The key issue here is that even at the level of individual fields do not treat your decisions lightly. Anyway, having specified your fields this defines what should go in each column, now you then need to put data in them for example see Table 10.3.

Table 10.3: Data and fields

First Name	Family Name
Fred	Smith
Peter	Jones

10.5.4 Problems with flat files

As noted above we are not only interested in customers but also our products. So what would happen if we tried to fit all the data illustrated in Table 10.4 in one file?

Table 10.4: Data for flat file

Description	Code
First Name	FiN
Family Name	FaN
Product Id	PI
Product Category	PC
Product Name	PN
Product Description	PD
Product Price	PP

If you think about the things you want to do with this data then to try to do it in one file would lead to incomplete records and wouldn't make any sense. For example if you are adding a new product you would add a record that used all the Product fields but didn't put anything in the other fields.

A similar thing would occur for our customer as illustrated in Table 10.5.

Table 10.5: Incomplete data records

FiN	FaN	PI	PC	PN	PD	PP
		1001	Video	Ice Age	Children	£7.99
		2003	DVD	XXX	Action	£19.99
Fred	Smith					
Peter	Jones					

10.6   Modelling a database system

What would make more sense is to store all the data once only and there needs to be some way of associating a record in one file with one in another file. That is the purpose of a database.

Dividing the data down into meaningful groups not only removes what are called *repeating groups* but also makes your system easier to maintain. In some systems this is achieved by having separate files. When one or more files are managed within a single application they are called a *database management system (DBMS)*. A DBMS allows for the creation, modification and deletion of data, as well as often providing the opportunity to create an interface that assists in the management of data.

We are going to concentrate on how data can be efficiently stored and how it can be effectively retrieved in the form of information. There are three traditional ways of modelling a system: Data, Process and Event. Each is independent but they have some areas of overlap, this is understandable since they are merely different views of the same thing.

10.6.1 Data modelling

In data modelling you determine what you want to store. This can be achieved either by thinking of the key things in your system that have characteristics you want to store (entities) and then determining what those characteristics are. Alternatively you can think of all possible bits of data that are of interest and then group them together into associated groups. You also need to be sure that, having put all your data into the system that it is possible to get out the bits you want. This overlaps with process modelling

10.6.2 Process modelling

In process modelling you are thinking about all the things you want your system to do; for example in the current system one of the processes will be Add a Product. This process will use data that comes out of the data model, or it may be necessary to put data into the system. In any event, it is important to know the steps that make up that process. In process modelling, you are not interested in the order that these steps occur because this overlaps with event modelling.

10.6.3 Event modelling

In event modelling you are looking at when things occur in your system. You are interested in low-level sequencing of actions as in a specific process, but you are also concerned with the sequences of actions performed by the user and the consequent reactions by the system. This in turn may involve a sequencing of processes.

10.6.4 Relational model

Databases that are based on the relational model are termed a *relational database management system (RDBMS)*. Microsoft Access is an example of a database system based on the relational model. Within an RDBMS separate files are re-named *tables/relations* the columns are *fields/attributes* and the rows are *records/tuples*. With our example we keep our two tables, see Table 10.6.

Table 10.6: Customer and product tables

Customer	Product
First Name	Id
Family Name	Category
	Name
	Description
	Price

One of the major benefits of creating separate tables for each entity is that when you are considering the entity you start to focus on it rather than the system. When you do that it is often the case that you recognise additional fields which in turn can influence the functions required of the system as can be seen in Table 10.7.

Table 10.7: Revised customer and product tables

Customer	Product
First Name	Id
Family Name	Category
Address	Name
Post Code	Description
Tel No.	Price
	Supplier Code
	Supplier Address
	Quantity in Stock

Each table is obtaining uniqueness. However, it should be noted that up to this point the tables are not linked to one another in any way. This means that so far it is not possible for the system to recognise any relationship between, for example, the customer and a particular product choice.

10.6.5 Keys

Each table contains one or more records, one of the important benefits of having a relational database system in that every one of those records must be unique in some identifiable way. This is achieved by specifying fields that can be used to uniquely identify the record (Keys). This means that the values stored in such key fields cannot have duplicates but that they must have a value. Using our example, looking at the fields available in the Customer table it is possible that there could be more than one customer with the same Family Name.

Similarly there could be more than one person living at the same address or post code. Consequently at the moment it is not possible to uniquely identify a customer from keys based on the existing fields. It is easier to find a key in the Product table as Id acts as a unique identifier for a product and as such can perform the same role in our database. The key (or keys) is marked with an "underline" to distinguish it from other fields, see Table 10.8.

Table 10.8: Customer and Product tables

Customer	Product
First Name	<u>Id</u>
Family Name	Category
Address	Name
Post Code	Description
Tel No.	Price
	Supplier Code
	Supplier Address
	Quantity in Stock

10.6.6 Data types

In a flat file all data, including numbers, are stored as text since they are generated in a text editor. Since everything is text, any piece of software that handles the text file has to determine how to handle that data (e.g. as a whole number, a decimal number, a date or just as text). In a database, fields can be specified as being of a particular data type. You need to think carefully about what data you want each field to contain and how you intend to process it into information. You should use the Access Help system to explain to you the different data types.

Each data type can also be formatted to ensure *consistency* and *efficiency*. This is achieved through the modification of the properties associated with that field. There are different properties for each data type.

When you first create a table you are required to specify the data type of every field you use. Once created the data type can be changed but in order to change the data type and its properties you need to open a table in design mode, since it is characteristics of data and not the data itself that you are changing. If you already have data in your tables you cannot change the data type. This is why it is important to think about your design before you spend too much time implementing your system.

The data types and properties shown in Table 10.9 and 10.10 are, in our opinion appropriate for this system. Remember you are the designer of the system and need to prepare yourself to be accountable should problems occur. As such you should have clear reasons for your design decisions.

Table 10.9: Customer data types and field size

Customer	Data Type	Field Size
First Name	Char	15
Family Name	Char	20
Address	Char	50
Post Code	Char	10
Tel No.	Char	15

All of these fields are of type Character (char) as they hold values that are only going to be referred to as text. This is the case even with Tel No. since the user may include parentheses surrounding the area code. Similarly whilst the Post Code does contain numbers an individual field value would be a combination of text and numbers and as such must be handled as a char.

In Table 10.10 we decided that the Id and Supplier Code were going to be Integers. This decision would obviously be influenced by the existing needs of the organisation that might have business rules for the generation of such codes. Whilst in previous chapters we have been keen to perform mathematical operations on money in this example we only need to display the value. As such any monetary value consists of numbers and characters so we have decided to treat this field as a char.

Table 10.10: Product data types and field size

Product	Data Type	Field Size
<u>Id</u>	Int	
Category	Char	15
Name	Char	30
Description	Char	10
Price	Char	10
Supplier Code	Int	
Supplier Address	Char	50
Quantity in Stock	Int	

10.7   How to create tables and fields

Web Matrix provides a relatively simple set of dialogues to create a table but it has some limitations. The first of these is that you cannot save a table unless that table has a key. Since the Customer table does not have a key at the moment we will demonstrate how to create a table by walking through the creation of the Product table. Assuming that you have created the Shopping database, your Data window should look still like Figure 10.4, a number of pages ago. Select the Tables object and then click New Item; this will display the Create New Table dialog as shown in Figure 10.5.

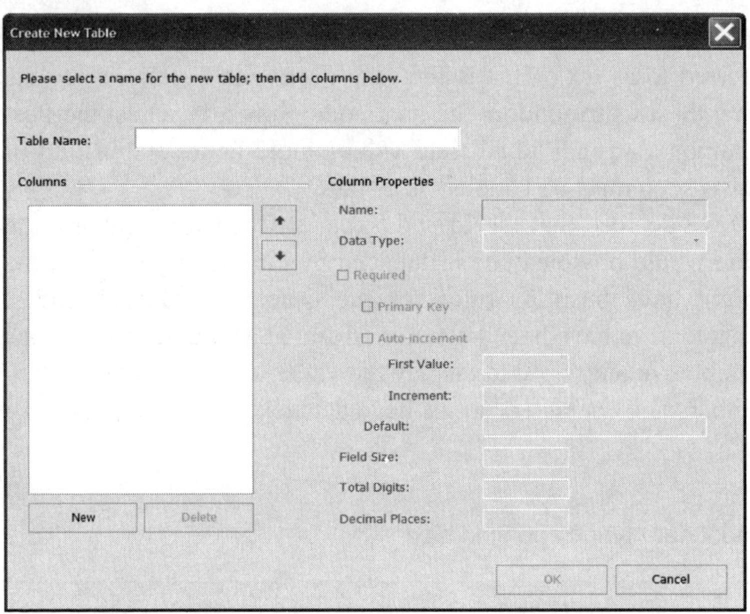

Figure 10.5: Create New Table dialog

In the Table Name textbox enter Product then click the New button under Columns. This will create a new field and enable its properties. Change the contents of the Name textbox to Id, select Int from the Data Type drop-down box. Then select Required, this will enable Primary Key which you should also select but do not select Auto-increment. Select Required for this field only. This completes the Id field so you can click New again. This will update the name of the field in the Columns window and create a new field.

Add the remaining fields from Table 10.10 until the dialog is the same as that shown in Figure 10.6. Make sure that when you do add the other fields that the correct Data Type is selected and for the Char data types you enter the correct Field Size in the correct textbox.

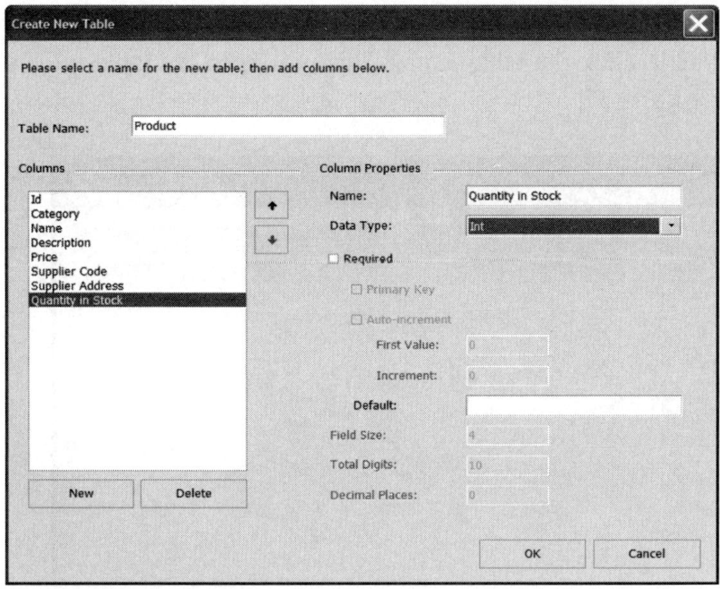

Figure 10.6: Complete table design for Product

Once you have completed this then select OK. This will add the table to the list of tables, see Figure 10.7.

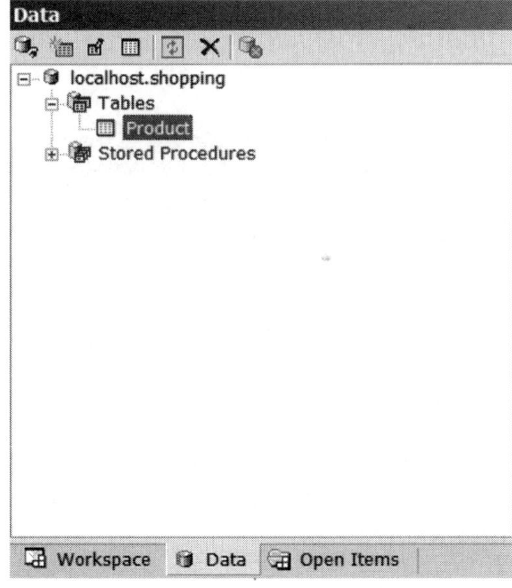

Figure 10.7: Updated Data window

Remember that at this time all you have done is design the table. In order to add data to the table double-click the table name. This will open the table in data entry view as in Figure 10.8.

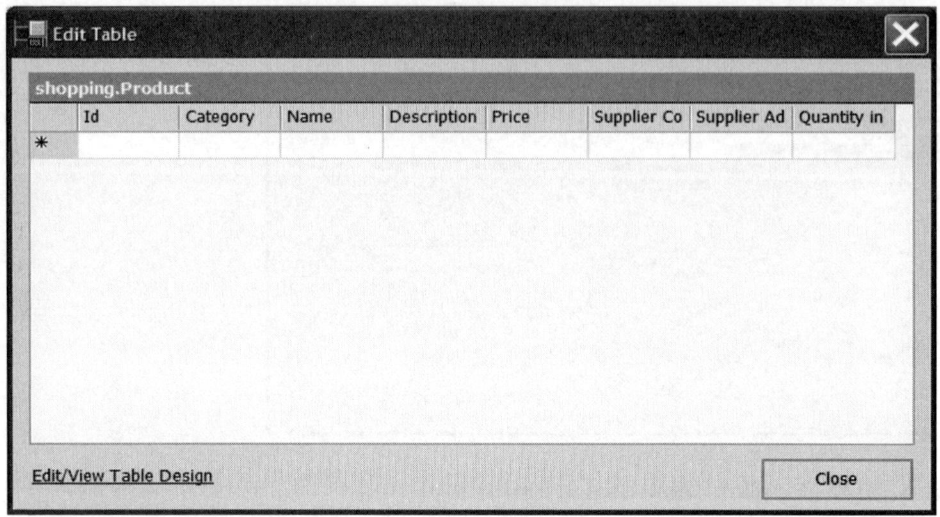

Figure 10.8: Product table in data entry view

You need to enter the data shown in Table 10.11 into the Product table.

Table 10.11: Data for Product table

Id	Category	Name	Description	Price	Supplier Code	Supplier Address	Quantity in Stock
1001	Video	Ice Age	Children	£7.99	1	Video Shack	111
1002	Video	Lord of the Rings	Fantasy	£9.99	1	Video Shack	86
1003	Video	XXX	Action	£9.99	1	Video Shack	200
2001	DVD	Ice Age	Children	£17.99	2	DVD Sales	145
2002	DVD	Lord of the Rings	Fantasy	£19.99	2	DVD Sales	150
2003	DVD	XXX	Action	£19.99	2	DVD Sales	200

In Section 10.6.5 we argued that it is not possible as yet to specify a key for the Customer table so at the moment we are not going to create it as Web Matrix will not allow you to save a table unless it has a key.

10.7.1 Relationships

So far, the discussion has been about developing tables that have a unique identity, that store common data and that the type and formatting of the data is determined in advance. However, remembering back there is a clear relationship between the data stored in the Product table and that in the Customer table. This means there should be some way to link these tables together.

Before you start to link tables it is necessary to think about the nature of the relationships between the tables. The most common and preferred type of relationship is known as a *one to many* (1:M) relationship; for example, as you can see from the Product table a *supplier* may provide many *products* (See Figure 10.9).

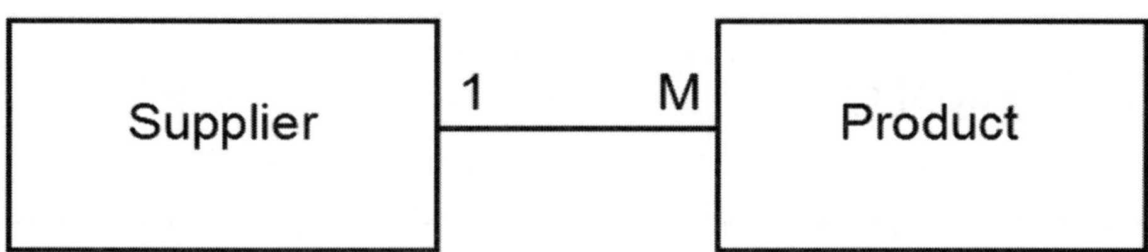

Figure 10.9: One to many relationship

In order to keep things simple, in our system we are not going to create separate tables for the Supplier and Product but in a larger system this would probably be recommended. Note that if you spelt the Supplier Address or Supplier code incorrectly as far as the system is concerned they are different suppliers. If there was a separate Supplier table then the key for Supplier would probably be Supplier Code and the Supplier Address would only appear once in that table.

When you think about your design there might be times where there might be a 1:1 relationship between records in one table and those in another. This often occurs when you create the system entities. For example there may be two or more entities in your system that are unique and have fields that only relate to that entity however there is a relationship between the entities such that when a record is created in one there will be an associated record in the other (Figure 10.10).

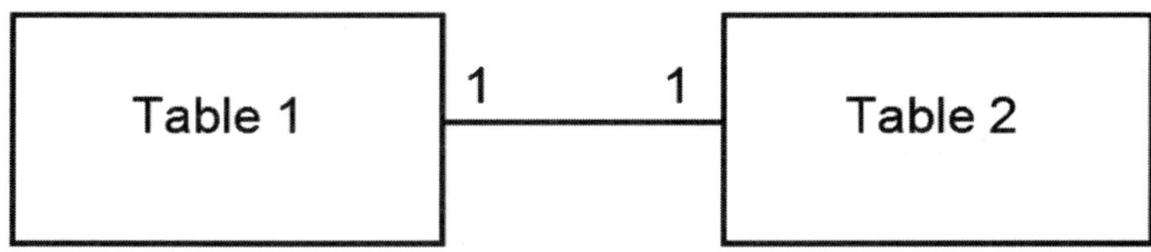

Figure 10.10: One to one relationship

In such circumstances you need to decide whether it makes sense to keep two separate tables or whether they could realistically be merged into a single table. As with all design decisions there may be good and bad choices but you should understand and be able to argue why you have made the decisions you have.

There is one other type of relationship that might occur between two entities. This is called a many to many relationship (M:M). Many to many relationships are not allowed in relational databases because of the need to be able to uniquely identify records. In our system such a link would be between Customer and Product.

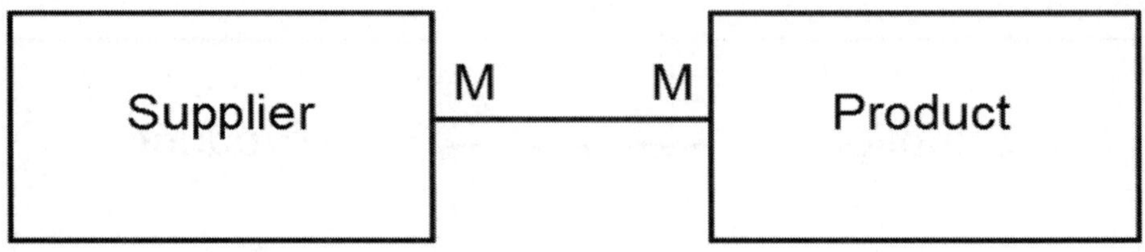

Figure 10.11: Many to many relationship

In a 1:M relationship it is important to be able to take any one record on the many side and know precisely which record on the one side it is associated with (a sort of 1:1). For example assume we did have a Supplier table that consisted of the Supplier Code as key and the Supplier Address. For every record in the Product table it is possible to take the Supplier Code and link back to an individual record in the Supplier table, see Tables 10.12 and 10.13.

Table 10.12: Supplier table

Supplier Code	Supplier Address
1	Video Shack
2	DVD Sales

Table 10.13: Product table

Id	Category	Name	Description	Price	Quantity in Stock	Supplier Code
1001	Video	Ice Age	Children	£7.99	111	1
1002	Video	Lord of the Rings	Fantasy	£9.99	86	1
1003	Video	XXX	Action	£9.99	200	1
2001	DVD	Ice Age	Children	£17.99	145	2
2002	DVD	Lord of the Rings	Fantasy	£19.99	150	2
2003	DVD	XXX	Action	£19.99	200	2

However, with a many to many (M:N) relationship that is not possible and this confuses the link. In order to get around this you need to create what is termed a link table. The link table contains all the possible combinations of the M:N but stands between the two tables and they are linked through this table rather than directly to each other. The relationship is 1:M between the tables and the link table. Our tables have a M:N relationship in that not only can a customer select many products but also a product may be selected by many customers. Therefore we need a link table here. Sometimes when you are modelling you must make arbitrary decisions to include link tables but that they do not bear any relationship to the system's entities. However in our system there is an entity that we have not considered yet that will act as a link between the two tables.

When a customer visits a site such as ours one of the most common features available is a *shopping cart*. A shopping cart is associated with a particular customer and can consist of a number of product items. Similarly the same product can appear in a number of different customer shopping carts. Once again at this stage we are not interested in how to create such a structure but rather what data we need to store about it. The first thing that is required is a key. The key for a link table is made up of the keys from the other two tables. But here we have a problem because the Customer table does not have a key. We have a number of options at this point.

The first is to create an arbitrary field in the Customer table that can act as a key. Usually this is some form of counter and Web Matrix does offer the opportunity to create such a field and provide a different value for the field for every record by means of the *Auto Increment* facility in field design. Whilst this facility can be useful we would tend to use it when no other option is available. The reason for this is you are adding to the requirements purely for system reasons rather than the needs of the user and data is stored that is never used and often not seen.

Another alternative is that you make a design decision that some combination of fields are highly unlikely to result in records that duplicate the value. In this table we could argue that a combination of Post Code and First Name is such that you will not get two people in the same household with the same first name. Whilst this may be true in a lot of circumstances there is no certainty to it.

The final option is that you re-visit the requirements of the system and see if there is some data that you have not included in the current table description but would provide added benefit. Currently we have the following fields in the Customer table, as illustrated in Table 10.14.

Having decided that we need a shopping cart we need some way to ensure that when a user enters the system and selects products to add to their shopping cart there is some way to uniquely identify their cart from other users. To do this you usually have some form of login system. Logging on to a system can often be done at a number of places within the system and requires the user to enter a valid user name and password. Since the user name and password are unique to an individual customer they can logically be stored in the Customer table.

Table 10.14: Customer data types and field size

Customer	Data Type	Field Size
First Name	Char	15
Family Name	Char	20
Address	Char	50
Post Code	Char	10
Tel No.	Char	15

In addition, the combination of both fields provides a unique identifier and as such can be used as the key for the Customer table. Hence the structure of the table can be updated as shown in Table 10.15.

Table 10.15: Customer data types and field size

Customer	Data Type	Field Size
Login	Char	10
Password	Char	10
First Name	Char	15
Family Name	Char	20
Address	Char	50
Post Code	Char	10
Tel No.	Char	15

10.7.2 Link tables

Now let us return to the link table that will handle the Shopping Cart. First we need to name the table, it should be called *CartItems*. In order to link tables it is necessary to have the key field(s) in the One-side of the relationship present in the Many-side as well. In the Customer table the key is the combination of the Family Login and Password fields, so in the CartItems table it is necessary to include those fields as well. In the CartItems table this is called a Foreign Key and in the table definition below this is marked by an asterisk (*). It is called a foreign key because it is a key from another table and is only in the foreign table to provide a link between the two tables. Remember earlier we argued that one of the major benefits of having multiple tables is to remove repetition of data; foreign keys are the exception to this. Similarly the key in the Product table is Id and so this must be included in the collection of fields in CartItems as a Foreign Key, as shown in Table 10.16.

Table 10.16: CartItems data types and field size

CartItems	Data Type	Field Size
*Id	Int	
*Login	Char	10
*Password	Char	10
Category	Char	15
Name	Char	30
Description	Char	10
Price	Char	10

The keys from the other tables become the key in a link table. This is necessary because if you used another fields(s) as the key for the link table then it would be possible for cart items to be duplicated; for example if there was a field called CartId and this was key then there could only be one instance of a value for CartItemsId but there is no restriction on other fields, see Table 10.17.

Table 10.17: CartItems data

CartIId	Id	Login	Password	Category	Name	Description	Price
1	2001	abc	123	DVD	Ice Age	Children	£17.99
2	2001	abc	123	DVD	Ice Age	Children	£17.99
3	1001	abc	123	Video	Ice Age	Children	£7.99
4	1001	xyz	789	Video	Ice Age	Children	£7.99
5	2001	xyz	789	DVD	Ice Age	Children	£17.99

The first two items of the CartItems table should not occur as this means that a particular user can have duplicate shopping cart entries. The rest of the table shows valid permutations.

In our system you would only expect the user to enter their login and password once and that in all other situations where these details are required, as in adding an item to the shopping cart, the values would be added automatically. The user would only see the relevant details of the shopping cart objects and not their login and password against every record. Now if we just made the Login and Password the key then it would be possible for user to select and add a product to the shopping cart but as soon as they tried to add another product it would result in an error caused by a duplicate value for the key, see Table 10.18.

Table 10.18: Duplicate login key

Id	Login	Password	Category	Name	Description	Price
2001	abc	123	DVD	Ice Age	Children	£17.99
1001	abc	123	Video	Ice Age	Children	£7.99

Similarly you would get an error if the Id field was made the key and more than one user attempted to add the same item to their cart, see Table 10.19.

Table 10.19: Duplicate Id key

Id	Login	Password	Category	Name	Description	Price
2001	abc	123	DVD	Ice Age	Children	£17.99
2001	xyz	789	DVD	Ice Age	Children	£17.99

However, if you use both of the foreign keys as the key for the link table duplications cannot occur, see Table 10.20.

Table 10.20: Both foreign keys solve problem

Id	Login	Password	Category	Name	Description	Price
2001	abc	123	DVD	Ice Age	Children	£17.99
1001	abc	123	Video	Ice Age	Children	£7.99
1001	xyz	789	Video	Ice Age	Children	£7.99
2001	xyz	789	DVD	Ice Age	Children	£17.99

Now each customer can have more than one item in the shopping cart and the same item can be added to more than one customer's shopping cart. Unfortunately we are still in the position where the user can add the same item to the cart more than once. We do not want this to happen. Obviously the key is effective as far as it goes but this final requirement must be added by code. We will see how that is achieved in Chapter 12.

As for the remaining fields: Category, Name, Description and Price the field descriptions are the same as those in the Product table but whereas in the Product table there would only be one instance of any individual product in the CartItems table potentially any number of records could use the values from that one Product record. The final design of the three tables is shown in Tables 10.21, 10.22 and 10.23.

Table 10.21: Product data types and field size

Product	Data Type	Field Size
Id	Int	
Category	Char	15
Name	Char	30
Description	Char	10
Price	Char	10
Supplier Code	Int	
Supplier Address	Char	50
Quantity in Stock	Int	

Table 10.22: Customer data types and field size

Customer	Data Type	Field Size
Login	Char	10
Password	Char	10
First Name	Char	15
Family Name	Char	20
Address	Char	50
Post Code	Char	10
Tel No.	Char	15

Table 10.23: CartItems data types and field size

CartItems	Data Type	Field Size
*Id	Int	
*Login	Char	10
*Password	Char	10
Category	Char	15
Name	Char	30
Description	Char	10
Price	Char	10

10.8   Summary

In this chapter we have investigated the design and implementation of databases within Web Matrix. Probably the most important point to draw from this chapter is that you need to think carefully about the system you are designing. This will include not only the data you are going to use but also the order in which this occurs. As noted you are likely to obtain a more thorough understanding of the system if you think about the data and the functions of the system as separate issues since understanding of one can highlight deficiencies that can be resolved by examining the other. It is always better to develop your design on paper before committing yourself to implementation. It will take slightly longer but ultimately your system will be more complete and result in a better structure that is easier to maintain. In addition having explained your system on paper you will also have the basis for documentation that will help you, or someone else, at a later date to understand why the system is constructed as it is.

10.9   Exercises

1.   Implement the database discussed in this chapter within Web Matrix. This will form the basis of the system to be developed over the next two chapters.

2.   You are going to design and implement a database that supports a web site devoted to making bookings for a dentist surgery. The dentist requires a web site that will store all the details for patient appointments and treatments for the three dentists who work at that surgery.

Through discussion with one of the dentists, the following data elements were isolated as being of importance to the system:

Address (Dentist), Address (Patient), Appointment Date, Appointment Time, Clean and Polish, Dentist Name, Extraction, Family Name (Patient), Filling, Given Name (Patient), Patient Id, Post Code (Dentist), Post Code (Patient), Telephone Number (Dentist), Telephone Number (Patient), Town (Dentist), Town (Patient).

Organise these on paper into potential tables including data types and formatting. Remember; tables should store data that is associated with one another. In order to do this exercise you will have to make assumptions about the functionality of the system and how it is likely to operate. This will influence the nature of your tables and the fields they contain. Note down any assumptions you make. Having done that, create a database called Dentist and then implement your designed tables.

11

Interacting with the database using SQL

11.1 Introduction

In this chapter we are going to examine some of the database development tools provided by Web Matrix and how they may be used. In order to do this you need to obtain an understanding of the Structured Query Language (SQL) and how it might be used to query a database. We are going to use the Shopping database that you created in the last chapter in our examples.

11.2 Objects provided by Web Matrix

Web Matrix offers a range of objects to display and manipulate data from a database. There are a number of ways to use these objects and each approach has its own strengths and weaknesses.

If you opened an ASP.NET page and connected and displayed the tables from a database you could drag and drop a table from the database window to the design window and this will insert two objects an *SqlDataSourceControl* and an *MxDataGrid*. To do this select the Data tab in the Data component window and then select the *New Connection* icon from the icons at the top of the window. Select the shopping database, as shown in Figure 11.1 and click OK.

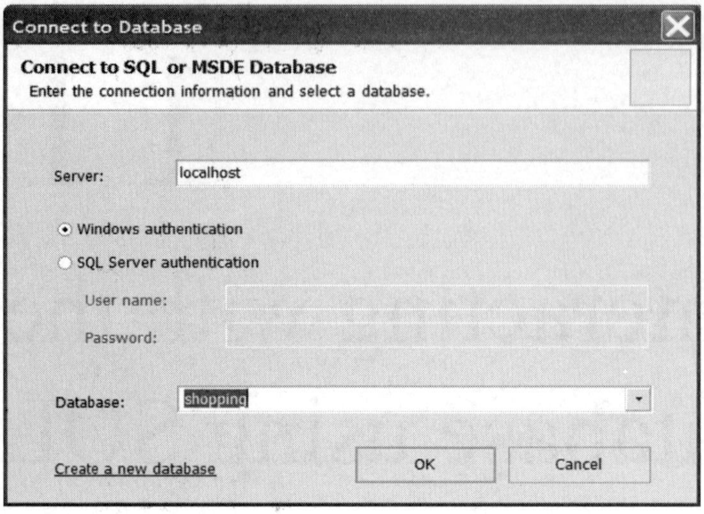

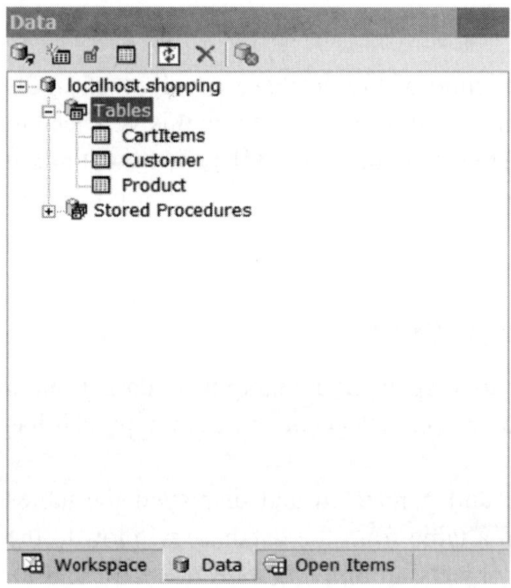

Figure 11.1: Selecting the shopping database

The Data component window should now look like that shown in Figure 11.2.

Figure 11.2: Data component window

Clicking and dragging the *Customer* table from the Data component window onto the Document window will result in the creation of the controls and table shown in Figure 11.3.

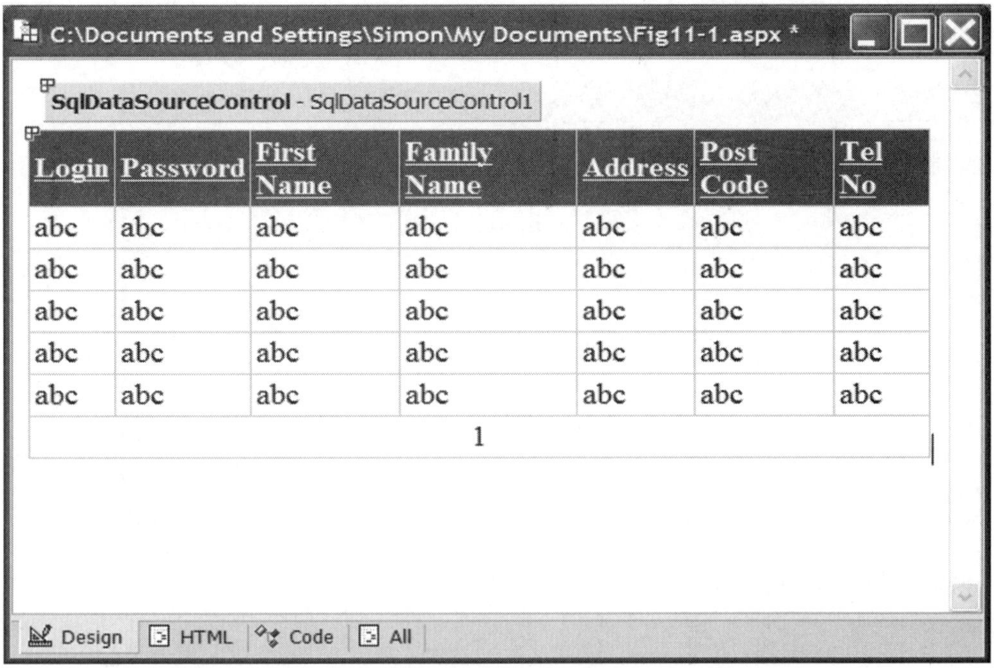

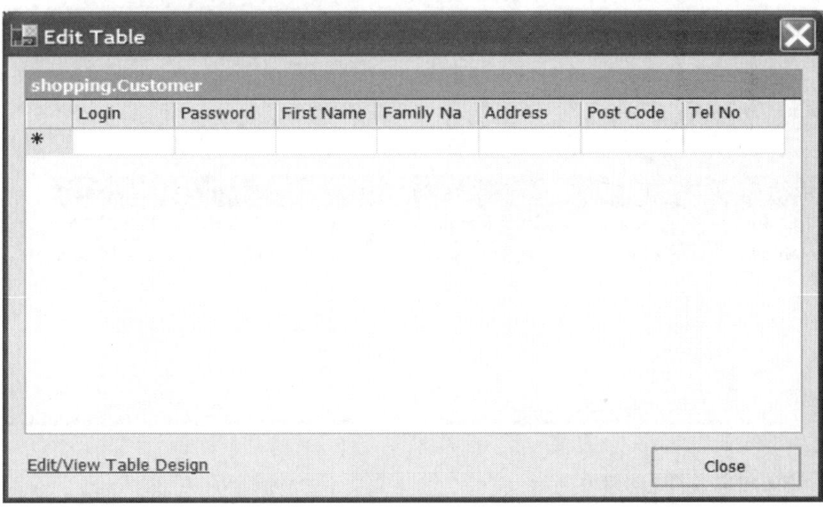

Figure 11.3: Drag and drop customer table

At present we have no data in our tables and so it would make sense to add some test data to one of the tables. If we connect to the *Shopping Database* and then from the Tables group double click *Customer* we are provided with a dialog to enter, edit and delete records as in Figure 11.4.

Figure 11.4: Edit Table dialog

Enter two records so that it corresponds with Figure 11.5

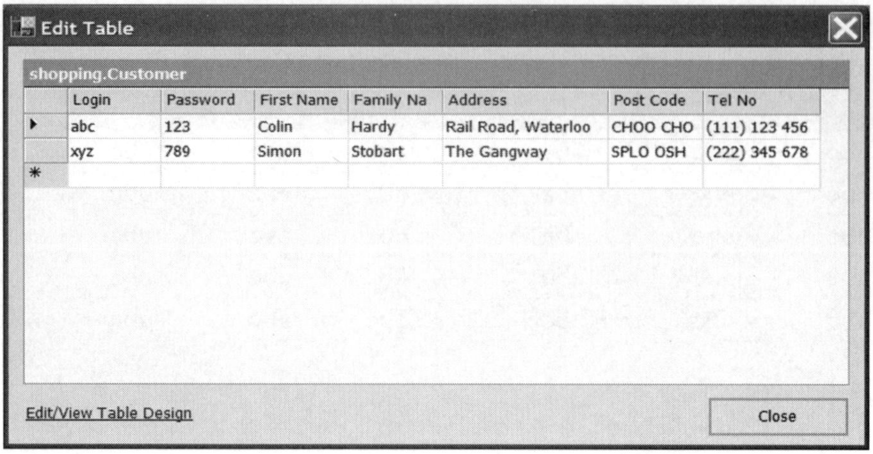

shopping.Customer

	Login	Password	First Name	Family Na	Address	Post Code	Tel No
▶	abc	123	Colin	Hardy	Rail Road, Waterloo	CHOO CHO	(111) 123 456
	xyz	789	Simon	Stobart	The Gangway	SPLO OSH	(222) 345 678
*							

Edit/View Table Design   Close

Figure 11.5: Completed Edit Table dialog

As an aside, if you clicked the *Edit/View Table Design* link at this point you would be taken to the Design dialog but it would be in Read-Only mode. Web Matrix does not allow you to change the design of a table when there is data in it. This is another reason why you should think carefully about the design of your tables as data entry is probably the most boring part of database work and should always be kept at a minimum. If you ran the drag and drop design shown in Figure 11.3, the output would be similar to Figure 11.6.

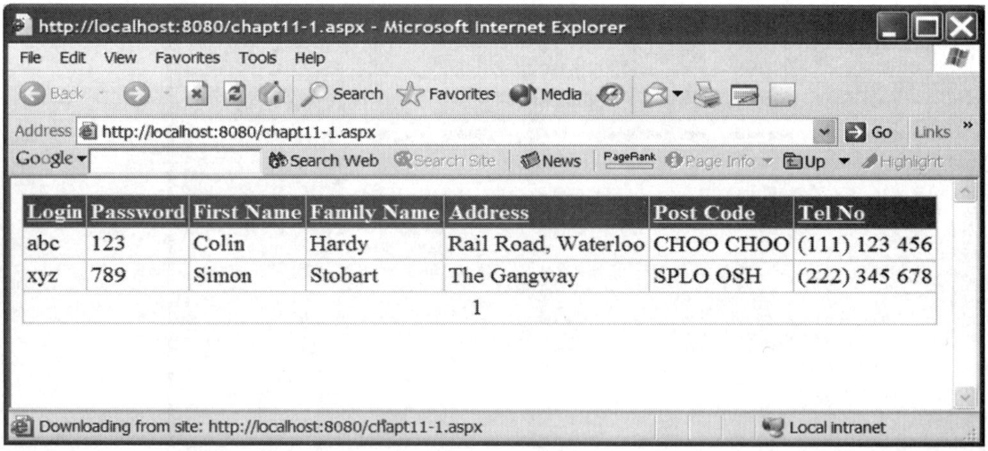

Login	Password	First Name	Family Name	Address	Post Code	Tel No
abc	123	Colin	Hardy	Rail Road, Waterloo	CHOO CHOO	(111) 123 456
xyz	789	Simon	Stobart	The Gangway	SPLO OSH	(222) 345 678

1

Figure 11.6: Drag and drop output

The code for this apparently simple action is below. Web Matrix does not do everything for you and so it is important to understand the code that is generated in order to modify it to your needs.

```
<%@ Page Language="VB" Explicit="True" Debug="True" %>
<%@ Register TagPrefix="wmx"
        Namespace="Microsoft.Saturn.Framework.Web.UI"
        Assembly="Microsoft.Saturn.Framework,
        Version=0.5.464.0,
        Culture=neutral,
        PublicKeyToken=6f763c9966660626" %>


<script runat="server">
</script>

<html>
<head>
</head>
<body>
  <form runat="server">
    <wmx:SqlDataSourceControl id="SqlDataSourceControl1" runat="server"
        UpdateCommand="" SelectCommand="SELECT * FROM [Customer]"
        AutoGenerateUpdateCommand="False"
        ConnectionString="server='localhost';
        trusted_connection=true;
        Database='shopping'"
        DeleteCommand=""></wmx:SqlDataSourceControl>
    <wmx:MxDataGrid id="MxDataGrid1" runat="server"
        DataSourceControlID="SqlDataSourceControl1"
        BorderColor="#CCCCCC"
        AllowSorting="True"
        AutoGenerateFields="False"
        DataMember="Customer"
        AllowPaging="True" BackColor="White" CellPadding="3"
        BorderWidth="1px" BorderStyle="None">
        <PagerStyle horizontalalign="Center" forecolor="#000066"
        backcolor="White" mode="NumericPages"></PagerStyle>
        <FooterStyle forecolor="#000066" backcolor="White"></FooterStyle>
        <SelectedItemStyle font-bold="True" forecolor="White"
        backcolor="#669999"></SelectedItemStyle>
        <ItemStyle forecolor="#000066"></ItemStyle>
        <Fields>
            <wmx:BoundField DataField="Login" SortExpression="Login"
                HeaderText="Login"></wmx:BoundField>
            <wmx:BoundField DataField="Password" SortExpression="Password"
                HeaderText="Password"></wmx:BoundField>
            <wmx:BoundField DataField="First Name" SortExpression="First Name"
                HeaderText="First Name"></wmx:BoundField>
            <wmx:BoundField DataField="Family Name" SortExpression="Family
                Name" HeaderText="Family Name"></wmx:BoundField>
```

```
                <wmx:BoundField DataField="Address" SortExpression="Address"
                    HeaderText="Address"></wmx:BoundField>
                <wmx:BoundField DataField="Post Code" SortExpression="Post Code"
                    HeaderText="Post Code"></wmx:BoundField>
                <wmx:BoundField DataField="Tel No" SortExpression="Tel No"
                    HeaderText="Tel No"></wmx:BoundField>
            </Fields>
            <HeaderStyle font-bold="True" forecolor="White"
                    backcolor="#006699"></HeaderStyle>
        </wmx:MxDataGrid>
      </form>
</body>
</html>
```

The first thing to note is that an additional line is added to the header to allow for the use of the two Web Matrix objects. The next line defines the *SqlDataSourceControl* object:

```
<wmx:SqlDataSourceControl id="SqlDataSourceControl1" runat="server"
    UpdateCommand="" SelectCommand="SELECT * FROM [Customer]"
    AutoGenerateUpdateCommand="False"
    ConnectionString="server='localhost';
    trusted_connection=true;
    Database='shopping'"
    DeleteCommand=""></wmx:SqlDataSourceControl>
```

An *SqlDataSourceControl* object specifies the data to be displayed in another object, in this case an *MxDataGrid*. Since the *SqlDataSourceControl* object is a Web Matrix object rather than a standard web object the line begins with *wmx*. This invokes the header line which in turn provides guidance to the system as to how the object is to be used. There are two more elements of this line that are of importance and are a common feature of database interaction. The first of these specifies the connection between this web page and a database:

```
ConnectionString="server='localhost'; trusted_connection=true;
    Database='shopping'"
```

This specifies that the server that hosts the database is our local host and that there is a safe connection between it and the web page. Finally it specifies the name of the database. The second element is our first introduction to SQL:

```
SelectCommand="SELECT * FROM [Customer]"
```

This is probably the simplest SQL statement that you will come across. At this point we will not go into detail about SQL as a language but will merely highlight that this statement retrieves all the records (*) from the *Customer* table. But we didn't ask for a query all we wanted was to display the contents of the *Customer* table. What you need to realise is that the tables and their data are secure and can only be accessed by means of an SQL statement from a secure source. This stops anyone from being able to access the tables directly without going through the interface.

The next line defines the *MxDataGrid*:

```
<wmx:MxDataGrid id="MxDataGrid1" runat="server"
   DataSourceControlID="SqlDataSourceControl1"
   BorderColor="#CCCCCC"
   AllowSorting="True"
   AutoGenerateFields="False"
   DataMember="Customer"
   AllowPaging="True" BackColor="White" CellPadding="3"
   BorderWidth="1px" BorderStyle="None">
```

Much of this is formatting information about the structure of the grid rather than its contents, but there are two elements that link the *SqlDataSourceControl* to this object:

```
DataSourceControlID="SqlDataSourceControl1"
DataMember="Customer"
```

The first of these creates the link between the two objects whilst the second specifies that the data is drawn from the *Customer* table.

The next block of code specifies the format of the grid. This is done in terms of a style guide.

```
<PagerStyle horizontalalign="Center" forecolor="#000066"
 backcolor="White" mode="NumericPages"></PagerStyle>
<FooterStyle forecolor="#000066" backcolor="White"></FooterStyle>
<SelectedItemStyle font-bold="True" forecolor="White"
 backcolor="#669999"></SelectedItemStyle>
<ItemStyle forecolor="#000066"></ItemStyle>
```

The final block of code provides the link between individual cells in the *MxDataGrid* and the fields in the table

```
<Fields>
   <wmx:BoundField DataField="Login" SortExpression="Login"
         HeaderText="Login"></wmx:BoundField>
   <wmx:BoundField DataField="Password" SortExpression="Password"
         HeaderText="Password"></wmx:BoundField>
   <wmx:BoundField DataField="First Name" SortExpression="First Name"
         HeaderText="First Name"></wmx:BoundField>
   <wmx:BoundField DataField="Family Name" SortExpression="Family
         Name" HeaderText="Family Name"></wmx:BoundField>
   <wmx:BoundField DataField="Address" SortExpression="Address"
         HeaderText="Address"></wmx:BoundField>
   <wmx:BoundField DataField="Post Code" SortExpression="Post Code"
         HeaderText="Post Code"></wmx:BoundField>
   <wmx:BoundField DataField="Tel No" SortExpression="Tel No"
         HeaderText="Tel No"></wmx:BoundField>
</Fields>
```

The final block of code defines the style of the Header for the grid

```
<HeaderStyle font-bold="True" forecolor="White"
           backcolor="#006699"></HeaderStyle>
```

11.3   Introduction to SQL

SQL or Structured Query Language is what is termed a *declarative* language. It differs from other programming languages such as VB.NET in that SQL achieves its purpose in a single statement. If you think about the programming you have done so far in VB.NET, subroutines are self-contained purposeful blocks of code and it is normally the case that each subroutine contains a number of lines of code. Subroutines are very flexible and you can use them to achieve a variety of functional needs. Conversely SQL has a single purpose namely to perform queries on a database. Whilst queries might be highly complex and a single query may contain sub-queries a query is a single action.

There are a variety of different queries that you can perform

- Select – selects a range of field values from one or more tables
- Insert – adds a record to a table
- Delete – deletes one or more records
- Update – modifies one or more records

In this chapter we will introduce each of these query types. Web Matrix offers support in creating appropriate SQL statements to meet your needs but it does not do all of the work for you. As with all web site design it is important to think carefully what you want to achieve. In the last chapter we created the Shopping database; in this chapter we are going to start to examine some of the functions of the web site that is going to use that database. Databases are not just used by customers they also need to be managed. An example of this with the Shopping database is that you may need to modify the current list of products. Figure 11.7 shows the interface we are going to develop that allows the owners of the site to manipulate the database through a web page.

This interface has been deliberately designed to highlight the use of different types of query we recognise that it is not ideal in terms of web usability. Before we go further your header for this example needs to refer to SQL server objects as follows:

```
<%@ Page Language="VB" Explicit="True" Debug="True" %>
<%@ import Namespace="System.Data" %>
<%@ import Namespace="System.Data.SqlClient" %>
```

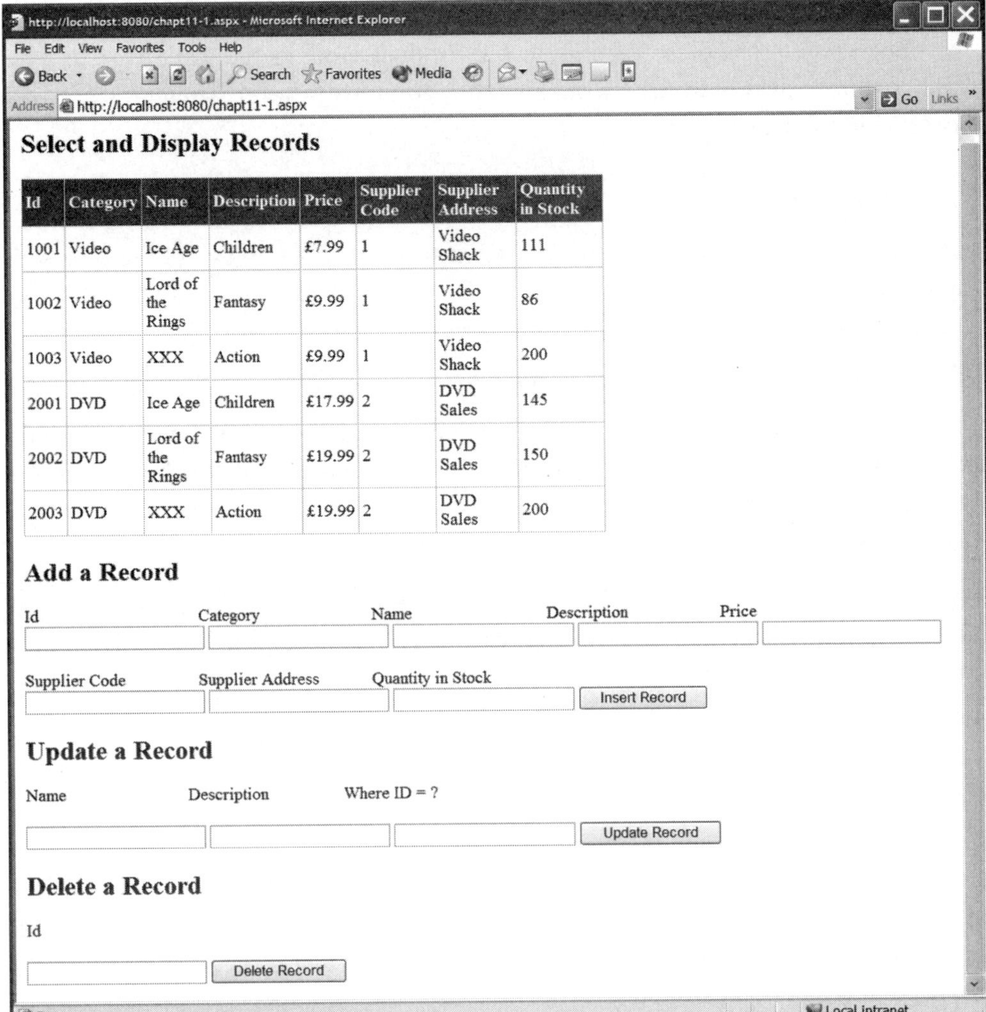

Figure 11.7: SQL in practice

Before we go any further we must ensure that our *Product* database table has some records. These records are illustrated in Table 11.1.

Table 11.1: Product table records

Id	Category	Name	Description	Price	Quantity in Stock	Supplier Address	Supplier Code
1001	Video	Ice Age	Children	£7.99	111	Video Shack	1
1002	Video	Lord of the Rings	Fantasy	£9.99	86	Video Shack	1
1003	Video	XXX	Action	£9.99	200	Video Shack	1
2001	DVD	Ice Age	Children	£17.99	145	DVD Sales	2
2002	DVD	Lord of the Rings	Fantasy	£19.99	150	DVD Sales	2
2003	DVD	XXX	Action	£19.99	200	DVD Sales	2

You should add these records to the Product table in the same way as you added customer details to the *Customer* table previously in this chapter. This was illustrated in Figures 11.4 and 11.5.

11.3.1 Select queries

Select queries are probably the most common form of query, they are the type you would use if you are wanting to display a set of records that match a particular set of criteria. The basic format of a *SELECT* statement is as follows:

```
SELECT field[s] FROM table[s] (WHERE field[s] match these criteria)
```

The actual syntax of a *SELECT* statement is more complex than this but this defines as much as you need. You will always need the *SELECT and FROM* elements, as in our next example that corresponds to the query for the *Select and Display Records* from Figure 11.7.

```
SELECT [Product].* FROM [Product]
```

This is a slight variation on our first example in that it uses *[Product].* * rather than simply *. This is a more complete form of the language in that it is possible to select items from more than one table.

11.3.2 Implementation of a Select query

The output from the Select query is displayed in an ASP.NET *DataGrid*. We have used a H2 heading for the title and then inserted a line and dragged a *DataGrid* onto the form. You should then select the AutoFormat option from the preferences for this object. This will display the dialog displayed in Figure 11.8 from which you need to select *Professional 2*.

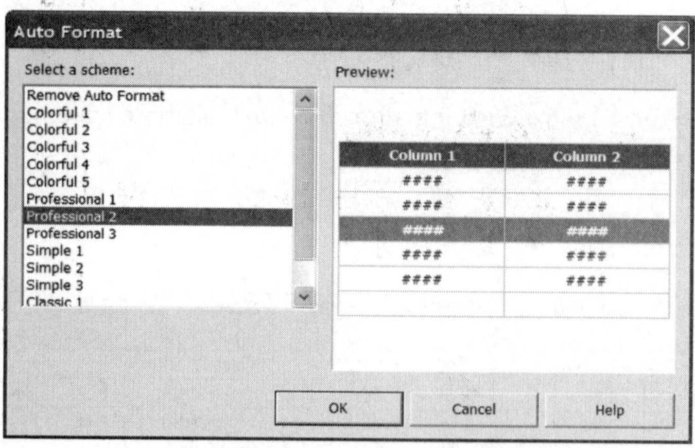

Figure 11.8: AutoFormat dialog

You should then select the *DataGrid* handles and increase its size. This provides us with a Design view in Figure 11.9 and the associated code which follows:

```
<h2>Select and Display Records
</h2>
<p>
   <asp:datagrid id="DataGrid1" runat="server" Width="493px"
          CellPadding="3" BackColor="White" EnableViewState="False"
          BorderStyle="None" BorderWidth="1px" BorderColor="#CCCCCC"
          Height="200px">
      <FooterStyle forecolor="#000066" backcolor="White"></FooterStyle>
      <HeaderStyle font-bold="True" forecolor="White"
          backcolor="#006699"></HeaderStyle>
      <PagerStyle horizontalalign="Left" forecolor="#000066"
          backcolor="White" mode="NumericPages"></PagerStyle>
      <SelectedItemStyle font-bold="True" forecolor="White"
          backcolor="#669999"></SelectedItemStyle>
      <ItemStyle forecolor="#000066"></ItemStyle>
   </asp:datagrid>
</p>
```

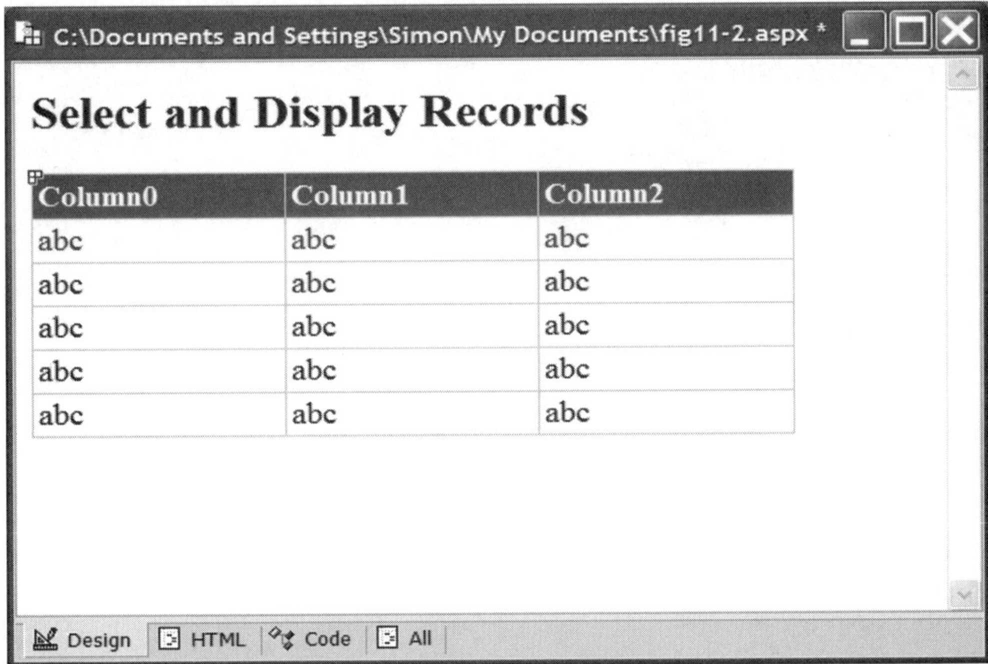

Figure 11.9: Select and Display Records Design view

You will notice that this is merely the definition of the grid and does not as yet associate any data with it. You should switch to code view. You will notice that the Toolbox has changed to Code Builders. The items available are designed to support the writing of code that includes SQL statements. You should drag the *SELECT* Data Method onto the code page. This presents you with the Connect to Database dialog. It will do this regardless of whether you have used the Workspace window to connect to a database already. What it is doing is generating the code that makes the connection. You should select the Shopping database from the Database drop-down list. This presents you with the Query Builder dialog in Figure 11.10.

By connecting to the Shopping database the dialog has retrieved its structure. It therefore knows that there are three tables and the fields within them as can be seen from the Columns window which is currently displaying the fields from the selected *CartItems* Table. We are interested in retrieving all of the field values from the *Product* table so you should select the *Product* table. This will display the following fields in the Columns window shown in Figure 11.11.

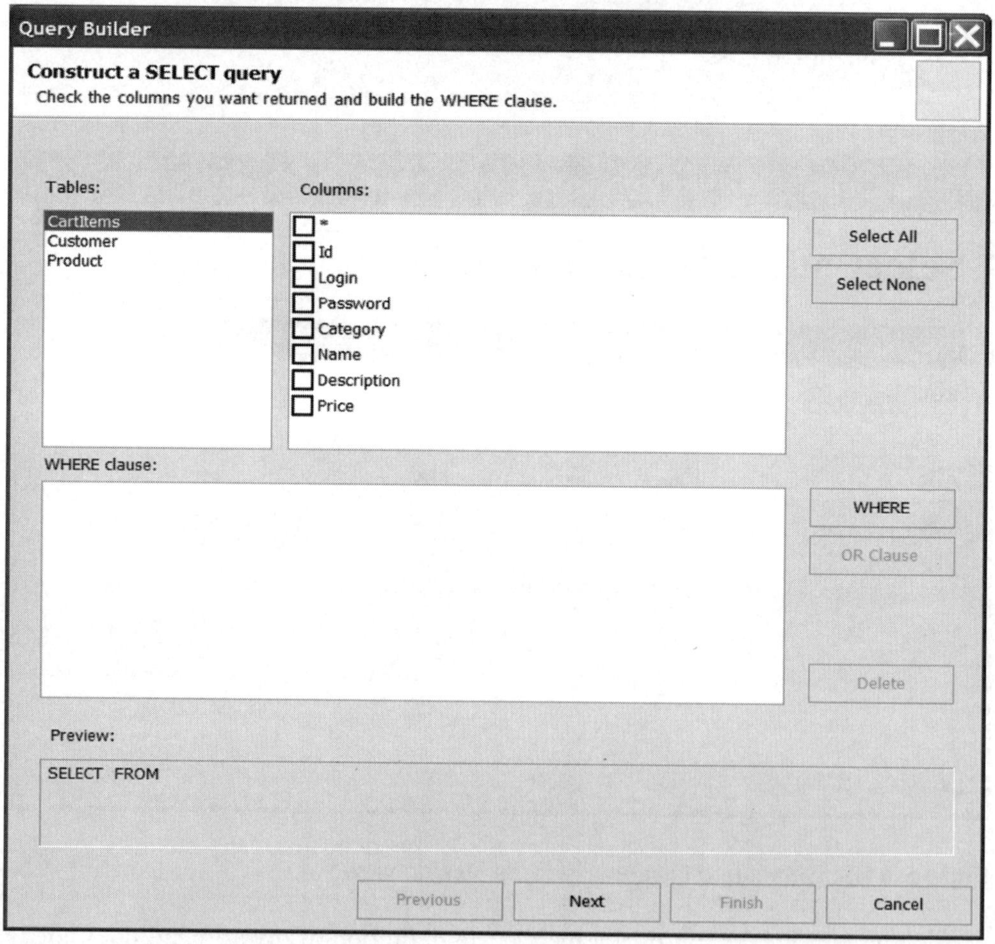

Figure 11.10: Query Builder dialog

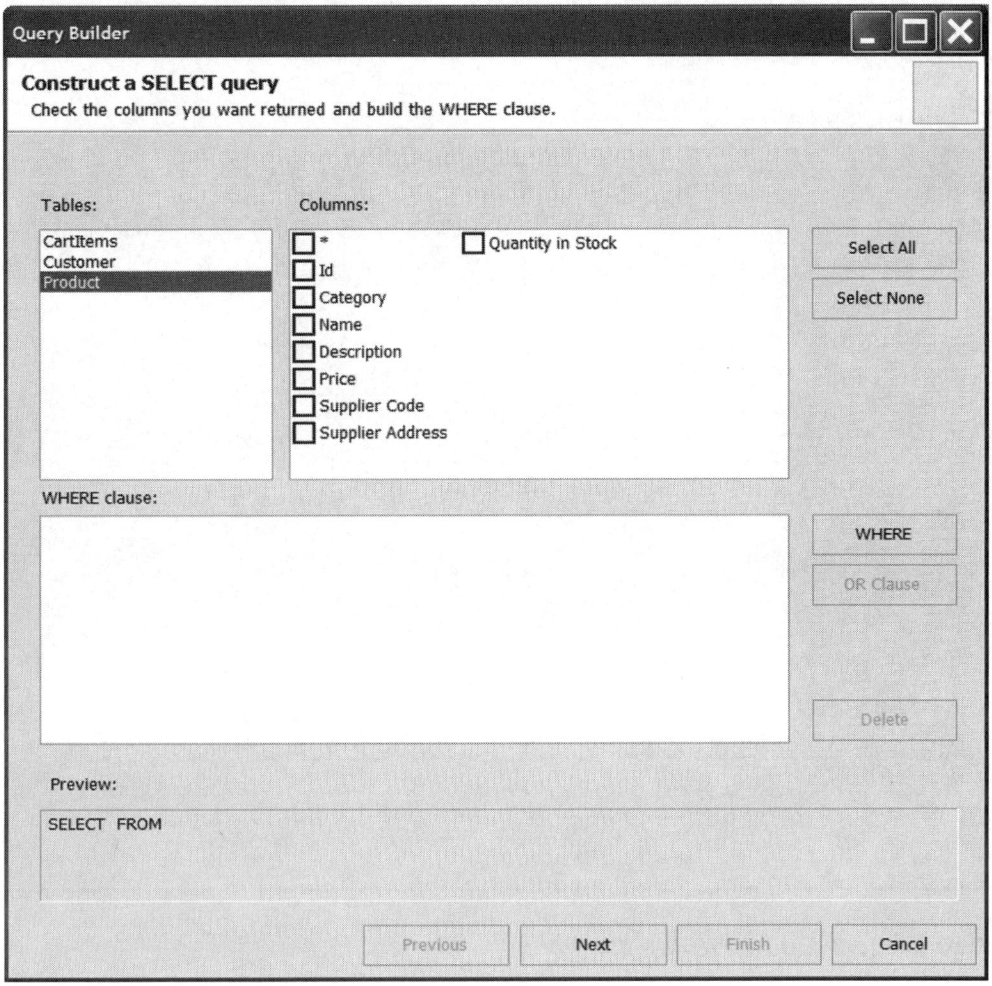

Figure 11.11: Product fields

You are able to select any number of fields as part of your query. You will notice that the first checkbox in the list is an asterisk (*). In SQL this means all fields. If you just want to display all fields without specifying, for example, their order or giving them more meaningful header names then the * is sufficient. If you do need to manipulate individual fields then you should not select the * but should select all of the individual fields. In this instance we are just going to display the field values unchanged so you should select the *. This will automatically change the value in the Preview window to: *SELECT [Product].* FROM [Product]* which as we already know means select all fields from the *Product* table. Click the Next button and you will see the *Query Preview* dialog, see Figure 11.12.

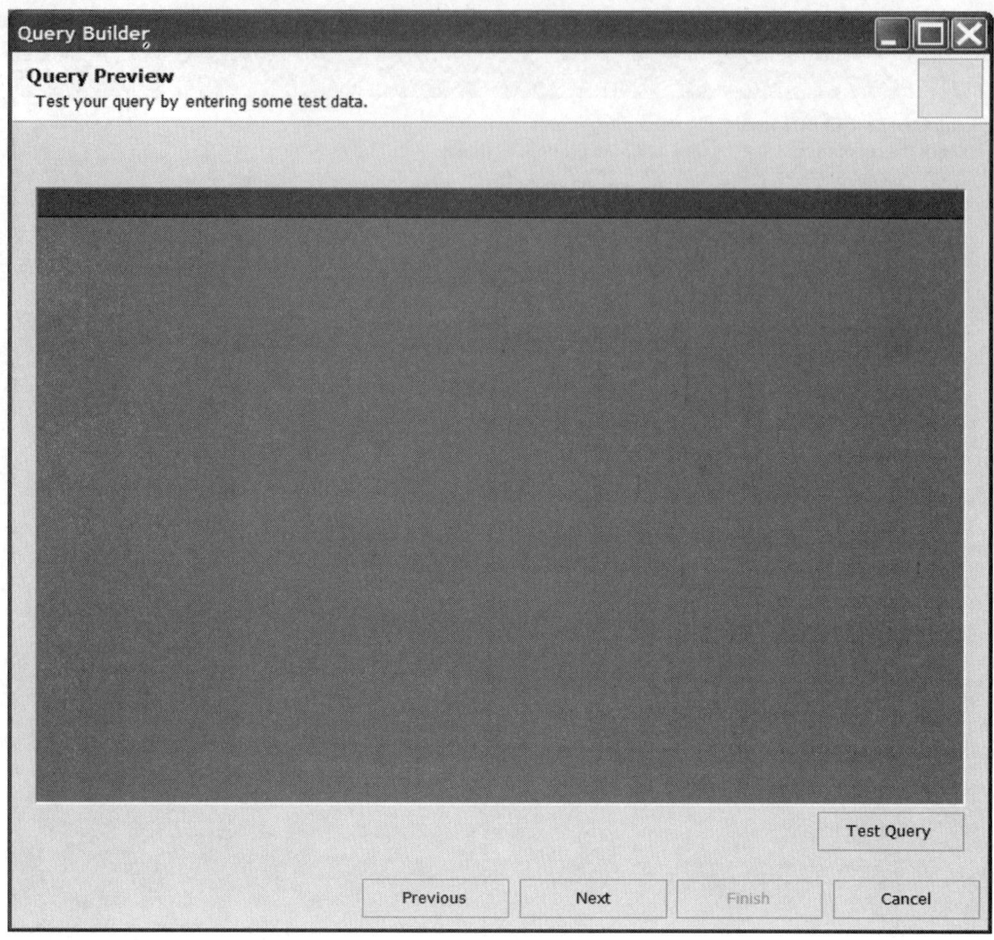

Figure 11.12: Query Preview dialog

By clicking the *Test Query* button you will see the output from the query as a table of values. This is illustrated in Figure 11.13. Click the *Next* button; this displays the final dialog in the wizard. This allows you to determine the name of the query and whether the output is in the form of a *DataSet* or a *DataReader*. You should change the default name to *Page_Load* (the reason for this will become apparent shortly.

You should also select *DataReader*. Really it doesn't matter whether you select *DataSet* or *DataReader* as you are going to change the code associated with the output. Click Finish.

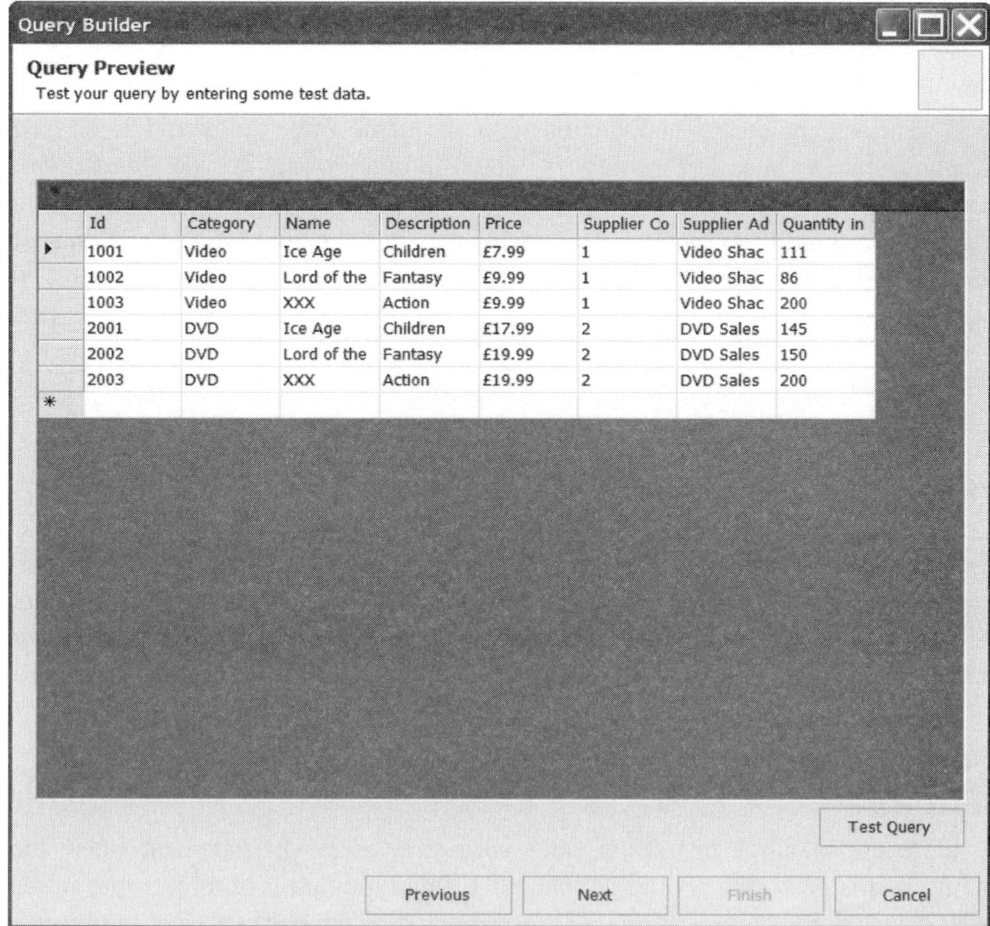

Figure 11.13: Test Query output

You should then be returned to the Code view where the following code has been inserted:

```
Function Page_Load() As System.Data.SqlClient.SqlDataReader
    Dim connectionString As String = "server='localhost'; trusted_connection=true;
        Database='shopping'"
    Dim sqlConnection As System.Data.SqlClient.SqlConnection = New
        System.Data.SqlClient.SqlConnection(connectionString)

    Dim queryString As String = "SELECT [Product].* FROM [Product]"
    Dim sqlCommand As System.Data.SqlClient.SqlCommand = New
        System.Data.SqlClient.SqlCommand(queryString, sqlConnection)

    sqlConnection.Open
    Dim dataReader As System.Data.SqlClient.SqlDataReader =
        sqlCommand.ExecuteReader(System.Data.CommandBehavior.CloseConn
        ection)
```

```
    Return dataReader
End Function
```

The wizard creates a Function with the name *Page_Load* and is of type *System.Data.SqlClient.SqlDataReader*, which in other words is type *DataReader*. But as we said we do not require a datareader function, what we need is a subroutine, so the first thing we need to change are the beginning and end lines of the function from:

```
Function Page_Load() As System.Data.SqlClient.SqlDataReader

End Function
```

To:

```
Sub Page_Load(Sender as Object, E as EventArgs)

End Sub
```

Page_Load(Sender as Object, E as EventArgs) is a special subroutine that will always run when the page is loaded. What we need to do is understand what this ex-function does so that we know where to change it. The first line creates a string variable that is then assigned the description for connecting the database:

```
Dim connectionString As String = "server='localhost'; trusted_connection=true;
    Database='shopping'"
```

In the next line this string value is used in an assign statement where the connection is passed to a variable that has a data type that is an object that stores SQL connections: *Data.SqlClient.SqlConnection*. Since the data type is an object it requires the keyword *New*:

```
Dim sqlConnection As System.Data.SqlClient.SqlConnection = New
    System.Data.SqlClient.SqlConnection(connectionString)
```

You will notice that both of these lines use a shortcut to declare and then assign values to a variable. We would argue that this is not good programming practice as it makes variable declaration hard to find as it is buried in the code. Nevertheless in this case we will leave the declarations as they are since we are more interested in you understanding what is happening in the code. The next line assigns the SQL statement to a string variable called *queryString*:

```
Dim queryString As String = "SELECT [Product].* FROM [Product]"
```

What is needed now is a command that will use the connection and the SQL statement; this is provided in the next line:

```
Dim sqlCommand As System.Data.SqlClient.SqlCommand = New
    System.Data.SqlClient.SqlCommand(queryString, sqlConnection)
```

The next line takes the SQL connection object and uses its *Open* method, this opens the connection for use:

```
sqlConnection.Open
```

Having opened the connection we then need to use the SQL command, but the remaining lines are assuming we are using an *SqlReader* when what we really want to do is display the output of the SQL in our DataGrid. Consequently we need to change the remaining lines. In the next line we want to change the object that is going to be assigned a value. Our original states that a *DataReader* object is defined and then assigned the SQL command

```
Dim dataReader As System.Data.SqlClient.SqlDataReader =
    sqlCommand.ExecuteReader(System.Data.CommandBehavior.CloseConn
    ection)
```

This needs to be changed to the following:

```
DataGrid1.DataSource =
    sqlCommand.ExecuteReader(CommandBehavior.CloseConnection)
```

This assigns the output of the command to the *DataSource* property of the object *DataGrid1*. We need one final command to make this subroutine work as required:

```
DataGrid1.DataBind()
```

You will also need to delete the line:

```
Return dataReader
```

The code for the updated subroutine is as follows:

```
Sub Page_Load(Sender as Object, E as EventArgs)
    Dim connectionString As String = "server='localhost';
trusted_connection=true; Database='shopping'"
    Dim sqlConnection As System.Data.SqlClient.SqlConnection = New
System.Data.SqlClient.SqlConnection(connectionString)

    Dim queryString As String = "SELECT [Product].* FROM [Product]"

    Dim sqlCommand As System.Data.SqlClient.SqlCommand = New
System.Data.SqlClient.SqlCommand(queryString, sqlConnection)

    sqlConnection.Open
    DataGrid1.DataSource =
sqlCommand.ExecuteReader(CommandBehavior.CloseConnection)
    DataGrid1.dataBind()
    End Sub
```

Now if we open the web page we will see Figure 11.14.

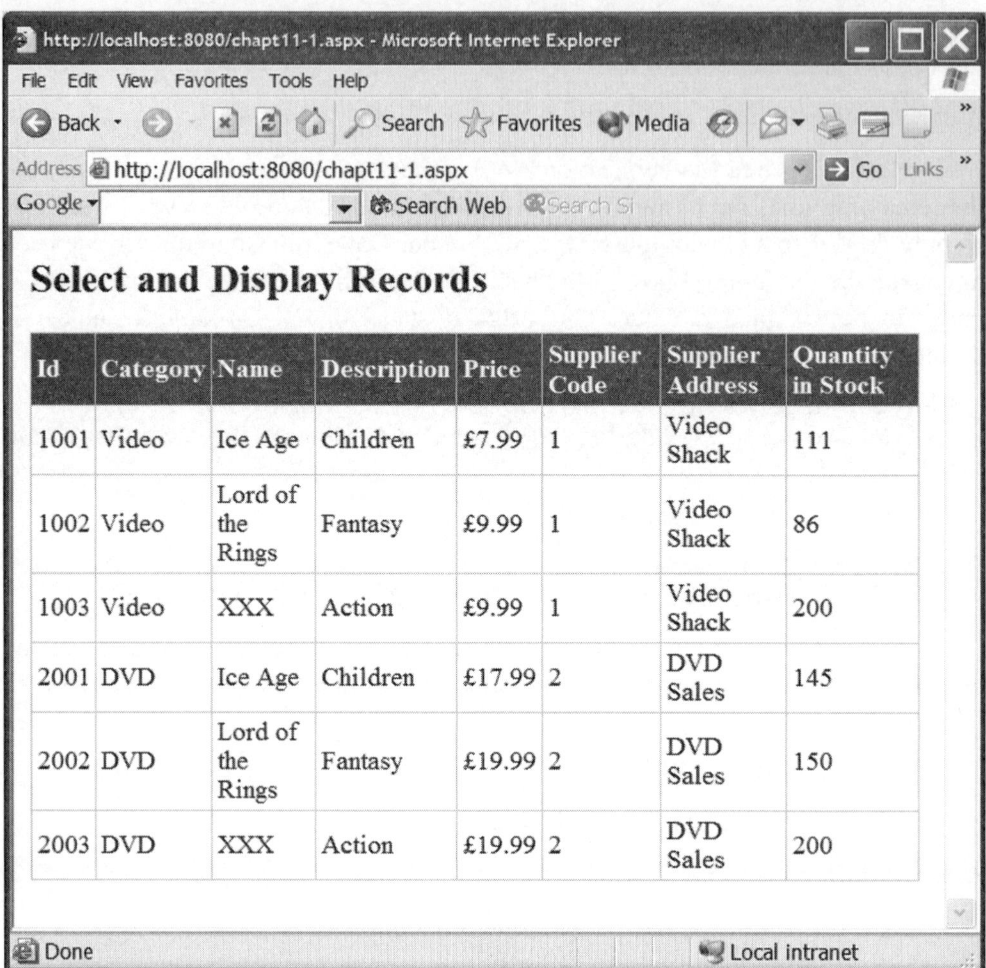

Figure 11.14: DataGrid output

11.3.3 Implementation of an Add query

To remind you, what we are trying to develop is shown in Figure 11.15.

Add a Record

Id   Category   Name   Description   Price

Supplier Code   Supplier Address   Quantity in Stock

Figure 11.15: Add a Record output

The code for the interface is as follows:

```
<h2>Add a Record
</h2>
<p>
  <asp:Label id="Label7" runat="server" Width="155px">Id</asp:Label>
  <asp:Label id="Label8" runat="server" Width="155px">Category</asp:Label>
  <asp:Label id="Label9" runat="server" Width="155px">Name</asp:Label>
  <asp:Label id="Label1" runat="server" Width="155px">Description</asp:Label>
  <asp:Label id="Label2" runat="server" Width="155px">Price</asp:Label>
  <br />
  <asp:TextBox id="txtId" runat="server"></asp:TextBox>
  <asp:TextBox id="txtCategory" runat="server"></asp:TextBox>
  <asp:TextBox id="txtName" runat="server"></asp:TextBox>
  <asp:TextBox id="txtDescription" runat="server"></asp:TextBox>
  <asp:TextBox id="txtPrice" runat="server"></asp:TextBox>
</p>
<p>
  <asp:Label id="Label3" runat="server" Width="155px">Supplier
Code</asp:Label>
  <asp:Label id="Label4" runat="server" Width="155px">Supplier
Address</asp:Label>
  <asp:Label id="Label5" runat="server" Width="155px">Quantity in
Stock</asp:Label>
  <br />
  <asp:TextBox id="txtCode" runat="server"></asp:TextBox>
  <asp:TextBox id="txtAddress" runat="server"></asp:TextBox>
  <asp:TextBox id="txtQuantity" runat="server"></asp:TextBox>
  <asp:Button id="Button1" onclick="insertcall" runat="server" Text="Insert
Record"></asp:Button>
</p>
```

You will need to add this code to your current ASP.NET web page. To do this click the HTML tab on the Document component window and add the code below the *</asp:DataGrid>* line. This is shown in Figure 11.16.

You will note that it consists of an H2 heading followed by five ASP.NET labels that have appropriate text values. In the next paragraph are five ASP.NET TextBoxes, their *id* values have been changed to reflect their type and purpose. Finally there is a button that has a meaningful text value and calls a subroutine called *insertcall* when the button is clicked.

We now need to add the appropriate code to make these objects work. In Section 11.3.2 we used the *SELECT Data Method* wizard to create and then modify a function to become a subroutine; we could do the same here but instead we are going to discuss the use of functions. In Chapter 8 we said that functions were blocks of code that returned a single value and as such were ideal if you wished to perform calculations. In addition we have used a number of VB.NET built-in functions like *ucase()*. In the current example we are going to use a function written, or at least manipulated by you. This is an arbitrary example and does not really show the power of functions but it does show how they are used.

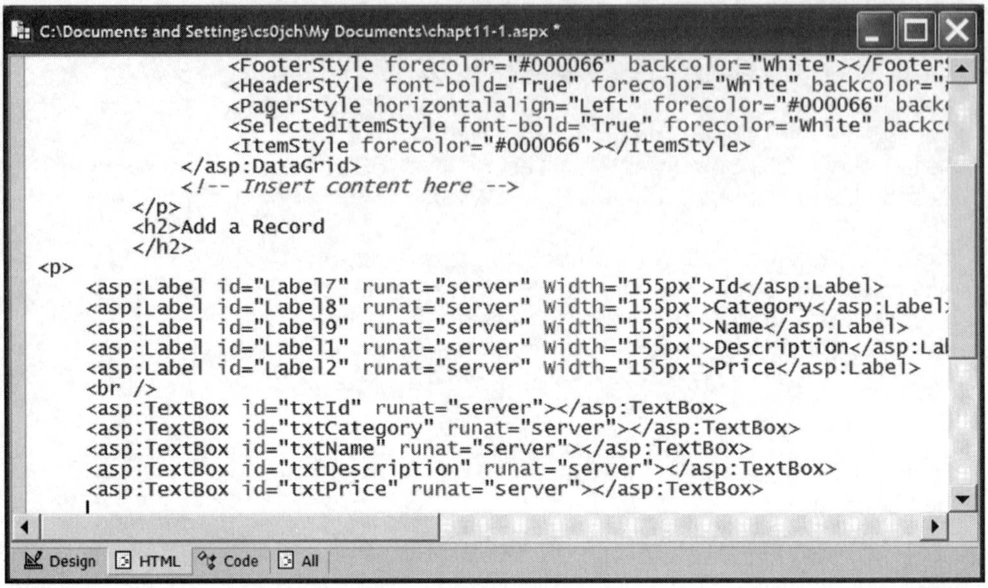

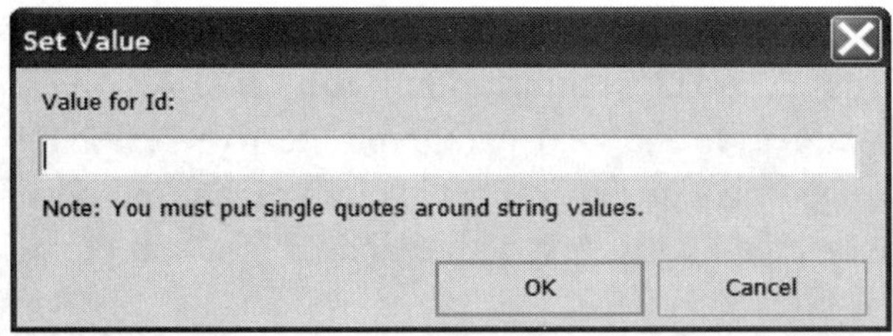

Figure 11.16: Add Record HTML

You need to be in Code view and then drag the *Insert Data Method* object from the toolbox and then select the Shopping database from the Connect to Database dialog. In the *Query Builder* select the *Product* table. As before this displays the fields from the table. We need to select all of the fields but if you attempt to select the *Id* field you will be presented with the dialog shown in Figure 11.17.

Figure 11.17: Set Value dialog

This dialog allows you to directly or indirectly enter values to this field. If you were entering a value for this field directly then you would enter the value in the textbox provided. With *Id* we know that its data type is Integer and so we could enter a numeric value for this field. Note the instruction provided in the dialog if the data type is text. We are going to add values to this field indirectly in that we are going to take the text values from textboxes on the web page. Consequently what is required is a filter that will hold the value to be stored in the field. This filter is like a variable but is indicated by an @ symbol in SQL. Consequently in this Value you should enter *@Id*. Repeat this process for the remaining fields using an @ symbol followed by the name of the field. Note, you should not include any spaces in the names of your filters. Therefore, *Supplier Code* should read *@SupplierCode*, *Supplier Address* should read *@SupplierAddress* and *Quantity* in Stock should read *@QuantityinStock*.

Once this has been done click the *Next* button. This will take you to the final dialog where you should name the function *InsertValue*. This will generate the following code:

```
Function InsertValue() As Integer
    Dim connectionString As String = "server='localhost';
trusted_connection=true; Database='shopping'"
    Dim sqlConnection As System.Data.SqlClient.SqlConnection = New
System.Data.SqlClient.SqlConnection(connectionString)

    Dim queryString As String = "INSERT INTO [Product] ([Id], [Category],
[Name], [Description], [Price], [Supplie"& _
"r Code], [Supplier Address], [Quantity in Stock]) VALUES (@Id, @Category,
@Name,"& _
" @Description, @Price, @SupplierCode, @SupplierAddress, @QuantityinStock)"

    Dim sqlCommand As System.Data.SqlClient.SqlCommand = New
System.Data.SqlClient.SqlCommand(queryString, sqlConnection)

    Dim rowsAffected As Integer = 0
    sqlConnection.Open
    Try
        rowsAffected = sqlCommand.ExecuteNonQuery
    Finally
        sqlConnection.Close
    End Try

    Return rowsAffected
End Function
```

The first two lines are familiar from the last section. The next line declares a string to store the SQL statement. This introduces the *SQL INSERT* statement. The first part of this statement defines the fields that are going to receive the inserted values:

```
INSERT INTO [Product] ([Id], [Category], [Name], [Description], [Price], [Supplier
Code], [Supplier Address], [Quantity in Stock])
```

The next part specifies the values to be inserted:

```
VALUES (@Id, @Category, @Name, @Description, @Price, @SupplierCode,
@SupplierAddress, @QuantityinStock)
```

Remember there are currently no values in the filters. The next line creates the SQL command from the connection and the SQL statement. The remainder of the code determines the number of rows affected by the operation of this query:

```
Dim rowsAffected As Integer = 0
sqlConnection.Open
Try
    rowsAffected = sqlCommand.ExecuteNonQuery
Finally
    sqlConnection.Close
End Try


Return rowsAffected
```

The *Try, Finally* and *End Try* construct is one that we are not going to cover in this book. Suffice to say, the connection is opened, the SQL command statement run and the rows affected returned and assigned to the initialised variable *rowsAffected* and then the connection is closed again.

None of the code in this function assigns values from the web page to the appropriate filters; therefore we need to write it. The code required is as follows and should be inserted after the declaration of *sqlCommand*:

```
    sqlCommand.Parameters.Add("@Id", System.Data.SqlDbType.Char).Value =
id
    sqlCommand.Parameters.Add("@Category",
System.Data.SqlDbType.Char).Value = category
    sqlCommand.Parameters.Add("@Name",
System.Data.SqlDbType.Char).Value = name
    sqlCommand.Parameters.Add("@Description",
System.Data.SqlDbType.Char).Value = description
    sqlCommand.Parameters.Add("@Price",
System.Data.SqlDbType.Char).Value = price
    sqlCommand.Parameters.Add("@SupplierCode",
System.Data.SqlDbType.Char).Value = SCode
    sqlCommand.Parameters.Add("@SupplierAddress",
System.Data.SqlDbType.Char).Value = SAddress
    sqlCommand.Parameters.Add("@QuantityinStock",
System.Data.SqlDbType.Char).Value = Quantity
```

We will explain the first of these lines as the other four use the same format for the other variables and associated filters:

```
sqlCommand.Parameters.Add("@Id", System.Data.SqlDbType.Char).Value = id
```

This uses the *Add* method which has two arguments/parameters: the filter to receive the value and its data type. The data type is set as Char because whilst the field is data type Integer the value is being passed from a Textbox which is of data type Char. The *Value* property is then assigned the value currently stored in the variable *id*.

There is something to note here; all of the elements in this statement are separated by dots. The reason for this is that it is a single object command that uses methods from within itself. This seems odd and really is quite difficult to explain in a few short words. Microsoft deals with what is termed the Common Object Model which is a variation on Object orientation. All objects have properties and methods but these objects are complex in structure and have a hierarchy. In order to assign a value to a particular property of an object you not only need to know the property name but also the place of that property within the object hierarchy and you must state this explicitly. For example an *SqlCommand* object is defined as being an element of SqlClient, which in turn is a Data element of System as in *System.Data.SqlClient.SqlCommand*. But that isn't the end because we wish to use that command and it in turn has elements of which one is Parameters, it in turn has an Add() method which has a property called Value. You need only be aware that this object model exists at this stage, however if you are going to be working with Microsoft's products extensively then it will be useful to you if you spent some time familiarising yourself with the various hierarchies involved.

This nearly completes the function but you would have noticed that the four Add commands assign variable values and that these variables are not defined. Consequently we need to modify the arguments passed to the Function so that it reads as follows:

```
Function insertvalue(ByVal id As String, ByVal category As String, ByVal name As String, ByVal description As String, ByVal price As String, ByVal SCode As String, ByVal SAddress As String, ByVal Quantity As String) As Integer
```

This means that each of the variables is passed into the function when it is called. The *ByVal* statement before each declaration means that it is only the current value of the variable that is passed and that any change made to it inside the function will not affect the original values. It is as though new local instances of the variables have been created that allow you to play around with their values but do not harm the main program. Unfortunately we cannot use functions in the same way as subroutines in that they cannot be called from, for example, a button's on click event. Therefore we need a subroutine to call the function which we will call *insertcall()*. The code for this subroutine is below:

```
sub insertcall(Sender as Object, E as EventArgs)
    Dim Id as string = txtId.text
    Dim Category as string = txtCategory.text
    Dim Name as string = txtName.text
    Dim Description as string = txtDescription.text
    Dim Price as string = txtPrice.text
    Dim SCode as string = txtCode.text
    Dim SAddress as string = txtAddress.text
    Dim Quantity as string = txtQuantity.text
```

```
    Dim rows as integer = insertvalue(Id, Category, Name, Description, Price,
SCode, SAddress, Quantity)
    txtId.text = ""
    txtCategory.text = ""
    txtName.text = ""
    txtDescription.text = ""
    txtPrice.text = ""
    txtCode.text = ""
    txtAddress.text = ""
    txtQuantity.text = ""
    Call Page_Load(Sender, E)
  end sub
```

This is a relatively simple subroutine, it starts with the declaration of five variables each of which is assigned the appropriate text property value from the web page. The next line calls the function we have just written. As with all functions the call is located on the right-hand side of the assign statement since the function must return a value. Reflecting back to the function, *insertvalue()* is of data type integer so the value that is returned from the function must also be assigned to an integer variable. This is the case in our subroutine where the variable *rows* has been declared to store the assigned value. The rows variable you will notice is not used beyond accepting the returned value from the function. As we indicated earlier this is an arbitrary use of a function to show how they could be applied rather than its ideal use. Having called the function the text properties of the text boxes are initialised to empty strings to allow the user to add another record. The final line of this subroutine is interesting in that it is a call to another subroutine, in this case the *Page_load()* subroutine we discussed in the last section. As you will remember this subroutine runs a query that selects all the records from the *Product* table and then displays them in the datagrid. In this case it has the effect of refreshing the display within the *datagrid* to include the record just added.

We are going to add a new record to the table. The new product record is illustrated in Table 11.2.

Table 11.2: New product record

Id	Category	Name	Description	Price	Quantity in Stock	Supplier Address	Supplier Code
1004	Video	X Men 2	Action	£10.99	50	Video Shack	1

Load the web page in a browser and in the form fields presented enter the data in Table 11.2. When you click the Insert Record button you should be presented with a screen similar to that in Figure 11.18.

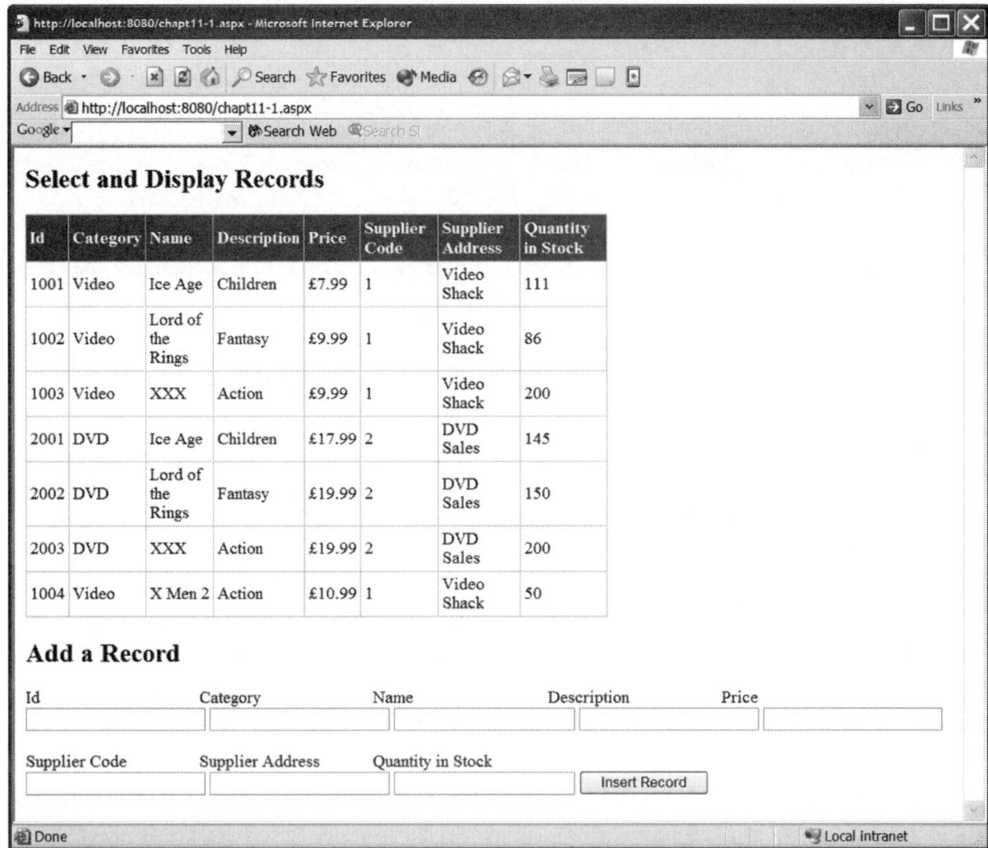

Figure 11.18: Add a Record

11.3.4 Implementation of an Update query

The next part of the interface involves the use of an *Update* query. This type of query is used when you want to update values stored in existing records. In our example we want the user to be able to select a particular record by its Id, which they can see from the datagrid. We have structured this element of the interface to conform to the syntax of the SQL *Update* statement, as such it is not necessarily the most intuitive layout. This element of the interface can be seen in Figure 11.19, where we have made the assumption that the user would only wish to update the Name and Description fields for a single record. The associated design code is as follows:

```
<h2>Update a Record </h2>
<p>
  <asp:Label id="Label10" runat="server" Width="145px">Name</asp:Label>
  <asp:Label id="Label11" runat="server" Width="139px">Description</asp:Label>
  <asp:Label id="Label12" runat="server">Where ID = ?</asp:Label>
</p>
```

```
<p>
  <asp:TextBox id="txtnamechange" runat="server"></asp:TextBox>
  <asp:TextBox id="txtdescriptionchange" runat="server"></asp:TextBox>
  <asp:TextBox id="txtWhere" runat="server"></asp:TextBox>
  <asp:Button id="Button2" onclick="updatecall" runat="server" Text="Update
      Record"></asp:Button>
</p>
```

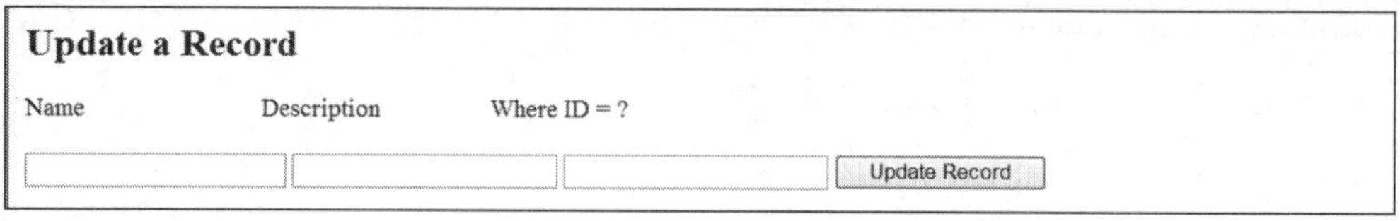

Update a Record

Name	Description	Where ID = ?	
			Update Record

Figure 11.19: Update a Record output

As with the Add record design code this consists of a heading followed by labels and then textboxes below that will receive the user input. Finally there is a button that when clicked will call a subroutine called *updatecall()*.

Having created the interface we now need the code. From the code view drag *UPDATE* data method below the current block of code. This opens the Connect to Database dialog from which you need to select the Shopping database. Once the Query Builder is displayed you need to select the Product table. You will see from Figure 11.19 that we will not be using all the fields and are only allowing the user to change the *Name* and *Description* fields for a particular record. You need to be aware that if the user only wishes to change one of these fields they would still need to enter the other original value. If the user just leaves it blank then when the system is updated that field will be blank.

In order to create the query code you need to be in Code view and then drag the *UPDATE* data method to a line below the last block of code. This gives you the Connect to Database dialog and as before you need to select the Shopping database. The *Query Builder* dialog is then displayed and you should select the Product Table. From the Columns window you should click the Name field. This will display the Set Value dialog in Figure 11.20.

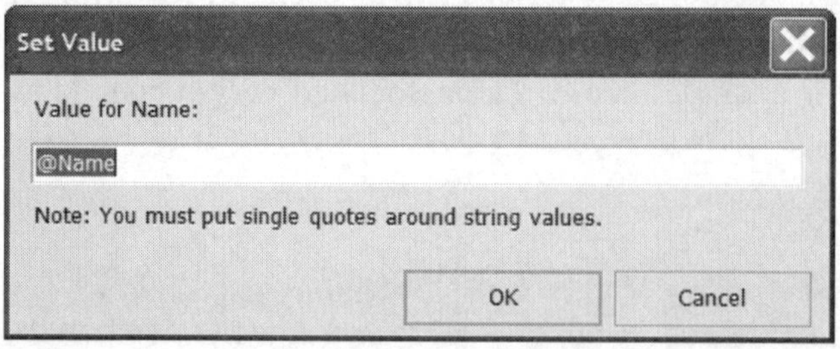

Figure 11.20: Set Value dialog for INSERT query

This automatically places a filter in the *Value* field and you should just click OK as it is appropriate for our needs. Do the same for the *Description* field, now you have a Preview output that states:

```
UPDATE [Product] SET [Name]=@Name, [Description]=@Description
```

However the statement so far does not say which record needs to be updated. This is where the *WHERE* part of the statement comes in. Click on the *WHERE* button and you are presented with the dialog shown in Figure 11.21.

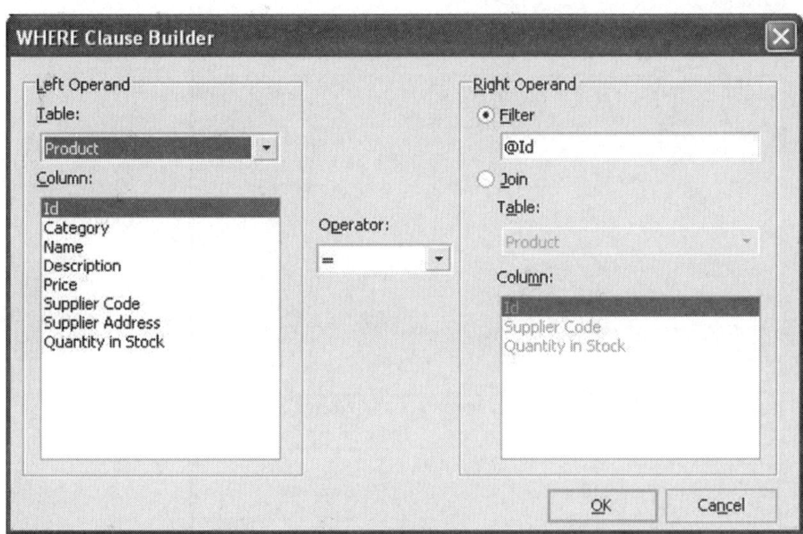

Figure 11.21: WHERE Clause Builder

This consists of two Operands (Left and Right) and an Operator. The left operand is the thing you want to test. The Table has defaulted to Product as we are currently using it and the column has defaulted to Id as it is the first field in the table. Luckily this is the field/table combination we need. What we are trying to do is to obtain a test that says we want to update the field *WHERE* the *Id* field in the Product table is equal to a value entered by the user. Since we are looking for something to be equal to *Id* then the default Operator is correct. The right operand allows you to use either a filter or a value from another table. Since we want to use a value from the web page the default filter is appropriate. So all you have to do is click *OK*. This will return you back to the Query Builder dialog which should now look like Figure 11.22.

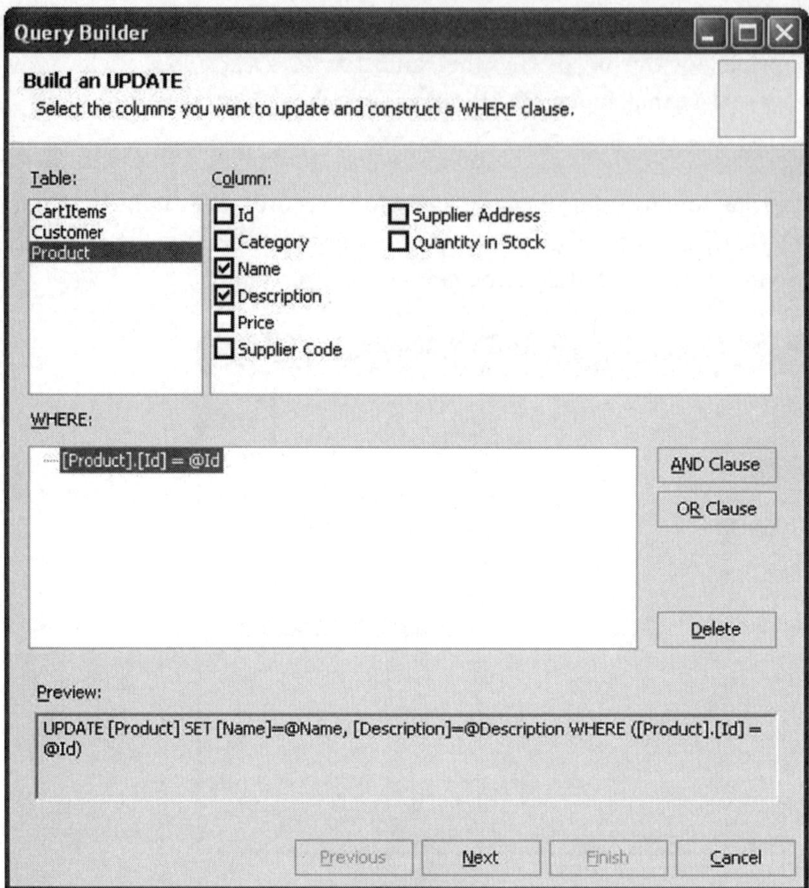

Figure 11.22: Completed Update query dialog

By clicking the *Next* button this will take you to the Preview screen, just click the Next button and rename the function as *updatevalue* and click *Finish*. This will create the following code:

```
Function updatevalue(ByVal id As Integer, ByVal name As String, ByVal
        description As String) As Integer
Dim connectionString As String = "server='localhost'; trusted_connection=true;
        Database='shopping'"
Dim sqlConnection As System.Data.SqlClient.SqlConnection = New
        System.Data.SqlClient.SqlConnection(connectionString)

Dim queryString As String = "UPDATE [Product] SET [Name]=@Name,
        [Description]=@Description WHERE ([Product].[Id] = @Id)"
Dim sqlCommand As System.Data.SqlClient.SqlCommand = New
        System.Data.SqlClient.SqlCommand(queryString, sqlConnection)

sqlCommand.Parameters.Add("@Id", System.Data.SqlDbType.Int).Value = id
sqlCommand.Parameters.Add("@Name", System.Data.SqlDbType.Char).Value =
```

```
name
sqlCommand.Parameters.Add("@Description",
        System.Data.SqlDbType.Char).Value = description

    Dim rowsAffected As Integer = 0
    sqlConnection.Open
    Try
        rowsAffected = sqlCommand.ExecuteNonQuery
    Finally
        sqlConnection.Close
    End Try

    Return rowsAffected
End Function
```

The wizard that controls the code construction for *UPDATE* queries provides more appropriate output than that of the *ADD* wizard. As such this code can remain unchanged. If you examine the code you will find that in principle it is structured the same way as the *ADD* query and we are going to call this function in the similar way. Therefore we need to write the following subroutine:

```
sub updatecall(Sender as Object, E as EventArgs)

    Dim Id as integer = cint(txtwhere.text)
    Dim Name as string = txtnamechange.text
    Dim Description as string = txtdescriptionchange.text

    Dim rows as integer = updatevalue(Id, Name, Description)

    txtwhere.text = ""
    txtnamechange.text = ""
    txtdescriptionchange.text = ""

    Call Page_Load(Sender, E)

end sub
```

There are minor differences; firstly you need to create three variables. The variable for Id we are going to convert to its appropriate data type, namely an Integer. However, as noted in the previous section the text property of an object returns a text value regardless of whether a numeric value is stored in it. Consequently we need to convert this value to an Integer before it is passed to the variable otherwise we would get an error. To do this we are introducing another in-built function of VB.NET called *cint()*. This takes a text value passed as an argument and returns its integer equivalent. The function is then called and the variable values passed as arguments. The returned value of the function is then assigned to the variable *rows*. The field values are then initialised to allow another update and the datagrid is refreshed by calling the *Page_Load* subroutine.

Load the web page into a web browser and in the Name field below the Update a record text type "*X Men 2*". In the *description* type "*Sci-Fi*" and in the *ID* field type "1004". Clicking the *Update Record* button should result in the X Men 2 Video record being updated, as shown in Figure 11.23.

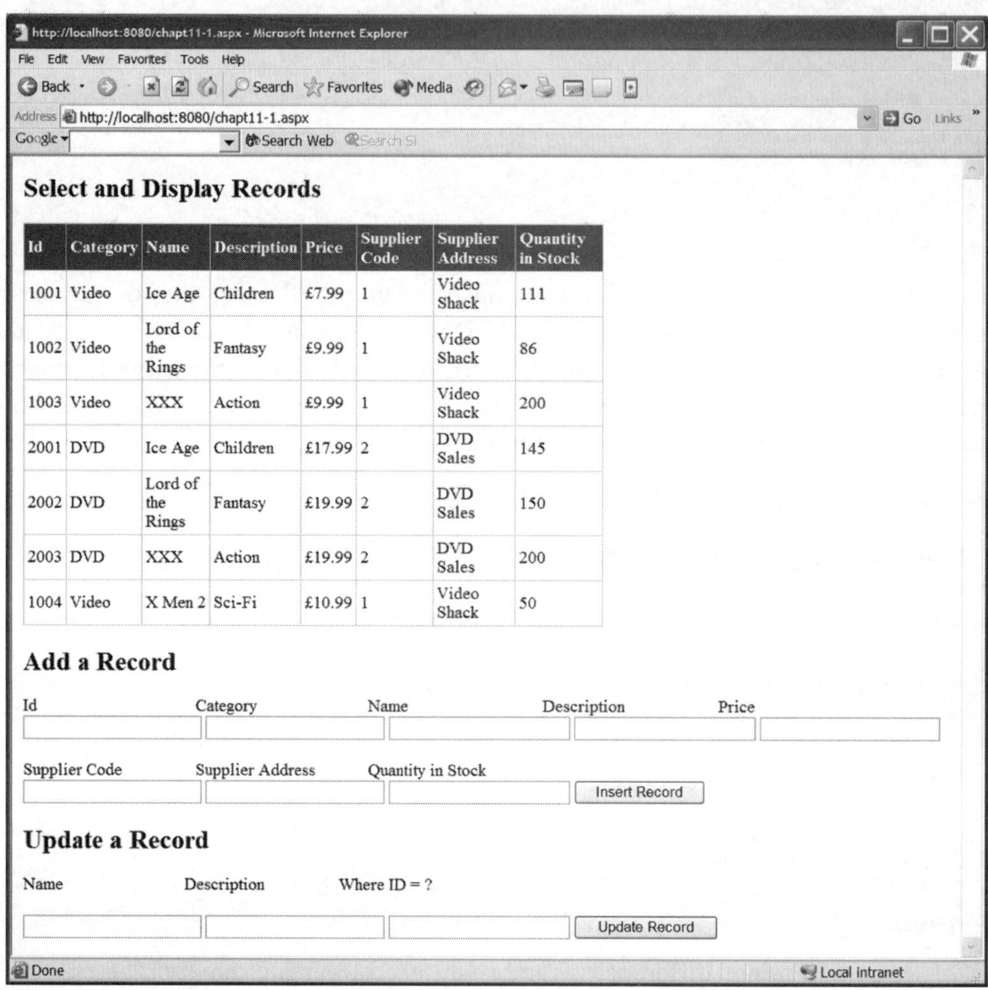

Figure 11.23: Updating a Record

11.3.5 Implementation of a Delete query

The final part of the interface requires the development of a *Delete* query. A delete query deletes one or more records that match specific criteria. In our case we want to be able to delete a single record and as such since the key value for the Product table uniquely identifies an individual record we will use the Id field to select the record for deletion. The interface is laid out as in Figure 11.24.

Delete a Record

Id

[________________] [Delete Record]

Figure 11.24: Delete a Record output

The code generated for this design is as follows:

```
<h2>Delete a Record
</h2>
<p>
    <asp:Label id="Label13" runat="server" Width="144px">Id</asp:Label>
</p>
<p>
    <asp:TextBox id="txtIdDelete" runat="server"></asp:TextBox>
    <asp:Button id="Button3" onclick="deletecall" runat="server" Text="Delete
        Record"></asp:Button>
</p>
```

This interface provides a single entry field as described above and a button. When the user clicks this button it calls a subroutine called *deletecall*. To implement the code for this part of the interface you need to switch to Code view and then drag *DELETE* data method to a line below the last block of code. You need to connect to the Shopping database and then you are passed to the Query Builder dialog. You should select the Product table and then click the *WHERE* button. This will display a dialog similar to the one shown in Figure 11.25.

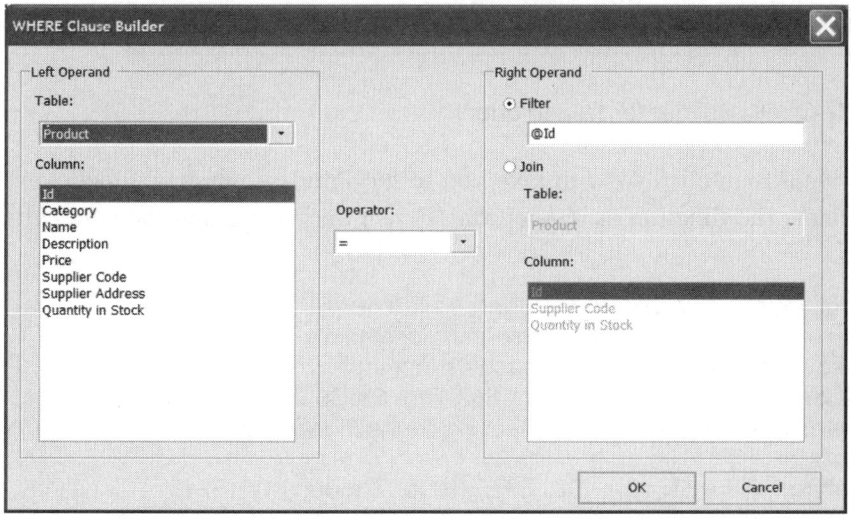

Figure 11.25: WHERE Clause Builder

You should accept the values displayed. This will return you to the Query Builder, where the output should look like Figure 11.26.

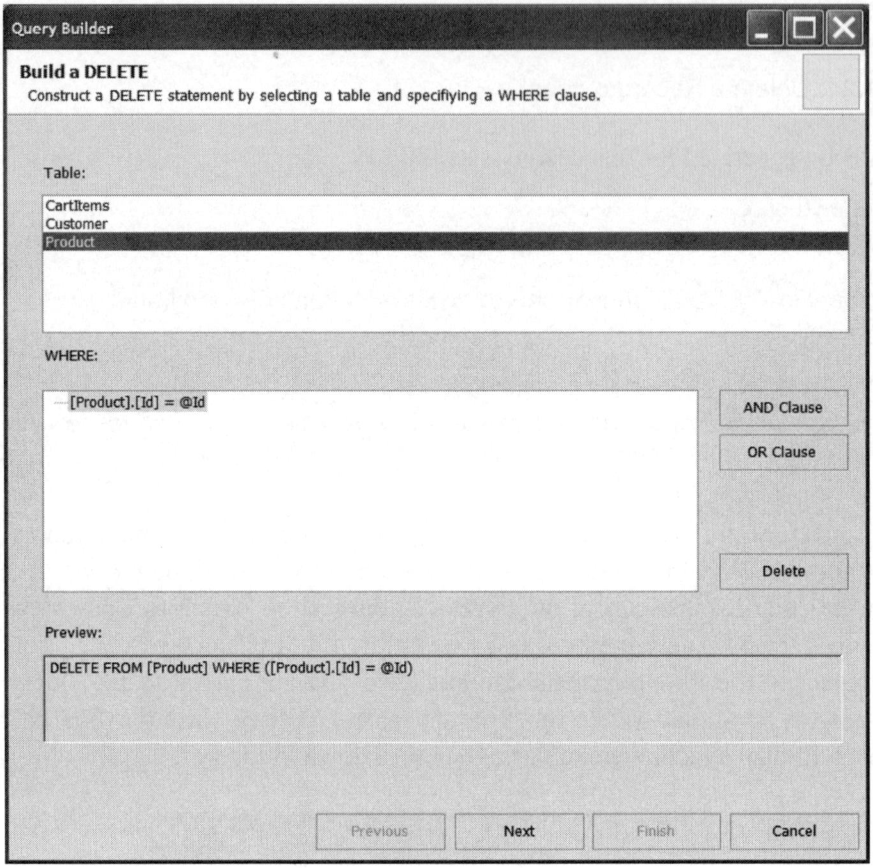

Figure **11.26**: Query Builder for Delete query

You should then click *Next* to take you to the Preview window. Click *Next* again and rename the function as *deletevalue*. Finish the wizard and the code will be as follows:

```
Function deletevalue(ByVal id As Integer) As Integer
    Dim connectionString As String = "server='localhost';
        trusted_connection=true; Database='shopping'"
    Dim sqlConnection As System.Data.SqlClient.SqlConnection = New
        System.Data.SqlClient.SqlConnection(connectionString)

    Dim queryString As String = "DELETE FROM [Product] WHERE
        ([Product].[Id] = @Id)"
    Dim sqlCommand As System.Data.SqlClient.SqlCommand = New
        System.Data.SqlClient.SqlCommand(queryString, sqlConnection)
```

```
    sqlCommand.Parameters.Add("@Id", System.Data.SqlDbType.Int).Value = id

    Dim rowsAffected As Integer = 0
    sqlConnection.Open
    Try
        rowsAffected = sqlCommand.ExecuteNonQuery
    Finally
        sqlConnection.Close
    End Try

    Return rowsAffected
End Function
```

As with the *Update* query we do not need to change this code but we do need to create the subroutine that calls it. The code for this is as follows:

```
sub deletecall(Sender as Object, E as EventArgs)

    Dim Id as integer = cint(txtIdDelete.text)

    Dim rows as integer = deletevalue(Id)

    txtIdDelete.text = ""

    Call Page_Load(Sender, E)

end sub
```

The meaning of this code should be apparent as it is a simpler version of that used in the *Update* query.

Load the web page into a browser and in the Id field under the Delete Record title enter "*1004*" and click the "*Delete Record*" Button. The new X Men record which we added to the database should be deleted.

11.3.6 The code for SQL example

This completes the example and what follows is the complete ASP.NET code:

```
<%@ Page Language="VB" Explicit="True" Debug="True" %>
<%@ import Namespace="System.Data" %>
<%@ import Namespace="System.Data.SqlClient" %>
<script runat="server">

  ' Insert page code here
  '
    Sub Page_Load(Sender as Object, E as EventArgs)
        Dim connectionString As String = "server='localhost';
trusted_connection=true; Database='shopping'"
        Dim sqlConnection As System.Data.SqlClient.SqlConnection = New
System.Data.SqlClient.SqlConnection(connectionString)
```

```
    Dim queryString As String = "SELECT [Product].* FROM [Product]"

    Dim sqlCommand As System.Data.SqlClient.SqlCommand = New
System.Data.SqlClient.SqlCommand(queryString, sqlConnection)

    sqlConnection.Open
    DataGrid1.DataSource =
sqlCommand.ExecuteReader(CommandBehavior.CloseConnection)
    DataGrid1.dataBind()
  End Sub


    Function insertvalue(ByVal id As String, ByVal category As String, ByVal
name As String, ByVal description As String, ByVal price As String, ByVal SCode
As String, ByVal SAddress As String, ByVal Quantity As String) As Integer
    Dim connectionString As String = "server='localhost';
trusted_connection=true; Database='shopping'"
    Dim sqlConnection As System.Data.SqlClient.SqlConnection = New
System.Data.SqlClient.SqlConnection(connectionString)

    Dim queryString As String = "INSERT INTO [Product] ([Id], [Category],
[Name], [Description], [Price], [Supplie"& _
  "r Code], [Supplier Address], [Quantity in Stock]) VALUES (@Id, @Category,
@Name,"& _
  " @Description, @Price, @SupplierCode, @SupplierAddress,
@QuantityinStock)"


    Dim sqlCommand As System.Data.SqlClient.SqlCommand = New
System.Data.SqlClient.SqlCommand(queryString, sqlConnection)

    sqlCommand.Parameters.Add("@Id", System.Data.SqlDbType.Char).Value
= id
    sqlCommand.Parameters.Add("@Category",
System.Data.SqlDbType.Char).Value = category
    sqlCommand.Parameters.Add("@Name",
System.Data.SqlDbType.Char).Value = name
    sqlCommand.Parameters.Add("@Description",
System.Data.SqlDbType.Char).Value = description
    sqlCommand.Parameters.Add("@Price",
System.Data.SqlDbType.Char).Value = price
    sqlCommand.Parameters.Add("@SupplierCode",
System.Data.SqlDbType.Char).Value = SCode
    sqlCommand.Parameters.Add("@SupplierAddress",
System.Data.SqlDbType.Char).Value = SAddress
    sqlCommand.Parameters.Add("@QuantityinStock",
System.Data.SqlDbType.Char).Value = Quantity


    Dim rowsAffected As Integer = 0
```

```vbnet
        sqlConnection.Open
        Try
            rowsAffected = sqlCommand.ExecuteNonQuery
        Finally
            sqlConnection.Close
        End Try

        Return rowsAffected
    End Function

    sub insertcall(Sender as Object, E as EventArgs)
        Dim Id as string = txtId.text
        Dim Category as string = txtCategory.text
        Dim Name as string = txtName.text
        Dim Description as string = txtDescription.text
        Dim Price as string = txtPrice.text
        Dim SCode as string = txtCode.text
        Dim SAddress as string = txtAddress.text
        Dim Quantity as string = txtQuantity.text

        Dim rows as integer = insertvalue(Id, Category, Name, Description, Price,
SCode, SAddress, Quantity)
        txtId.text = ""
        txtCategory.text = ""
        txtName.text = ""
        txtDescription.text = ""
        txtPrice.text = ""
        txtCode.text = ""
        txtAddress.text = ""
        txtQuantity.text = ""

        Call Page_Load(Sender, E)
    end sub


    Function updatevalue(ByVal id As Integer, ByVal name As String, ByVal
description As String) As Integer
        Dim connectionString As String = "server='localhost';
trusted_connection=true; Database='shopping'"
        Dim sqlConnection As System.Data.SqlClient.SqlConnection = New
System.Data.SqlClient.SqlConnection(connectionString)

        Dim queryString As String = "UPDATE [Product] SET [Name]=@Name,
[Description]=@Description WHERE ([Product].[I"& _
    "d] = @Id)"
        Dim sqlCommand As System.Data.SqlClient.SqlCommand = New
System.Data.SqlClient.SqlCommand(queryString, sqlConnection)

        sqlCommand.Parameters.Add("@Id", System.Data.SqlDbType.Int).Value =
id
```

```
        sqlCommand.Parameters.Add("@Name",
System.Data.SqlDbType.Char).Value = name
        sqlCommand.Parameters.Add("@Description",
System.Data.SqlDbType.Char).Value = description

        Dim rowsAffected As Integer = 0
        sqlConnection.Open
        Try
           rowsAffected = sqlCommand.ExecuteNonQuery
        Finally
           sqlConnection.Close
        End Try

        Return rowsAffected
    End Function

  sub updatecall(Sender as Object, E as EventArgs)

    Dim Id as integer = cint(txtwhere.text)
    Dim Name as string = txtnamechange.text
    Dim Description as string = txtdescriptionchange.text

    Dim rows as integer = updatevalue(Id, Name, Description)

    txtwhere.text = ""
    txtnamechange.text = ""
    txtdescriptionchange.text = ""

    Call Page_Load(Sender, E)

  end sub


    Function deletevalue(ByVal id As Integer) As Integer
        Dim connectionString As String = "server='localhost';
trusted_connection=true; Database='shopping'"
        Dim sqlConnection As System.Data.SqlClient.SqlConnection = New
System.Data.SqlClient.SqlConnection(connectionString)

        Dim queryString As String = "DELETE FROM [Product] WHERE
([Product].[Id] = @Id)"
        Dim sqlCommand As System.Data.SqlClient.SqlCommand = New
System.Data.SqlClient.SqlCommand(queryString, sqlConnection)

        sqlCommand.Parameters.Add("@Id", System.Data.SqlDbType.Int).Value =
id

        Dim rowsAffected As Integer = 0
        sqlConnection.Open
        Try
```

```
          rowsAffected = sqlCommand.ExecuteNonQuery
        Finally
          sqlConnection.Close
        End Try

        Return rowsAffected
      End Function

      sub deletecall(Sender as Object, E as EventArgs)

        Dim Id as integer = cint(txtIdDelete.text)

        Dim rows as integer = deletevalue(Id)

        txtIdDelete.text = ""

        Call Page_Load(Sender, E)

      end sub

</script>
<html>
<head>
</head>
<body>
  <form runat="server">
    <h2>Select and Display Records
    </h2>
    <p>
      <asp:DataGrid id="DataGrid1" runat="server" BorderStyle="None"
BorderWidth="1px" BorderColor="#CCCCCC" BackColor="White" CellPadding="3"
Width="532px">
        <FooterStyle forecolor="#000066" backcolor="White"></FooterStyle>
        <HeaderStyle font-bold="True" forecolor="White"
backcolor="#006699"></HeaderStyle>
        <PagerStyle horizontalalign="Left" forecolor="#000066"
backcolor="White" mode="NumericPages"></PagerStyle>
        <SelectedItemStyle font-bold="True" forecolor="White"
backcolor="#669999"></SelectedItemStyle>
        <ItemStyle forecolor="#000066"></ItemStyle>
      </asp:DataGrid>
      <!-- Insert content here -->
    </p>
    <h2>Add a Record
    </h2>
    <p>
      <asp:Label id="Label7" runat="server" Width="155px">Id</asp:Label>
      <asp:Label id="Label8" runat="server"
Width="155px">Category</asp:Label>
      <asp:Label id="Label9" runat="server" Width="155px">Name</asp:Label>
```

```
    <asp:Label id="Label1" runat="server"
Width="155px">Description</asp:Label>
    <asp:Label id="Label2" runat="server" Width="155px">Price</asp:Label>
    <br />
    <asp:TextBox id="txtId" runat="server"></asp:TextBox>
    <asp:TextBox id="txtCategory" runat="server"></asp:TextBox>
    <asp:TextBox id="txtName" runat="server"></asp:TextBox>
    <asp:TextBox id="txtDescription" runat="server"></asp:TextBox>
    <asp:TextBox id="txtPrice" runat="server"></asp:TextBox>
  </p>
  <p>
    <asp:Label id="Label3" runat="server" Width="155px">Supplier
Code</asp:Label>
    <asp:Label id="Label4" runat="server" Width="155px">Supplier
Address</asp:Label>
    <asp:Label id="Label5" runat="server" Width="155px">Quantity in
Stock</asp:Label>
    <br />
    <asp:TextBox id="txtCode" runat="server"></asp:TextBox>
    <asp:TextBox id="txtAddress" runat="server"></asp:TextBox>
    <asp:TextBox id="txtQuantity" runat="server"></asp:TextBox>
    <asp:Button id="Button1" onclick="insertcall" runat="server" Text="Insert
Record"></asp:Button>
  </p>
  <h2>Update a Record
  </h2>
  <p>
    <asp:Label id="Label10" runat="server" Width="145px">Name</asp:Label>
    <asp:Label id="Label11" runat="server"
Width="139px">Description</asp:Label>
    <asp:Label id="Label12" runat="server">Where ID = ?</asp:Label>
  </p>
  <p>
    <asp:TextBox id="txtnamechange" runat="server"></asp:TextBox>
    <asp:TextBox id="txtdescriptionchange" runat="server"></asp:TextBox>
    <asp:TextBox id="txtWhere" runat="server"></asp:TextBox>
    <asp:Button id="Button2" onclick="updatecall" runat="server" Text="Update
Record"></asp:Button>
  </p>

    <h2>Delete a Record
</h2>
<p>
    <asp:Label id="Label13" runat="server" Width="144px">Id</asp:Label>
</p>
<p>
    <asp:TextBox id="txtIdDelete" runat="server"></asp:TextBox>
    <asp:Button id="Button3" onclick="deletecall" runat="server" Text="Delete
Record"></asp:Button>
</p>
```

```
    </form>
</body>
</html>
```

11.4   Editable data grid

We have just written a lot of code to achieve something that is relatively simple and not particularly elegant. Web Matrix provides an object that does a very similar thing and most of the code is written for you. It is called an editable data grid. However, using such a grid requires you to understand the sort of code we have just written so that you can edit it to get it to work. Once again Web Matrix takes you so far but then requires you to do the rest.

We deliberately left the introduction of the editable data grid until now so that you are more likely to understand and modify the relatively complex code that it generates. So far when we have created a new ASP.NET file we have used an ASP.NET Page however there are a number of partial interfaces that are available from the Data Pages option as in Figure 11.27.

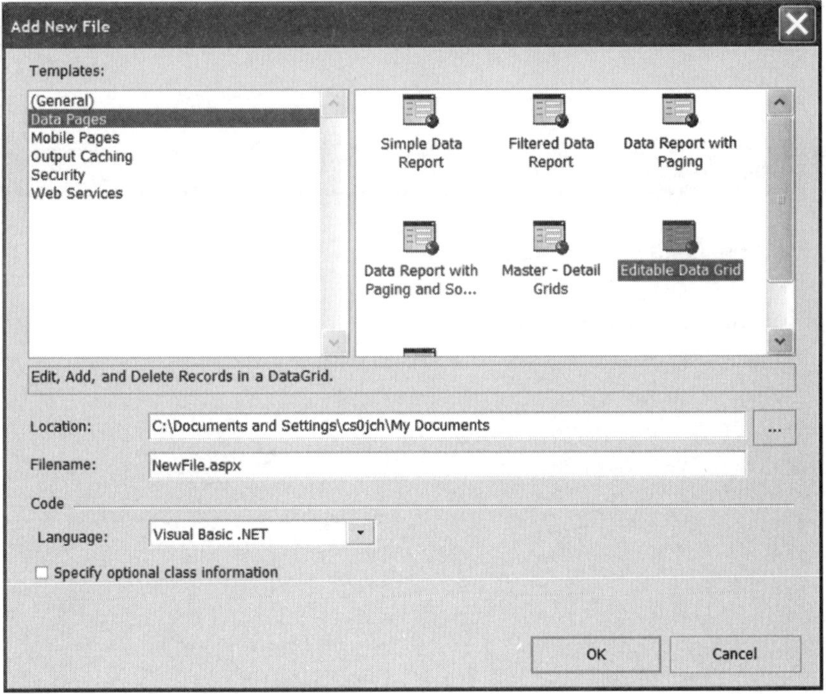

Figure 11.27: New File dialog

If you select the Editable Data Grid and then click *OK* Web Matrix will generate the design as shown in Figure 11.28.

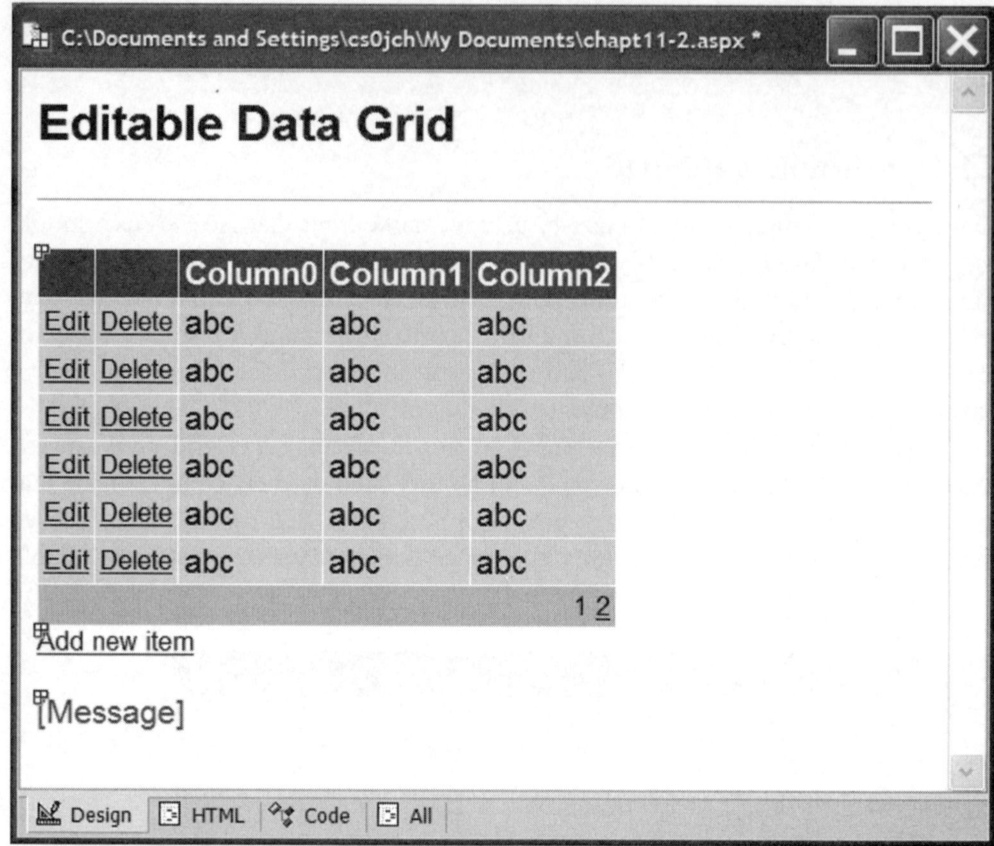

Figure 11.28: Editable Data Grid design

The code for this interface is as follows:

```
<html>
<head>
</head>
<body style="FONT-FAMILY: arial">
  <h2>Editable Data Grid
  </h2>
  <hr size="1" />
  <form runat="server">
    <asp:datagrid id="DataGrid1" runat="server" width="80%" CellSpacing="1"
        GridLines="None" CellPadding="3" BackColor="White" ForeColor="Black"
        OnPageIndexChanged="DataGrid_Page" PageSize="6"
        AllowPaging="true"
        OnDeleteCommand="DataGrid_Delete"
        OnCancelCommand="DataGrid_Cancel"
        OnUpdateCommand="DataGrid_Update"
        OnEditCommand="DataGrid_Edit"
        OnItemCommand="DataGrid_ItemCommand"
        DataKeyField="Id">
```

```
            <HeaderStyle font-bold="True" forecolor="white"
            backcolor="#4A3C8C"></HeaderStyle>
            <PagerStyle horizontalalign="Right" backcolor="#C6C3C6"
            mode="NumericPages" font-size="smaller"></PagerStyle>
            <ItemStyle backcolor="#DEDFDE"></ItemStyle>
            <FooterStyle backcolor="#C6C3C6"></FooterStyle>
            <Columns>
               <asp:EditCommandColumn ButtonType="LinkButton"
                    UpdateText="Update" CancelText="Cancel" EditText="Edit"
                    ItemStyle-Font-Size="smaller" ItemStyle-
                    Width="10%"></asp:EditCommandColumn>
               <asp:ButtonColumn Text="Delete" CommandName="Delete" ItemStyle-
                    Font-Size="smaller" ItemStyle-
                    Width="10%"></asp:ButtonColumn>
            </Columns>
         </asp:datagrid>
         <br />
         <asp:LinkButton id="LinkButton1" onclick="AddNew_Click" runat="server"
            Font-Size="smaller" Text="Add new item"></asp:LinkButton>
         <br />
         <br />
         <asp:Label id="Message" runat="server" width="80%" ForeColor="red"
            EnableViewState="false"></asp:Label>
      </form>
</body>
</html>
```

This interface consists of a *datagrid,* a link *button* and a **label.** The *datagrid* has been formatted to include two Bound columns. The first of these is an Edit/Update/Cancel link button that will display by default Edit but if selected will display Update and Cancel. Each of these are links that will result in a subroutine being called. The second column displays a link button called *Delete* which will similarly call an appropriate subroutine. The subroutines are specified by the following lines where the name of the subroutine is assigned to the event:

```
OnDeleteCommand="DataGrid_Delete"
OnCancelCommand="DataGrid_Cancel"
OnUpdateCommand="DataGrid_Update"
OnEditCommand="DataGrid_Edit"
OnItemCommand="DataGrid_ItemCommand"
```

This datagrid is generated by a wizard that supplies links to a default database which is not Shopping and the table used is not Products. As such the changes we need to make are to the elements that refer to the database and tables. There is only one such change to the design and that is the line which reads

```
DataKeyField="au_id">
```

The key field we need to point to is *Id* so we need to change the value between quotes. The code that adds functionality to the datagrid is as follows, you will note that this is quite extensive and if you hadn't done some SQL work already it would largely be meaningless:

```vb
<%@ Page Language="VB" %>
<%@ import Namespace="System.Data" %>
<%@ import Namespace="System.Data.SqlClient" %>

<script runat="server">

  ' TO DO: update the ConnectionString and Command values for your application

  Dim ConnectionString As String =
"server=(local);database=pubs;trusted_connection=true"
  Dim SelectCommand As String =
"SELECT au_id, au_lname, au_fname from Authors"

  Dim isEditing As Boolean = False

  Sub Page_Load(Sender As Object, E As EventArgs)

    If Not Page.IsPostBack Then

      ' Databind the data grid on the first request only
      ' (on postback, bind only in editing, paging and sorting commands)

      BindGrid()
    End If
  End Sub

  ' -------------------------------------------------------------
  '
  ' DataGrid Commands: Page, Sort, Edit, Update, Cancel, Delete
  '

  Sub DataGrid_ItemCommand(Sender As Object, E As
DataGridCommandEventArgs)

    ' this event fires prior to all of the other commands
    ' use it to provide a more graceful transition out of edit mode
    CheckIsEditing(e.CommandName)
  End Sub

  Sub CheckIsEditing(commandName As String)

    If DataGrid1.EditItemIndex <> -1 Then

      ' we are currently editing a row
      If commandName <> "Cancel" And commandName <> "Update" Then

        ' user's edit changes (If any) will not be committed
```

```
        Message.Text = "Your changes have not been saved yet.  Please press
update to save your changes, or cancel to discard your changes, before selecting
another item."
        isEditing = True
      End If
    End If
  End Sub

  Sub DataGrid_Edit(Sender As Object, E As DataGridCommandEventArgs)

    ' turn on editing for the selected row
    If Not isEditing Then

      DataGrid1.EditItemIndex = e.Item.ItemIndex
      BindGrid()
    End If
  End Sub

  Sub DataGrid_Update(Sender As Object, E As DataGridCommandEventArgs)

    ' update the database with the new values

    ' get the edit text boxes
    Dim id As String = CType(e.Item.Cells(2).Controls(0), TextBox).Text
    Dim lname As String = CType(e.Item.Cells(3).Controls(0), TextBox).Text
    Dim fname As String = CType(e.Item.Cells(4).Controls(0), TextBox).Text

    ' TODO: update the Command value for your application
    Dim myConnection As New SqlConnection(ConnectionString)
    Dim UpdateCommand As SqlCommand = new SqlCommand()
    UpdateCommand.Connection = myConnection

    If AddingNew = True Then
      UpdateCommand.CommandText = "INSERT INTO authors(au_id,
au_lname, au_fname, contract) VALUES (@au_id, @au_lname, @au_fname, 0)"
    Else
      UpdateCommand.CommandText = "UPDATE authors SET au_lname =
@au_lname, au_fname = @au_fname WHERE au_id = @au_id"
    End If
    UpdateCommand.Parameters.Add("@au_id", SqlDbType.VarChar, 11).Value
= id
    UpdateCommand.Parameters.Add("@au_lname", SqlDbType.VarChar,
40).Value = lname
    UpdateCommand.Parameters.Add("@au_fname", SqlDbType.VarChar,
20).Value = fname

    ' execute the command
    Try
      myConnection.Open()
      UpdateCommand.ExecuteNonQuery()
```

```
    Catch ex as Exception
      Message.Text = ex.ToString()
    Finally
      myConnection.Close()
    End Try


    ' Resort the grid for new records
    If AddingNew = True Then
      DataGrid1.CurrentPageIndex = 0
      AddingNew = false
    End If


    ' rebind the grid
    DataGrid1.EditItemIndex = -1
    BindGrid()
  End Sub

Sub DataGrid_Cancel(Sender As Object, E As DataGridCommandEventArgs)

    ' cancel editing
    DataGrid1.EditItemIndex = -1
    BindGrid()
    AddingNew = False
  End Sub

Sub DataGrid_Delete(Sender As Object, E As DataGridCommandEventArgs)

    ' delete the selected row

    If Not isEditing Then

      ' the key value for this row is in the DataKeys collection
      Dim keyValue As String = CStr(DataGrid1.DataKeys(e.Item.ItemIndex))

      ' TODO: update the Command value for your application
      Dim myConnection As New SqlConnection(ConnectionString)
      Dim DeleteCommand As New SqlCommand("DELETE from authors where
au_id='" & keyValue & "'", myConnection)

      ' execute the command
      myConnection.Open()
      DeleteCommand.ExecuteNonQuery()
      myConnection.Close()
      ' rebind the grid
      DataGrid1.CurrentPageIndex = 0
      DataGrid1.EditItemIndex = -1
      BindGrid()

    End If
```

```vb
End Sub

Sub DataGrid_Page(Sender As Object, E As DataGridPageChangedEventArgs)

   ' display a new page of data

   If Not isEditing Then
     DataGrid1.EditItemIndex = -1
     DataGrid1.CurrentPageIndex = e.NewPageIndex
     BindGrid()
   End If
End Sub

Sub AddNew_Click(Sender As Object, E As EventArgs)

   ' add a new row to the end of the data, and set editing mode 'on'

   CheckIsEditing("")

   If Not isEditing = True Then

      ' set the flag so we know to do an insert at Update time
      AddingNew = True

      ' add new row to the end of the dataset after binding

      ' first get the data
      Dim myConnection As New SqlConnection(ConnectionString)
      Dim myCommand As New SqlDataAdapter(SelectCommand,
myConnection)

      Dim ds As New DataSet()
      myCommand.Fill(ds)

      ' add a new blank row to the end of the data
      Dim rowValues As Object() = {"", "", ""}
      ds.Tables(0).Rows.Add(rowValues)

      ' figure out the EditItemIndex, last record on last page
      Dim recordCount As Integer = ds.Tables(0).Rows.Count

      If recordCount > 1 Then

         recordCount -= 1
         DataGrid1.CurrentPageIndex = recordCount \ DataGrid1.PageSize
         DataGrid1.EditItemIndex = recordCount Mod DataGrid1.PageSize

      End If

      ' databind
```

```
        DataGrid1.DataSource = ds
        DataGrid1.DataBind()
    End If
End Sub


' --------------------------------------------------------------
'
' Helpers Methods:
'

' property to keep track of whether we are adding a new record,
' and save it in viewstate between postbacks

Property AddingNew() As Boolean

    Get
        Dim o As Object = ViewState("AddingNew")
        If o Is Nothing Then
            Return False
        End If
        Return CBool(o)
    End Get

    Set(ByVal Value As Boolean)
        ViewState("AddingNew") = Value
    End Set

End Property

Sub BindGrid()

    Dim myConnection As New SqlConnection(ConnectionString)
    Dim myCommand As New SqlDataAdapter(SelectCommand, myConnection)

    Dim ds As New DataSet()
    myCommand.Fill(ds)

    DataGrid1.DataSource = ds
    DataGrid1.DataBind()

End Sub
```

The code is quite well laid out and there are comments throughout that give some information about the code. The first comment to note provides guidance as to what to do next

```
'TO DO: update the ConnectionString and Command values for your application
```

This states that you need to go through the code and exchange the default links to the database, fields, variables and filters. It is not our intention to go through the code line by line but we have provided you with before and after code which we suggest you compare to see how changes have been made. The finished output is displayed in Figure 11.29.

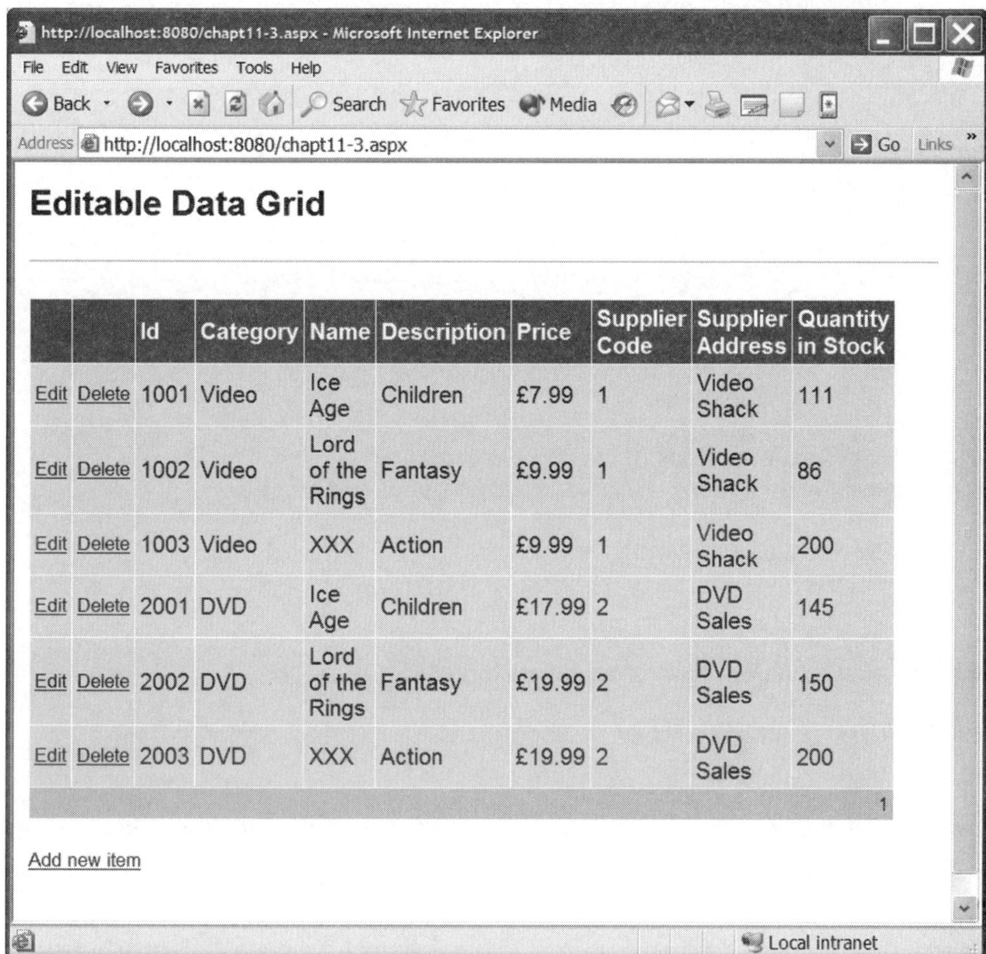

Figure 11.29: Output from complete Editable Data Grid

The completed code is supplied below:

```
' TODO: update the ConnectionString and Command values for your application
Dim ConnectionString As String =
"server=(local);database=shopping;trusted_connection=true"
Dim SelectCommand As String = "SELECT * FROM Product"

Dim isEditing As Boolean = False

Sub Page_Load(Sender As Object, E As EventArgs)
```

```vb
If Not Page.IsPostBack Then

    ' Databind the data grid on the first request only
    ' (on postback, bind only in editing, paging and sorting commands)

    BindGrid()

End If

End Sub

'--------------------------------------------------------------
'
' DataGrid Commands: Page, Sort, Edit, Update, Cancel, Delete
'

Sub DataGrid_ItemCommand(Sender As Object, E As
DataGridCommandEventArgs)

    ' this event fires prior to all of the other commands
    ' use it to provide a more graceful transition out of edit mode

    CheckIsEditing(e.CommandName)

End Sub

Sub CheckIsEditing(commandName As String)

  If DataGrid1.EditItemIndex <> -1 Then

      ' we are currently editing a row
      If commandName <> "Cancel" And commandName <> "Update" Then

        ' user's edit changes (If any) will not be committed
        Message.Text = "Your changes have not been saved yet.  Please press
update to save your changes, or cancel to discard your changes, before selecting
another item."
        isEditing = True

      End If

  End If

End Sub

Sub DataGrid_Edit(Sender As Object, E As DataGridCommandEventArgs)

    ' turn on editing for the selected row

  If Not isEditing Then
```

```vb
    DataGrid1.EditItemIndex = e.Item.ItemIndex
    BindGrid()

  End If

End Sub

Sub DataGrid_Update(Sender As Object, E As DataGridCommandEventArgs)

  ' update the database with the new values

  ' get the edit text boxes
  Dim id As String = CType(e.Item.Cells(2).Controls(0), TextBox).Text
  Dim category As String = CType(e.Item.Cells(3).Controls(0), TextBox).Text
  Dim name As String = CType(e.Item.Cells(4).Controls(0), TextBox).Text
  Dim description As String = CType(e.Item.Cells(5).Controls(0), TextBox).Text
  Dim Price As String = CType(e.Item.Cells(6).Controls(0), TextBox).Text
  Dim SCode As String = CType(e.Item.Cells(7).Controls(0), TextBox).Text
  Dim SAddress As String = CType(e.Item.Cells(8).Controls(0), TextBox).Text
  Dim Quantity As String = CType(e.Item.Cells(9).Controls(0), TextBox).Text

  ' TODO: update the Command value for your application
  Dim myConnection As New SqlConnection(ConnectionString)
  Dim UpdateCommand As SqlCommand = new SqlCommand()
  UpdateCommand.Connection = myConnection

  If AddingNew = True Then
    UpdateCommand.CommandText = "INSERT INTO Product(id, category,
name, description, price, [Supplier Code], [Supplier Address], [Quantity in Stock])
VALUES (@Id, @Category, @Name, @Description, @Price, @SCode,
@SAddress, @Quantity)"
  Else
    UpdateCommand.CommandText = "UPDATE Product SET id = @Id,
category = @Category, name = @Name, description = @Description, price =
@Price, [Supplier Code] = @SCode, [Supplier Address] = @SAddress, [Quantity in
Stock] = @Quantity WHERE id = @Id"
  End If

  UpdateCommand.Parameters.Add("@Id", SqlDbType.Int, 4).Value = id
  UpdateCommand.Parameters.Add("@Category", SqlDbType.VarChar,
15).Value = category
  UpdateCommand.Parameters.Add("@Name", SqlDbType.VarChar, 30).Value =
name
  UpdateCommand.Parameters.Add("@Description", SqlDbType.VarChar,
16).Value = description
  UpdateCommand.Parameters.Add("@Price", SqlDbType.VarChar, 8).Value =
price
  UpdateCommand.Parameters.Add("@SCode", SqlDbType.Int, 4).Value =
SCode
```

```
    UpdateCommand.Parameters.Add("@SAddress", SqlDbType.VarChar,
50).Value = SAddress
    UpdateCommand.Parameters.Add("@Quantity", SqlDbType.Int, 4).Value =
Quantity


  ' execute the command
  Try
     myConnection.Open()
     UpdateCommand.ExecuteNonQuery()

  Catch ex as Exception
     Message.Text = ex.ToString()

  Finally
     myConnection.Close()

  End Try

  ' Resort the grid for new records
  If AddingNew = True Then
     DataGrid1.CurrentPageIndex = 0
     AddingNew = false
  End If

  ' rebind the grid
  DataGrid1.EditItemIndex = -1
  BindGrid()

End Sub

Sub DataGrid_Cancel(Sender As Object, E As DataGridCommandEventArgs)

  ' cancel editing

  DataGrid1.EditItemIndex = -1
  BindGrid()

  AddingNew = False

End Sub

Sub DataGrid_Delete(Sender As Object, E As DataGridCommandEventArgs)

  ' delete the selected row

  If Not isEditing Then

     ' the key value for this row is in the DataKeys collection
     Dim keyValue As String = CStr(DataGrid1.DataKeys(e.Item.ItemIndex))
```

```
      ' TODO: update the Command value for your application
      Dim myConnection As New SqlConnection(ConnectionString)
      Dim DeleteCommand As New SqlCommand("DELETE from Product where
Id='" & keyValue & "'", myConnection)

      ' execute the command
      myConnection.Open()
      DeleteCommand.ExecuteNonQuery()
      myConnection.Close()

      ' rebind the grid
      DataGrid1.CurrentPageIndex = 0
      DataGrid1.EditItemIndex = -1
      BindGrid()

   End If

End Sub

Sub DataGrid_Page(Sender As Object, E As DataGridPageChangedEventArgs)

   ' display a new page of data

   If Not isEditing Then

      DataGrid1.EditItemIndex = -1
      DataGrid1.CurrentPageIndex = e.NewPageIndex
      BindGrid()

   End If

End Sub

Sub AddNew_Click(Sender As Object, E As EventArgs)

   ' add a new row to the end of the data, and set editing mode 'on'

   CheckIsEditing("")

   If Not isEditing = True Then

      ' set the flag so we know to do an insert at Update time
      AddingNew = True

      ' add new row to the end of the dataset after binding

      ' first get the data
      Dim myConnection As New SqlConnection(ConnectionString)
      Dim myCommand As New SqlDataAdapter(SelectCommand, myConnection)
```

```vb
        Dim ds As New DataSet()
        myCommand.Fill(ds)

        ' add a new blank row to the end of the data
        Dim rowValues As Object() = {0, "", "", "", "", 0, "", 0}
        ds.Tables(0).Rows.Add(rowValues)

        ' figure out the EditItemIndex, last record on last page
        Dim recordCount As Integer = ds.Tables(0).Rows.Count

        If recordCount > 1 Then

            recordCount -= 1
            DataGrid1.CurrentPageIndex = recordCount \ DataGrid1.PageSize
            DataGrid1.EditItemIndex = recordCount Mod DataGrid1.PageSize

        End If

        ' databind
        DataGrid1.DataSource = ds
        DataGrid1.DataBind()

    End If


End Sub

' --------------------------------------------------------------
'
' Helpers Methods:
'


' property to keep track of whether we are adding a new record,
' and save it in viewstate between postbacks

Property AddingNew() As Boolean

    Get
        Dim o As Object = ViewState("AddingNew")
        If o Is Nothing Then
            Return False
        End If
        Return CBool(o)
    End Get

    Set(ByVal Value As Boolean)
        ViewState("AddingNew") = Value
    End Set
```

```
End Property

Sub BindGrid()

   Dim myConnection As New SqlConnection(ConnectionString)
   Dim myCommand As New SqlDataAdapter(SelectCommand, myConnection)

   Dim ds As New DataSet()
   myCommand.Fill(ds)

   DataGrid1.DataSource = ds
   DataGrid1.DataBind()

End Sub
```

11.5 Summary

In this chapter we have introduced the major SQL statements and how these can be used within ASP.NET. It is clear that Web Matrix offers some support for on-line database developers but that there requires some initial skills developed before a novice would be able to develop a web-based database. Nevertheless you now have the basic skills to use SQL to develop an interface that has clear functionality. In the next chapter we are going to develop this site further.

11.6 Exercises

1. Implement the editable datagrid discussed in Section 11.4. You should attempt to do this without copying the code in Section 11.4, but if you get stuck you can refer to it.

2. You are going to develop an interface that allows the user to view the purchases for each Customer. This requires the use of two tables, Customer and CartItems. If you used CartItems alone you would not see the Customer's name. There is a One:Many relationship between the two tables with the Customer table on the 'One' side. This cannot be easily shown in a single grid and so most database systems offer the possibility of a Master-Detail grid. This consists of two grids one above the other with the 'One' table above the 'Many' table and when a record is selected in the 'One' table its associated records are displayed in the 'Many' table. The link between the two tables is the key; in this case it is a combination of Login and Password. To keep things simple we are only going to use the Login field as the link. You need to create a new ASPX form using Master-Detail Grids from Data Pages. You need to modify the items in

both grids so that you obtain an output below. This shows the output where the details are selected for Colin Hardy.

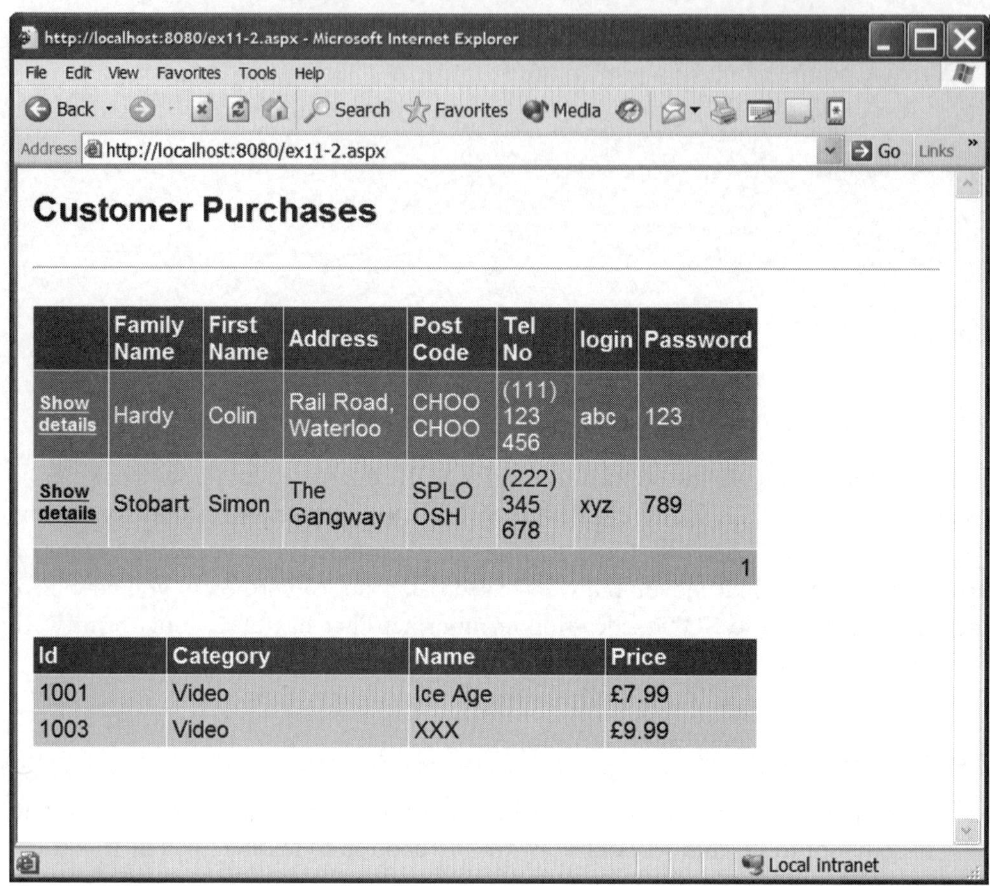

12

Developing a simple online shop

12.1 Introduction

In this chapter we will bring all of the elements of the book together in the development of an interactive on-line e-shop. This will build on the Video Store presented in the last chapter. In Chapter 11 we examined the development of what may be termed back-end operations, these are maintenance activities that the owner of the site would need to do such as the addition/modification of products. In this chapter we are going to develop the front-end operations that are seen and used by the visitors to this site. The major new elements are the login process, display and selection of products and adding and removing items from a personalised shopping cart. It should be noted however that this does not provide a complete e-shop but covers the major developmental issues. It is assumed that if you can follow and develop the system described in Chapter 11 and this chapter that you should be able to complete a site to meet your needs.

12.2 Login page

A login page usually provides access to a system or part of a system for individuals who have valid identifiers. In an e-shop the concept is often used in a slightly different way. You require anyone to be able to enter the site but only individuals who have registered should be allowed to purchase. The reason for this is that the registration process formally adds the user to the system and collects vital information such as name and address as well as payment details. Many e-shops allow a user to log on at any time during their visit to the site. This requires not only a login option on every screen but also a way of monitoring the users' actions to ensure that any attempt to access transaction related sections of the site results in a check to ensure that the user is logged in. If the user is not logged on at that point the system usually offers a login option or registration for new users. In this chapter we are not going to go into such detail. We are going to work on a more linear and hence sequential approach to developing this site in that the user will log on when entering the system. Consequently from the login page the user would be presented with the products from which they would be able to add items to their shopping cart. They would then be able to move from there to the shopping cart to check what they have selected and also have the opportunity to remove items.

Web Matrix provides a default login page that we are going to modify to suit our needs. We need to open a new document and then select Security from Templates and Login Page option, see Figure 12.1.

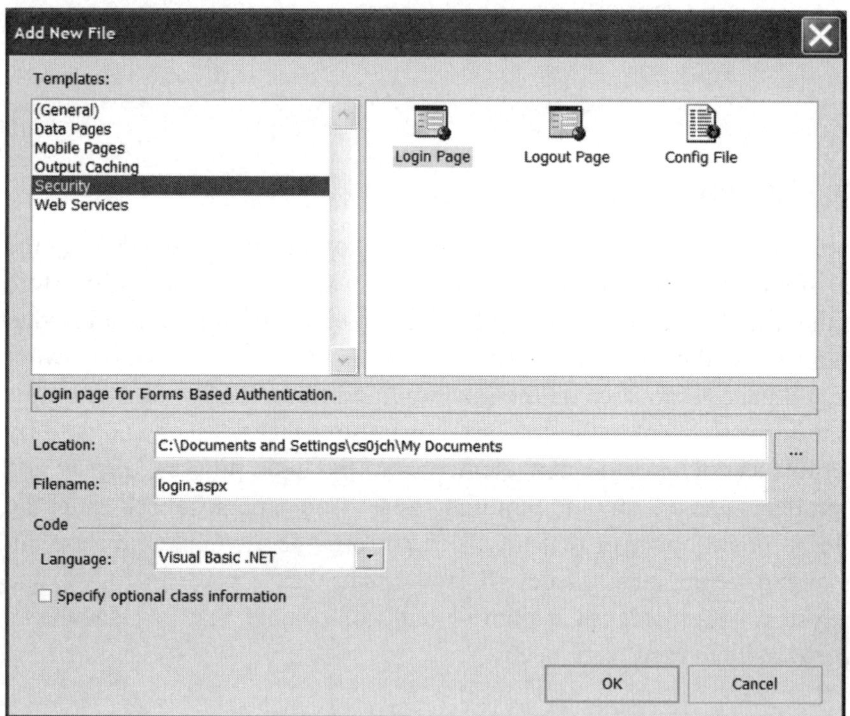

Figure 12.1: New Login dialog

This will result in the creation of the interface provided in Figure 12.2

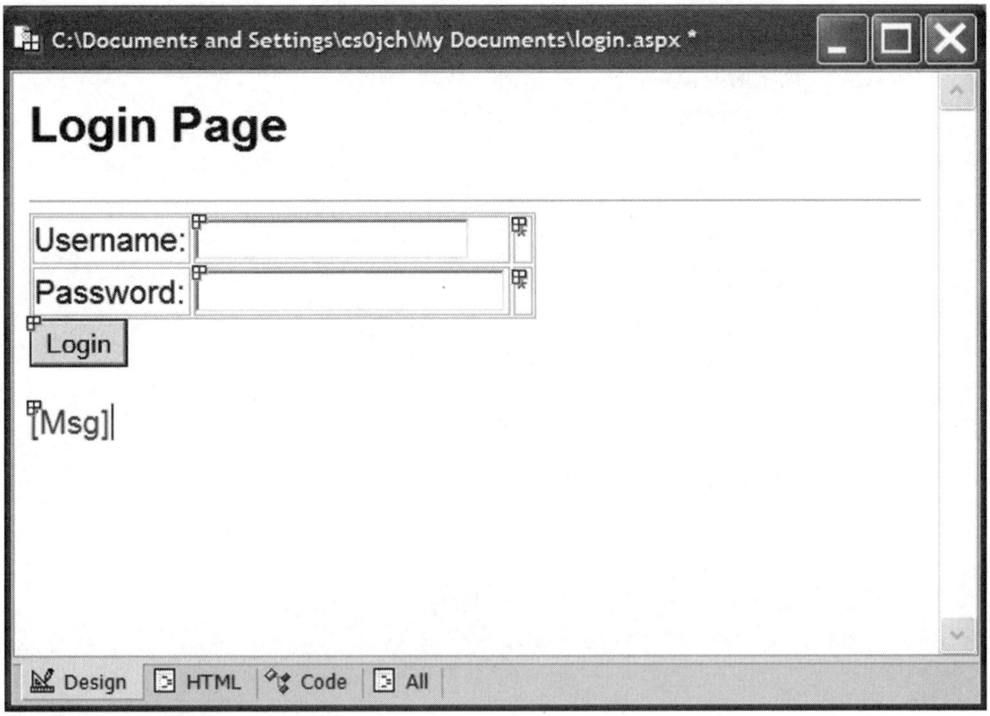

Figure 12.2: New Login design

As with all ASP.NET pages we need to deal with both the design and the functionality. The code for the design is as follows. We will talk through this to argue how it might be changed to meet our needs:

```
<html>
<head>
</head>
<body style="FONT-FAMILY: arial">
  <form runat="server">
    <h2>Login Page
    </h2>
    <hr size="1" />
    <table>
      <tbody>
        <tr>
          <td>
            Username:</td>
          <td>
            <asp:TextBox id="UserName" runat="server"></asp:TextBox>
          </td>
          <td>
            <asp:RequiredFieldValidator
              id="Requiredfieldvalidator1"
              runat="server"
```

```
                    ErrorMessage="*"
                    Display="Static"
                    ControlToValidate="UserName">
                    </asp:RequiredFieldValidator>
              </td>
          </tr>
          <tr>
            <td>
               Password:</td>
            <td>
               <asp:TextBox id="UserPass" runat="server"
               TextMode="Password"></asp:TextBox>
            </td>
            <td>
               <asp:RequiredFieldValidator
               id="Requiredfieldvalidator2"
               runat="server"
               ErrorMessage="*"
               Display="Static"
               ControlToValidate="UserPass">
               </asp:RequiredFieldValidator>
            </td>
         </tr>
       </tbody>
    </table>
    <asp:button id="LoginBtn" onclick="LoginBtn_Click" runat="server"
       text="Login"></asp:button>
    <p>
       <asp:Label id="Msg" runat="server" ForeColor="red"></asp:Label>
    </p>
  </form>
</body>
</html>
```

The *H2* heading is followed by a horizontal rule and then a table that has two rows and three columns. In the first column are the labels Username and Password, we prefer User Name to Username but apart from that they are fine. The second column consists of ASP.NET textboxes with id UserName and Password respectively. We decided to change UserName to Login. The final column contains required field validators. You need to ensure that the Control to Validate matches the appropriate field id. At present if the user fails to type in either a User Name or a password then an asterisk is displayed indicating that this is a required field. Whilst the use of an asterisk for this purpose is becoming more common we feel that it would be more helpful to provide a message. Consequently we have modified the Error Message. Below the table is an ASP.NET button that when clicked will call the subroutine ***LoginBtn_Click***. Finally there is a *label* with the *id Msg*.

This finished design should look like Figure 12.3

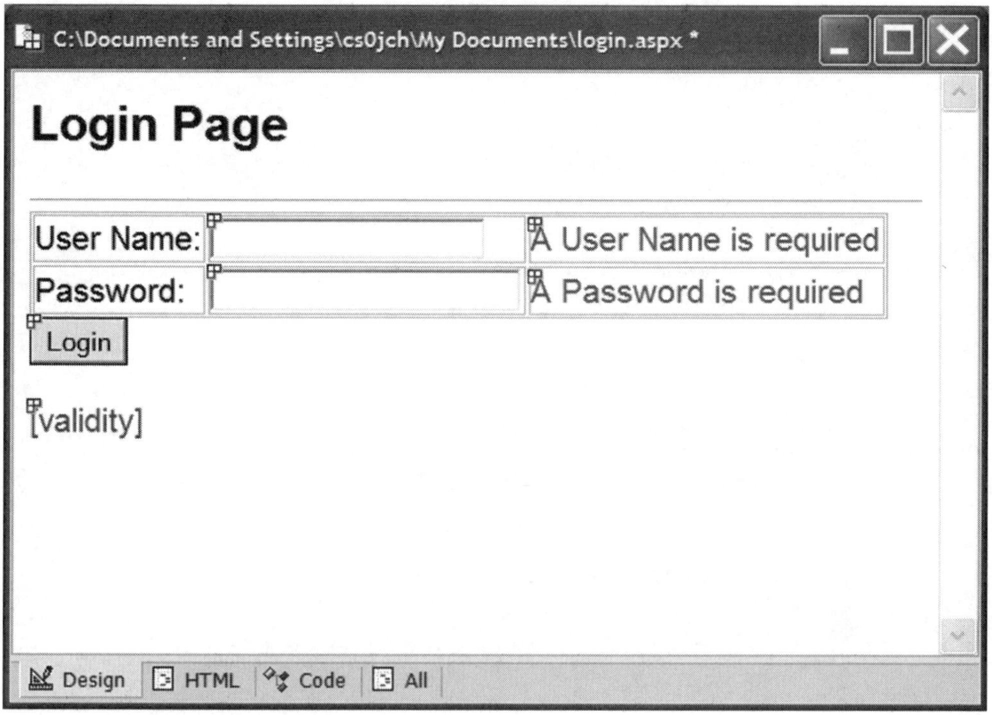

Figure 12.3: Modified Login design

The modified design code is as follows

```
<html>
<head>
</head>
<body style="FONT-FAMILY: arial">
  <form runat="server">
    <h2>Login Page
    </h2>
    <hr size="1" />
    <table>
      <tbody>
        <tr>
          <td>
              User Name:</td>
          <td>
              <asp:TextBox id="Login" runat="server"></asp:TextBox>
          </td>
          <td>
              <asp:RequiredFieldValidator
                id="Requiredfieldvalidator1"
                runat="server"
                ControlToValidate="Login"
                Display="Static"
```

```
                ErrorMessage="A User Name is required">
                </asp:RequiredFieldValidator>
          </td>
        </tr>
        <tr>
          <td>
            Password:</td>
          <td>
            <asp:TextBox id="Password" runat="server"
            TextMode="Password"></asp:TextBox>
          </td>
          <td>
            <asp:RequiredFieldValidator
            id="Requiredfieldvalidator2"
            runat="server"
            ControlToValidate="Password"
            Display="Static"
            ErrorMessage="A Password is required">
            </asp:RequiredFieldValidator>
          </td>
        </tr>
      </tbody>
    </table>
    <asp:button id="LoginBtn" onclick="LoginBtn_Click" runat="server"
      text="Login"></asp:button>
    <p>
      <asp:Label id="validity" runat="server" ForeColor="red"></asp:Label>
    </p>
  </form>
</body>
</html>
```

The subroutine code provided by default for the button is as follows:

```
Sub LoginBtn_Click(Sender As Object, E As EventArgs)

  If Page.IsValid Then
    If (UserName.Text = "jdoe@somewhere.com") And
      (UserPass.Text = "password") Then
      FormsAuthentication.RedirectFromLoginPage(UserName.Text, true)
    Else
      Msg.Text = "Invalid Credentials: Please try again"
    End If
  End If

End Sub
```

This is very simplistic and assumes that there is only one valid user of the system. It tests the text properties of the *UserName* and *Password* against specific values (*"jdoe@somewhere.com"* and *"password"* respectively). Note the use of the logical operator AND this tests that both values are correct, if only one is true the test fails. If the test fails then a message is displayed in the *Msg* label, but if the test is true and this is the valid user then the method in the next line redirects the system to the first web page. We need to change this code so that it accesses the details of valid users in our Customer table. The code for this is as follows:

```
Sub LoginBtn_Click(Sender As Object, E As EventArgs)

    If Page.IsValid Then
        Dim members As New System.Data.DataSet

        members = TestLogin(Login.Text, Password.Text)

        If members.Tables(0).Rows.Count = 1 Then
            FormsAuthentication.RedirectFromLoginPage(Login.Text, true)
            response.cookies("Details")("Login") = Login.Text
            response.cookies("Details")("Password") = Password.Text
        Else
            validity.Text = "Please try again"
        End If
    End If

End Sub




Function TestLogin(ByVal login As String, ByVal password As String) As
System.Data.DataSet

Dim connectionString As String = "server='localhost'; trusted_connection=true;
        Database='shopping'"
Dim sqlConnection As System.Data.SqlClient.SqlConnection = New
        System.Data.SqlClient.SqlConnection(connectionString)
Dim queryString As String = "SELECT [Customer].* FROM [Customer] WHERE
    ((([Customer].[Login] = @Login) AND ([Customer].[Password] = @Password))"
Dim sqlCommand As System.Data.SqlClient.SqlCommand = New
        System.Data.SqlClient.SqlCommand(queryString, sqlConnection)
sqlCommand.Parameters.Add("@Login", System.Data.SqlDbType.Char).Value =
        login
sqlCommand.Parameters.Add("@Password",
        System.Data.SqlDbType.Char).Value = password
Dim dataAdapter As System.Data.SqlClient.SqlDataAdapter = New
        System.Data.SqlClient.SqlDataAdapter(sqlCommand)
Dim dataSet As System.Data.DataSet = New System.Data.DataSet
dataAdapter.Fill(dataSet)

Return dataSet
End Function
```

This creates a *dataset* object called *members* and then assigns to it the returned value from the function *TestLogion()*. As the code logically jumps to the function at this point we will describe it and then return to the button click code.

The function receives the values of the text properties of the Login and Password textboxes and then assigns them to the variables *Login* and *password*. The values are then used in a *SELECT* query that retrieves those records that match the combination of login and password. As these are the key fields for the Customer table the result will either be a single matching record or no record if there is no match. The remainder of the code creates a *dataSet* and when the query is run this object is filled with the output from the query and the value returned.

We now move back to the button click subroutine where the returned value is assigned to *members*. The next line begins an If statement that tests the values stored in members. The test counts the numbers of rows in the dataset (number of records). If there are no rows then the test is false and the message *"Please try again"* is displayed in the textbox Validity. If the test is true then the page is redirected in the next line. However the subroutine is not complete and so the remainder of the code is run before the page is displayed.

The next two lines introduce the concept of Cookies. What we want to do is to pass the login and password values to another web page. Unfortunately there is no direct way of passing values from one page to another since when a web page is replaced by another all values on the first page are destroyed with the web page. One way around this is to use cookies. You may have come across cookies before for example when the system prompts you if it should remember your password. A cookie is a temporary or permanent file that is like a record in that it can hold values in a number of fields. To a certain extent you can think of them as variables but instead of values being stored in memory they are stored on your hard disk. Once a value is copied to a cookie from a field on your webpage they can then be retrieved from the cookie by commands on another page.

Cookies have gained themselves a negative reputation in that they are under the control of the web developer and as such they can create files on your system and store anything in them. As a user you do not know when these files are created. Consequently web browsers come with the ability to deny cookies. Unfortunately this reputation is not always deserved and there are a lot of cookies that serve useful work, such is the intention in this chapter. What we want to do is to store the value temporarily on the hard disk of the user but that the value is deleted along with the cookie when the web session ends.

In order to use a cookie you need a pair of commands in this web page we will use the command to create and add a value to a cookie whilst in the next section we will introduce the command to retrieve a value from a cookie:

```
response.cookies("Details")("Login") = Login.Text
```

Response.cookies requires two values; the first is the name of cookie record (Details) the second is the "field name" in that record (Login). The value to the right of the assign statement is assigned to the Login field in the cookie. If the cookie did not exist then this command will create it and assign the value. If the cookie already exists then the assign statement will overwrite it. There are additional options that can be added to the response.cookie statement that will determine how long the cookie remains on the system. As it stands this cookie will only be created and available for use during this current session. As soon as the user closes the browser the cookie will be deleted.

```
response.cookies("Details")("Password") = Password.Text
```

In this second line the value in the Password textbox is assigned to the Password "field" in the Details cookie. This ends the subroutine and so the following line can be activated.

```
FormsAuthentication.RedirectFromLoginPage(Login.Text, true)
```

This command acts as a link between three pages, namely this login web page a web configuration page that is not displayed but serves a potentially key role (see next section) and the next web page to appear which will always be called Default.aspx. The output from the Login Page can be seen in Figure 12.4 where the password has not been entered and Figure 12.5 where an incorrect login/password has been entered.

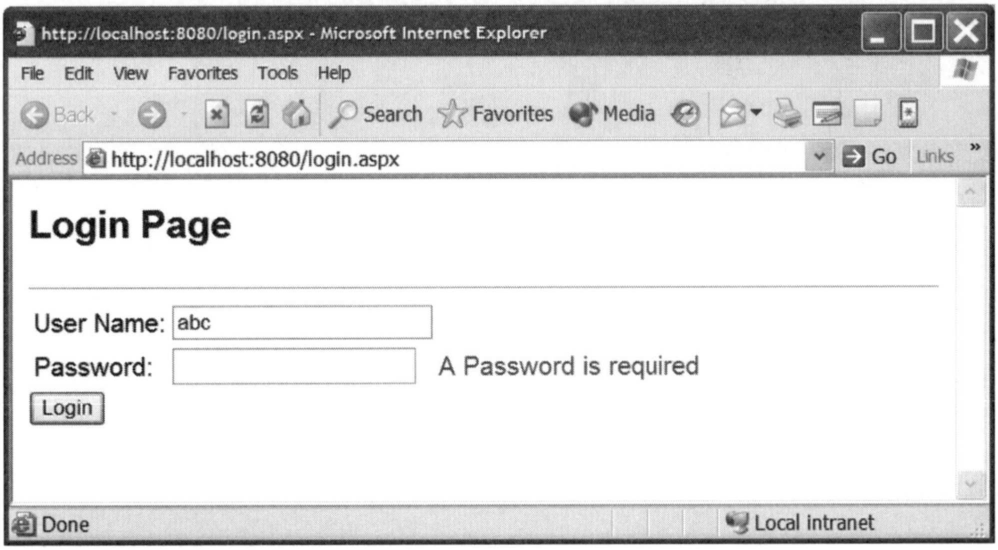

Figure 12.4: Omitted password

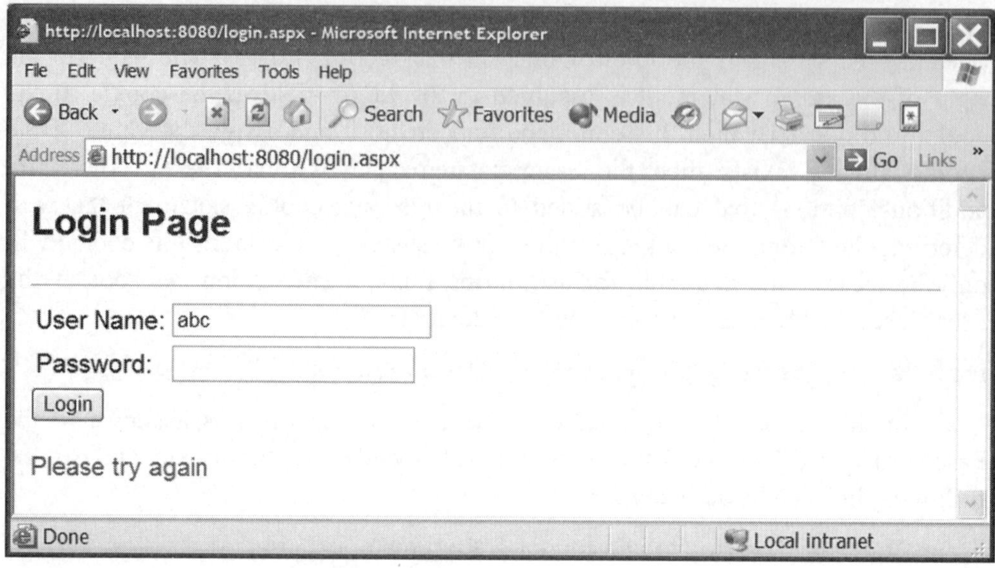

Figure 12.5: Incorrect login/password

12.3 Web configuration file

The web.config file is available from the Security template as in Figure 12.6.

Figure 12.6: Web configuration file

Note that when you select Config File the file name is automatically set to web.config and this should not be changed. As noted earlier this page is not displayed but it does let the developer specify controls to the environment beyond this point. Remember that having authorised a user to access pages beyond this point there may be controls you wish to put in place. Having said that we are not going to use the facilities offered by this file and so will not make any changes to the file. As long as it appears as follows it will work effectively:

```
<?xml version="1.0" encoding="UTF-8" ?>

<configuration>

  <!--

      The <appSettings> section is used to configure application-specific
        configuration settings.  These can be fetched from within apps by calling
        the "ConfigurationSettings.AppSettings(key)" method:

      <appSettings>
        <add key="connectionstring"
        value="server=localhost;trusted_connection=true;database=pubs"/>
      </appSettings>

  -->

  <system.web>

    <!--

      The <sessionState" section is used to configure session state for the
        application. It supports four modes: "Off", "InProc", "StateServer", and
        "SqlServer".  The later two modes enable session state to be stored off the
        web server machine - allowing failure redundancy and web farm session
        state scenarios.

      <sessionState mode="InProc"
              stateConnectionString="tcpip=127.0.0.1:42424"
              sqlConnectionString="data
              source=127.0.0.1;trusted_connection=true"
              cookieless="false"
              timeout="20" />

    -->

    <!--

      The <customErrors> section enables configuration of what to do if/when an
        unhandled error occurs during the execution of a request.  Specifically, it
        enables developers to configure html error pages to be displayed in place
```

```
of a error stack trace:

<customErrors mode="RemoteOnly"
defaultRedirect="GenericErrorPage.htm">
  <error statusCode="403" redirect="NoAccess.htm"/>
  <error statusCode="404" redirect="FileNotFound.htm"/>
<customErrors>

-->

<!--


The <authentication> section enables configuration of the security
authentication mode used by ASP.NET to identify an incoming user.  It
supports a "mode" attribute with four valid values: "Windows", "Forms",
"Passport" and "None":

The <forms> section is a sub-section of the <authentication> section,
and supports configuring the authentication values used when Forms
authentication is enabled above:

<authentication mode="Forms">

    <forms name=".ASPXAUTH"
        loginUrl="login.aspx"
        protection="Validation"
        timeout="999999" />

</authentication>

-->


<!--


The <authorization> section enables developers/administrators to configure
whether a user or role has access to a particular page or resource.  This is
accomplished by adding "<allow>" and "<deny>" sub-tags beneath the
<authorization> section - specifically detailing the users/roles allowed or
denied access.

Note: The "?" character indicates "anonymous" users (ie: non authenticated
users).  The "*" character indicates "all" users.

<authorization>
  <deny users="*" />
</authorization>

-->
```

```
</system.web>

</configuration>
```

12.4   Product selection

As noted in the last section we need to create a web page with the name
Default.aspx as this is the page the system 'defaults' to when the login is
successful. This web page is going to allow the user to view existing products and
then add items to their shopping cart. In order to ease the browsing process we are
also going to categorise the displays so that the user can select whether they want
to see the stock for videos or DVDs. The interface is provided in Figure 12.7.

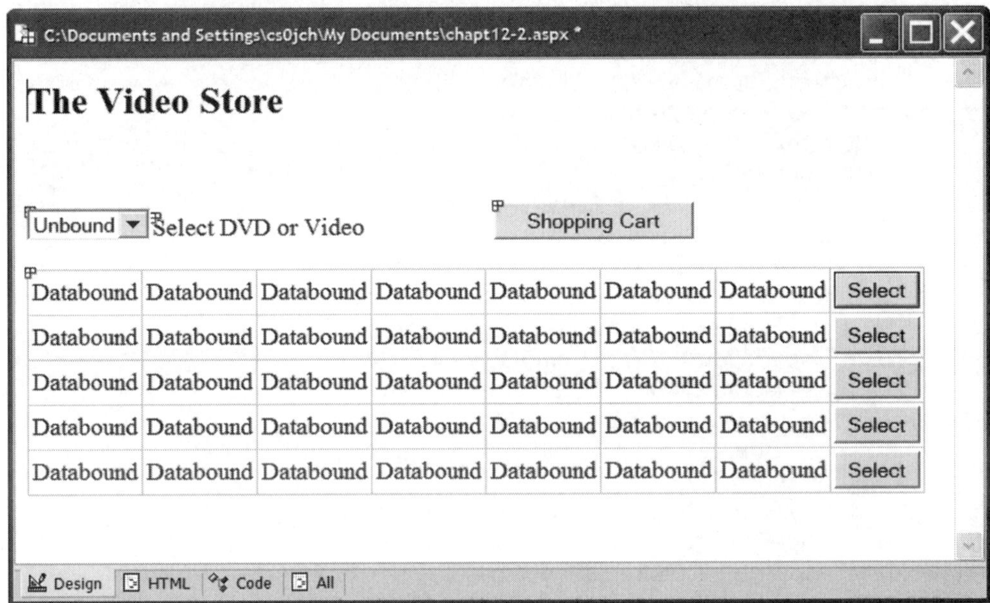

Figure 12.7: Product selection design

This interface uses familiar objects in a more advanced way than in earlier
chapters. The code for the design is as follows. Don't type this in at the moment:

```
<html>
<head>
</head>
<body>
  <form runat="server">
    <h2>The Video Store
    </h2>
    <br />
    <br />
```

```
    <p>
        <asp:DropDownList id="DDList" runat="server"
onselectedindexchanged="DDL" AutoPostBack="True"></asp:DropDownList>
        <asp:Label id="Label1" runat="server" Width="274px">
         Select DVD or Video</asp:Label>
        <asp:Button id="Cart" onclick="gotocart" runat="server" Text="Shopping
Cart"></asp:Button>
    </p>
    <p>
        <asp:DataGrid id="grid" runat="server" onitemcommand="Update"
BorderColor="#CCCCCC" BackColor="White" CellPadding="3" BorderWidth="1px"
BorderStyle="None" ShowHeader="False" AutoGenerateColumns="False">
        <FooterStyle forecolor="#000066" backcolor="White"></FooterStyle>
        <HeaderStyle font-bold="True" forecolor="White"
backcolor="#006699"></HeaderStyle>
        <PagerStyle horizontalalign="Left" forecolor="#000066"
backcolor="White" mode="NumericPages"></PagerStyle>
        <SelectedItemStyle forecolor="#000066"
backcolor="White"></SelectedItemStyle>
        <ItemStyle forecolor="#000066"></ItemStyle>
        <Columns>
          <asp:BoundColumn DataField="Id"
HeaderText="Id"></asp:BoundColumn>
          <asp:BoundColumn DataField="Name"
HeaderText="Name"></asp:BoundColumn>
          <asp:BoundColumn DataField="Description"
HeaderText="Description"></asp:BoundColumn>
          <asp:BoundColumn DataField="Price"
HeaderText="Price"></asp:BoundColumn>
          <asp:BoundColumn DataField="Supplier Code" HeaderText="Supplier
Code"></asp:BoundColumn>
          <asp:BoundColumn DataField="Supplier Address"
HeaderText="Supplier Address"></asp:BoundColumn>
          <asp:BoundColumn DataField="Quantity in Stock"
HeaderText="Quantity"></asp:BoundColumn>
          <asp:ButtonColumn Text="Select" ButtonType="PushButton"
CommandName="Select">
            <HeaderStyle width="30px"></HeaderStyle>
          </asp:ButtonColumn>
        </Columns>
      </asp:DataGrid>
    </p>
  </form>
</body>
</html>
```

This code begins with an H2 header. This is followed by three objects on the same row, a dropdown list, a label and a button. The dropdown list is not populated here and will receive values from a subroutine DDL that is called when the value selected by the user is changed. There is a slight limitation with using this particular method in that when the interface is run DVD is displayed by default. If the user requires DVDs they need to select Videos first and then DVDs as the subroutine only occurs on a change and the grid is not initially displayed. This is a minor glitch as long as everything else works. The label provides instructions to the user. It has been extended beyond the width of the characters to force the button to appear more to the right of the web page. This is not ideal as the width of characters will be influenced by the font used on the host browser. A table would have been more reliable as we have used in previous examples. The button allows the user to go to their shopping cart and as such when clicked it will call a subroutine called *gotocart*.

Below this is a datagrid and this consists of five bound columns. Before we talk about column binding there are a number of minor alterations that need to be made. If you select the object in design mode you will see its properties. You should select Auto Format and from the dialog select Professional 2 as this is consistent with the rest of the site. You will notice that this provides you with a blue heading row which is not present in our design. To remove the heading set the *ShowHeader* property to False. We also need to set the *AutoGenerateColumns* property to False. Web Matrix attempts to help the developer and based on the properties we set will create columns to match. However in this instance we want to be in complete control of the design and setting this property to False stops Web Matrix from generating unwanted columns. When the interface is complete set this property to True and see the effect! There is one last change to be made to the code for the design at this point in that it requires the call to the subroutine that will be called when the button is clicked against a particular record. This is done with the command:

```
onitemcommand="Update"
```

We now need to bind the required columns. To do this from Design View click on the dataGrid and then from the Properties component window select the *"Property Builder ..."* link. This will display the dialog shown in Figure 12.8. Select the Columns option from the list in the dialog, the output is shown in Figure 12.9.

This dialog can also be reached by selecting Property Builder and then the Columns option. We will be building individual columns to fields from the Product table.

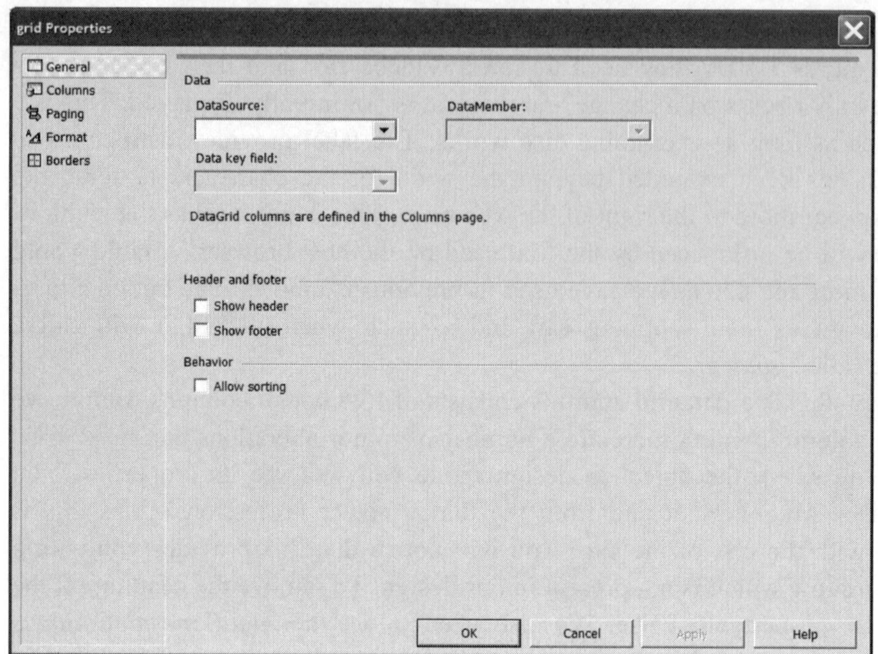

Figure 12.8: General datagrid properties

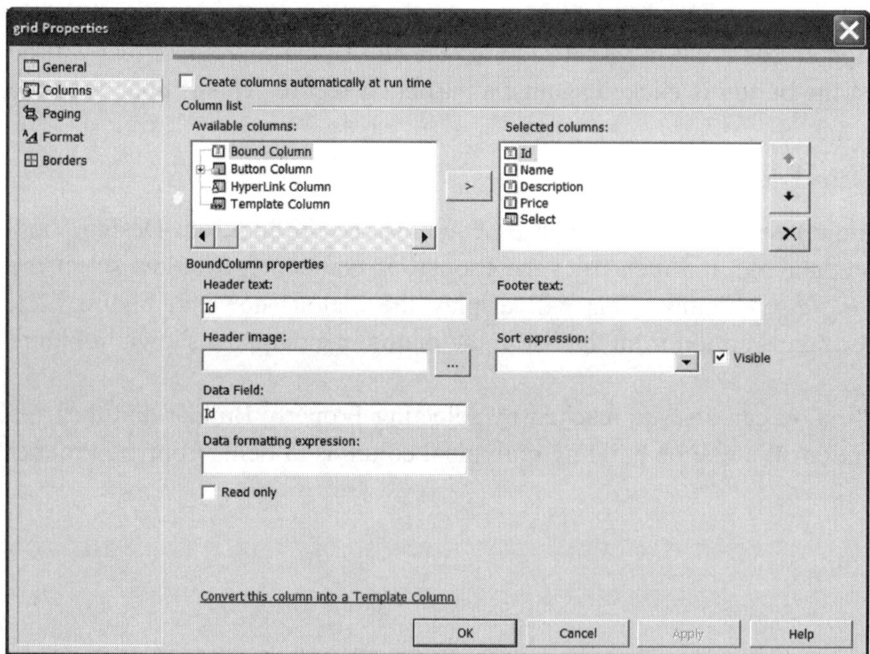

Figure 12.9: Column datagrid properties

We need to add a number of bound columns one by one. If we select Bound Column from the Available columns list and click the greater than symbol (>) we will be presented with the following dialog, see Figure 12.10.

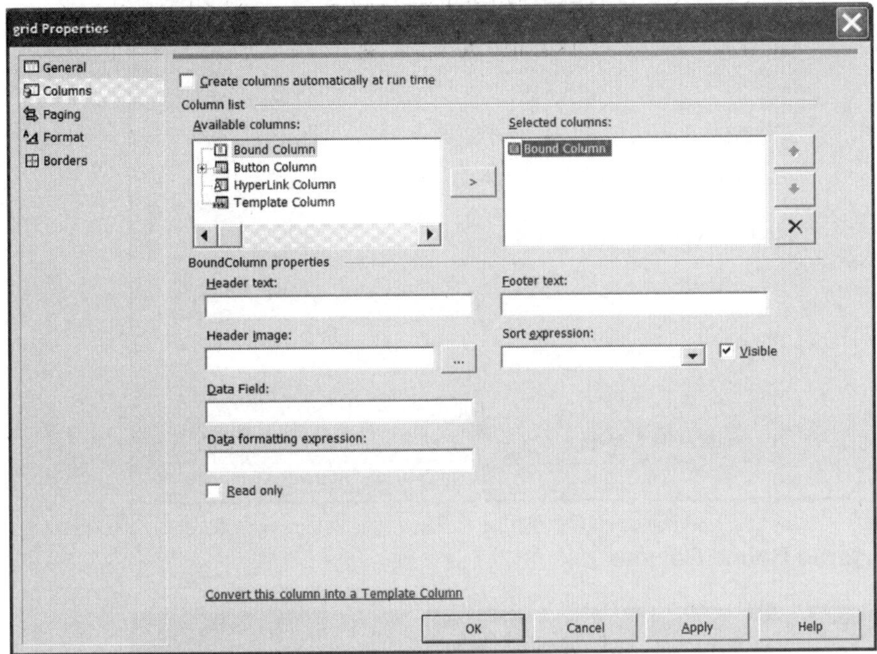

Figure 12.10: Bound column design

This first column is going to display the Id field from the Product table so we need to modify the Header Text field to *Id* and do the same under Data Field. As far as this interface is concerned it does not know what Id is or its value, this we will add with code later. The name of the column in the Selected Columns window has now changed to Id. This is shown in Figure 12.11.

We can add the next column by clicking the greater than symbol. The new column is going to represent the Name column and so we need to change the Header text and Data field in line with the field name. Having done this we can do the same for the other fields in our Product table. These fields are Description, Price, Supplier Code, Supplier Address and Quantity in Stock.

The final column is a button that will allow the user to add an item to their shopping cart. Under Available columns there is a Button column option that can be expanded and the Select type selected as in Figure 12.12.

Figure 12.11: Id Bound Column

Figure 12.12: Select button

By default the button type is a *LinkButton*, which needs to be changed to a PushButton. This completes the design now we need to add functionality. The code for this is as follows:

```
' Creates contents of drop-down list

    Function list() As System.Data.DataSet
        Dim connectionString As String = "server='localhost';
            trusted_connection=true; Database='shopping'"
        Dim sqlConnection As System.Data.SqlClient.SqlConnection = New
            System.Data.SqlClient.SqlConnection(connectionString)
        Dim queryString As String = "SELECT DISTINCT [Product].[Category]
            FROM [Product]"
        Dim sqlCommand As System.Data.SqlClient.SqlCommand = New
            System.Data.SqlClient.SqlCommand(queryString, sqlConnection)
        Dim dataAdapter As System.Data.SqlClient.SqlDataAdapter = New
            System.Data.SqlClient.SqlDataAdapter(sqlCommand)
        Dim dataSet As System.Data.DataSet = New System.Data.DataSet
        dataAdapter.Fill(dataSet)
        Return dataSet
    End Function


' Populates the drop-down list

    Sub Page_Load(Sender as Object, E as EventArgs)
        If not page.ispostback Then
        DDList.DataTextField = "Category"
        DDList.datasource = list()
        DDList.databind()
        End If
    End Sub

' Creates contents of grid

    Function GridContent(ByVal category As String) As System.Data.DataSet
        Dim connectionString As String = "server='localhost';
            trusted_connection=true; Database='shopping'"
        Dim sqlConnection As System.Data.SqlClient.SqlConnection = New
            System.Data.SqlClient.SqlConnection(connectionString)
        Dim queryString As String = "SELECT [Product].* FROM [Product] WHERE
            ([Product].[Category] = @Category)"
        Dim sqlCommand As System.Data.SqlClient.SqlCommand = New
            System.Data.SqlClient.SqlCommand(queryString, sqlConnection)
    sqlCommand.Parameters.Add("@Category",
            System.Data.SqlDbType.Char).Value = category
        Dim dataAdapter As System.Data.SqlClient.SqlDataAdapter = New
            System.Data.SqlClient.SqlDataAdapter(sqlCommand)
        Dim dataSet As System.Data.DataSet = New System.Data.DataSet
        dataAdapter.Fill(dataSet)
        Return dataSet
```

```vb
    End Function

' Populates the grid

    sub DDL(Sender as Object, E as EventArgs)
        grid.datasource = GridContent(DDList.items(DDList.selectedindex).text)
        grid.databind()
    end sub


Function TestCartEntry(ByVal Id As String, ByVal Login As String, ByVal Password _
        As String) As System.Data.DataSet
    Dim connectionString As String = "server='localhost'; trusted_connection=true;
        Database='shopping'"
    Dim sqlConnection As System.Data.SqlClient.SqlConnection = New
        System.Data.SqlClient.SqlConnection(connectionString)
    Dim queryString As String = "SELECT [CartItems].* FROM [CartItems] WHERE
(([CartItems].[Id] = @Id) AND ([CartItems].[Login] = @Login) AND
        ([CartItems].[Password] = @Password))"
    Dim sqlCommand As System.Data.SqlClient.SqlCommand = New
        System.Data.SqlClient.SqlCommand(queryString, sqlConnection)

    sqlCommand.Parameters.Add("@Id", System.Data.SqlDbType.Char).Value = Id
    sqlCommand.Parameters.Add("@Login", System.Data.SqlDbType.Char).Value =
        Login
    sqlCommand.Parameters.Add("@Password",
System.Data.SqlDbType.Char).Value = Password
    Dim dataAdapter As System.Data.SqlClient.SqlDataAdapter = New
        System.Data.SqlClient.SqlDataAdapter(sqlCommand)
    Dim dataSet As System.Data.DataSet = New System.Data.DataSet
    dataAdapter.Fill(dataSet)
    Return dataSet
End Function


Sub Update(Sender As Object, E As DataGridCommandEventArgs)
    Dim members As New System.Data.DataSet
    Dim Login as String = request.cookies("Details")("Login")
    Dim Password as string = request.cookies("Details")("Password")

    members = TestCartEntry(e.Item.Cells(0).Text, Login, Password)
    If members.Tables(0).Rows.Count <> 1 Then
        Dim Id As String = e.Item.Cells(0).Text
        Dim Name As String = e.Item.Cells(1).Text
        Dim Category As String = DDList.items(DDList.selectedindex).value
        Dim Description As String = e.Item.Cells(2).Text
        Dim Price As String = e.Item.Cells(3).Text
        Dim ConnectionString As String = "server='localhost'; trusted_connection=true;
            Database='shopping'"
        Dim myConnection As New SqlConnection(ConnectionString)
        Dim UpdateCommand As SqlCommand = new SqlCommand()
```

```
        UpdateCommand.Connection = myConnection
        UpdateCommand.CommandText = "INSERT INTO CartItems(Login,
            Password, Id, Name, Category, Description, Price) VALUES (@Login,
            @Password, @Id, @Name, @Category ,@Description, @Price)"

        UpdateCommand.Parameters.Add("@Login", SqlDbType.VarChar, 10).Value
            =  Login
        UpdateCommand.Parameters.Add("@Password", SqlDbType.VarChar,
            10).Value =  Password
        UpdateCommand.Parameters.Add("@Id", SqlDbType.VarChar, 4).Value =  Id
        UpdateCommand.Parameters.Add("@Name", SqlDbType.VarChar, 30).Value
            = Name
        UpdateCommand.Parameters.Add("@Category", SqlDbType.VarChar,
            10).Value = Category
        UpdateCommand.Parameters.Add("@Description", SqlDbType.VarChar,
            10).Value = Description
        UpdateCommand.Parameters.Add("@Price", SqlDbType.VarChar, 10).Value
            = Price


        ' execute the command
        Try
            myConnection.Open()
            UpdateCommand.ExecuteNonQuery()


        Finally
         myConnection.Close()
        End Try
    End If
End Sub


Sub gotocart(Sender as Object, E as EventArgs)
    response.redirect("Shopping Cart.aspx")
End Sub
```

We are going to deal with the dropdown list first. This is handled by the
Page_Load() subroutine that calls the function *list()*. The function list is a *SELECT*
query much like those we examined in the last chapter. A connection is made to the
database Shopping and then a select statement is assigned to a string variable. The
difference with the query is the use of the key word *DISTINCT*:

```
Dim queryString As String = "SELECT DISTINCT [Product].[Category] FROM
[Product]"
```

If the *DISTINCT* key word was not present then the Category value for every
record in the Product table would be displayed. For example if there were 100
DVDs in the Product table then the query would return the value DVD 100 times.
We do not need this; all we need is DVD to occur once and the same to happen for
Video. You may ask yourself why we are using a query rather than populating the
dropdown list with explicit values. There are two reasons for this, firstly it shows

you have to populate a dropdown list from a database and secondly we would like the opportunity to allow the system to grow automatically. If new categories of products are added to the system we do not want to come into the code and manually change the values. This way the dropdown list will automatically update with a change to the Product table.

Returning to the function the connection to the database and the query are then assigned to a command that is then run with the output being assigned to a dataset. This dataset is returned to the subroutine *Page_Load()*. As we know a *Page_Load()* subroutine will automatically run when the web page is loaded. The *If* statement tests if this is the first time the page has been loaded so that the dropdown list is only populated once. The following line assigns the value Category to the textfield property of the dropdown list:

```
DDList.DataTextField = "Category"
```

Next the datasource for the dropdown list is assigned the dataset from the function and then the data is bound to the object and the output displayed.

The next function/subroutine pair populates the datagrid, namely Function *GridContent()* and *Sub DDL()*. The *GridContent()* function is another *SELECT* query but this time introduces the *WHERE* clause:

```
Dim queryString As String = "SELECT [Product].* FROM [Product] WHERE
        ([Product].[Category] = @Category)"
```

This SQL statement selects all records from the Product table but only where the category field matches a particular value. The *@Category* represents whatever is the current value of the Category field. This is passed to the function as a string variable from the subroutine. So for example if the user selects DVD then the query selects all records from the Product table where the Category field is DVD. As with previous queries the query and connection are then generated into a command that is run and the output assigned to a dataset that is returned to the subroutine. The subroutine calls the function and then assigns the returned dataset to the datasource of the datagrid. This is then bound to the grid and displayed. Note that in this case we do not need the *If* statement because we would like this function/subroutine to be run every time the user selects a value from the dropdown list.

The final subroutine/function combination is concerned with handling when the user selects an item to be added to their shopping cart and the call is specified in the design of the datagrid:

```
onitemcommand="Update"
```

Consequently the subroutine is called *update()* and the function *TestCartEntry()*. *TestCartEntry()* receives three arguments from the subroutine *Id, Login* and *Password* these are the key fields for the *CartItems* table. The function performs a *SELECT* query that uses a logical operator in the *WHERE* clause:

```
Dim queryString As String = "SELECT [CartItems].* FROM [CartItems] WHERE
(([CartItems].[Id] = @Id) AND ([CartItems].[Login] = @Login) AND
([CartItems].[Password] = @Password))"
```

The datagrid displays all values for either DVD or Video, what this query must do is to select the one record from that set. To do this it needs the key value and as such we need all three values. As in previous functions the database connection and the SQL statement are converted into a command that is run and the output assigned to a dataset. This dataset is then returned to the subroutine.

This subroutine is more complex than previous ones because it has a more specific purpose than merely calling the function and displaying output. In this subroutine the aim is to use the dataset from the function to determine firstly if the user has the selected item in their shopping cart and if they do not to add it to the CartItems table. An object called members is declared as a dataset. The call to the function shows how it is possible to refer to a value in a datagrid. E is defined in the subroutine and allows the code to refer to it using the object. Therefore e.Item.Cells(1) states that the datagrid object has an item that is a cell and that we wish to refer to the text property of the first cell of the selected record. It is the first cell because cells are numbered from zero. The second and third values to be passed to the function are variable values obtained from the cookie Details:

```
Dim Login as String = request.cookies("Details")("Login")
Dim Password as string = request.cookies("Details")("Password")
members = TestCartEntry(e.Item.Cells(0).Text, Login, Password)
```

The *If* statement that follows this tests if the user already has that item in the shopping cart, in that it would only return a row count of one if a record existed. Consequently the test is that the count is not equal to one (<>). The variables declared next: Id, Name, Description and Price obtain their values from the datagrid and the Category value is obtained from the dropdown list. All of these variables are needed because they represent the fields in the CartItems table and the remainder of the subroutine performs an INSERT SQL statement. To achieve this, a connection is made to the Shopping database and an SQL statement constructed.

```
UpdateCommand.CommandText = "INSERT INTO CartItems(Login, Password, Id,
     Name, Category, Price) VALUES (@Login, @Password, @Id, @Name,
     @Category, @Description, @Price)"
```

This statement Inserts a record into the CartItems table and then populates the Login, Password, Id, Name Category, Description and Price with relevant filters. The next seven lines of code perform Add statements that assign the variable values to the filters. Finally the Try statement performs the update to the CartItems table.

The final subroutine in this code is *gotocart()* that opens the Shopping Cart webpage using the *response.redirect()* method. The above program generates the web page shown in Figure 12.13.

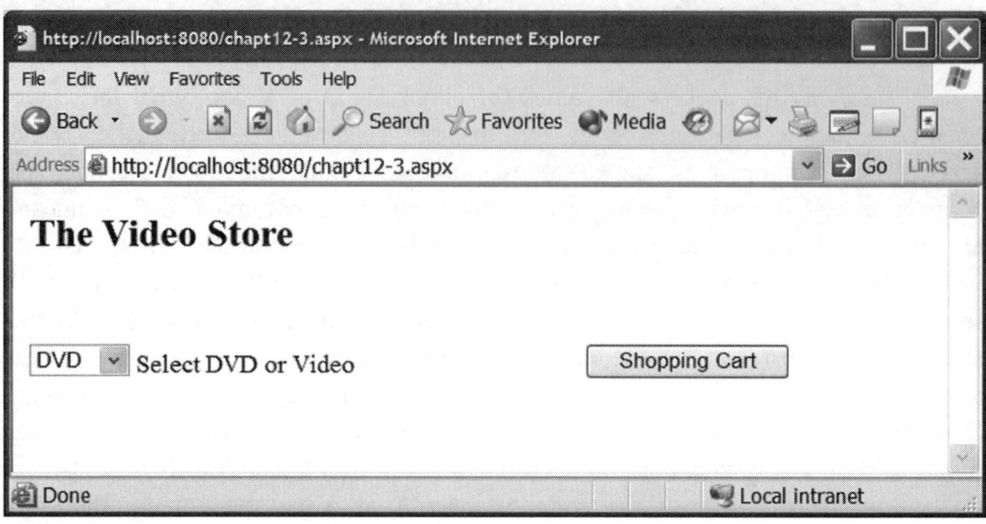

Figure 12.13: Video Store web page

Selecting the Video option from the drop down list provides a list of items to purchase. This is illustrated in Figure 12.14.

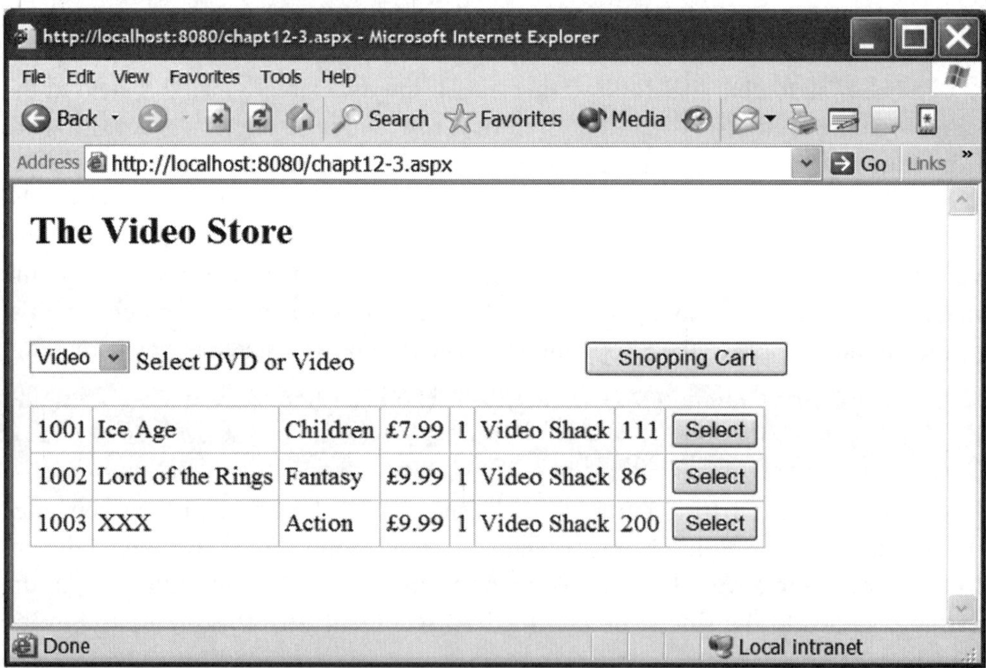

1001	Ice Age	Children	£7.99	1	Video Shack	111	Select
1002	Lord of the Rings	Fantasy	£9.99	1	Video Shack	86	Select
1003	XXX	Action	£9.99	1	Video Shack	200	Select

Figure 12.14: Video Store list

12.5   Shopping Cart

The last part of our system is the Shopping Cart web page where the user can view and delete items from their shopping cart. The interface design is in Figure 12.15.

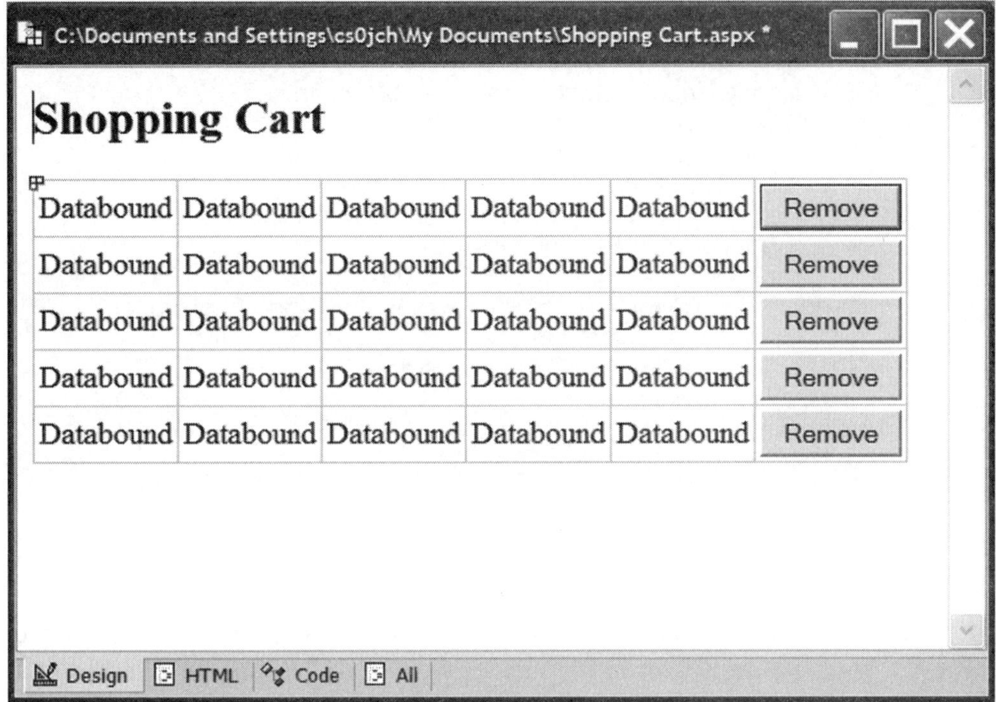

Figure 12.15: Shopping Cart design

The code for the design is as follows:

```
<html>
<head>
</head>
<body>
   <form runat="server">
     <h2>Shopping Cart
     </h2>
     <p>
       <asp:DataGrid id="grid" runat="server" AutoGenerateColumns="False"
       ShowHeader="False" BorderStyle="None" BorderWidth="1px"
       CellPadding="3" BackColor="White" BorderColor="#CCCCCC"
       onitemcommand="Remove">
         <FooterStyle forecolor="#000066" backcolor="White"></FooterStyle>
         <HeaderStyle font-bold="True" forecolor="White"
               backcolor="#006699"></HeaderStyle>
         <PagerStyle horizontalalign="Left" forecolor="#000066"
```

```
            backcolor="White" mode="NumericPages"></PagerStyle>
        <SelectedItemStyle forecolor="#000066"
            backcolor="White"></SelectedItemStyle>
        <ItemStyle forecolor="#000066"></ItemStyle>
        <Columns>
          <asp:BoundColumn DataField="Id"
            HeaderText="Id"></asp:BoundColumn>
          <asp:BoundColumn DataField="Name"
            HeaderText="Name"></asp:BoundColumn>
          <asp:BoundColumn DataField="Category"
            HeaderText="Category"></asp:BoundColumn>
          <asp:BoundColumn DataField="Description"
            HeaderText="Description"></asp:BoundColumn>
          <asp:BoundColumn DataField="Price"
            HeaderText="Price"></asp:BoundColumn>
          <asp:ButtonColumn Text="Remove" ButtonType="PushButton"
            CommandName="Remove">
            <HeaderStyle width="30px"></HeaderStyle>
          </asp:ButtonColumn>
        </Columns>
      </asp:DataGrid>
    </p>
  </form>
</body>
</html>
```

The code for this design is, as you would expect, very similar to the Product Selection page we dealt with in the last section. A H2 heading is followed by a datagrid that consists of five bound columns (Name, Category, Description and Price) these represent the fields from the CartItems table that the user needs to know the other two fields (Login and Password) the user already knows. The final column is a pushbutton that when clicked would call the appropriate subroutine

```
onitemcommand="Remove"
```

The functionality of this page is concerned with displaying in the datagrid those records from CartItems that are associated with a particular user. In addition the user has the opportunity to delete an item from the cart. The code is as follows:

```
' Creates contents of grid

Function GridContent() As System.Data.DataSet
    Dim Login as String = request.cookies("Details")("Login")
    Dim Password as string = request.cookies("Details")("Password")
    Dim connectionString As String = "server='localhost'; trusted_connection=true;
        Database='shopping'"
    Dim sqlConnection As System.Data.SqlClient.SqlConnection = New
        System.Data.SqlClient.SqlConnection(connectionString)
```

```
   Dim queryString As String = "SELECT [CartItems].* FROM [CartItems] WHERE
       [CartItems].[Login] ='" & Login & "' AND [CartItems].[Password] ='" &
       Password & "'"
   Dim sqlCommand As System.Data.SqlClient.SqlCommand = New
       System.Data.SqlClient.SqlCommand(queryString, sqlConnection)

   Dim dataAdapter As System.Data.SqlClient.SqlDataAdapter = New
       System.Data.SqlClient.SqlDataAdapter(sqlCommand)
   Dim dataSet As System.Data.DataSet = New System.Data.DataSet
   dataAdapter.Fill(dataSet)

   Return dataSet
End Function

' Populates the grid

sub Page_Load(Sender as Object, E as EventArgs)
   if not page.ispostback then
      grid.datasource = GridContent()
      grid.databind()
   end if
end sub

' Creates item to be deleted

Sub DeleteItem(ByVal Id as string)
   Dim connectionString As String = "server='localhost'; trusted_connection=true;
       Database='shopping'"
   Dim sqlConnection As System.Data.SqlClient.SqlConnection = New
       System.Data.SqlClient.SqlConnection(connectionString)
   Dim queryString As String = "DELETE from [CartItems] WHERE [CartItems].[Id]
       ='" & Id & "'"
   Dim DeleteCommand As System.Data.SqlClient.SqlCommand = New
       System.Data.SqlClient.SqlCommand(queryString, sqlConnection)

   DeleteCommand.Parameters.Add("@Id", System.Data.SqlDbType.Char).Value
       = Id

   Dim dataAdapter As System.Data.SqlClient.SqlDataAdapter = New
       System.Data.SqlClient.SqlDataAdapter(DeleteCommand)
   Dim dataSet As System.Data.DataSet = New System.Data.DataSet
   dataAdapter.Fill(dataSet)

End Sub

' Populates the grid after delete

Sub Remove(Sender As Object, E As DataGridCommandEventArgs)
   dim Id as string = e.item.cells(0).text
   Call DeleteItem(Id)
```

```
grid.datasource = GridContent()
grid.databind()
End Sub
```

As with other blocks of code the population of the datagrid consists of a function and subroutine pair *GridContent()* and *Page_Load()* respectively. The *GridContent()* function performs a *SELECT* query. To do this it requests the Login and Password from the Details cookie and places them in appropriate variable declarations. A connection is made to the Shopping database and the SQL statement constructed:

```
Dim queryString As String = "SELECT [CartItems].* FROM [CartItems] WHERE
     [CartItems].[Login] ='" & Login & "' AND [CartItems].[Password] ='" &
     Password & "'"
```

This query highlights another aspect of SQL use. In this query we wish to use values taken from variables but we are unable to use variables directly within SQL. An SQL statement is used as a string and as such can be built up by a concatenation of strings. As such we can split an SQL statement to allow the inclusion of variable values. Note we say variable values. If you look carefully at the SQL statement you will see that where a variable is concatenated it is surrounded by single and double quotes ("'"). Quotation marks mark the ends of strings but they also mark the end of SQL statements and so we need both when we are splitting an SQL statement as well as using it as a string to be assigned to a variable. Therefore, when the value is passed to the variable it must retain one of the quotation marks to show that the SQL is paused at that point. Beyond this line the structure is familiar with the SQL command constructed, run and then returned to the subroutine as a dataset. The *Page_Load()* subroutine is also familiar in that it assigns the dataset to the datasource of the datagrid and then binds and displays the output.

The final blocks of code in this web page consists of a pair of subroutines *DeleteItem()* and *Remove()*. *Remove()* is called when the user clicks the button to delete an item from the shopping cart. When we used a function/sub-routine pairing the function was of type dataset and returned a dataset to the subroutine before it was bound to an object. In this final piece of code we do not need to bind the code and so there is nothing to return; consequently we are using a subroutine. DeleteItem accepts the Id of the shopping basket item. The subroutine performs a DELETE query and as such creates a connection to the Shopping database and then builds the SQL statement:

```
Dim queryString As String = "DELETE from [CartItems]
      WHERE [CartItems].[Id] = '" & Id & "'"
```

This query uses the concatenation process we discussed earlier in order to use the value from the Id variable. The SQL command is then built and the dataset generated. The generation of the dataset in this case deletes the record. At this point the subroutine has performed its task and so the control of the program returns to the subroutine.

The subroutine creates a variable and assigns to it the value stored in the Id column of the selected record. This is then passed to the *DeleteItem()* subroutine which is then called. The final two lines in this subroutine call the function *GridContent()* that we discussed earlier and then binds the returned dataset to the datagrid thereby updating what the user sees. This is a good example of code reuse in that if we had not used a function to update the grid then we would have had to write the code more than once.

Selecting some of the products to purchase and then clicking the Shopping Cart button will display the Shopping Cart screen as shown in Figure 12.16.

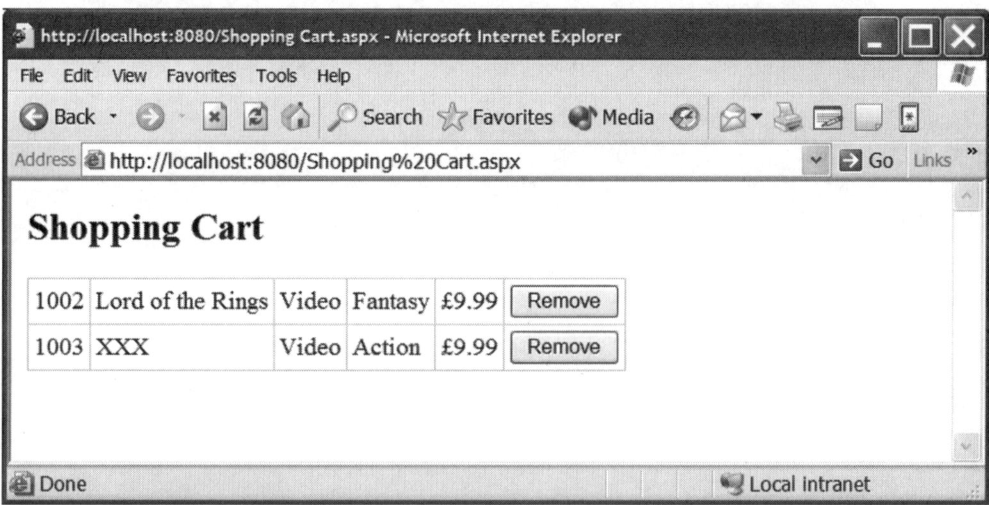

Figure 12.16: Shopping Cart

12.6 Summary

That completes our system. It should be clear from this and earlier chapters that although Web Matrix does offer a number of time-saving tools you do need to understand what you want and how to achieve it before you start. Building interactive web pages for the first time can be daunting as there is a lot to learn. However if you have followed this book so far and have attempted the code described you will recognise that a lot of things get repeated. If you can see where this occurs and you understand what is going on then Web Matrix can truly take a lot of the work away from you. In this chapter we moved away from developing individual web pages to the development of a web site. We said earlier that the system described here was very linear and we took that decision to assist in your understanding, but to develop effective web sites you need to allow your users controlled freedom. It should appear to them that they can do anything at any time but this should be controlled by you. The more flexible the interface is the more complex the design and implementation. I'm sure you are aware by now that web design is not a trivial task and hopefully we have provided you with a range of design ideas as well as guidance on how they may be implemented.

12.7 Exercises

1. There is only one exercise that will offer you immediate benefits and that is to implement the system described in this chapter. Where possible develop the interface and code without copying the code.

13

The Web Matrix community

13.1 Introduction

The Web Matrix ASP.NET development environment is somewhat special in that it was designed to be community supported from its inception. The Web Matrix tool even has in-built links to the on-line community. In this chapter we examine what support the on-line community can provide and where you can go for advice and further information.

13.2 In-built community support

As mentioned way back in Chapter 4 the Properties component window has a tab labelled Community. Selecting this tab will display the hyperlinks which have been incorportated into Web Matrix. This is shown in Figure 13.1. The hyperlinks will have been divided up into different categories. These are:

• ASP.NET Web Matrix Online	Web pages concerning Web Matrix and ASP.NET
• Web Matrix Forums	Web Matrix discussion forums
• ASP.NET Forums	ASP.NET discussion forums
• Newsgroups	Various newsgroup postings
• Listservs	ASP.NET Friends Yahoo Discussion Groups

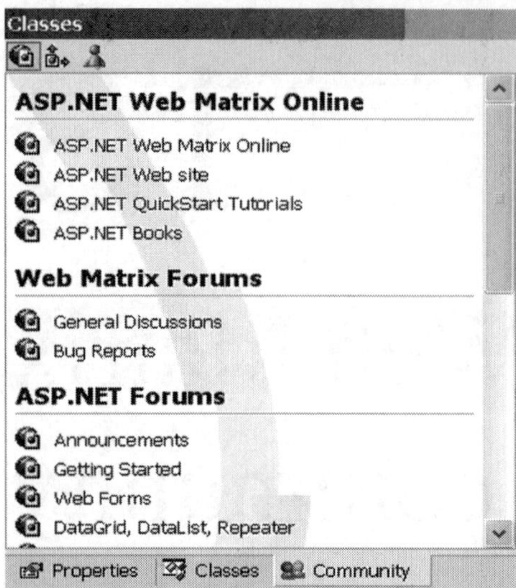

Figure 13.1: Community window view

13.2.1 ASP.NET Web Matrix Online

The ASP.NET Web Matrix Online link loads Microsoft's Web Matrix page. The URL is http://www.asp.net/WebMatrix/ and is illustrated in Figure 13.2.

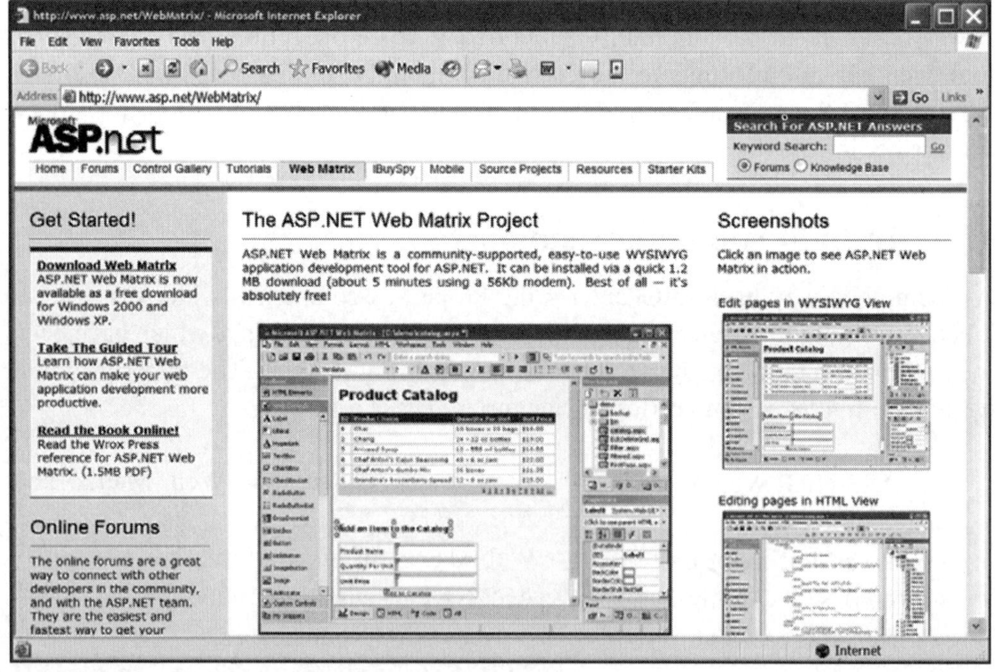

Figure 13.2: ASP.NET Web Matrix

The page provides details on the Web Matrix tool, tutorials, screenshots and a link to download the Web Matrix environment. The ASP.NET web site link provides access to the ASP.NET home page. The URL is http://www.asp.net/ and this is illustrated in Figure 13.3. The web page provides a means to download the ASP.NET environment, provides information about why you should use ASP.NET as well as some quick start tutorials.

Figure 13.3: ASP.NET

Clicking the ASP.NET Quickstart Tutorials link from either the ASP.NET home page or from the Web Matrix community list launches the Quickstart tutorials page. The tutorials provide a brief introduction to the ASP.NET environment and languages. Examples are provided in C#, VB or Jscript languages. The URL of the page is http://www.asp.net/tutorials/quickstart.aspx and it is illustrated in Figure 13.4.

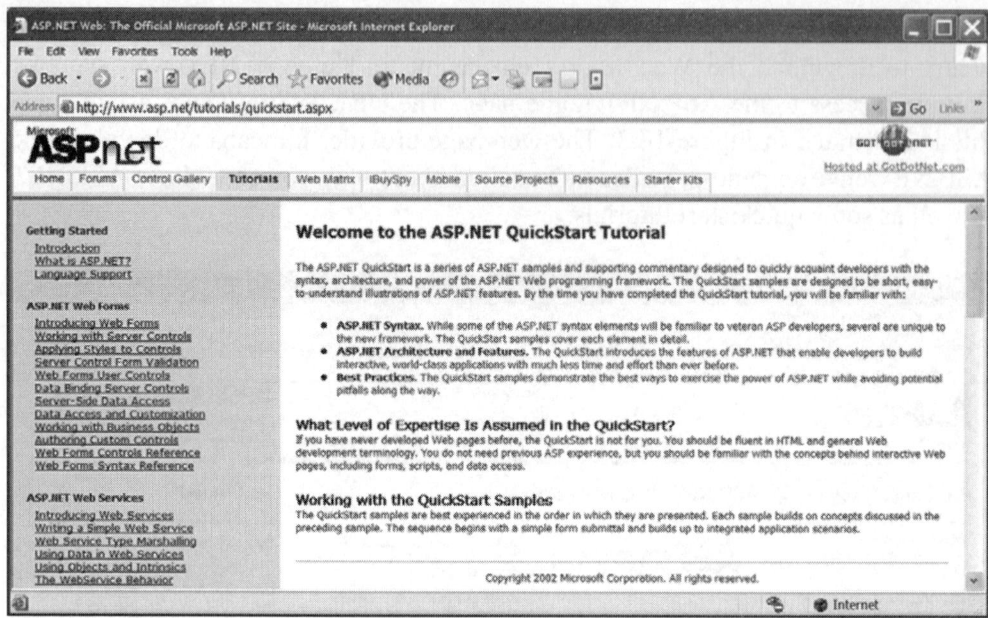

Figure 13.4: QuickStart Tutorials

The ASP.NET book link as you may quess displays a web page with a selection of the most popular books on ASP.NET. The URL for the web page is: http://www.asp.net/Modules/MoreBooks.aspx which is illustrated in Figure 13.5.

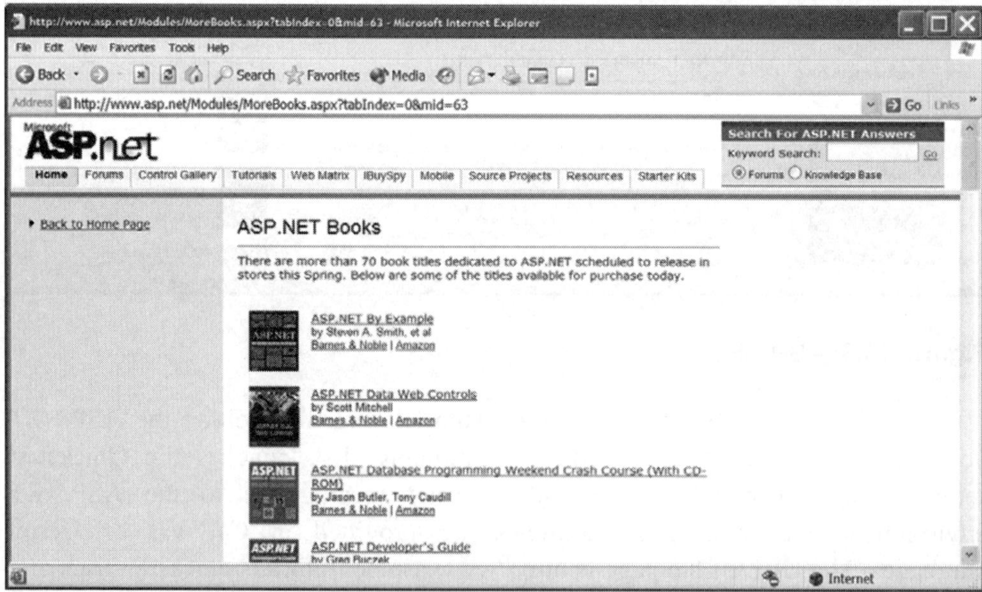

Figure 13.5: ASP.NET Books

13.2.2 Web Matrix Forums

The Web Matrix Forums section provides two links to forums on Web Matrix. The first is a General Discussion forum and the second is a list of Bug Reports. Figure 13.6 illustrates the General Disscussion forum. The URL of this forum is: http://www.asp.net/Forums/ShowForum.aspx.

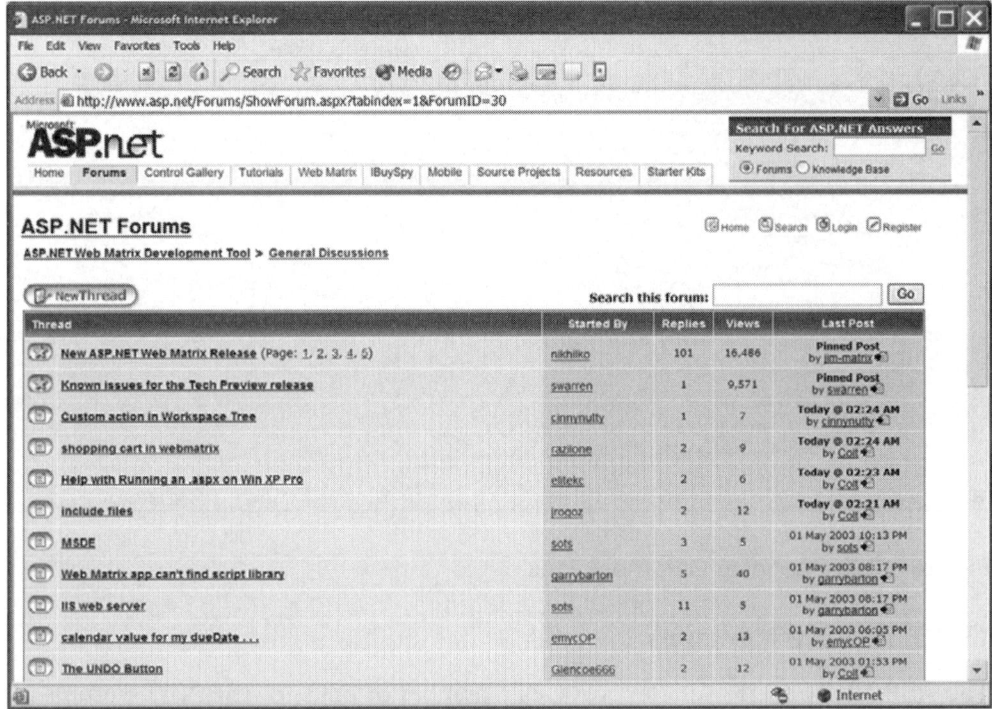

Figure 13.6: General Discussion forum

The forums are a list of topic areas in which users have posted questions and replies to these questions. Anyone can log into the forum and start posting messages. You don't even have to log in to read the messages which have been posted. Figure 13.7 illustrates the contents of a forum on shopping carts. The forums are an excellent resource for finding answers to your questions. If you cannot find an answer straightaway leave a message asking the community and then check back in a few days' time. You will be surprised by the knowledge and willingness of people to help youn solve your problem.

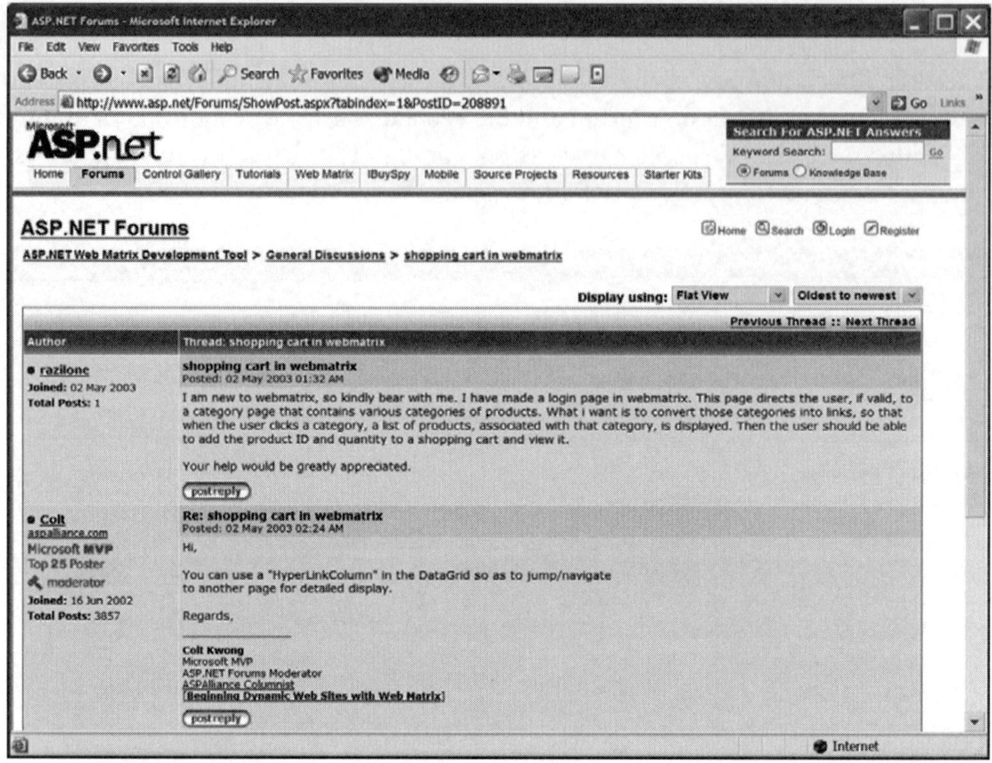

Figure 13.7: Shopping Cart messages

13.2.3 ASP.NET Forums

The ASP.NET Forums section provides a number of links to ASP.NET Forums on specific topics. The different forums cover the following topics:

- Announcements
- Getting Started
- Web Forms
- DataGrid, DataList, Repeater
- Data Access
- Security
- Caching
- Mobile
- XML
- XML Web services

The ASP.NET forums look exactly the same as those on the subject of Web Matrix.

13.2.4 Newsgroups

The Newsgroups section provides a series of links to different ASP.NET related newsgroups. These news groups are:

- dotnet.framework.aspnet
- dotnet.framework.aspnet.webcontrols
- dotnet.framework.aspnet.datagridcontrol
- dotnet.framework.aspnet.mobile
- dotnet.framework.aspnet.webservices
- dotnet.framework.aspnet.security
- dotnet.framework.aspnet.caching
- dotnet.framework.adonet

Newsgroups are similar to forums but require different software to access them. Figure 13.8 illustrates the dotnet.framework.aspnet newsgroup displayed in Microsoft Outlook Newsreader.

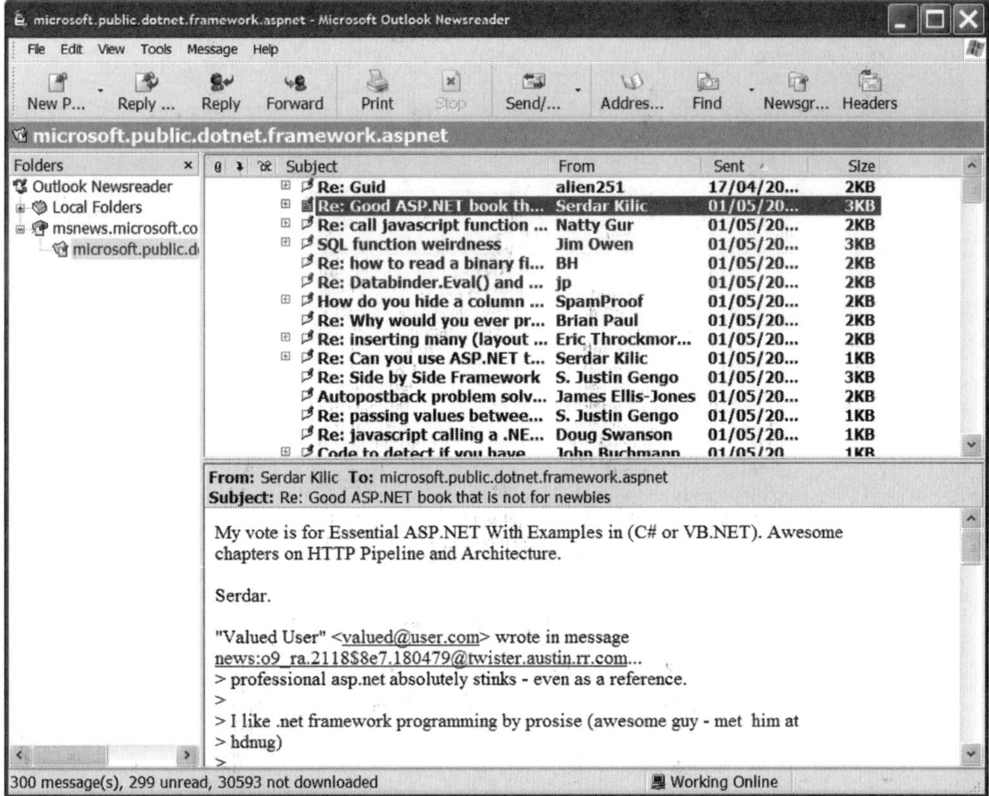

Figure 13.8: Newsgroup

13.2.5 Listservs

The ASPFriends link under the Listservs section launches a web page which lists all Yahoo groups you can join to discuss the topic areas displayed. The URL for this page is http://www.aspfriends.com/aspfriendshome/ and is illustrated in Figure 13.9.

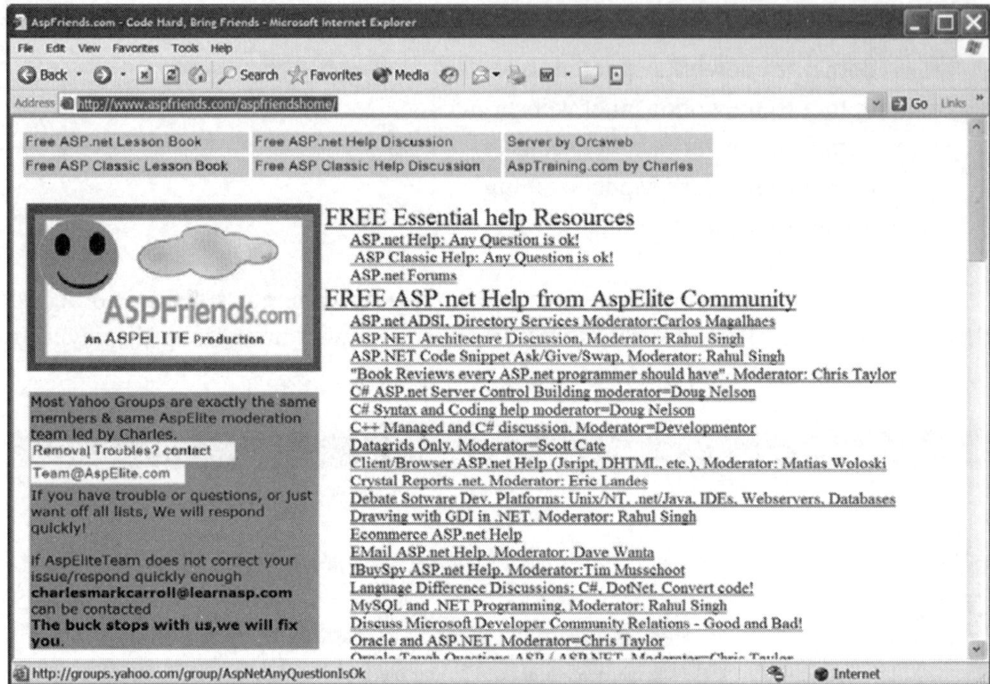

Figure 13.9: Listservs

13.3   Other community support

In addition to the hyperlinks which have been in-built into Web Matrix there are a large number of other web sites which provide useful information to the ASP.NET Web Matrix developer.

Table 13.1 illustrates the names of these web pages and their URLs. Remember that some of these web pages are very good and are independent communities of their own. Just because they are not Microsoft sponsored or created doesn't mean that they are not very good. Many of these web sites include example pieces of code, tutorials and their own forums for discussion.

Table 13.1: Community web sites

Name	URL
4 Guys From Rolla	http://aspnet.4guysfromrolla.com
Dot Net Junkies	http://www.dotnetjunkies.com/
ASP Today	http://www.asptoday.com/
123 ASPX	http://www.123aspx.com/
411 ASP	http://www.411asp.net/

13.4 Summary

This chapter has described some of the resources that are available on-line where you can go for help and assistance and to expand your knowledge of ASP.NET and Web Matrix.

14

Model solutions

14.1   Introduction

In this chapter we provide some model solutions for the exercises which were included at the end of each chapter. Remember that these are model solutions and there are always a number of different ways to solve the same problem. To compare your solution with these simply open your solution in Web Matrix and click the All tab at the bottom of the document window.

14.2   Chapter 1 – Solutions

There are no solutions for this chapter.

14.3   Chapter 2 – Solutions

There are no solutions for this chapter.

14.4   Chapter 3 – Solutions

Exercise 1

```
<%@ Page Language="VB" %>
<script runat="server">
```

```
    ' Insert page code here
    '

    Sub Button1_Click(sender As Object, e As EventArgs)
    Label1.Text = "You clicked Button One"
    End Sub

    Sub Button2_Click(sender As Object, e As EventArgs)
    Label1.Text = "You clicked Button Two"
    End Sub

    Sub TextBox1_TextChanged(sender As Object, e As EventArgs)

    End Sub

</script>
<html>
<head>
</head>
<body>
   <form runat="server">
     <p>
       <asp:Label id="Label1" runat="server">Label</asp:Label>
     </p>
     <p>
       <asp:Button id="Button1" onclick="Button1_Click" runat="server"
Text="Button"></asp:Button>
       <asp:Button id="Button2" onclick="Button2_Click" runat="server"
Text="Button"></asp:Button>
     </p>
     <!-- Insert content here -->
   </form>
</body>
</html>
```

Exercise 2

```
<%@ Page Language="VB" %>
<script runat="server">

   ' Insert page code here
   '

   Sub Button1_Click(sender As Object, e As EventArgs)
   Label1.Text = TextBox1.Text
   Label2.Text = TextBox2.Text
   End Sub

</script>
<html>
```

```
<head>
</head>
<body>
  <form runat="server">
    <p>
      <asp:Label id="Label1" runat="server">Label</asp:Label>
    </p>
    <p>
      <asp:Label id="Label2" runat="server">Label</asp:Label>
    </p>
    <p>
      <asp:TextBox id="TextBox1" runat="server"></asp:TextBox>
    </p>
    <p>
      <asp:TextBox id="TextBox2" runat="server"></asp:TextBox>
    </p>
    <p>
      <asp:Button id="Button1" onclick="Button1_Click" runat="server"
Text="Button"></asp:Button>
    </p>
    <!-- Insert content here -->
  </form>
</body>
</html>
```

14.5   Chapter 4 – Solutions

Exercise 1

```
<%@ Page Language="VB" %>
<script runat="server">

  ' Insert page code here
  '

  Sub DropDownList1_SelectedIndexChanged(sender As Object, e As EventArgs)

  End Sub

</script>
<html>
<head>
</head>
<body>
  <form runat="server">
    <p>
      <!-- Insert content here -->
    </p>
    <p>
```

```
        Welcome to my web page.
        <hr align="left" color="black" noshade="noshade" size="4" />
        This is a horizontal rule.
    </p>
    <p>
    </p>
  </form>
</body>
</html>
```

Exercise 2

```
<%@ Page Language="VB" %>
<script runat="server">

  ' Insert page code here
  '

  Sub Calendar1_SelectionChanged(sender As Object, e As EventArgs)
  Label1.Text = "The Date is " & Calendar1.SelectedDate
  End Sub

  Sub Calendar2_SelectionChanged(sender As Object, e As EventArgs)
  Label2.Text = "The Date is " & Calendar2.SelectedDate
  End Sub

</script>
<html>
<head>
</head>
<body>
  <form runat="server">
    <p>
      <asp:Label id="Label1" runat="server">Label</asp:Label>
    </p>
    <p>
      <asp:Calendar id="Calendar1" runat="server"
OnSelectionChanged="Calendar1_SelectionChanged"></asp:Calendar>
    </p>
    <p>
      <asp:Label id="Label2" runat="server">Label</asp:Label>
    </p>
    <p>
      <asp:Calendar id="Calendar2" runat="server"
OnSelectionChanged="Calendar2_SelectionChanged"></asp:Calendar>
    </p>
    <!-- Insert content here -->
  </form>
</body>
</html>
```

14.6   Chapter 5 – Solutions

Exercise 1

```html
<html>
<head>
</head>
<body>
  <form runat="server">
    <p align="center">
        <img src="fishing.jpg" align="center" border="5" />
    </p>
  </form>
</body>
</html>
```

Exercise 2

```html
<html>
<head>
</head>
<body>
  <form runat="server">
    <p>
        This is Page One
    </p>
    <p>
        Click <a href="page2.aspx">here</a> to go to page 2.
        <!-- Insert content here -->
    </p>
  </form>
</body>
</html>
```

```html
<html>
<head>
</head>
<body>
  <form runat="server">
    <p>
        This is Page Two
    </p>
    <p>
        Click <a href="page1.aspx">here</a> to go to page 1.
        <!-- Insert content here -->
    </p>
  </form>
</body>
</html>
```

Exercise 3

```
<html>
<head>
</head>
<body>
  <form runat="server">
    <table>
      <tbody>
        <tr>
          <td bgcolor="#ff8080">
            A</td>
          <td bgcolor="yellow">
            B</td>
        </tr>
        <tr>
          <td bgcolor="#80ffff">
            C</td>
          <td bgcolor="silver">
            D</td>
        </tr>
        <tr>
          <td bgcolor="#ffc0ff">
            E</td>
          <td bgcolor="#c0c0ff">
            F</td>
        </tr>
        <tr>
          <td bgcolor="#ffc080">
            G</td>
          <td bgcolor="#c0c000">
            H</td>
        </tr>
      </tbody>
    </table>
    <!-- Insert content here -->
  </form>
</body>
</html>
```

Exercise 4

```
<html>
<head>
</head>
<body>
  <form runat="server">
    <table>
      <tbody>
        <tr>
          <td>
```

```
            <img src="fishing.jpg" /></td>
        <td>
            <img src="fishing.jpg" /></td>
        <td>
            <img src="fishing.jpg" /></td>
      </tr>
    </tbody>
  </table>
  <!-- Insert content here -->
  </form>
</body>
</html>
```

14.7   Chapter 6 – Solutions

Exercise 1

```
<%@ Page Language="VB" %>
<script runat="server">

  ' Insert page code here
  '

  Sub Button1_Click(sender As Object, e As EventArgs)
  Label2.Text = TextBox1.Text
  Label3.Text = TextBox2.Text
  Label1.Text = DropDownList1.SelectedItem.Text
  End Sub

</script>
<html>
<head>
</head>
<body>
  <form runat="server">
    <p>
      <asp:Label id="Label1" runat="server"></asp:Label>
      <asp:Label id="Label2" runat="server"></asp:Label>
      <asp:Label id="Label3" runat="server"></asp:Label>
    </p>
    <p>
      Title:
      <asp:DropDownList id="DropDownList1" runat="server">
        <asp:ListItem Value="Mr">Mr</asp:ListItem>
        <asp:ListItem Value="Ms">Ms</asp:ListItem>
        <asp:ListItem Value="Miss">Miss</asp:ListItem>
        <asp:ListItem Value="Mrs">Mrs</asp:ListItem>
        <asp:ListItem Value="Dr">Dr</asp:ListItem>
      </asp:DropDownList>
```

```
        </p>
        <p>
          Firstname:
          <asp:TextBox id="TextBox1" runat="server"></asp:TextBox>
        </p>
        <p>
          Surname:
          <asp:TextBox id="TextBox2" runat="server"></asp:TextBox>
        </p>
        <p>
          <asp:Button id="Button1" onclick="Button1_Click" runat="server"
BorderColor="#FF8080" BackColor="#FFC0C0" ForeColor="DimGray"
Text="Submit the form"></asp:Button>
        </p>
        <!-- Insert content here -->
    </form>
</body>
</html>
```

Exercise 2

```
<%@ Page Language="VB" %>
<script runat="server">

  ' Insert page code here
  '

  Sub Button1_Click(sender As Object, e As EventArgs)
  Label2.Text = DropDownList1.SelectedItem.Text
  Label1.Text = RadioButtonList1.SelectedItem.Text
  End Sub

</script>
<html>
<head>
</head>
<body>
  <form runat="server">
    <table>
      <tbody>
        <tr>
          <td>
            <asp:Label id="Label1" runat="server"></asp:Label>
          </td>
          <td>
            <asp:Label id="Label2" runat="server"></asp:Label>
          </td>
        </tr>
        <tr>
          <td>
```

```
                <asp:RadioButtonList id="RadioButtonList1" runat="server">
                    <asp:ListItem Value="Red">Red</asp:ListItem>
                    <asp:ListItem Value="Orange">Orange</asp:ListItem>
                    <asp:ListItem Value="Yellow">Yellow</asp:ListItem>
                    <asp:ListItem Value="Green">Green</asp:ListItem>
                    <asp:ListItem Value="Blue">Blue</asp:ListItem>
                    <asp:ListItem Value="Indigo">Indigo</asp:ListItem>
                    <asp:ListItem Value="Violet">Violet</asp:ListItem>
                </asp:RadioButtonList>
            </td>
            <td>
                <asp:DropDownList id="DropDownList1" runat="server">
                    <asp:ListItem Value="Red">Red</asp:ListItem>
                    <asp:ListItem Value="Orange">Orange</asp:ListItem>
                    <asp:ListItem Value="Yellow">Yellow</asp:ListItem>
                    <asp:ListItem Value="Green">Green</asp:ListItem>
                    <asp:ListItem Value="Blue">Blue</asp:ListItem>
                    <asp:ListItem Value="Indigo">Indigo</asp:ListItem>
                    <asp:ListItem Value="Violet">Violet</asp:ListItem>
                </asp:DropDownList>
            </td>
        </tr>
        <tr>
            <td colspan="2">
                <asp:Button id="Button1" onclick="Button1_Click" runat="server"
Text="Submit the form" ForeColor="DimGray" BackColor="#FFC0C0"
BorderColor="#FF8080"></asp:Button>
            </td>
        </tr>
      </tbody>
    </table>
    <!-- Insert content here -->
  </form>
</body>
</html>
```

14.8 Chapter 7 – Solutions

Exercise 1

```
<%@ Page Language="VB" %>
<script runat="server">

  ' Insert page code here
  '

  Sub Button1_Click(sender As Object, e As EventArgs)

  End Sub
```

```
</script>
<html>
<head>
</head>
<body>
  <form runat="server">
    <p>
      Enter your personal details:
    </p>
    <table>
      <tbody>
        <tr>
          <td>
            Firstname:</td>
          <td>
            <asp:TextBox id="TextBox1" runat="server"
Width="225px"></asp:TextBox>
          </td>
          <td>
            <asp:RequiredFieldValidator id="RequiredFieldValidator1"
runat="server" ErrorMessage="Enter Firstname"
ControlToValidate="TextBox1"></asp:RequiredFieldValidator>
          </td>
        </tr>
        <tr>
          <td>
            Surname:</td>
          <td>
            <asp:TextBox id="TextBox2" runat="server"
Width="225px"></asp:TextBox>
          </td>
          <td>
            <asp:RequiredFieldValidator id="RequiredFieldValidator2"
runat="server" ErrorMessage="Enter Surname"
ControlToValidate="TextBox2"></asp:RequiredFieldValidator>
          </td>
        </tr>
        <tr>
          <td valign="top">
            Address:</td>
          <td>
            <asp:TextBox id="TextBox3" runat="server" TextMode="MultiLine"
Height="85px"></asp:TextBox>
          </td>
          <td valign="top">
            <asp:RequiredFieldValidator id="RequiredFieldValidator3"
runat="server" ErrorMessage="Enter Address"
ControlToValidate="TextBox3"></asp:RequiredFieldValidator>
          </td>
```

```
          </tr>
          <tr>
            <td colspan="3">
              <asp:Button id="Button1" onclick="Button1_Click" runat="server"
BorderColor="#FF8080" BackColor="#FFC0C0" ForeColor="DimGray"
Text="Submit the form"></asp:Button>
            </td>
          </tr>
        </tbody>
      </table>
      <!-- Insert content here -->
    </form>
  </body>
</html>
```

Exercise 2

```
<%@ Page Language="VB" %>
<script runat="server">

  ' Insert page code here
  '

  Sub Button1_Click(sender As Object, e As EventArgs)

  End Sub

  Sub DropDownList1_SelectedIndexChanged(sender As Object, e As EventArgs)

  End Sub

</script>
<html>
<head>
</head>
<body>
  <form runat="server">
    <p>
      Please select your first and second choices of music:
    </p>
    <table>
      <tbody>
        <tr>
          <td>
            First choice:</td>
          <td>
            <asp:DropDownList id="DropDownList1" runat="server"
OnSelectedIndexChanged="DropDownList1_SelectedIndexChanged">
              <asp:ListItem Value="Pop">Pop</asp:ListItem>
              <asp:ListItem Value="Rock">Rock</asp:ListItem>
```

```
                    <asp:ListItem Value="Classical">Classical</asp:ListItem>
                    <asp:ListItem Value="Punk">Punk</asp:ListItem>
                    <asp:ListItem Value="Country">Country</asp:ListItem>
                </asp:DropDownList>
            </td>
            <td>
              Second choice:</td>
            <td>
                <asp:DropDownList id="DropDownList2" runat="server"
OnSelectedIndexChanged="DropDownList1_SelectedIndexChanged">
                    <asp:ListItem Value="Pop">Pop</asp:ListItem>
                    <asp:ListItem Value="Rock">Rock</asp:ListItem>
                    <asp:ListItem Value="Classical">Classical</asp:ListItem>
                    <asp:ListItem Value="Punk">Punk</asp:ListItem>
                    <asp:ListItem Value="Country">Country</asp:ListItem>
                </asp:DropDownList>
            </td>
        </tr>
        <tr>
            <td align="middle" colspan="4">
                <asp:CompareValidator id="CompareValidator1" runat="server"
ErrorMessage="First choice cannot be the same as the second"
ControlToValidate="DropDownList2" ControlToCompare="DropDownList1"
Operator="NotEqual"></asp:CompareValidator>

            </td>
        </tr>
        <tr>
            <td align="middle" colspan="4">
                <asp:Button id="Button1" onclick="Button1_Click" runat="server"
Text="Submit the form" ForeColor="DimGray" BackColor="#FFC0C0"
BorderColor="#FF8080"></asp:Button>
            </td>
        </tr>
      </tbody>
    </table>
    <!-- Insert content here -->
  </form>
</body>
</html>
```

14.9   Chapter 8 – Solutions

Exercise 1

```
<%@ Page Language="VB" Explicit="True" Debug="True" %>
<script runat="server">

  Sub testname(Sender as Object, E as EventArgs)
```

```
      Dim userpath as string

      If TxtInput.Text = "Fred" Then
         userpath = "fred.aspx"
         response.redirect(userpath)
      Else
         TxtOutput.Text = "I don't know anyone called " & TxtInput.Text
         cmdTest.Visible = false
         cmdClear.Visible = true
         TxtOutput.Visible = true
      End If
   End Sub

   Sub clear(Sender as Object, E as EventArgs)
      TxtInput.Text = ""
      TxtOutput.Text = ""
      TxtOutput.Visible = false
      cmdClear.Visible = false
      cmdTest.Visible = true
   End Sub

</script>
<html>
<head>
</head>
<body>
   <form runat="server">
      <div align="center">
         <asp:Label id="Label1" runat="server" Font-Bold="True" Font-Size="X-Large">Does the system know you?</asp:Label>
      </div>
      <div align="center">
      </div>
      <h1 align="center">
         <asp:TextBox id="TxtInput" runat="server"></asp:TextBox>
      </h1>
      <div align="center">
         <asp:Label id="Label2" runat="server">Please enter your name and then click Check</asp:Label>
      </div>
      <div align="center">
      </div>
      <h1 align="center">
         <asp:Button id="cmdTest" onclick="testname" runat="server" Text="Check"></asp:Button>
         <asp:Button id="cmdClear" onclick="clear" runat="server" Text="Try Again" Visible="False"></asp:Button>
      </h1>
      <div align="center">
      </div>
```

```
    <div align="center">
       <asp:TextBox id="TxtOutput" runat="server" Visible="False"
Width="279px"></asp:TextBox>
    </div>
  </form>
</body>
</html>
```

```
<%@ Page Language="VB" %>
<script runat="server">

  ' Insert page code here
  '

</script>
<html>
<head>
</head>
<body>
  <form runat="server">
    <p align="center">
       <asp:Label id="Label1" runat="server" Font-Size="XX-Large"
Height="60px" Width="240px">Hello Fred!</asp:Label>
       <!-- Insert content here -->
    </p>
  </form>
</body>
</html>
```

Exercise 2

```
<%@ Page Language="VB" Explicit="True" Debug="True" %>
<script runat="server">

  Sub testname(Sender as Object, E as EventArgs)
     Dim userpath as string

     If lcase(TxtInput.Text) = "fred" Then
        userpath = "Fred.aspx"
        response.redirect(userpath)
     Else
        TxtOutput.Text = "I don't know anyone called " & TxtInput.Text
        cmdTest.Visible = false
        cmdClear.Visible = true
        TxtOutput.Visible = true
     End If
  End Sub

  Sub clear(Sender as Object, E as EventArgs)
```

```
      TxtInput.Text = ""
      TxtOutput.Text = ""
      TxtOutput.Visible = false
      cmdClear.Visible = false
      cmdTest.Visible = true
   End Sub

</script>
<html>
<head>
</head>
<body>
   <form runat="server">
     <div align="center">
        <asp:Label id="Label1" runat="server" Font-Size="X-Large" Font-
Bold="True">Does the system know you?</asp:Label>
     </div>
     <div align="center">
     </div>
     <h1 align="center">
        <asp:TextBox id="TxtInput" runat="server"></asp:TextBox>
     </h1>
     <div align="center">
        <asp:Label id="Label2" runat="server">Please enter your name and then
click Check</asp:Label>
     </div>
     <div align="center">
     </div>
     <h1 align="center">
        <asp:Button id="cmdTest" onclick="testname" runat="server"
Text="Check"></asp:Button>
        <asp:Button id="cmdClear" onclick="clear" runat="server" Text="Try Again"
Visible="False"></asp:Button>
     </h1>
     <div align="center">
     </div>
     <div align="center">
        <asp:TextBox id="TxtOutput" runat="server" Visible="False"
Width="279px"></asp:TextBox>
     </div>
   </form>
</body>
</html>
```

14.10 Chapter 9 – Solutions

Exercise 1

```
<%@ Page Language="VB" Explicit="True" Debug="True" %>
```

```
<%@ import Namespace="system.drawing" %>
<script runat="server">

  sub calculate(Sender as Object, E as EventArgs)

    dim total as integer

    total = 0

    if RBList1.selectedindex = 1 then
      total = total + 1
      row1.visible = "false"
    end if

    if RBList2.selectedindex = 2 then
      total = total + 1
      row2.visible = "false"
    end if

    if RBList3.selectedindex = 2 then
      total = total + 1
      row3.visible = "false"
    end if

    if RBList4.selectedindex = 0 then
      total = total + 1
      row4.visible = "false"
    end if

  textbox1.text = total

  end sub

</script>
<html>
<head>
</head>
<body>
  <form runat="server">
    <p align="left">
      <asp:Label id="Label1" runat="server" Font-Size="XX-Large" Font-
Bold="True">Test your knowledge of code</asp:Label>
    </p>
    <p>
      <asp:Table id="Table1" runat="server" width="100%" BackColor="White">
        <asp:TableRow BorderStyle="Solid" ID="row1">
          <asp:TableCell BorderStyle="Solid" Text="What is the name of the
function that converts a string to upper case?"></asp:TableCell>
          <asp:TableCell BorderStyle="Solid">
            <asp:RadioButtonList runat="server" ID="RBList1">
```

```
                <asp:ListItem Value="toupper()">toupper()</asp:ListItem>
                <asp:ListItem Value="ucase()">ucase()</asp:ListItem>
                <asp:ListItem Value="upper()">upper()</asp:ListItem>
            </asp:RadioButtonList>
          </asp:TableCell>
        </asp:TableRow>
        <asp:TableRow BorderStyle="Solid" ID="row2">
          <asp:TableCell BorderStyle="Solid" Text="In the ASP.NET header
what is the meaning of Explicit='True'?"></asp:TableCell>
          <asp:TableCell BorderStyle="Solid">
            <asp:RadioButtonList runat="server" ID="RBList2">
              <asp:ListItem Value="Be true to yourself">Be true to
yourself</asp:ListItem>
              <asp:ListItem Value="All code must be correct">All code must be
correct</asp:ListItem>
              <asp:ListItem Value="Declare all variables before use">Declare
all variables before use</asp:ListItem>
            </asp:RadioButtonList>
          </asp:TableCell>
        </asp:TableRow>
        <asp:TableRow BorderStyle="Solid" ID="row3">
          <asp:TableCell BorderStyle="Solid" Text="Concatenation is the way to
do what?"></asp:TableCell>
          <asp:TableCell BorderStyle="Solid">
            <asp:RadioButtonList runat="server" ID="RBList3">
              <asp:ListItem Value="Concentrate on your coding">Concentrate
on your coding</asp:ListItem>
              <asp:ListItem Value="Cheat cats">Cheat cats</asp:ListItem>
              <asp:ListItem Value="Glue text strings together">Glue text
strings together</asp:ListItem>
            </asp:RadioButtonList>
          </asp:TableCell>
        </asp:TableRow>
        <asp:TableRow BorderStyle="Solid" ID="row4">
          <asp:TableCell BorderStyle="Solid" Text="An array takes advantage
of?"></asp:TableCell>
          <asp:TableCell BorderStyle="Solid">
            <asp:RadioButtonList runat="server" ID="RBList4">
              <asp:ListItem Value="A subscript">A subscript</asp:ListItem>
              <asp:ListItem Value="A transcript">A transcript</asp:ListItem>
              <asp:ListItem Value="A substitute">A substitute</asp:ListItem>
            </asp:RadioButtonList>
          </asp:TableCell>
        </asp:TableRow>
      </asp:Table>
    </p>
    <p align="center">
    </p>
    <p align="center">
```

```
        <asp:TextBox id="TextBox1" runat="server" Font-Size="X-Large"
Width="31px" Height="45px"></asp:TextBox>
    </p>
    <p align="center">
        <asp:Button id="Button1" onclick="calculate" runat="server"
Text="Calculate"></asp:Button>
    </p>
    <p align="center">
    </p>
  </form>
</body>
</html>
```

Exercise 2

```
<%@ Page Language="VB" Explicit="True" Debug="True" %>
<%@ import Namespace="system.drawing" %>
<script runat="server">

  sub calculate(Sender as Object, E as EventArgs)

    dim total as integer

    total = 0

    if RBList1.selectedindex = 1 then
       total = total + 1
       row1.backcolor = color.green
    else
       row1.backcolor = color.red
    end if

    if RBList2.selectedindex = 2 then
       total = total + 1
       row2.backcolor = color.green
    else
       row2.backcolor = color.red
    end if

    if RBList3.selectedindex = 2 then
       total = total + 1
       row3.backcolor = color.green
    else
       row3.backcolor = color.red
    end if

    if RBList4.selectedindex = 0 then
       total = total + 1
       row1.backcolor = color.green
    else
```

```
            row1.backcolor = color.red
        end if

    textbox1.text = total

    end sub

</script>
<html>
<head>
</head>
<body>
    <form runat="server">
        <p align="left">
            <asp:Label id="Label1" runat="server" Font-Bold="True" Font-Size="XX-
Large">Test your knowledge of code</asp:Label>
        </p>
        <p>
            <asp:Table id="Table1" runat="server" BackColor="White" width="100%">
                <asp:TableRow BorderStyle="Solid" ID="row1">
                <asp:TableCell BorderStyle="Solid" Text="What is the name of the
function that converts a string to upper case?"></asp:TableCell>
                <asp:TableCell BorderStyle="Solid">
                    <asp:RadioButtonList runat="server" ID="RBList1">
                        <asp:ListItem Value="toupper()">toupper()</asp:ListItem>
                        <asp:ListItem Value="ucase()">ucase()</asp:ListItem>
                        <asp:ListItem Value="upper()">upper()</asp:ListItem>
                    </asp:RadioButtonList>
                </asp:TableCell>
                </asp:TableRow>
                <asp:TableRow BorderStyle="Solid" ID="row2">
                <asp:TableCell BorderStyle="Solid" Text="In the ASP.NET header
what is the meaning of Explicit='True'?"></asp:TableCell>
                <asp:TableCell BorderStyle="Solid">
                    <asp:RadioButtonList runat="server" ID="RBList2">
                        <asp:ListItem Value="Be true to yourself">Be true to
yourself</asp:ListItem>
                        <asp:ListItem Value="All code must be correct">All code must be
correct</asp:ListItem>
                        <asp:ListItem Value="Declare all variables before use">Declare
all variables before use</asp:ListItem>
                    </asp:RadioButtonList>
                </asp:TableCell>
                </asp:TableRow>
                <asp:TableRow BorderStyle="Solid" ID="row3">
                <asp:TableCell BorderStyle="Solid" Text="Concatenation is the way to
do what?"></asp:TableCell>
                <asp:TableCell BorderStyle="Solid">
                    <asp:RadioButtonList runat="server" ID="RBList3">
```

```
                    <asp:ListItem Value="Concentrate on your coding">Concentrate
on your coding</asp:ListItem>
                    <asp:ListItem Value="Cheat cats">Cheat cats</asp:ListItem>
                    <asp:ListItem Value="Glue text strings together">Glue text
strings together</asp:ListItem>
                </asp:RadioButtonList>
            </asp:TableCell>
        </asp:TableRow>
        <asp:TableRow BorderStyle="Solid" ID="row4">
            <asp:TableCell BorderStyle="Solid" Text="An array takes advantage
of?"></asp:TableCell>
            <asp:TableCell BorderStyle="Solid">
                <asp:RadioButtonList runat="server" ID="RBList4">
                    <asp:ListItem Value="A subscript">A subscript</asp:ListItem>
                    <asp:ListItem Value="A transcript">A transcript</asp:ListItem>
                    <asp:ListItem Value="A substitute">A substitute</asp:ListItem>
                </asp:RadioButtonList>
            </asp:TableCell>
        </asp:TableRow>
    </asp:Table>
</p>
<p align="center">
</p>
<p align="center">
    <asp:TextBox id="TextBox1" runat="server" Font-Size="X-Large"
Height="45px" Width="31px"></asp:TextBox>
</p>
<p align="center">
    <asp:Button id="Button1" onclick="calculate" runat="server"
Text="Calculate"></asp:Button>
</p>
<p align="center">
</p>
  </form>
</body>
</html>
```

14.11 Chapter 10 – Solutions

There are no solutions for this chapter.

14.12 Chapter 11 – Solutions

Exercise 2

```
<%@ Page Language="VB" Explicit="True" Debug="True" %>
<%@ import Namespace="System.Data" %>
<%@ import Namespace="System.Data.SqlClient" %>
```

```
<script runat="server">

  Sub Page_Load(Sender As Object, E As EventArgs)

    If Not Page.IsPostBack Then

      ' Databind the master grid on the first request only
      ' (viewstate will restore these values on subsequent postbacks).

      MasterGrid.SelectedIndex = 0
      BindMasterGrid()
      BindDetailGrid()

    End If

  End Sub

  Sub MasterGrid_Select(Sender As Object, E As EventArgs)
    BindDetailGrid()
  End Sub

  Sub MasterGrid_Page(Sender As Object, E As
DataGridPageChangedEventArgs)

    If MasterGrid.SelectedIndex <> -1 Then

      ' unset the selection, details view
      MasterGrid.SelectedIndex = -1
      BindDetailGrid()

    End If

    MasterGrid.CurrentPageIndex = e.NewPageIndex
    BindMasterGrid()

  End Sub

  Sub BindMasterGrid()

    ' TODO: Update the ConnectionString and CommandText values for your
application
    Dim ConnectionString As String =
"server=(local);database=Shopping;trusted_connection=true"
    Dim CommandText As String = "select [Family Name], [First Name], Address,
[Post Code], [Tel No], login, Password from Customer order by [Family Name]"

    Dim myConnection As New SqlConnection(ConnectionString)
    Dim myCommand As New SqlDataAdapter(CommandText, myConnection)

    Dim ds As New DataSet()
```

```
        myCommand.Fill(ds)

        MasterGrid.DataSource = ds
        MasterGrid.DataBind()

    End Sub

    Sub BindDetailGrid()

        ' get the filter value from the master Grid's DataKeys collection
        If MasterGrid.SelectedIndex <> -1 Then

            ' TODO: update the ConnectionString value for your application
            Dim ConnectionString As String =
"server=(local);database=Shopping;trusted_connection=true"

            ' TODO: update the CommandText value for your application
            Dim filterValue As String =
CStr(MasterGrid.DataKeys(MasterGrid.SelectedIndex)).Replace("'", "''")
            Dim CommandText As String = "select Id, Category, Name, Price from
CartItems where Login = '" & filterValue & "'"

            Dim myConnection As New SqlConnection(ConnectionString)
            Dim myCommand As New SqlCommand(CommandText, myConnection)

            myConnection.Open()

            DetailsGrid.DataSource =
myCommand.ExecuteReader(CommandBehavior.CloseConnection)

        End If

        DetailsGrid.DataBind()

    End Sub

</script>
<html>
<head>
</head>
<body style="FONT-FAMILY: arial">
  <h2>Customer Purchases 
  </h2>
  <hr size="1" />
  <form runat="server">
    <p>
      <asp:datagrid id="MasterGrid" runat="server" DataKeyField="Login"
OnSelectedIndexChanged="MasterGrid_Select" AllowPaging="true" PageSize="6"
OnPageIndexChanged="MasterGrid_Page" ForeColor="Black" BackColor="White"
CellPadding="3" GridLines="None" CellSpacing="1" width="80%">
```

```
            <HeaderStyle font-bold="True" forecolor="white"
backcolor="#4A3C8C"></HeaderStyle>
            <SelectedItemStyle forecolor="White"
backcolor="#9471DE"></SelectedItemStyle>
            <PagerStyle horizontalalign="Right" backcolor="#C6C3C6"
mode="NumericPages"></PagerStyle>
            <ItemStyle backcolor="#DEDFDE"></ItemStyle>
            <Columns>
              <asp:buttoncolumn text="Show details" commandname="Select"
ItemStyle-Font-Bold="true" ItemStyle-Font-Size="smaller"></asp:buttoncolumn>
            </Columns>
          </asp:datagrid>
          <br />
          <br />
          <asp:datagrid id="DetailsGrid" runat="server" ForeColor="Black"
BackColor="White" CellPadding="3" GridLines="None" CellSpacing="1"
width="80%" EnableViewState="False">
            <HeaderStyle font-bold="True" forecolor="white"
backcolor="#4A3C8C"></HeaderStyle>
            <PagerStyle horizontalalign="Right" backcolor="#C6C3C6"
mode="NumericPages"></PagerStyle>
            <ItemStyle backcolor="#DEDFDE"></ItemStyle>
          </asp:datagrid>
        </p>
      </form>
  </body>
</html>
```

14.13 Chapter 12 – Solutions

There are no solutions for this chapter.

14.14 Chapter 13 – Solutions

There are no solutions for this chapter.